Method, Context, and Meaning in New Testament Studies

Method, Context, and Meaning in New Testament Studies

C. Kavin Rowe

William B. Eerdmans Publishing Company
Grand Rapids, Michigan

Wm. B. Eerdmans Publishing Co.
4035 Park East Court SE, Grand Rapids, Michigan 49546
www.eerdmans.com

Published 2024

Book design by Lydia Hall

Printed in the United States of America

30 29 28 27 26 25 24 1 2 3 4 5 6 7

ISBN 978-0-8028-8273-8

Library of Congress Cataloging-in-Publication Data

A catalog record for this book is available from the Library of Congress.

To those who have helped to carry our lives

Contents

Preface

It is too easy to forget a basic fact about scholarly practice, which is this: scholarship pursues truth. Scholars may often think that we are engaged in an additive enterprise—a piling up of information as we do more and more research, a kind of increase in knowledge-by-addition. We do, of course, learn some things we did not know by increasing the scope of our awareness or filling out many of the details of the larger pictures we create. But all the studies produced presuppose the question of truth. Whether we focus on historical information (what was it like then?), philosophically descriptive patterns of thought (how do we think?), philosophically normative patterns of thought (how should we order our thoughts?), exegetical puzzles (what could this mean?), or any number of other things, scholarly studies attempt to track the truth, to show what is—or is most likely—the case and to persuade others to assent to what we have argued.[1] Our studies say, in effect, "here is something true; assent to this, and you will know the truth." Indeed, human beings cannot help but

1. This is true even in studies whose genre makes them seem rather removed from "arguments." An example could be the collating of manuscripts. Even with collation there is argument and attempt at persuasion, viz., that we should agree that the texts belong to this grouping or that grouping, based on these criteria or those. The entirety of the collating enterprise is built on arguments and the effort to say that these particular arrangements are the correct—or most correct—way to understand the age, provenance, grouping, etc., of these manuscripts.

assent to whatever we perceive as true.[2] Actual scholarly learning thus turns out to be growing in our knowledge of the truth.[3]

Truth is not purely a matter of intellectual assent, however, for the simple reason that humans do not think apart from our lives but within them. Truth is therefore also a becoming, an assent with our living to a shape of existence. Some people assent, for example, to a tradition of life and undergo the induction and transformation of the self that such a tradition claims is necessary for those who know the truth. Others, to take another powerful example in the modern North Atlantic West, assent to liberal notions of the human and its rights and attempt to make their way through the world attached to causes that champion these views. Even if we were to assent to the idea that life has no normative pattern, we would be living with the pattern of the life we think means that we do not assent to the idea of a normative pattern.[4] In short, human beings live out what we take to be true whether we wish to do this or not, and we are continuously making judgments through the shape of our living about truth and about its implications.[5] Truth has implications, as it turns out, and we are all implicated.

2. Hence the importance of argument. On the other side of the matter, we cannot assent to something we know is not true. See the classic work of John Henry Newman, *An Essay in Aid of a Grammar of Assent* (New York: Catholic Publication Society, 1870). What exactly goes into how we assent to things is complicated, not least because the matters to which we assent can themselves be complicated. But we can do things to make it more and less likely that we will assent to certain claims, statements, the correctness of a decision, etc. Experiencing peace as the fruit of practicing temperance in relationships, for example, makes it more likely, as it turns out, that we could assent to arguments about the necessity of the virtues for the pursuit of peace. When it comes to self-deception and our ability to convince ourselves of the truth of lies we nevertheless know to be lies, the complexity increases. See Gary Saul Morson, *Wonder Confronts Certainty: Russian Writers on the Timeless Questions and Why Their Answers Matter* (Cambridge, MA: Belknap, 2023), especially 263–66.

3. Such growth does not by any means always follow a straight line of progress. We may, for example, have to return to earlier moments of insight or arguments that we thought were discarded and rediscover their power. And there are countless revisions in our current understandings. Moreover, we can be deceived and assent to things that are not true (this just means, however, that we think such things are true when they are not). Scholarship, in one way of looking at it, is a practice that attempts to keep us on the path of truth. When criticisms cause us to revise our understanding, we learn by moving toward the truth as we then more clearly see it.

4. The fact that we are here self-deceived does not make it any less true that our lives turn out to be ordered toward and by things we take to be true.

5. This fact does not mean that we are always self-consistent, i.e., we can be aware of living a lie. For example, many Christians and other religious people are acutely aware of the (sometimes vast) distance between what they believe about how they ought to be living

The first essay makes some of this plain. The rest of the essays presuppose it. In the last several years, I have often been asked whether there is a particular method to my thinking. To my knowledge, I do not have a particular method if by method one means a kind of stepwise hermeneutics or one whose basic features are proximately derived from a particularly powerful school of thought (Kantian, say). Nor do I advocate for a distinctive hermeneutics that is phenomenologically of one identifiable sort rather than another. I thus prefer to think of these essays as "studies in" method, context, and meaning rather than as a series of essays that articulates how we ought to be going about things all the time.

All thinking is, after all, a response. We cannot think ex nihilo. Put differently, as we think we are thinking answers to questions that have been posed.[6] What the New Testament does is to pose the kind of question that means that thinking about its texts involves us in answers that manifest the density of human thought—or, to put a finer point on it, answers that show the fact that thoughts are but a way of speaking about the shape of our lives.

---

and how they actually live. Indeed, the reality of this distance is embedded in the purpose of regular confession, and it simultaneously highlights the risk of hypocrisy: for those who look to the lives of religious people to see what their traditions are about, the distance is at best confusing and often disillusioning and disconfirming.

6. And, of course, going on to ask (new) questions as a result. Thus begins the question/answer dialectic that marks human thought. Plato's dialogues never go out of style for many reasons, but their basic apprehension and display of this mark of thinking are at the heart of their enduring power.

Abbreviations

BTCB	Brazos Theological Commentary on the Bible
BTONT	*Biblical Theology of the Old and New Testaments* (Childs)
BZNW	Beihefte zur Zeitschrift für die neutestamentliche Wissenschaft
HBT	*Horizons in Biblical Theology*
HThKNT	Herders Theologischer Kommentar zum Neuen Testament
ICR	*Institutes of the Christian Religion* (Calvin)
JAAR	*Journal of the American Academy of Religion*
JRE	*Journal of Religious Ethics*
JSNT	*Journal for the Study of the New Testament*
JSOT	*Journal for the Study of the Old Testament*
JTI	*Journal of Theological Interpretation*
LCL	Loeb Classical Library
LNTS	Library of New Testament Studies
LXX	Septuagint
MT	Masoretic Text
NT	New Testament
NTC	*The New Testament in Comparison* (Barclay and White)
NTS	*New Testament Studies*
OT	Old Testament
ProEccl	*Pro Ecclesia*
SJT	*Scottish Journal of Theology*
ThTo	*Theology Today*
WBC	Word Biblical Commentary
WUNT	Wissenschaftliche Untersuchungen zum Neuen Testament

Part 1

BIBLICAL STUDIES AND THEOLOGY

What If It Were True?

◆ WHY STUDY THE NEW TESTAMENT

> How hard I find it to see what is *right in front of my eyes*![1]

> An anxious desire for interposition, for explicative-evaluative mediation between ourselves and the primary, permeates our condition.[2]

The Problem

In 2005 the widely respected NT scholar Wayne Meeks published his Society for New Testament Studies presidential address, "Why Study the New Testament?" Among the many reasons Meeks offered, there was a conspicuous absence: we should study the NT because it might tell the truth about God.[3]

1. Ludwig Wittgenstein, *Culture and Value* (London: Wiley-Blackwell, 1995), 39e.

2. George Steiner, *Real Presences* (Chicago: University of Chicago Press, 1989), 39.

3. Wayne A. Meeks, "Why Study the New Testament?," *NTS* 51 (2005): 155–70. Meeks gives five reasons why the NT "must" be studied. The first is religious/sociological (part of the foundation of Christian communities), the second is aesthetic/intellectual (pervasive influence in art, literature, and thought), and the last three are moral (it has been abused as often as used; we damage ourselves and others when we lose sight of our situation in the stream of history; we should be future-oriented because we don't have the last word). In some ways, these reasons are just fine as far as they go—partly because they are so unobjectionable—but under scrutiny one can see that they are simply assertions about the importance of things whose importance is just another assertion. We may agree or we may not. Who's to compel us? This layering of assertion on top of another assertion as if on a foundation and not just

"What If It Were True? Why Study the New Testament" was originally published in *NTS* 68 (2022): 144–55. It is reproduced with permission.

Nowhere is modernity's effect on the interpretation of the NT more evident than in the fact that we can manage to read the NT and avoid acknowledging the question it puts about truth. Of course, we have learned all sorts of interesting things by focusing on matters other than the main question the NT directly puts to its readers. Indeed, the signal contribution of modern study of the NT behind which we are unlikely to go is the delineation of the historical conditions under which the texts came to be and in which they made their sense. All our thinking in the West is now historical in one way or another, after all, and it is thus unsurprising that we have tasted—and quite enjoyed—the fruit borne of over two centuries of historical labor.[4]

But no matter how much information we amass, there remains a vast difference between learning some interesting things or playing various methodological games and facing the ever-present challenge posed by the NT. Søren Kierkegaard, whose treasure trove of insights into the NT is far too seldom searched by NT scholars, saw clearly what was at stake in the difference when he said that losing sight of the main thing is not simply opting for a different way of doing things, as if one could just say, "I'm not interested in *that*; I'm interested in *this*," and move on. Losing focus, rather, changes the terms of our understanding altogether, of what "serious" reading of the NT actually is.[5]

---

another layer of assertion is a common way of writing when you want to find something to hang your convictions on but don't want to use words like "truth" or "God" or "theology" (Meeks admonishes us to jettison the language of biblical and NT theology).

4. Even those who want to use history to get free of it—genealogists, for example—do their work by history (see Nietzsche's *The Use and Abuse of History*). Try as we might, we cannot think on this side of the historical turn without the historical turn. We all now know, and cannot not know, that the NT documents have particular histories of composition, destination, purpose, and so on. All supposedly non- or ahistorical reflection gets its critical launch angle from what has come before it, what it finds unsatisfying in that "before," and thus situates itself historically as yet one more mode of human reflection. All complications of "objective" historiography just mean the "objective" part is complicated. The historical part—that we turn to the past for reflection of any sort—remains firmly in place, even for those who think they have left it behind. In the end, this dependence on history is a feature of our humanity—we are finite creatures who emerge "after" what has come "before" and cannot do without what has come before—and it will inflect our thinking one way or the other regardless of our theoretical attempts to embrace or reject particular forms of historiography.

5. Søren Kierkegaard, *For Self-Examination*, in *For Self-Examination, and Judge for Yourselves!*, trans. W. Lowrie (Princeton: Princeton University Press, 1944), 58–59. A more recent translation of *For Self-Examination*—but less elegant in this particular passage—is *For Self-Examination/Judge for Yourself!*, trans. Howard V. Hong and Edna H. Hong (Princeton: Princeton University Press, 1990), 33–34.

"Every blessed day," said Kierkegaard, "there comes out an interpretation more learned than the last, more acute, more elegant, more profound, more ingenious, more wonderful, more charming, and more wonderfully charming. . . . Indeed criticism itself has become a literature so prolix that it is impossible to attain a survey of the criticism." And yet the sheer amount was not the main trouble in itself. It was rather that the torrent of scholarly works resulted in a monumental shift in consciousness and concentration: "At the same time the point of view for determining what seriousness is was altered, and to be busy about interpretation became real seriousness."[6] The problem, Kierkegaard argued, was that our attention was swept away from the NT by a surge of scholarship, and we came to think that what it is to be serious as an NT scholar is to be serious about NT scholarship.

The flood has only risen since Kierkegaard's day. The temptation to believe that being a serious scholar is being serious about scholarship is greater than it has ever been. "Book engenders book, essay breeds essay, article spawns article."[7] And never have we been more unable to see the field of NT criticism as a whole. Even the most learned among us work only in relatively well-defined areas, pursuing our questions and issuing our proposals almost entirely to the neglect of those whose research falls outside our particular ambit. Is there a way to recover our seriousness about the main thing, the NT itself and the questions it puts to its readers? Can we swim out of the flood and "go upstream, to the living streams of 'first being'"?[8] I think so.

Naturally, I recognize this essay's participation in the problem it names. But, of course, there is no other way to do it.[9] In what follows, I thus argue something rather simple but with far-reaching consequences not only for our discipline's focus and energy expenditure but also for the way that we conceive of what we are doing and what "serious" study of the NT entails. To make this argument I will first engage a recent article as a representative of "not-theology," a long-running but ultimately incoherent position within modernity about how to read the NT with critical seriousness. I will then turn to the problem of "deflection" and to Hans-Georg Gadamer to help us comprehend

6. Kierkegaard, *For Self-Examination*, 58–59.

7. Steiner, *Real Presences*, 39. He finishes the sentence: "the primary text is only the remote font of autonomous exegetic proliferation."

8. Steiner, *Real Presences*, 40.

9. Even the Bible itself is often commentary on commentary, the Chronicler's on Kings and Samuel, Luke's on Isaiah, or Matthew's on Mark, or 1 John on the Gospel of John, for that matter. Still, part of the point of returning regularly to the primary texts is surely to return to the primary texts.

why questions of truth are inherent to understanding the NT, discuss the sort of truth at which the NT aims as lived truth, and conclude with a concise recommendation for renewal within our discipline.

Being Serious . . . or Not

In a recent article entitled "'Let's Take the Text Seriously': The Protectionist *Doxa* of Mainstream New Testament Studies," Stephen Young argues against one kind of seriousness and for another.[10] Young's article contains some caricatures of the work he seeks to criticize, but he nevertheless raises a crucial question: What is it to be serious about the texts of the NT?

Young's constructive answer is hard to discern amid the jargonese, but his negative case is easier to spot. And it is this: despite their admonitions to take the texts seriously, those who interpret the NT in line with its claims are not serious. They are "protectionist," out to "protect" the NT from the truly serious critics who interrogate both the NT and its "confused" interpreters. The Protectionists reason theologically with the NT texts, privilege the "insider" perspectives of those texts, ignore "etic" interpretations, and "invalidate" serious criticism that wishes to "historicise" the ancient materials.[11]

According to Young, Protectionist John Barclay, for example, is confused because he argues, in broad terms, that there are theological claims in Paul's letters that cannot be reduced to an anthropological base.[12] The origin of Christian identity ultimately lies beyond the human horizon and, precisely because it comes from the God who is simultaneously the God of Israel and the only God of the cosmos, is able to hold together both a universalism and a commitment to Israel's particularity; such "irreducibly theological" understanding is not simply one more socio-psychological take on Israel/race/ethnicity. To make it so is not to offer an "etic" interpretation but to contest the reasonableness and truth of the theological claim by transforming the "emic" reasoning into "mythological ideology."[13]

Though "presumably unintended," says Young, Barclay's logic here exhibits a fencing-off strategy in which the only perspective that is taken seriously is that

10. Stephen L. Young, "'Let's Take the Text Seriously': The Protectionist *Doxa* of Mainstream New Testament Studies," *Method & Theory in the Study of Religion* (2019): 1–36.

11. See, for instance, Young, "'Let's Take the Text Seriously,'" 3, 11–13.

12. For Young's treatment of Barclay, see Young, "'Let's Take the Text Seriously,'" 13–18.

13. John M. G. Barclay, "An Identity Received from God: The Theological Configuration of Paul's Kinship Discourse," *Early Christianity* 8 (2017): 372.

of Paul himself. Never mind that Barclay's driving point is hardly what Young describes; the main thing is (apparently) that Barclay's focus on "emic" language somehow traps him inside a pattern of thought he cannot exit. Barclay's captivity is so profound, in fact, that he cannot detect his problem because he literally cannot think in terms other than Paul's (or at least the scholarly elucidation of Paul's). Barclay is entirely inscribed within the boundary of what Young, taking a term from Pierre Bourdieu, calls *doxa*: the thinkable. Barclay's thought is imprisoned within "the commonsense that shapes what is and is not thinkable, the questions that seem obvious, or the self-evident or taken-for-granted categories that govern available discourses in a field."[14] J. Louis Martyn, N. T. Wright, Volker Rabens, and I are the other mainstream scholarly examples of oblivious Protectionists whose work evidences "no concern to defend" its intellectual moves and substitutes "description—or repetition—for analysis."[15] Blithely unaware of what we cannot think—the *unthinkable*—the Protectionists "prohibit inquiry that could transgress or think beyond emic theories."[16]

Young's non sequiturs notwithstanding—surely Protectionist blindness would not ipso facto "prohibit" or "invalidate" inquiry from other quarters—the question of whether we know what we are doing or are merely trapped within the noetic boundaries of hermeneutical ignorance touches on a fundamental matter endemic to serious study of the NT. The best way to see it is to begin with some questions. What if, contrary to Young's assertions, we know quite well what we are doing and do it in order to press a particular point, a point about the language of the NT and the inherent claim to the truth about God embedded in that language? And what if this point leads to a second, a point about the inherent positions of interpretative languages that interface with the NT's language and how that interface is best construed?

My *One True Life* book that Young discusses, for example, displays considerable awareness of the emic/etic distinction. In fact, I argue explicitly and

14. Young, "'Let's Take the Text Seriously,'" 3.

15. Young, "'Let's Take the Text Seriously,'" 3.

16. Young, "'Let's Take the Text Seriously,'" 6. In Young's view, we do offer some arguments, but they are only "further protectionist arguments." There is a real question about whether Young has interpreted Bourdieu correctly. I think not, or at least not entirely, for the rather simple reason that his explanation of Bourdieu stands in tension with his analysis of Protectionist scholarly work on his own terms. For Bourdieu, *doxa* is a level of assumption that is deeper than reflection; at this level one cannot reflect upon what is assumed, at least not until some fundamental conditions that go beyond scholarly paradigms change (of society, of culture, etc.). Young's use of Bourdieu does not show (a) an awareness of this problem and/or (b) that the conditions have changed so that we can now see the "protectionist" assumptions that undergird NT studies that we were earlier unable to see.

at length that this distinction is conceptually far too clunky to cope with the complexities generated by the grammar of invitation and rejection, claim and conflict, that pervade both the Christian and Roman Stoic sources. The nature and telos of the "emic" language of these traditions disclose "etic" language as something other than what it claims to be: etic is not "outside" or observational in some sort of existentially protected sense; contrary to interpreters who claim that their "etic" analyses have no bearing on truth, etic language is instead just one more evaluative judgment about the truth of the traditions it claims to study. I thus reject the distinction as a way to think productively about interpreting the texts of religious/philosophical traditions of the sort that Christianity and Stoicism are—traditions that claim truth for their way of being. I may be wrong in what I argue (and/or in many other things), but the problem posed by the emic/etic distinction is not *un*thinkable to me. Quite to the contrary, the point is that I think very differently about it in relation to questions of truth, and in a way that challenges the sort of inquiry represented by Young.

Young's essay is styled as avant-garde, but in reality he simply sings a familiar old tune with some different words. Had Bruce Lincoln, for example, decided to write with a smattering of Bourdieu's terms, he would not have needed to change the notes. Nor would Russell McCutcheon for that matter, whose 1997 essay sounds remarkably like something Young wants to voice over: the need to "historicise," to be "transgressive" in our questioning, to steer free of religious commitments in our analyses, and so forth.[17] Further back, William Wrede would have seen much with which to agree, as would, more recently, Heikki Räisänen. Though there are obvious differences between these scholars and their many disciples, they share a significant commitment that binds them together: the commitment to what Paul Griffiths once cleverly called "not-theology."[18]

The advocates of not-theology zealously proclaim the possibility of theology-free interpretation and assert (or intimate) the inadmissibility of theological reasoning within scholarly discourse.[19] They use words such as

17. See Russell T. McCutcheon, "A Default of Critical Intelligence: The Scholar of Religion as Public Intellectual," *JAAR* 65 (1997): 443–68, which presages his book *Critics Not Caretakers: Redescribing the Public Study of Religion* (Albany: State University of New York Press, 2001).

18. Paul J. Griffiths, "On the Future of the Study of Religion in the Academy," *JAAR* 74 (2006): 66–74.

19. See, e.g., Young's approval of Bruce Lincoln's comment: "When one permits those whom one studies to define the terms in which they will be understood . . . one has ceased to

"critical" or "history" or, in Young's case, "protectionist" that are supposed to sound more analytically serious than the theological vocabularies of either the ancient sources or their current readers. Perhaps the rhetorical move is also intended to intimidate or frighten the confused theological counterparts out of the scholarly debate. Such words are, however, little more than "charms" waved around to ward off exactly the kind of rigorous questioning of presuppositions that the not-theologians allegedly mean to invite.[20] They tell us nothing about the things that must be true for not-theology to be a viable way to think (such as that God does not exist, or that God, if he exists, is unnecessary to take account of in matters of truth, or that interpreters have the ability to bracket God out of their thinking, or that anthropology and theology are epistemically competitive arenas, and so on). In fact, no arguments for not-theology are given at all. The assertions of Young, Lincoln, and others, when it comes to what we should and should not do, are little more than the proclamation of preference, an academic's kind of homiletical self-expression.[21] They also

function as historian or scholar" (Young, "Let's Take the Text Seriously," 3, citing B. Lincoln, "Theses on Method," *Method and Theory in the Study of Religion* 8 [1996]: 225–27). A representative work within NT studies of this widespread position is Heikki Räisänen's *Beyond New Testament Theology: A Story and a Programme* (London: SCM, 1990). Räisänen attempts some nuance in his article "A Religious Studies Alternative to New Testament Theology: Reflections on a Controversial Enterprise," in *The Bible among Scriptures and Other Essays* (Tübingen: Mohr Siebeck, 2017), 15–29, which explains his overall sense of his work. But the basic idea that not-theology is a viable way to think is simply restated. For an excellent treatment of this question in relation to reading strategies that explicitly presuppose faith, see Richard B. Hays, "Reading the Bible with the Eyes of Faith: The Practice of Theological Exegesis," *JTI* 1 (2007): 5–21. Hays discusses Meeks, Räisänen, Michael Fox, and Hector Avalos.

20. "Charms" is Griffiths's apt word ("On the Future," 73).

21. The program of the not-theologians, while veiled in the language of "historicising" and so forth, often functions as a mask behind which various moralisms and exhortations are smuggled in—all presented as self-evident, thrown out to their audience without any justification. Though he derides the "mainstream" Protectionists for their way of reading, Young, for example, makes a convenient exception to his claim that Protectionist interpretation is problematical. As it turns out, there are some Protectionists whose protecting work is actually to be lauded ("dominated Protectionists"). Why? For the moral end that the work serves: "One should not leverage examples of dominated-protectionism to legitimate protectionism in biblical studies since the latter reproduces the privilege of long-privileged texts and functions within a larger disciplinary apparatus of domination. . . . There remains an important place for promoting scholarship with modestly empiricist, socially 'realist,' and critical orientations since sexist, colonial, and other dominations are social realities that require non-protective interrogation and resistance" (9–10). It apparently does not bother Young that by calling it Protectionist he admits that the hermeneutical moves of this type of Protectionist are formally no different from the mainstream type of Protectionist schol-

evidence a particular interpretative posture, one that is common among their ilk and constitutive of those who think the question of truth emanating from that which they study somehow avoids reaching them. In short, while claiming to be serious about studying, what the not-theologians actually display is a posture of deflection.

Deflection: Truth and Method; Knowing and Acknowledging

The term "deflection" derives from the thought of philosopher Stanley Cavell and applies to the significant difference between what we know to be true and what we acknowledge as truth. We may know another person is in pain, for example, but that is not the same thing as acknowledging that fact. We may keep silent or, if we are academics, become mired in philosophical questions about how we really know that we know another person is in pain. Either way, the truth of the case, a truth that we know—namely, someone is in pain—is deflected rather than acknowledged.[22] Recently Cora Diamond developed Cavell's notion in relation to the work of thinking in particular. Diamond argued that deflection is a particular existential posture that results from converting things that call us fundamentally into question or resist our thinking into intellectual "issues." The texts, lectures, and novel (in Diamond's chief

arship, which would, of course, suggest that the approved Protectionists are just as confused as the mainstream since the former commit the exact same formal intellectual errors as the latter. Young tries to avoid this problem by naming the difference "structural" and by moral exhortation/preaching, but his basic grammar gives the game away. What matters to Young is (a) to exhort his readers to embrace the moral ends he likes (I say "likes" because no justification is given for his preferences—with the result that the exhortations appear purely as a matter of taste), and (b) probably not to be heard as criticizing the sort of current moral commitments you simply can't criticize if you want acceptance and employment at an American university. Young is for all that sort of thing, even if it is Protectionist on his own definition (and therefore "confused"). His basic typology seems to be: evangelical Protectionist (confused and bad); mainstream Protectionist (confused and confused); "dominated" protectionist (confused and good). McCutcheon, to take another example of a modern academic moralist, thinks we should be public intellectuals; Lincoln that we owe something to society, and so on. Whether one agrees with Young or McCutcheon or Lincoln, or some combination thereof, is beside the point. They all exhort as if they have made arguments or have a moral or metaphysical background against which such positions are self-evidently compelling to all people.

22. Stanley Cavell, "Knowing and Acknowledging," in *Must We Mean What We Say?*, 2nd ed. (Cambridge: Cambridge University Press, 2002), 220–45.

example) cease to be what they clearly are—their confrontation with us over the truth of our embodied life and time-bound existence is deflected—as we turn them into contributions to this or that individual question, or as we subsume them into wider methodological reflections or ethical deliberations as examples of X or Y. We deflect when we move "from the appreciation, or attempt at appreciation, of a difficulty of reality to a philosophical or moral problem apparently in the vicinity."[23] Deflection, that is, is the posture of defensive reading, a way in which intellectual skills and habits are used as an existential prophylactic to shield us from texts that question us with the possibility of their truth in the midst of our lives.[24]

To name the reading style of the not-theology advocates as deflection may at first seem somewhat strange or even hyperbolic. Why, after all, can't not-theology simply be just another way of interpreting ancient texts? The answer has to do with the way it attempts to inhabit the space between knowing and acknowledging—it knows what it refuses to acknowledge—and turns from the question of truth to the issue of method.

To the extent that NT scholars have invoked Gadamer, they have often assumed that he argued for the "fusion of horizons" as the central goal of hermeneutics and that to achieve this "fusion" was exactly the point of their historical labor.[25] Gadamer's argument, however, was not about a particular method of inquiry but about the entirety of the human experience of understanding (*Erfahrung*).[26] He explicitly rejected accounts of his work that described it in

23. Cora Diamond, "The Difficulty of Reality and the Difficulty of Philosophy," *Partial Answers: Journal of Literature and the History of Ideas* 1 (2003): 12.

24. Diamond also says that deflection occurs when we face things too difficult to think. But I take her "to think" to mean too difficult to deal with. For surely there is some thinking of the problem that makes it known to us that it is the sort of thing we find too difficult to think.

25. As if one has a modern horizon and an ancient horizon and the scholar's job is to merge them. This is a misunderstanding of Gadamer. To take only one small example, see his remarks in the afterword to Hans-Georg Gadamer, *Truth and Method*, 2nd ed. (New York: Continuum, 1996), 576–77 (e.g., "working out the historical horizon of a text is always already a fusion of horizons," 577; cf. xxxiv in the foreword to the second edition). There are of course exceptions within NT studies. See, e.g., J. Louis Martyn's use of Gadamer to critique Troels Engberg-Pedersen's *Paul and the Stoics* ("De-apocalypticizing Paul: An Essay Focused on *Paul and the Stoics* by Troels Engberg-Pedersen," *JSNT* 86 [2002]: 68–69); or, with an insightful attempt to put Gadamer in conversation with J. G. Hamann, Jonathan A. Linebaugh, "Relational Hermeneutics and Comparison as Conversation," in *The New Testament in Comparison: Validity, Method, and Purpose in Comparing Traditions*, ed. John M. G. Barclay and B. G. White, LNTS (London: T&T Clark, 2020), esp. 147.

26. *Erfahrung* names for Gadamer something like "the entirety of the human experience

terms of "method" and insisted instead on the dialectical nature of question/answer and the claim to truth as ingredient to all understanding.[27] All statements/propositions/declarations (*Aussagen*) encountered in a text, thought Gadamer, presuppose questions, and understanding is the experience of being asked those questions. Furthermore, those questions are by their nature as questions put to the interpreter as questions of truth, questions that demanded one answer or another. The point is that interpretation is not something we can objectify methodologically but is rather a dialogical confrontation with truth.[28] As he puts it near the end of *Truth and Method*, "The whole value of hermeneutical experience—like the significance of history for human knowledge in general—[consists] in the fact that here we are not simply filing things in pigeonholes but that what we encounter in a tradition says something to us. Understanding, then, does not consist in a technical virtuosity of 'understanding' everything written. Rather, it is a genuine experience (*Erfahrung*)—i.e., an encounter with something that asserts itself as truth."[29] According to Gadamer, readers of an ancient text are thus put in the position—whether wittingly or not—of having to decide on the truth of that which confronts them: "The written word makes the argued reader the arbiter of its claim to truth. . . . What [the reader] understands is always more than an unfamiliar opinion: it is always possible truth."[30]

Confronting truth in the form of a question that demands an answer does not mean that the answer an interpreter gives is a foregone conclusion, even if the question itself—in its *Situationshorizont*—comes from a text whose situation implied a particular answer.[31] But, for Gadamer, the idea that we could understand a text and avoid its question-putting force is incoherent. Understanding and dialogue with the text are one and the same thing.[32] Exactly to

of understanding," not an isolated aspect of that understanding (as if there were such a thing as experience qua experience).

27. Gadamer is clear that the question/answer dialectic does not mean that there can be only one question. There are often questions (plural); but the hermeneutical point remains exactly the same.

28. Hence the title of his most famous work.

29. Gadamer, *Truth and Method*, 489.

30. Gadamer, *Truth and Method*, 394.

31. On the point about *Situationshorizont* and, e.g., the role of historical research, see briefly his "Was ist Wahrheit?," in *Kleine Schriften* (Tübingen: Mohr Siebeck, 1967), esp. 1:55.

32. To understand something at all is to be able to understand it as *said* to oneself (otherwise it is just gibberish and we do not understand it: *Truth and Method*, 442). This is the truth that language reveals to us: exactly to the extent that we understand it at all, we understand it as said to us, as spoken to us, as in dialogue with us (cf. 446). Cf. Donald

the degree that we understand a text, we know that it offers more than an "unfamiliar opinion"; we know it questions us with the possibility of truth.[33]

The advocates of not-theology pretend this isn't so. They catalogue as "unfamiliar opinions" the questions of truth the NT puts to its readers and insist on the seriousness of method instead. In short, where the NT "asserts itself as truth" and requires an answer, the not-theologians simply try to avoid the question and change the subject. This is deflection: the realization that the NT puts questions of truth with the simultaneous attempt to avoid acknowledging them.

We could pick any number of compositions or verses from the NT to illustrate the point, but for the sake of space we will mention only five. These have been selected because they are indicative of the wider theological grammar of the NT; that is, they are not isolated verses of this or that unusual moment within the NT but are instances of regular, large-scale patterns across multiple texts and time periods.[34]

(1) John 3:15–17: the Son of Man will be lifted up "so that everyone who believes in him will have eternal life. For God so loved the cosmos that he gave his only begotten Son so that everyone who believes in him will not perish but will have eternal life. For God did not send his Son into the cosmos in order that the cosmos might be judged but in order that the cosmos might be saved through him." No three verses can summarize the complexity of John's Gospel, of course, but these three get about as close as possible.[35] The point for the present essay is that the questions that go with the truth assertion are crystal clear and, significantly, do not disappear even when the text is "historicised." That is, within the horizon of John's Gospel, the truth claim applies to any

Marshall's concise remark on Gadamer's view: "If we understand a text that has come down to us from the past, then that understanding has the character of a dialogue" (D. G. Marshall, "On Dialogue: To Its Cultural Despisers," in *Gadamer's Repercussions: Reconsidering Philosophical Hermeneutics*, ed. B. Kajewski [Berkeley: University of California Press, 2003], 130).

33. This would be the case even for what we initially see as fantastical, reject as false, and so forth. The very fact that we reject something as false or outrageous, for example, tells us that we understand its implicit claim to be possible truth.

34. To say it only slightly differently: they are focal instances of larger narratives—whether explicit or implicit—in which they are found and that give them the sense they have. On the indispensability of narrative for word meaning, see my "Making Friends and Comparing Lives," esp. 157–63, and "A Response to Friend-Critics," esp. 188–92, in part 2 of this volume.

35. These verses have been overused in popular evangelism, but such overuse does not make it any less true that they summarize well the gospel's main themes. In fact, the popularity may have something to do with an intuitive grasp of their overall importance.

and all—the correlation of God and cosmos is universal—and no amount of first-century reading can reduce this claim.[36] To understand the text is to understand that it asks whether or not overcoming death depends on a response to the Son of God—and that it asks this question to any and all of its readers.[37] There is no moment in human history at which the death of any reader of John would cease to be on that reader's horizon. The gospel asserts that there is a way to deal with our impending death, and exactly to the degree that we understand the gospel's claim do we understand that we have been asked the question about our death.

(2) Romans 10:9: "If you confess with your mouth that Jesus is Lord and believe in your heart that God raised him from the dead, you will be saved." While all NT scholars would affirm that this text was meant for the Roman Christians as a word on target, it is equally clear that only if we deflect the "you" could we fail to realize that the text puts the question to all "yous" who have come since Paul penned the epistle. Any time Romans is understood, the text asserts that what it says here is true.[38] One could, of course, extract this verse from Romans and assign it a different meaning, but there is no case in which Romans could be the text of *Romans* where this assertion would not be meant as true. Contextualizing the sentence in first-century Rome or arguing about the meaning of "saved" in the ancient world does nothing whatsoever to blunt or alter its truth claim for other readers. For all readers, it is there for

36. The idea that we cannot understand a text until we know its historical occasion is, as Gadamer shows, far too simplistic an account of historical understanding. For Gadamer, "occasionality" is not a barrier to understanding but a part of all understanding. We understand the text in some ways upon the first reading, and as a result are impelled to look for a particular occasion, which when found helps us to understand more of the text, which then enriches our sense of the occasion of the text, and so forth. But, note, Gadamer does not think that this is a linear process or a step-wise one: it is schematized like that so that he can draw our attention to the various features of the work of understanding, but the actual working out of a particular occasion of a text—and the hermeneutics that allow us to name this as what is going on—is simply a part of the whole experience of understanding. Put differently, the dialectic that is the relation between part and whole includes the working out of the occasion of the text as part of the interplay of part/whole. Put differently still, the *Vorverständnis* that goes with us whenever we read and interpret will always include occasionality. See Gadamer, *Truth and Method*, esp. 497.

37. There are other questions here, too, of course. Is there a God? What about death? Who's the Son? What's belief? and so on. The multiplicity of crucial questions only highlights the fact that there are questions embedded in understanding.

38. An easy way to see this is to try imagining a case where Paul would not think this is true. There is no such case.

you. The meant is the meaning; the assertion of truth comes precisely as we understand what is said.[39]

(3) Galatians 4:4–6: "When the fullness of time came, God sent forth his son, born of a woman, born under the law, so that he might deliver/redeem those under the law so that we might receive adoption/sonship." The central argument in Galatians is conducted along the axis of time/age (Lou Martyn was right about this, among other things). The fundamental problem in Galatia is that the "teachers" have missed the significance of Christ's death and resurrection for the shift of the ages and have gotten the time wrong; those Christians who follow them are attempting to live in the wrong time. The question that comes to the readers of the letter is, In what time do you live? Is time itself affected by Jesus Christ? How do we mark time so that we know what to do because we know when we are living? Is it true that we can or need to know what time it is in the cosmos? Again, exactly to the degree that we can understand these questions, we understand that Galatians presupposes them and asserts the truth of a particular answer. Precisely to the degree that we can articulate the argument of the letter to the Galatians do we show that we have already understood the questions it asks.[40] Insisting that these are not questions that confront current readers of Galatians is akin to insisting that they are not questions at all (and is a simultaneous admission that we have not understood the letter).

(4) Mark 8:27–29 (Matt. 16:13–16//Luke 9:18–20): "And Jesus asked his disciples, 'Who do the people say that I am?' And they said to him, 'John the Baptist, and others Elijah, and others that you're one of the prophets.' And he answered them, 'But who do you say that I am?' And Peter answered, 'You are the Messiah.'" In the synoptic accounts, Jesus puts the central question directly. It is the question that funds the dramatic tension in the gospel literature and

39. This does not mean that there would be no differences in how we fill out the picture: how we understand salvation, for example, would naturally be construed differently in different epochs or places. But—and here's the point—in none of these construals would the claim Paul makes be taken to express Paul's opinion of the matter which he could just as easily take as leave.

40. Cf. Gadamer's perceptive remark that in questioning what we are to believe, we reveal that our questioning "arrives too late," that is, post-understanding: "Someone who understands is always already drawn into an event through which meaning asserts itself. . . . When we understand a text, what is meaningful in it captivates us just as the beautiful captivates us. It has asserted itself and captivated us before we can come to ourselves and be in a position to test the claim to meaning that it makes. . . . In understanding we are drawn into an event of truth and arrive, as it were, too late, if we want to know what we are supposed to believe" (*Truth and Method*, 490).

reverberates throughout the early Christian sources: Who is Jesus? Of course, the reader of Mark (and Matthew and Luke) can answer this question in light of the story: according to the narrative, Peter gets Jesus's identity right. But that is obviously just another way to ask the main question: Is the narrative right to present Jesus this way—as the Jewish Messiah? Is that who he was—in fact no less than in claim? The assertion of the truth here cannot be missed for the simple reason that we understand the claim so clearly. The text says that Jesus was the Messiah. It meant and means that. As Gadamer would point out, the perception of the question that goes with this assertion entails the realization that we understand exactly what confronts us. Assuming that we are not asked this question is, once again, the same thing as saying that we do not understand it (which in this instance is for NT scholars rather preposterous). We may of course want to say all kinds of things about the meaning of *Christos* in its first-century context, but as we do we will still discover when reading the Gospels that the question/answer dialectic turns out to be exactly the way the claim to truth about Jesus's identity is made. The basic assertion of truth and its necessary question remain: Is that who Jesus is?[41]

(5) Revelation 1:8 (Lord God); 21:6 (God); 22:13 (Jesus): "'I am the Alpha and Omega,' says the Lord God, 'the One who Is, the One who Was, and the One who is To Come'" (1:8); "And the One on the throne said to me, 'I am the Alpha and the Omega, the beginning and the end'" (21:6); Jesus says, "I am the Alpha and the Omega, the first and the last, the beginning and the end" (22:13; we know from 22:16, along with other evidence, that it is Jesus speaking). It may well be harder to find the questions Revelation works with—that is, to understand the text—than it is to land upon them in the Gospels or Paul, for example, but these three Alpha/Omega sayings assert the truth that all of human life is encompassed within the parentheses of God's self-identification, revelation, and act in Jesus of Nazareth. Once again, situating Revelation within a context of imperial domination and ad hoc persecution may help to illuminate such a claim as a claim to God's ultimate sovereignty over the emperor and the violent death he deals.[42] But such historicizing does nothing whatsoever to qualify the statements as claims to truth. To understand the text is to understand that it asserts that the answer to the question

41. For an interpretation that presses the significance of the Gospels' truth assertion, see Richard B. Hays, *Echoes of Scripture in the Gospels* (Waco, TX: Baylor University Press, 2016), esp. 365.

42. See, e.g., Steven J. Friesen, *Imperial Cults and the Apocalypse of John: Reading Revelation in the Ruins* (New York: Oxford University Press, 2001).

of origin and end—the question of the encompassing of all human life—lies in God's identification with Jesus. Understanding *that* it is this question and this answer simply means that one understands it is *this*—which, in turn, means that the reader of the Apocalypse is inescapably asked the question of whether the assertion is true.

In all of these passages, the work of understanding comes as "an encounter with something that asserts itself as truth." Reading as if this is not so—assuming that understanding the text is possible without grasping its claim to truth—is deflection, a defensive substitution of the issue of method for something that aims at truth.

Truth

To speak with Gadamer of the hermeneutical event of reading the NT texts as an encounter with the assertion of truth begs for additional clarification and elaboration. There are, after all, many kinds of truth. The kind of truth at which the NT aims is what I have elsewhere called lived truth, truth that is inseparable from a pattern of human existence through which the truth about God is understood and displayed.[43] If Gadamer was right that understanding a text requires the recognition of the assertion of truth—the question/answer that the text puts to its readers—what he left out was the fact that some questions and answers are not simply those of the dialogical intellect (as if there were such a thing as a "reading mind" that could be divorced from the person whose mind it is).[44]

The NT does not, for example, primarily ask its readers to evaluate the correspondence of its assertions with the exterior world; its emphasis is rather on trusting the truth enough to live by it, a kind of hanging of your existence on the truth by the style of life you adopt and exhibit. Sentences such as "God so loved the world" are not so much to be met with an "I agree with or assent to that" or a "That is the way it is with the world in actual fact" as they are with a pattern of life that shows what its truth means. The entire Gospel of John, that is, assumes that "God so loved the world" is a way of life; its truth shows up for

43. See C. Kavin Rowe, *World Upside Down: Reading Acts in the Graeco-Roman Age* (New York: Oxford University Press, 2009), 160–76, and *One True Life: The Stoics and Early Christians as Rival Traditions* (New Haven: Yale University Press, 2016), 215–58.

44. I use "mind" here colloquially, not as a way to endorse a view of "mind" that takes it to be a "thing" that is fundamentally different from the body (or brain), which would be taken to be yet another "thing," and so on.

what it is in the patterns of the community that exhibit trusting belief (*pistis*) in God's Son. One "does" the truth (3:21). John's Gospel refuses the modern separation of intellect and life, so powerful since at least Descartes, and locates truth in the full trajectory of a human life: thinking, willing, being—in short, living. In fact, the whole sweep of the NT texts is virtually unintelligible apart from the basic sense that the assertions of truth are built on questions about the lives of its readers. This is what Kierkegaard saw so clearly when he provocatively said that original "Christianity wanted to protect itself against acquiring characterless assistant professors instead of witnesses."[45] The question/answer "dialectic" is embodied in the life of the reader.

Deflection, then, not only turns from truth to method but also positions readers of the NT existentially in an attempt to "tear apart the act of thinking from the act of living."[46] If we learn from Diamond that thinking can be deflected, we also learn from the NT itself that the sort of thinking that is "deflection" is existentially committed whether one wants it to be or not. Precisely because of the kinds of questions put to the reader through the NT's claims to truth, the response to the truth of the NT can never be other than a lived response. To put it simply now: Jesus of Nazareth can either be the Jewish Messiah or not, and whether we take him to be or not is a decision that inflects the lives we live even as the lives we live display what we take to be true. When it comes to this kind of truth, there is no such thing, in George Steiner's pointed phrase, as the "immunity of indirection."[47] The advocates of not-theology—and any and all of their cousins—thus take positions on the lives we live even as they proclaim their skill in avoiding central theological questions. Their proclamation is self-deceived, of course, as it must be if they understand what they read, but the deeper trouble is their false commentary on the possibility of lives of indifference.[48]

45. Søren Kierkegaard, "Was Bishop Mynster a 'Truth-Witness,' One of 'the Authentic Truth-Witnesses'—Is This the Truth?," in *"The Moment" and Late Writings*, ed. Howard V. Hong and Edna H. Hong (Princeton: Princeton University Press, 1998), 4.

46. Rudolf Bultmann, *Theology of the New Testament*, 2 vols. (New York: Scribner, 1951–1955), 2:250–51, with reference to Adolf Schlatter's famous essay "The Theology of the NT and Dogmatics" (cf. 249).

47. Steiner, *Real Presences*, 39 (he uses the plural "immunities").

48. To take an example of someone who detested Christianity but understood that its truth claims had to do with life, we may think of Nietzsche. Nietzsche's version of Christianity was often a caricature—and he relied on a false division between Jesus the "one true Christian" and all others who were nothing of the kind—but he grasped what was put to him as a style of life and saw it for the canker it was to his own conception of authentic, powerful existence.

Implications

The proposal, then, for going back upstream in NT studies is rather simple: read for truth. Scholarship on the NT will probably not cease proliferating, but we can reclaim a seriousness in our study that matches the gravity of the texts that fund our inquiry.

Reading for truth obviously does not *eo ipso* entail an "acceptance" of the claims of the NT, but it does require us to take the NT seriously as the possibility of "God's question to us"—and, further, to dispense with self-deceptive interpretative grammars that claim to have no position on this question and try interminably to inhabit the distance Cavell saw between knowing and acknowledging.[49] Insofar as we understand what we read in the NT, we already know that our humanity is implicated in the question it puts to us about its truth and the shape of the lives that follow our answers. Acknowledging this simply makes explicit what we already know hermeneutically from the texts we understand—and thereby makes available to critical scrutiny of a thick, existential kind exactly what it is that we claim to know.

If, in addition to the ancients, our conversation partners on the question of truth become for a time more like Kierkegaard and even Nietzsche—who knew enough about seriousness to realize that NT Christianity had to be rejected if not accepted—then that is all to the good. They, and those like them, are not doves with olive leaves, but they do know that when the NT claims to be true, it means what it meant.

49. "God's question to us" (Gadamer, *Truth and Method*, Supp. I, 527).

The Kerygma of the Earliest Church

With the aging and retirement of scholars who knew the power of Bultmann's thought first- or secondhand, we risk losing our habits of grappling seriously with a remarkable theological thinker. The volume in which this essay originally appeared, *Beyond Bultmann: Reckoning a New Testament Theology*, is therefore to be welcomed if for no other reason than that it helps to ensure sophistication in reflection upon issues of NT interpretation: an educated engagement with Bultmann's *Theology of the New Testament* requires an awareness of a staggeringly wide range of both subtle and complicated issues. If we are to move beyond Bultmann, we will have to display the requisite level of thought needed to engage him. For that, we may well need a whole volume of contributors.

In this essay my focus is primarily restricted to the section of Bultmann's *Theology* titled "The Kerygma of the Earliest Church."[1] Despite endorsing the need to move "beyond Bultmann," I first identify two features of his thinking in that section that we should continue to make our own. I then discuss three other features that are problematical and require either considerable refinement or wholesale rejection. I conclude with some brief reflections on the significance of the *Theology* as a whole.

Bultmannian Insights

The German original of Bultmann's *Theology* is structured in three parts. Part 1 contains "The Presuppositions" of NT theology; part 2 offers an interpreta-

1. All citations of Bultmann's *Theology* refer to *Theology of the New Testament*, 2 vols. (Waco, TX: Baylor University Press, 2007).

"The Kerygma of the Earliest Church" was originally published in Bruce W. Longenecker and Mikeal C. Parsons, eds., chapter 2 of *Beyond Bultmann: Reckoning a New Testament Theology* (Waco, TX: Baylor University Press, 2014), 23–37. It is included with the permission of Baylor University Press.

tion of Paul and John that forms the material theological center of the work; part 3 traces the development toward the ancient church. "The Kerygma of the Earliest Church" is the second chapter of part 1 and follows Bultmann's reconstruction of Jesus's preaching and teaching. The location of this chapter makes a significant statement about Bultmann's understanding of its place within NT theology. He opens the *Theology* with the well-known statement that "the message of Jesus is a presupposition for the theology of the New Testament rather than a part of that theology itself" (1.3). He continues, "Christian faith did not exist until there was a Christian kerygma; i.e., a kerygma proclaiming Jesus Christ—specifically Jesus Christ the Crucified and Risen One—to be God's eschatological act of salvation. He was first so proclaimed in the kerygma of the earliest Church, not in the message of the historical Jesus. . . . Thus, theological thinking—the theology of the New Testament—begins with the kerygma of the earliest Church and not before" (1.3). Justifying the fact that he reconstructs Jesus's message anyway, Bultmann goes on to say that of course the preaching of the historical Jesus is not irrelevant for discerning the theology of the NT, since in fact Jesus's preaching is "among" the historical presuppositions for the rise of ecclesial kerygma. But it should not be mistaken for a part of the kerygma itself. Ecclesial kerygma, for Bultmann, is the beginning of real theology.

By framing things hermeneutically in this way, Bultmann establishes a dialectic that is central to his overall thought: on the one hand, there is a distance between the historical Jesus and the church, and, on the other, there is a trajectory from the historical Jesus to the church's kerygma, an unfolding of the significance of Jesus in historical time.

"The Kerygma of the Earliest Church," then, presents the first stuff of NT theology. It is not simply a theologically elaborate repetition of what the historical Jesus was about, but it nevertheless follows from him as the content of his significance. On the way to delineating the first kerygma about Jesus, Bultmann makes two highly significant points that remain either self-evidently or defensibly true.

(1) First, he famously says that "the proclaimer became the proclaimed" (1.33). By this Bultmann means that the "essential thing to see" in the earliest period is that "he who formerly had been the bearer of the message was drawn into it and became its essential content" (1.33). The historical Jesus did not, so Bultmann thinks in light of his extensive study of the Synoptic Gospels,[2] arrive on the Galilean scene proclaiming himself as God's Messiah

2. See Rudolf Bultmann, *The History of the Synoptic Tradition*, rev. ed., trans. John Marsh

or Savior. He instead announced "the radical demand of God" (1.34). It was the church that shifted the preaching by Jesus to the preaching about Jesus. Recognizing this fact, however, raises the "central" christological question: "In what sense?" (1.33). In what sense, Bultmann asks, did the Proclaimer become the Proclaimed?

Making his way to an answer, Bultmann rejects four options that historically have been important to the way Christians have conceived of the significance of Jesus. First, the movement from Proclaimer to Proclaimed did not happen because the church recognized Jesus as the Messiah in his earthly life. "Earthly Messiah," in Bultmann's view, did not explicate Jesus's significance. Why? Because initially the church did not think that Jesus was Messiah in his earthly life. "It is clear . . . that when Jesus was proclaimed as Messiah it was as the coming Messiah, in other words as the Son of Man. Not his return as Messiah, but his coming as Messiah was expected. That is, his then past activity on earth was not yet considered messianic by the earliest Church" (1.33; cf. 1.28–32). As far as "Messiah" goes, the earliest church thought of Jesus only as the future/coming Messiah.

Second, the movement from Proclaimer to Proclaimed cannot be explained on the basis of Jesus's teaching or prophetic role. Even Jesus's messianic identity "does not rest upon the fact that he was prophet and teacher" (1.34). The reason? "However much [Jesus's] preaching in its radicality is directed against Jewish legalism, still its content is nothing else than true Old Testament-Jewish faith in God radicalized in the direction of the great prophets' teaching" (1.34). Jesus's teaching and prophetic critique, that is, show no fundamental originality. Indeed, Bultmann argues, Jesus's "concepts of God, world, and man, of law and grace, of repentance and forgiveness . . . are not new in comparison with those of the Old Testament and Judaism, however radically they may be understood" (1.34). Even his radical interpretation of the Torah "stands within the scribal discussions about it" (1.35). Because the content of Jesus's message is still altogether Jewish, his significance cannot, so Bultmann thinks, be seen in this light.[3]

Third, the movement from Proclaimer to Proclaimed cannot be explained in terms of the greatness of Jesus's personality, as if what the earliest church saw in him was an "impressive power behind his teaching" or a "numinous

(Peabody, MA: Hendrickson, 1994), originally published as *Die Geschichte der synoptischen Tradition* (Göttingen: Vandenhoeck & Ruprecht, 1921).

3. For Bultmann this lack of originality also explains a potentially confusing fact of the NT—namely, why so little of Jesus's synoptic (or synoptic-like) language appears in Paul's letters or the Gospel of John. So, too, does Jesus's rootedness within Judaism explain why "modern liberal Judaism" can esteem him as a teacher (1.35).

figure" (1.35). True, Jesus worked miracles and the like, but the earliest church understood him neither as someone to "imitate" nor as "one who heroically sacrifices himself for his cause" nor, again, as a supernatural "divine man of the Hellenistic world" (1.35). "The personality of Jesus," says Bultmann, "has no importance for the kerygma either of Paul or of John or for the New Testament in general. Indeed the tradition of the earliest Church did not even unconsciously preserve a picture of his personality. Every attempt to reconstruct one remains a play of subjective imagination" (1.35). Jesus's gravitas, his charisma, his ability to call disciples to himself—none of this explains the move from Proclaimer to Proclaimed.

Fourth, the movement from Proclaimer to Proclaimed cannot be explained on the basis of the church's understanding of Jesus's unique place in history, as if the church originally conceived of him as the most significant event to occur in time. Nor was his ministry "understood as a decisive event for Israel's history like the call of Moses, the exodus from Egypt, the giving of the law on Sinai, or God's raising up of kings and prophets" (1.36). The church does not look back to Jesus because his "importance as Messiah-Son-of-Man lies not at all in what he did in the past, but entirely in what is expected of him for the future. And once this expectation is fulfilled by the eschatological drama, that event will never become, like the crossing of the Red Sea, a past to which one could look back thankfully . . . but it will be God's last deed of all, by which he puts history to an end" (1.36). In what, then, does the movement from Proclaimer to Proclaimed consist? In what "sense" does Bultmann think we should understand this transformation?

Bultmann's answer turns on his coordination of implicit claim with explicit understanding (a mirror image, of course, of the movement from Jesus's proclamation to the proclamation about him). By means of its self-understanding as the eschatological congregation, the earliest church implicitly commented upon the significance of Jesus's life: it was the eschatological occurrence. Jesus's proclamation, that is, entailed eschatological existence, and the church's form of life translated this proclamation by focusing it upon the person of Jesus himself and the one who called all things into being. Proclaiming Jesus explicated Jesus's proclamation precisely in its ability to see Jesus as the eschatological event (1.33–37; cf. esp. 1.43). The earliest church was not as clear on this point as was Paul, for example, but it was nevertheless conscious of "being already the called and chosen Congregation of the end of days" (1.42). Focusing on Bultmann's thesis about Jesus and the eschatological event takes us immediately to the second major theme of this section—the church as the eschatological community.

(2) So, second, in "The Kerygma of the Earliest Church" Bultmann argues that the best way to describe "church" is to speak of it as "the eschatological congregation." Both Paul and the synoptic tradition testify to the earliest church's self-understanding as the "vestibule, so to speak, of God's Reign that is shortly to appear" (1.37). The Twelve are not so much a dozen men appointed as apostles as they are "eschatological regents," those who will "rule the tribes of Israel" (1.37).[4] Subsequent to Jesus's resurrection appearances in Galilee, his followers did not stay put but gathered in Jerusalem, thus signifying their understanding of the central city as the focus of God's coming reign (1.37). And, rather tellingly of course, the church referred to itself as the *ekklēsia*, the principal term the Septuagint used to render the OT's theologically pregnant "congregation of Yahweh (קְהַל־יְהוָה)." Its members were "the chosen," "the elect," and "the saints"—all terms that point to a consciousness of eschatological existence (1.37–38).

Moreover, the earliest church engaged in five practices that evidenced the church's eschatological existence. Baptism was an initiation rite that both made people members of the eschatological congregation and purified them from sin. Common meals brought them together with a feeling of joy (ἀγαλλίασις). Speaking prophecies and in tongues testified to the Spirit's presence. Reading (OT) scripture—especially the prophecies—interpreted the current time as the end, the final fulfillment of God's promises made long ago. And the church's mission reflected its sense that the "immediately impending end" required a hastening to spread the news of the coming of God's reign (1.39–42). Individually, these practices may or may not be particularly significant vis-à-vis other first-century Jewish groups. But taken together they signify a community that is "distinguished from other sects and trends" by the fact of its eschatological determination (1.42 et passim).

Of course the history of NT scholarship has made it somewhat difficult to know what "eschatological" actually means (whether it is the same as or fundamentally different from apocalyptic, for example). Mercifully, however, Bultmann is clear. Applied to the earliest church, eschatological means a community that is living under the expectation of an imminent end and with a substantively different sense of time than that of the normal, everyday running of the world. It means, further and more specifically, a community that roots its own existence in the fact "that Jesus' having come was itself the decisive event" (1.43). For Bultmann, therefore, the eschatological church and the life of Jesus were inextricably bound.

4. Bultmann of course does not really think that the historical Jesus called twelve (1.37).

Indeed, it is exactly "Jesus' meaning" to the earliest church that provides the unity in Bultmann's overarching argument in this section of the *Theology*; to the church that proclaimed him, the Proclaimer means that the eschaton is on its way. That is why, after all, the congregation exists at all.

In a broad sense, these two points of Bultmann's *Theology* should, I think, remain central to the way in which we think about NT theology. This is not to say that Bultmann is right in the details of his reconstruction or even that he conceptualizes the material theological concerns in a way that we should emulate (see below). But it is to say that he saw something of the fundamental or underlying questions that confront the inquisitive modern reader of the NT.

All moderns are aware of the fact that the rise of the "historical Jesus" creates the need to decide whether or not—or to what degree—NT theology should deal with scholarly reconstructions of the man from Nazareth. In one sense, Bultmann, too, obviously takes a clear position on this matter—that is, the historically reconstructed Jesus should play no part in a theology of the NT.[5] In another sense, however, with his distinction between the Proclaimer and the Proclaimed, Bultmann merely relocates the same crucial question about the distance between Jesus and the NT to the NT texts themselves. Any reader of the Synoptic Gospels, he suggests, can see that Jesus does not talk about himself as much as he does about other things—the kingdom of God, the seeking of the lost, the coming of the Son of Man, the poor and downtrodden, the last days, and so forth. And any reader of the Gospel of John or the apostle Paul can see that something has changed. In John's Gospel, Jesus speaks about himself continuously, and in Paul's letters the focus is not upon Jesus's earthly teaching—either that he taught or the things about which he taught—but upon the implications of the profound change from old to new creation effected by Jesus's death and resurrection. Indeed, outside of Matthew, Mark, and Luke, the whole of the NT shows little interest in repeating Jesus's message. Bultmann, in short, may well reject the idea that scholarly reconstructions of Jesus should be admitted into NT theology proper, but his conception of the division between synoptic tradition and other NT witnesses requires him to conceive an answer to the same basic question of distance posed by the historical Jesus.

While recent studies have shown that the Synoptic Gospels are more concerned with articulating the identity of the Proclaimer than Bultmann ever ap-

5. In this he is right, as I suggest in "New Testament Theology: The Revival of a Discipline," in part 1 of this volume.

preciated,[6] his basic point that the inside of the NT itself displays a movement from words of Jesus to words about Jesus remains critically important. We may well now disagree with Bultmann about the hermeneutical viability of form criticism, but no theology of the NT that attends to the literary surface area of the NT itself can fail to account for the shift that takes place as one moves from the Synoptic Gospels into the rest of the NT. As Bultmann saw,[7] this shift contains *in nuce* the essential question of the specific connection between Jesus and the church, or, to state it slightly differently, how Christology and ecclesiology are mutually informing and inseparably intertwined. Systematic theologians have thought long and repeatedly about this connection (or lack thereof). But those who would directly engage in NT interpretation need to as well. The reason is simple: the question is endemic to the NT itself.

It is no accident, therefore, that Bultmann next moved to consider the church as the eschatological congregation. In broad terms, this understanding of the church is exactly what is to be expected if one sees Jesus as the decisive revelation of God. It is true, thankfully, that more current research on the NT has shown that the development of a sense of history and the need for ecclesial order—such as we find in the Acts of the Apostles and the Pastoral Epistles, for example—are not inversely related to a sense of the end. But it remains the case that Bultmann has clearly seen the result of the advent of Jesus. The time in which the community of his followers finds itself differs profoundly from that of the steady running of the world, and the community engages in regular practices that mark this difference. We do not have to agree with Bultmann about the early Christians' understanding of Jesus's return as the (first) coming of the Messiah to see the general accuracy of Bultmann's reading of the church as a community whose sense of time has radically changed in direct relation to God's act in Jesus.

But there are significant problems with "The Kerygma of the Earliest Church." To these we now turn.

Bultmannian Problems

There are, of course, many small matters that would bring disagreement from a variety of scholars, but this is no more significant than the nature of scholar-

6. C. Kavin Rowe, *Early Narrative Christology: The Lord in the Gospel of Luke*, BZNW 139 (Berlin: de Gruyter, 2006; repr., Grand Rapids: Baker Academic, 2009).

7. Bultmann was not much concerned with the literary surface area of the NT. Writing well after Wrede's *Messiasgeheimnis*, he knew the Synoptics were theological portraits. My point is that even those who understand now that the sort of form criticism Bultmann practiced has been hermeneutically problematized will still have to deal with the question he posed.

ship itself: we do not always agree. But there are at least three more substantive problems with this section of the *Theology* that call for serious criticism.

First, as is the case with much pre-Sanders scholarship, Bultmann's discussion of things Jewish is problematic. Jesus, he says, criticizes "Jewish legalism" (1.54). The early church failed "to achieve freedom from the Law"; indeed, a "retrogression had taken place so that the old scruples and fidelity to the law had gradually gained ground" (1.54). The antinomian conclusions of "the Hellenists" were "terrifying," and led to the creation of fear-stopping, Torah-upholding sayings by Jesus (e.g., Matt. 5:17). The church may well have tried to maintain "a critical attitude toward Jewish legalism" and to break with "the Jewish idea of merit," but it could not free itself because it "clung to the Law" as a "characteristic of the Chosen People which it was conscious of embodying" (1.54–55). The growth of the "church concept" in the earliest Christian community was "of course hindered . . . by its ties to the Jewish congregation. The Church as eschatological Congregation had not yet found appropriate expression in a cult of its own, since it had not cut itself loose from the temple cult" (1.57). In short, one of the problems of the early church was that it was too Jewish. It was Paul who was able to break the mold and to reach for true freedom from merit.[8]

For all the spinning of the wheels in NT scholarship, this is one instance in which research really has moved on. Perhaps it is no fault of his own, but it is nevertheless the case that Bultmann is here woefully out of date. First-century Jews were not "legalists," and their faithful adherence to Torah was not "legalism," a style of living before God that attempted to earn "merit" in his eyes. The Torah was a gift, the sign of God's covenant with his beloved people, the pattern of life by which they testified to his steadfast and loving kindness. Where they failed, God had provided ways by which they could be forgiven and restored, ways that were given in the Torah itself. Bultmann did not live to see NT scholars' "new perspective" on the Judaism of the time, but for all of us on this side of it, we have to consider it "beyond" him.

As he progresses through the *Theology* (and in much of his other work), it becomes clear, however, that Bultmann's presentation of ancient Judaism is not only a claim to historical understanding. Judaism, for Bultmann, also represents a deficient theological anthropology—namely, the view that the human problem is something that can be overcome by training the will to

8. For Bultmann's reading of Paul, see Richard B. Hays's and John M. G. Barclay's essays in the volume in which this essay originally appeared: Hays, "Humanity Prior to the Revelation of Faith," in *Beyond Bultmann*, 61–78; Barclay, "Humanity under Faith," in *Beyond Bultmann*, 79–100.

obey the law(s) of God. Bultmann is correct that this is a naive and bad anthropology—as Kierkegaard definitively showed in his discussion of the ethical man—but it was not Judaism's anthropology. It cannot, therefore, be used as the historical foil for the Christian understanding of humanity. At this point at least, scholarship on ancient Judaism would move us beyond Bultmann philosophically as well.[9]

Second, as is well known, Bultmann assigns a remarkably important role to the kerygma. Not only does the title of the section in focus (and the following section) already suggest that what is most important to know about the early church is its kerygma; it is also the case that a close reading of this section helps to shape the understanding of kerygma as a whole that will be employed throughout the *Theology*.

And just here is the problem. If in light of the subsection's title one asks the rather simple question that comes naturally to mind, "What is the kerygma of the earliest church?" the answer is surprisingly elusive. It is elusive, first, because Bultmann does not actually thematize "kerygma" to the degree that one might expect but instead simply uses the language throughout the section as a way to talk about what he's getting at, the telos, as it were, of his investigations. And, second, the kerygma of the early church is elusive because, sensu stricto, Bultmann does not think that kerygma has a specific conceptual content. It is conceptually received and interpreted, to be sure, but the thing itself does not subsist in concepts. To those unfamiliar with his broader theological corpus, this view of kerygma may seem surprising or even strange, but it is a structurally crucial aspect of Bultmann's larger thought.[10]

It is true, of course, that he can speak of "the specifically Christian kerygma" in contrast and connection to Jesus's message (e.g., 1.59). And it is true, more generally, that he talks frequently of "faith in the kerygma" as if faith had a specific content—for example, faith in "God's dealing in the man Jesus of Nazareth" (2.239 et passim). But such statements are misleading if understood to say that the kerygma itself could ever correspond to, for example, the Apostles' Creed, or some earlier creedal-like formulation. As he puts it in the epilogue, the kerygma "is just what theology can never seize in definitive form; it can

9. Lest this further significance go unnoticed: it is not only historical inaccuracy that is at stake here but also certain philosophical judgments about human beings that are coordinated with a particular picture of history; with Bultmann's historical picture now gone, his philosophical judgments should follow—or find independent ground.

10. It is an essential corollary to his emphasis on the preaching of the Word as that which calls for an existential decision: it is the event, not the specific content, of preaching that brings one to decision.

always take hold of it only as something conceptually stated, and that means as something already theologically interpreted" (2.240). Indeed, throughout the epilogue Bultmann explicitly discusses the kerygma in a way that makes his work in the earlier parts of the book intelligible.

Kerygma, for Bultmann, is "God's word addressing man as a questioning and promising word, a condemning and forgiving word" (2.240). Crucial here is the axis God-word-address; it is this connection that is meant both to negate the idea that the kerygma is something that can arise from within humanity's natural capacities and to affirm the way in which kerygma is free to remain kerygma. The kerygma is from God's side of things and reaches us as an addressing word that calls us to faith—a self-understanding that results from the decision to hear the address. Precisely because it confronts us as decision-requiring-address, the kerygma does not "offer itself to critical thought but speaks into one's concrete existence" (2.240). Kerygma that could be objectified by critical thought, Bultmann holds, would cease to address the hearer and, hence, cease to be the free gift of God's summons to new self-understanding in an authentic life.

Yet, once one has heard the kerygma and responded in faith, conceptual formulation must occur. The new self-understanding that is faith unfolds itself through "theological thoughts." Both "the kerygma and faith's self-understanding always appear in the texts, so far as they are expressed in words and sentences, already interpreted in some particular way—i.e., in theological thoughts" (2.239). Hence the Bultmannian dialectic: the kerygma both is and is not in the NT. It is not there because it does not consist in "theological thoughts"; it is there because it is already interpreted by "theological thoughts."

For some, a dialectic; for others, a pickle. In Bultmann's dialectic, the particularities of the NT's message are accidental. Christological content is not fundamentally wed to them; indeed, the content itself is not even really all that important. As he says in a statement that summarizes much of his thinking about the early church, "for the Church, as for Jesus himself, the content of his message was not the decisive thing. In his lifetime he had demanded decision for his person as the bearer of the Word; the Church has now made this decision" (1.43). In practice this means that Bultmann will not be able to find what he is seeking, that a great deal of exegetical groping is done after something that in principle cannot be grasped. In short, for all his emphasis upon the "act of existing" and the existential uptake that is the hearing of the kerygma, the kerygma for Bultmann is finally an abstraction.[11]

11. The kerygma is "real only in the act of existing" (2.241 et passim). For the argument

As Alasdair MacIntyre convincingly argued, however, we cannot know things such as action or word or person in abstraction but only within wider arenas of meaning that make these things intelligible to us.[12] There is no such thing, in other words, as kerygma or event or even the person of Jesus without the content that makes it intelligible.[13] The content of Jesus's message mattered (and matters) if for no other reason than that it cannot be otherwise. Absent such content we literally cannot know who or what "Jesus" is. However much Bultmann may wish to divide Jesus's message from Jesus or the church's teaching from the church's decision, therefore, he simply cannot do it. Bultmann's abstraction "kerygma" is at bottom only the fictitious creature of his intellect.

It is this problem, perhaps more than any other, that prohibits Bultmann from fully grasping the connection between the Proclaimer and the Proclaimed, which is exactly the unity of person/content through time.[14] Insofar as we recognize the Gospels are gospels, the Proclaimer is already the Proclaimed. The claim for unity is there in the very existence of the Gospels themselves; in the gospel form, Jesus's preaching is the proclamation of Jesus. The literary surface difference between the Synoptics and much of the rest of

---

that certain kinds of abstractions make it impossible to know what we are really talking about anymore, see Alasdair MacIntyre, "Colors, Cultures, and Practices," in *Selected Essays*, vol. 1, *The Tasks of Philosophy* (Cambridge: Cambridge University Press, 2006), esp. 38. MacIntyre's chief example that is directly applicable here is that of an imagined person whose language was entirely his own (Wittgenstein's "private language"). This figure, MacIntyre argues against those who try to reason from this imagined experience, is so abstract as to become philosophically meaningless: since all of our language is nonprivate, we literally have no conceptual possibilities for knowing how to speak well about such an imaginary figure.

12. Alasdair MacIntyre, *After Virtue*, 3rd ed. (Notre Dame, IN: University of Notre Dame Press, 2007), and MacIntyre, "The Intelligibility of Action," in *Rationality, Relativism, and the Human Sciences*, ed. J. Margolis, M. Krausz, and R. M. Burian (Dordrecht: Reidel, 1986), 63–80.

13. When Bultmann says that even a simple sentence such as "Jesus is Lord" already contains interpretation (of Lord, e.g.), he is hot on the trail of this insight. But he loses it again when he subsequently uses this example as proof that we cannot take the already interpreted NT statements as the kerygma.

14. Bultmann himself might reply that if we could find it by exegesis, we would have mastered it and it would no longer be address. There is a certain way in which this would be right, but more deeply such a view cuts out a significant part of the theological telos of exegesis, which is to test the faith against the biblical witness and clarify the content of whatever formulations we could ever dream up. It is true, of course, that Bultmann does use implicit/explicit language as a way to think about continuity. And this is good as far as it goes. The trouble is that it does not go far enough; we need more precision. What exactly is the implicit/explicit language meant to convey theologically?

the NT is simply a matter of theologically shaped history—that is, the claim that the content of the church's proclamation is the same as the person who proclaimed the church into being.[15] NT theology would do well to move beyond Bultmann at this point. Bultmann is right to focus on kerygma inasmuch as all Christian language is inescapably kerygmatic. But his focus turns out to be misleading because, in the end, he speaks not of Christian kerygma but of something that does not exist.[16]

Finally, though many of Bultmann's immediate intellectual forebears were considered Radical Critics (Bousset, Wrede, et al.), and though Bultmann himself often received the same laud/opprobrium, much of the textual work that provides the foundation for such judgments is—in hindsight—something more like guesswork or "uncritical" hypothesis making, a way of reasoning about history that lacks the disciplined historian's reserve and sobriety, or a willingness to be boring. To put it slightly differently, the invention of theories about the dynamics of the early church abounds where textual evidence is remarkably scant. It is true that it is better to be philosophically aware and sophisticated in one's views about history and religion than it is to be naive or simply confused—and, like F. C. Baur well before him, Bultmann was obviously both aware and sophisticated—but it is no less true that philosophical commitments to *Religionsgeschichte* will not (magically) supply what is left unsaid in the primary sources (even if such commitments turn out to be both defensible and correct). One need not deny, in fact, the basic *religionsgeschichtliche* claim that many things in the NT have their roots in "Jewish" or "Hellenistic" soil to appreciate the point that we often cannot see these roots.[17] Again and again, however, Bultmann attempts to see where we cannot. He says, for example, that baptism in the name of Christ "probably goes back to the usage of the Hellenistic-Christian congregations," and then continues, "But perhaps very early exorcistic effect (by means of naming 'the name of Jesus

15. Ecclesiology, to return to our earlier question, is thus communal Christology; or, in directly NT terms, the church is the body of Christ.

16. Another major problem with this section is Bultmann's treatment of the resurrection/empty tomb (esp. 1.44–45), but he states things more elaborately elsewhere, hence my decision not to thematize it here. On this problem in general, see Richard B. Hays, "Reading Scripture in Light of the Resurrection," in *The Art of Reading Scripture*, ed. Ellen F. Davis and Richard B. Hays (Grand Rapids: Eerdmans, 2003), 216–38.

17. Of course Jewish *or* Hellenistic has now long been seen as a problematic dichotomy (Martin Hengel and legions after him). The point here, however, is not about whether these are the right terms as much as it is about the philosophical commitment to the kind of history that makes this way of talking inevitable.

Christ' . . .) was already attributed to baptism. From what time the positive effect of endowment with the 'Spirit' was also attributed to it, is uncertain. It probably arose as a Hellenistic-Christian conception" (1.40). Later, he draws from his book on the synoptic tradition and asserts "that [Jesus's] sending meant doom for Jerusalem is expressed by the saying Lk. 13:34f. par., probably in origin a Jewish prophecy concerning 'Wisdom,' perhaps once quoted by Jesus, but as we now have it, reinterpreted by the church and put back into his mouth: It was he who had desired in vain to gather Jerusalem's 'children' together, so that it now was forsaken" (1.44). Or, to take only one more example from this indelible feature of the *Theology* as a whole, Bultmann argues that Jesus's saying in Matthew 10:5–6 ("go nowhere . . . but to the lost sheep of the house of Israel") "shows that in the earliest church there was at least a party which altogether rejected the mission to the Gentiles" (1.55).[18] To all this sort of thing, we can only shrug our shoulders and reply: well, maybe or maybe not; how could one possibly know?[19]

Drastically oversimplifying this last point, we could say that Bultmann is far quicker to offer speculative historical reconstructions than he is to accept the academic's inevitable limit of knowledge, the epistemic correlation, that is, to our dreaded confession "we just don't know and never will."[20] Much in the

18. F. C. Baur's legacy is not hard to discern here: behind awkward texts we have to find a real group of people with a controversial opinion (a "party"). This is yet another way we can move beyond Bultmann: it is simply unnecessary to posit actual groups for literary characters. Unless there are other reasons to assume the existence of various groups—such as the letters to the Corinthians or Galatians provide, for example—creating parties on the basis of literary characters is building castles in the air.

19. The discerning reader will note that I do not debate with Bultmann on the particulars here. The reason is that I reject the idea that serious debate is possible. Conducting a mock debate over origins that we simply cannot see would reproduce the Bultmannian assumption that I am here criticizing (viz., that there is enough or the right kind of information for historians to have a meaningful debate in the first place). I would not deny in general, of course, that historical work requires great imagination, nor that the so-called final form of the text raises the kinds of questions that Bultmann pursues. There are seams, tensions, outright awkwardness, and so forth, not to mention what seem to be differing accounts of the same events—all these matters require both imagination and restraint.

20. Bultmann's book on Jesus begins of course with the admission that we do not know much about Jesus (*Jesus and the Word*, trans. Louise Pettibone Smith [New York: Scribner, 1958], 8; of course, he does then go on to tell us quite a bit about Jesus). Bultmann obviously knows how to say "information is lacking" and "about that we know nothing" (57). My points are that he should say it far more frequently than he does and that he engages in the same basic inventive task as he takes the NT itself to engage in (i.e., create legend-ish mate-

Theology, therefore, that has passed as rigorous historical work should instead be redescribed by another genre, indeed, by one of Bultmann's own favorites: "tales about the life of the early church."

Arguing that we should move "beyond Bultmann" at these three points is less a disagreement with him about three separate issues than it is a suggestion that we should move beyond Bultmann in a rather complete sense. His understanding of Judaism and its anthropology, his conception of a kerygma that stands beyond our formulations, and his pervasive textual dismantling and speculative positing of trajectories/parties on the meager basis of the leftover textual bits are both cognitively and operatively basic to the *Theology*. Other essays in *Beyond Bultmann*, the volume in which this essay originally appeared, deal with additional ways in which the fundamental aspects of the *Theology* can no longer be taken as a guide. But even if they did not, these three matters are deeply enough embedded in the *Theology* as a whole that to see their significance is to question the viability of the *Theology* as a hermeneutical enterprise.[21]

---

rial about the church). By disciplined historian, I have in mind something like the reserve of the great Theodor Mommsen and those in Mommsen's tradition: one can think, e.g., of Mommsen's admonishment of Adolf Harnack when the latter suggested that the period of the Roman emperors should receive a more thorough teaching in the schools. Said Mommsen, "I too am in favour of this in general, but in specifics I believe that provisions and qualifications are called for. In general, the teaching of this field is in part impracticable and in part dangerous, since the tradition consists too much in court tittle-tattle or even worse things. In my view, teaching would specifically have to focus first on the Caesarian-Augustan period, which the Republican age leads into . . . and second on the age of Constantine. I regard what lies in between as unsuitable for fruitful treatment in schools." Mommsen continued, "If the question is put: what was the best period of the age of the emperors as a whole, the ancient Romans themselves answer: the first ten years of Nero's rule. No, try representing . . . that the first ten years of Nero's rule were the best period, and one of the most fortunate epochs in human history! Is this possible? Of course it would be, if every teacher could be equipped with the ability required to extract the kernel concealed inside the shell or sordid court gossip. I have been studying this period ever since I have been able to think. I have not succeeded in extracting this kernel, and if I were a teacher I would refuse the task of teaching the history of the emperors in general. Much as I regret having to water down Mr. Harnack's wine, I have to say I cannot accept this." Theodor Mommsen, *A History of Rome under the Emperors*, ed. Thomas Wiedermann, trans. Clare Krojzl (New York: Routledge, 1996), 5–6.

21. These are three threads that—if unraveled—would cause the garment to become completely tattered.

Conclusion

No essay on Bultmann's *Theology* would be complete without at least some reflection on the significance of the work as a whole. In my judgment, the significance of the work as a whole is primarily twofold. First, the *Theology* is a unified interpretation of the NT and continues to stand as a model for those who wish to conceptualize the totality of the NT's message. In an area of scholarship in which an almost rabid specialization is the norm, Bultmann actually knows what he thinks the whole NT is basically about—and this in connection to particular contemporary currents of thought that profoundly shape reflection's historicity. This is no small feat. The textual problems are unavoidable, the historical questions legion, the theological complexities ubiquitous, the current philosophical landscape difficult, and, yet, for all that, Bultmann conceptualizes the whole of the thing in a single, unified interpretation.

Moreover, in contrast to some of his revered teachers and his contemporaries, his interpretation is not self-deceptively cast as a detached observer's report on the NT documents and their history. It is instead the constructive thought of one who aims to think constructively with the theology of the NT. And he is clear where others remain opaque or uncommitted: Paul and John matter most. To be sure, Bultmann thinks, we can learn some things worth knowing from other parts of the canon (and Ignatius), but as a whole the rest of it matters little in comparison to these two towering theologians. It is these two who best understand the way in which the *Sache* of the Christian faith is to be thought and lived. The form of the *Theology*, therefore, is exactly its material content. Bultmannian *Sachkritik* places Paul and John at the center of the NT's theology.

Second, the *Theology* is an attempt to keep together two patterns of thought that in the early and mid-twentieth century were generally opposed—namely, *religionsgeschichtliche* investigation and theological interpretation for the present. Bultmann inherited this opposition, and, rather than opt for one side of it or the other, he tried to think through the opposition to a more complex or tensive unity. The hybrid that resulted was ultimately a failure—but not because he was wrong in the effort to engage the questions of intellectual unity and truth that go with work on the NT. Bultmann failed because the *Theology* reproduced the problem to which he sought the solution. Parts 1 and 3 display *religionsgeschichtliche* irrelevance; part 2 is contemporary existential theology. To be sure, parts 1 and 3 have some existentially relevant moments, and part 2 contains many *religionsgeschichtliche* proposals. But taken as a whole, the

Theology reinstantiates the distance it tried to overcome.[22] Bultmann is finally of two minds.[23]

Of course, in this way he is simply a man of his time. Twentieth-century theology was occupied with many different things, but it would not be much of an overstatement to say that the predominant hermeneutical question asked in relation to the Bible was how to deal with the rise of historical criticism. Nor would it be much of an overstatement to say that the most influential answers given from within biblical scholarship were varieties of two-mind thinking. Precisely because so many NT scholars in the twenty-first century are still asking a version of this question and remain of two minds about issues such as "theology *and* history"—as if they were ultimately different things—Bultmann's brilliant failure is almost as good for us as if it were a success. For what is true of him is surely true of lesser mortals: thinking constructively about NT theology cannot be done in two minds.

22. Careful readers will discern that the structure of the *Theology* is thus simultaneously a great strength (it beautifully displays the theological judgments of the Bultmannian program) and a great weakness (it rebuilds the cul-de-sac out of which Bultmann was trying to move).

23. I grant that Bultmann would not think he is of two minds; I deny, however, that he would be right to think that about his book.

Biblical Studies

◆ WITH RICHARD B. HAYS

Were the early Christians to hear of "systematic theology," they would probably be astonished to find that it is something different from "biblical studies," to discover that in contemporary theological education one usually encounters systematic theology and biblical studies as two separately conceived disciplines, each with its own rules of inquiry and corresponding community of discourse. In the postmodern period, we may experience the opposite surprise upon finding a biblical studies essay in a handbook of systematic theology.[1] Are these not two different disciplines?

This essay will analyze the relationship between biblical studies and systematic theology by surveying the history of their original unity and subsequent separation. It is impossible to trace every detail of this complex development, but a strategic selection of crucial figures and critical moments will provide the background for reflection about the relation between the two disciplines today.

Unity: The New Testament through the Post-Reformation Period

In the earliest period of Christianity, theology was essentially reflection upon the significance of the life, death, and resurrection of Jesus Christ in connec-

1. As the note below indicates, this essay on biblical studies originally appeared in a handbook of systematic theology.

"Biblical Studies" (with Richard B. Hays) was originally published in *The Oxford Handbook of Systematic Theology*, ed. John Webster, Kathryn Tanner, and Iain Torrance (Oxford: Oxford University Press, 2007), 435–55.

tion with scripture. In one of the oldest fragments of Christian tradition, Paul states explicitly that he passed on what he had received—namely, that "Christ died for our sins *in accordance with the scriptures*, and that he was buried, and that he was raised on the third day *in accordance with the scriptures*" (1 Cor. 15:3–4). This basic conviction—that of the inseparability of Jesus Christ from Israel's scripture—is not peculiar to Paul, or to the tradition that he preserves, but is indigenous to the NT as a whole. In the Gospel of Matthew, for example, one encounters again and again the formula citation, "This took place to fulfill what had been spoken" (Matt. 1:22; etc.). Likewise, the Gospel of Luke, long considered by modern scholars to be the most "Gentile" of the four canonical gospels, begins its narrative with a seamless transition from the tone and atmosphere of the OT to "the events that have been fulfilled" (Luke 1:1) and ends the story with two successive scenes in which Jesus himself instructs his followers in how to interpret the scriptures christologically (Luke 24:13–35, 36–48). Even in the letter to the Hebrews, where the "law" is regarded as only "a shadow of the good things to come" (Heb. 10:1), the imagery used for christological construction is itself derived from the OT and Jewish tradition; the Christology of Hebrews is unintelligible—indeed, inconceivable—apart from the deep theological well of the OT.

This basic unity between theological reflection and the interpretation of scripture continued through the patristic period, though with the substantial difference that the writings of the NT itself were now placed alongside Israel's scripture to form a two-testament hermeneutical matrix. Even so, the integration of theological reflection and scriptural interpretation remained. Irenaeus's *regula fidei*, for example, is not simply identical with scripture. Yet neither is it a deposit of doctrine logically independent of scripture; instead, the rule of faith is the very content of scripture itself as understood in the apostolic tradition. Only so can it function as the criterion of correct interpretation.[2] "The quest which Irenaeus accomplishes is basically the discovery of a principle of interpretation in the apostolic Rule of faith. At the same time . . . it is in another sense scripture itself that supplies the categories in which the principle of interpretation is expressed. Text and interpretation are like twin brothers; one can scarcely tell the one from the other."[3] Similarly, in his *Adversus Marcionem*, Tertullian does not attempt to refute Marcion first on

2. Irenaeus, *Against Heresies* 1.9.4, in *Ante-Nicene Fathers: The Writings of the Fathers Down to A.D. 325*, ed. A. Roberts and J. Donaldson (Edinburgh: T&T Clark, 1990), 1:330.

3. R. A. Greer, "The Christian Bible and Its Interpretation," in *Early Biblical Interpretation*, ed. J. Kugel and R. Greer (Philadelphia: Westminster, 1986), 157.

a philosophical or theological level and then draw out the implications of his argument regarding the accurate interpretation of scripture. Rather, his overall polemic is inextricably bound to both the Old and the New Testament. To separate Tertullian's use of scripture from his "systematic" theological argument is to dismantle the argument altogether.

One might object that, in light of his *De principiis*, we ought to consider Origen an early exception. On this construal of the evidence, *De principiis* would be read as a systematic or philosophical theology, while Origen's commentaries and homilies would be taken as his biblical, exegetical work. Yet such a view is inaccurate, for Origen's treatment of "first principles" is not a general systematic construction but rather a hermeneutical defense of the proper (i.e., Christian) understanding of scripture. Moreover, the treatments of the theological topics of books I–III are unthinkable without the manner of exegesis described in book IV. *De principiis* thus attempts to justify established, if controversial, exegetical practice and in this way both arises out of and is written for the interpretation of scripture.[4]

So, too, as his preface to the work makes clear, Augustine's *De doctrina Christiana* is not a systematic treatment of Christian doctrine articulated independently of scripture: "There are certain rules for the interpretation of Scripture which I think might with great advantage be taught to earnest students of the word. . . . These rules I propose to teach."[5] Indeed, for Augustine, Christian doctrine is itself derived from scripture taken as a whole—the "sense" of its "wording"—even as the "doctrinal tradition provides the principal criterion" for correct exegesis and understanding.[6]

To highlight the unity of exegesis and theology is not to say that reflective theology was *only* exegetical commentary. That would be an exaggeration. Yet Greer's point that "for the church fathers the true meaning of scripture was a theological one" can hardly be overstressed.[7] As Robert Wilken notes, in the patristic period "biblical exegesis was not a specialized discipline carried on independently of theology; it *was* theology. The church thought about the mysteries of the faith by expounding the text of the Bible. In the church fathers

4. Frances Young, "Alexandrian and Antiochene Exegesis," in *A History of Biblical Interpretation*, vol. 1, *The Ancient Period*, ed. Alan J. Hauser and Duane F. Watson (Grand Rapids: Eerdmans, 2003), esp. 335–38.

5. *De doctrina Christiana*, preface 1, in *Select Library of the Nicene and Post-Nicene Fathers of the Christian Church*, ed. Philip Schaff, 1st series (Edinburgh: T&T Clark, 1980), 2:519.

6. Frances M. Young, "The 'Mind' of Scripture: Theological Readings of the Bible in the Fathers," *International Journal of Systematic Theology* 7, no. 2 (2005): 130–31.

7. Greer, "The Christian Bible and Its Interpretation," 177.

one will seldom find arguments that stand on logical or philosophical grounds alone. Behind most theological discussions was a biblical text or texts, and it was on the basis of these texts that the church's first teachers gave expression to the central truths of faith and morals."[8] As Henri de Lubac has demonstrated, this interdependence of theology and exegesis continued throughout the medieval period. This is not to imply that the theological ratiocinations of Anselm, Abelard, and Aquinas are, to those who read with modern eyes, recognizably biblical. Nonetheless, the Bible and ecclesial theology were still assumed to exist in a complementary relationship, if not one of synonymity.

We may take Aquinas's *Summa Theologiae* as an example. Aquinas's metaphysical articulations of *sacra doctrina* are intimately intertwined with his reading of scripture. If we focus, for example, upon questions of "being" in relation to God's identity, it would be a gross misunderstanding of Aquinas to view his theology as simply a kind of Christianized Aristotelian metaphysics. As Matthew Levering has argued, the name YHWH "does not on Aquinas' interpretation trap Israel's God within the limitations of Aristotle's (idolatrous) prime mover. Rather, the name belongs to the history of Israel's and the church's striving *against* idolatrous conceptions of the divine being."[9] Aquinas does not, in other words, contemplate God "generically, but specifically as revealed through Moses to Israel."[10] The God about whom Aquinas speaks metaphysically is at every point—to the properly trained eye—the God of the Bible.

Despite the considerable ecclesial upheaval engendered by the Reformation, the essential unity between biblical interpretation and theological reflection remained unbroken. It is true, of course, that cries of *sola scriptura* and *ad fontes* were employed in an effort to reform and simplify the church's practices. Yet this corrective effort took place essentially within the parameters given by the early church's theological canon. Reformation exegesis was not interested, for example, in overturning the christological claims made at Nicaea. Nor, despite certain criticisms of "allegory," were the authorities of the patristic period spurned. Augustine is cited frequently not only in Aquinas's *Summa* but also by Calvin; indeed, in Calvin's *Institutes of the Christian Religion*, Augustine is cited more often than any source except scripture itself.

8. Robert Louis Wilken, foreword to *Medieval Exegesis*, by Henri de Lubac (Grand Rapids: Eerdmans, 2000), x.

9. Matthew Levering, *Scripture and Metaphysics: Aquinas and the Renewal of Trinitarian Theology* (Oxford: Blackwell, 2004), 65.

10. Levering, *Scripture and Metaphysics*, 53. Levering's thesis is articulated in conscious opposition to Rahner's well-known criticism of Aquinas's discussion of the divine essence as unbiblical (Karl Rahner, *The Trinity* [New York: Crossroad, 1998]).

For Calvin, moreover, systematic theology was itself derived from scripture. Thus conceived, it was not a separate field in which deliberation could take place apart from scripture. Rather, the telos of systematic theology was in fact hermeneutical; it existed for the sake of biblical interpretation: "It has been my purpose in this labor [writing the *Institutes*] to prepare and instruct candidates in sacred theology for the reading of the divine Word. . . . For I believe I have so embraced the sum of religion in all its parts, and have arranged it in such an order, that if anyone rightly grasps it, it will not be difficult for him to determine what he ought especially to seek in scripture and to what end he ought to relate its contents."[11] The unity envisioned by Calvin between doctrine and exegesis—the "sum of religion" and the "divine Word"—was not a simple hermeneutical circle of biblical prooftexts employed in the service of already-known doctrine. Nor was theology arranged in "order" merely to underwrite a particular mode of Reformed exegesis. Instead, the unity described here was in practice deeply dialogical: there was a mutually interactive relationship between the biblical text and the systematizing or ordering of theology. On the one hand, Calvin's theology was in effect *biblical* theology, and, on the other, his exegesis operated under the guidance of systematic theology. This dialogical unity allowed Calvin to attend concurrently to the shape and particularities of the biblical texts themselves and to the larger attempt to relate his exegetical findings ("contents") to the "sum of religion."

There was, however, a crucial point at which the exegesis of the Reformation did prefigure modern developments: the notion of *Sachkritik* in relation to the biblical canon. *Sachkritik* is a type of criticism that exposes theological inconsistencies within a text and criticizes an author's contingent formulations in light of the allegedly more fundamental truth (or subject matter) to which the text points. Clear indications of such an approach are found in Luther, though *Sachkritik* is hardly the sum of his hermeneutics.

To be sure, the earlier history of exegesis amply demonstrates interpreters' uneasiness with a wide range of biblical problems. Yet, before Luther, the tradition's characteristic strategy for dealing with intracanonical tensions was harmonization (e.g., the gospel harmonies of Tatian, the *Diatessaron*, and Augustine, *consensu evangelistarum*). No hermeneutical move had been made from within the Christian tradition that entailed a plain theological rejection of parts of scripture that were long considered canonical. In his preface to the epistle of James, however, Luther made just such a move.[12]

11. "John Calvin to the Reader," in *Institutes of the Christian Religion*, ed. John T. McNeill, trans. Ford Lewis Battles, 2 vols. (Philadelphia: Westminster, 1960), 4.

12. Luther's rather negative view of Jude, Hebrews, and especially Revelation is also well

Luther criticizes James on the grounds that (1) "it is flatly against St Paul and all the rest of scripture in ascribing justification to works," and (2) "in all this long teaching it does not once mention the Passion, the resurrection, or the Spirit of Christ. He names Christ several times; however he teaches nothing about him."[13] It is well known that for Luther the central doctrine of the Christian faith is justification by faith (not works) and that the center of scripture is Christ: "all the genuine sacred books . . . preach and inculcate Christ."[14] Thus, in Luther's reading, James "mangles the scripture, and thereby opposes Paul and all scripture." In this light Luther concludes: "Therefore, I will not have him in my Bible to be numbered among the true chief books. . . . How should this single man alone avail against Paul and all the rest of scripture?"[15]

Thus, even though Luther does not regard biblical interpretation and theology as different disciplines, his doctrine of justification and his conviction that "all the genuine sacred books . . . preach and inculcate Christ" are separated from explicit exegetical engagement and are worked out on a reflective level with considerable sophistication. At least in the preface to James, Luther approaches the exegetical task with a pre-understanding that is construed systematically. In light of this pre-understanding, he then moves to criticize a portion of scripture as theologically deficient.

Still, the theological position that leads Luther to criticize James is conceivable only on the basis of a prior unity between biblical exegesis and constructive theology. Luther's hermeneutical process moves from his exegesis of Paul to his view of justification, which he then develops systematically into a doctrinal criterion for right reading of the Bible. Subsequently, he returns to (canonical) scripture with this systematic structure in place. Even if Luther's particular interpretation of Paul would not find wide support among NT scholars today (at least outside Germany),[16] Luther himself evidently endeavors to speak theologically with the voice of the biblical Paul. Thus, if we may say that Luther operates under the guidance of a systematically developed *Sachkritik*, we must also say that this is for him emphatically biblical.

---

known (see the prefaces in *Luther's Works*, vol. 35 [St. Louis: Concordia, 1959]). But "what is not so well known is that in the table of contents of his September Bible of 1522 he openly separated them from the other twenty-three and according to him true New Testament writings, thus characterizing them at once as deutero-canonical" (Karl Barth, *Church Dogmatics* I/2 [Edinburgh: T&T Clark, 1956], 476).

13. *Luther's Works*, 35:395–97.

14. *Luther's Works*, 35:396.

15. *Luther's Works*, 35:397 nn. 54–55.

16. Cf. Douglas Harink, *Paul among the Postliberals* (Grand Rapids: Eerdmans, 2004), 13–65.

In his willingness to criticize canonical texts in light of doctrinal criteria, Luther differed from other Reformation leaders (e.g., Calvin). But, in that his criteria were biblically funded, he also differed widely from many scholars in the so-called post-Reformation period for whom—to oversimplify the matter—theology overran exegesis: the Bible functioned largely as a set of prooftexts (the *dicta classica* or *collegia biblica*) or a springboard for established doctrine.[17] This insertion of biblical texts into doctrinal schemata and discussions did not amount to a strict disciplinary separation between biblical studies and systematic theology. Viewed retrospectively, however, it allowed systematics to swallow up exegesis: no longer did the biblical narratives decisively impart their shape to dogmatic constructions.[18] Thus, in the midst of the burgeoning philosophies of the Enlightenment, when the early historical critics (e.g., Reimarus) returned to the Bible, it is no great surprise that what they found there bore scant resemblance to the systematic theology of the post-Reformation period.

Separation: The Eighteenth to the Early Twentieth Century

The beginnings of a fundamental separation between biblical exegesis and theology are notoriously difficult to determine with any precision. What is clear in general is that in light of certain philosophical-theological developments in Britain (especially deism) and the subsequent bloom of the Enlightenment in Germany, two interrelated possibilities arose: a historical, biblical exegesis set in conscious opposition to established ecclesial theology and a "systematic" theology whose content was distinguished from that of the Bible. The unity between the Bible as a whole and the theological content prescribed by the *regula fidei* was dissolved. This is not to say that historical exegesis was devoid of ecclesial elements, or that constructive theology had entirely rid itself of biblical content. In practice, many of the emerging historical critics saw their biblical work as theologically significant and, conversely, theologians even in the speculative Hegelian tradition continued to grapple with at least parts of

17. E.g., H. Diest's *Theologica biblica* of 1643, the earliest extant "biblical theology," organizes variously collected biblical texts under twenty-three different dogmatic topics.

18. Hans W. Frei, *The Eclipse of Biblical Narrative: A Study in Eighteenth and Nineteenth Century Hermeneutics* (New Haven: Yale University Press, 1974). Cf. Paul M. Blowers, "The *Regula Fidei* and the Narrative Character of Early Christian Faith," *ProEccl* 6, no. 2 (1997): 199–228.

the Bible. Yet biblical exegesis and systematic-theological reflection increasingly became two different disciplines.

Johann Philipp Gabler's famous inaugural address (1787) is often treated as the starting point for modern, descriptive biblical study. This perception doubtless oversimplifies the matter but is not without foundation. Gabler's address does evidence a particularly clear collocation of convictions and presuppositions that led to the erection of a wall between biblical studies and systematic and dogmatic theology. If the materials for this dividing wall were shaped earlier during the seventeenth and eighteenth centuries, it was here at the end of the eighteenth century that the wall itself began to be built.

In his address Gabler argued for the necessity of three crucial distinctions. First, he distinguished between "religion" and "theology." Religion is "everyday, transparently clear knowledge," whereas theology is "subtle, learned knowledge, surrounded by a retinue of many disciplines."[19] The Bible was the former rather than the latter, though scripture could furnish dogmatics with the material to be explained. Second, Gabler distinguished between historically conditioned statements and timeless, universal truths, and he affirmed that the Bible contained both. Finally, Gabler distinguished between "true" and "pure" biblical theology. The task of "true" biblical theology was carefully "to collect and classify" the "sacred ideas" of the biblical authors.[20] In other words, it was conceived as a *historically descriptive* discipline—although the "history" in question was strictly a history of ideas. On the basis of this classification, "pure" biblical theology would then differentiate the historically conditioned ("true") material from the ("pure") timeless, "universal ideas." As a result of this final differentiation, which "peel[ed] off everything local and temporal, everything individual and particular,"[21] dogmatics was provided with a secure foundation upon which to build: "After we have separated those things which in the sacred books refer most immediately to their own times from those pure notions which divine providence wished to be characteristic of all times and places, let us then construct the foundation of our philosophy [i.e., systematic theology] upon religion."[22]

19. J. P. Gabler, *De iusto discrimine theologiae biblicae et dogmaticae regundisque recte utriusque finibus* (1787), in "J. P. Gabler and the Distinction between Biblical and Dogmatic Theology: Translation, Commentary, and Discussion of His Originality," ed. and trans. J. Sandys-Wunsch and L. Eldredge, *SJT* 33, no. 2 (1980): 136.

20. Gabler, *De iusto discrimine*, 139–40.

21. Rudolf Bultmann, *Theology of the New Testament*, 2 vols. (New York: Scribner, 1951–1955), 2:243.

22. Gabler, *De iusto discrimine*, 138.

Although later scholars were not necessarily seeking to work out Gabler's program, his crisp delineations exemplify a certain way of conceptualizing the larger theological task that framed the ensuing history of discussion through the early twentieth century. Gabler's distinctions (1) split cleanly the discipline of historical exegesis of the Bible from dogmatic and systematic theology; (2) assigned a proper order to the relationship of the two disciplines that consisted of stages: first historical exegesis, then systematic reflection on the basis of the results; and (3) designated the contents of the Bible as "religion" in explicit contrast to reflective theology.

Taking these matters together, it becomes apparent that Gabler's model of the theological enterprise mandates a wall between historical exegesis and systematic reflection, since systematic theology in itself is *in principle* incapable of inquiring into the biblical text. It is the wrong tool for the task—like trying to eat soup with a fork—for the Bible is not theology but religion. Systematic theology is thus removed from the Bible and placed in a separate sphere of inquiry. Systematic theology, if it seeks to be "biblical," will have to wait for the completed results of historical exegesis.

The corollary, furthermore, to the notion that *historical* exegesis is the science proper to biblical interpretation is that the biblical texts are situated first of all not in the immediate life of the church but in the past. A sense of the vast chronological distance between the genesis of the texts and present theological reflection thus became a constitutive feature of biblical interpretation. In that the Bible could no longer speak directly from its time to ours—it needed mediation through historical research—the space was opened for the (now perennial) question of "development" to arise: How did we get from there to here? It was but a short step from this question to the inference that truly historical interpretation—that which attends to phenomena in their proper chronological sequence—not only entails the bracketing out of later ecclesial doctrine and systematic theology but also potentially undermines it.

By the middle of the nineteenth century, the separation between biblical studies and systematic theology had become firmly institutionalized in the disciplinary structure of European universities. This is not to say that theologians entirely shied away from interpreting the Bible (Schleiermacher, for example, wrote on source-critical questions in his essay on Luke) or that biblical scholars were unaware of the theological implications of their research (Strauss was acutely aware of the impact of his 1835 *Life of Jesus*). Nonetheless, both systematicians and exegetes, many of whom differed widely in the particulars of their theological perspective, agreed that accurate historical examination of the biblical texts divided these texts, in their original meaning, from later

Christian systematics. In *The Christian Faith*, for example, Schleiermacher assumes historical distance between the Gospel of John and later systematic theology. By focusing on the gospel prologue, he elucidates the noetic difference between the gospel's author and those who fashioned the doctrine of the Trinity:

> If the Trinity had been in the Apostle's mind, his exposition would very easily have lent itself to a similar introduction of the Holy Spirit, whose name occurs so often in . . . John; nor would John have lacked opportunity . . . to speak here of the Spirit as that which was "in the beginning with God and was God." Assuming, however, that John here declares that the dual nature of Christ existed in God in distinct form from all eternity, it would still not follow by any means that this was meant in the sense of the doctrine of the Trinity, and that that doctrine is therefore the true and the only natural completion of the Johannine statements. . . . John was not on the way to the doctrine of the Trinity as we have it.[23]

Even where there was a push to see the roots of doctrinal development in the NT itself, such as in the work of Ferdinand Christian Baur, the distance between the biblical texts and later systematic theology was assumed, and thoroughgoing historical study was considered the method appropriate to biblical interpretation. In practice, of course, Baur's Hegelian philosophy functioned as the unifying factor for the various pieces of the historical puzzle, but in principle Baur knew no method other than radical historical criticism by which to interpret the NT texts. Speaking of biblical theology, Baur wrote that "one calls this branch of theological science 'theology' in order to distinguish it with this general and non-specific name from 'dogmatics,' i.e., *systematic* theology. As distinct from dogmatics and other similar modes of inquiry, biblical theology should be a purely historical discipline."[24]

By the end of the nineteenth and beginning of the twentieth century, the disciplinary divisions were taken for granted to the point that the NT scholar William Wrede could declare to a group of German pastors that historical study of the NT should be "totally indifferent to all dogma and systematic

23. Friedrich Schleiermacher, *The Christian Faith* (Edinburgh: T&T Clark, 1928), 740. Cf. F. D. E. Schleiermacher, *Der christliche Glaube: nach den Grundsätzen der evangelischen Kirche im Zusammenhange dargestellt, Zweite Auflage*, in *Kritische Gesamtausgabe*, I. 13, 1 and I. 13, 2, ed. R. Schäfer (Berlin: de Gruyter, 2003), ii. 517.

24. Ferdinand Christian Baur, *Vorlesungen über neutestamentliche Theologie* (Darmstadt: Wissenschaftliche Buchgesellschaft, 1973 [1864]), 1 (emphasis added).

theology."[25] Reading the Bible in light of later dogmatic or systematic theology perverted the truth of historical conditioning and development and therefore was a hindrance to historical study of the biblical documents. On this latter point, if not on others, Albert Schweitzer agreed with Wrede: "Chalcedon . . . cut off the last possibility of a return to the historical Jesus. . . . This dogma had first to be shattered before men could once more go out in quest of the historical Jesus. . . . That the historical Jesus is something different from the Jesus Christ of the doctrine of the Two Natures seems to us now self-evident."[26] Later ecclesial theology, he wrote in a memorable phrase, binds the historical Jesus "like Lazarus of old . . . [in] the grave-clothes of the dogma of the Dual Nature."[27] Thus was Gabler's programmatic distinction carried forward, as doctrinal theology was taken to be the wrong instrument for investigation of the Bible.

The conviction that later theological categories were inappropriate for biblical exegesis found sophisticated systematic expression in the work of Ernst Troeltsch, the recognized "dogmatician" of the history-of-religions school. In an essay designed to introduce American theology to "a dogmatics working with the presuppositions and in the spirit of this school," Troeltsch argued forcefully for the historical determination of theology: "Jesus' life and teaching must be interpreted not by reference to later Christology and metaphysics but exclusively in the light of prophetism and late eschatological Judaism."[28] Troeltsch's point was that all knowledge is fundamentally historical in character; theological knowledge (dogmatic theology), therefore, was dependent upon historical reality. For Troeltsch, the "history" in question was of course that which could be reconstructed by the historical-biblical scholars. In this sense, in principle if not in practice, the historical determination of dogmatic theology conformed to Gabler's two-stage process in which the task of the dogmatician followed and was dependent upon that of the historian. The obvious effect was to remove dogmatic concerns further from the mind of the historians. As Wrede put it, "How the systematic theologian gets on with the results [of historical criticism] and deals with them—that is his own affair."[29]

25. William Wrede, "The Task and Methods of 'New Testament Theology,'" in *The Nature of New Testament Theology*, ed. Robert Morgan (Naperville, IL: Allenson, 1973 [1897]), 69.

26. Albert Schweitzer, *The Quest of the Historical Jesus: A Critical Study of Its Progress from Reimarus to Wrede* (Baltimore: Johns Hopkins University Press, 1998 [1906]), 3.

27. Schweitzer, *Quest of the Historical Jesus*, 3.

28. Ernst Troeltsch, "The Dogmatics of the History-of-Religions School," in *Religion and History*, ed. J. Adams and W. Bense (Minneapolis: Fortress, 1991 [1913]), 93.

29. Wrede, "The Task and Methods of 'New Testament Theology,'" 69.

Around the turn of the century, there was, of course, considerable debate about these matters within wider academic theology, and one can sense, looking back through Karl Barth, an almost prophetic tone in the dissenting voices of Martin Kähler[30] and Adolf Schlatter.[31] Yet the conviction that historical exegesis and systematic theology were independent and separate disciplines—each with its own primary sources of knowledge and rules of inquiry—dominated across the larger theological spectrum.

Unity and Separation: The Twentieth Century through the Present

Despite the virtual consensus in the late nineteenth and early twentieth century, the relation of biblical studies to systematic theology underwent profound change later in the twentieth century. The complexity involved in this change can best be seen by concentrating on the way in which Karl Barth and Rudolf Bultmann attempted to reintegrate theology with exegesis, the subsequent reaction to Barth and Bultmann, and finally, in this light, the more recent and competing tendencies within the field of biblical studies.

Karl Barth's break with the liberal Protestantism of his day changed decisively the course of both biblical studies and theology for the twentieth century. This shift, however, was arguably not a new direction as such. Indeed, on Barth's own terms, it was more of a return to a well-worn ecclesial path, walked first by the biblical writers themselves and subsequently by certain doctors of the church. Barth's was a return, to switch the metaphor, to an "ancestral line which runs back through Kierkegaard to Luther and Calvin, and so to Paul and Jeremiah."[32]

The crucial difference between the historians in the exegetical disciplines and himself, so Barth maintained, was that the former attempted mainly to think *about* Paul whereas Barth's attempt was to think *with* Paul. "The reigning biblical science saw [Paul] as an object of interest in his own right; Barth saw him as *witness*."[33] Historical-critical interpretation as practiced in the early

30. Martin Kähler, *The So-Called Historical Jesus and the Historic Biblical Christ* (Philadelphia: Fortress, 1988 [1896]).

31. Adolf Schlatter, "The Theology of the New Testament and Dogmatics," in Morgan, *The Nature of New Testament Theology*, 117–66.

32. Karl Barth, "The Word of God and the Task of the Ministry," in *The Word of God and the Word of Man* (New York: Harper & Row, 1957), 195.

33. Bruce McCormack, "Historical Criticism and Dogmatic Interest in Karl Barth's Theo-

twentieth century concentrated upon matters anthropological—human religious experience as reflected by the biblical texts. This concentration, in Barth's view, neglected the true subject matter (*die Sache*) of scripture, that to which Paul and Jeremiah witnessed and with which Calvin and Luther had attempted to grapple actively in their exegesis. Barth insisted that, in its character as witness to God, the Bible itself called for explicitly *theological* exegesis. In this way, Barth reversed Gabler and maintained that dogmatic theology was in principle required for the interpretation of scripture. To eliminate the theology of the church from biblical exegesis was to ignore the subject matter of scripture and, hence, not to *interpret* scripture at all.

Yet dogmatic or systematic theology was not itself an independent discipline in which a preconceived system was forced upon the biblical texts with a heavy hand. Despite charges to the contrary, Barth himself claimed never to have called for the abandonment of historical exegesis. "The demand that the Bible should be read and understood and expounded historically is, therefore, obviously justified and can never be taken too seriously. The Bible itself posits this demand: even where it appeals expressly to divine commissionings and promptings, in its actual composition it is everywhere a human word, and this human word is obviously intended to be taken seriously and read and understood as such. To do anything else would be to miss the reality of the Bible and therefore the Bible itself as the witness of revelation."[34] His protests were "not directed against historical research as such but against the *historicism* of the historians who sought to reduce . . . explanation of the biblical texts to historical explanation and that alone."[35] In point of fact, as Bruce McCormack has argued, Barth can be understood to view historical exegesis as both a starting point for and a "relative control" over the interpretative proposals of theological exegesis.[36]

Moreover, the "science" of dogmatics was itself to be biblical, both in the sense that it was dependent upon the pointing of the biblical witness for its view of the subject matter and in the sense captured by the old ecclesial notion of the

---

logical Exegesis of the New Testament," in *Biblical Hermeneutics in Historical Perspective: Studies in Honor of Karlfried Froehlich on His Sixtieth Birthday*, ed. M. Burrows and P. Rorem (Grand Rapids: Eerdmans, 1991), 327.

34. Barth, *Church Dogmatics* I/2, 464.

35. Bruce McCormack, "The Significance of Karl Barth's Theological Exegesis of Philippians," in *Epistle to the Philippians: 40th Anniversary Edition with Introductory Essays by Bruce L. McCormack and Francis B. Watson*, by Karl Barth (Louisville: Westminster John Knox, 2002), viii–ix.

36. McCormack, "Historical Criticism and Dogmatic Interest," 333–34.

relation between the *norma normans* (scripture) and the *norma normata* (dogmatic and systematic theology): systematic or dogmatic theology was subject to the formative and corrective witness of scripture. As opposed to "modern biblicism"—a prooftexting application of "what one thinks one has already heard from [the Bible] simply by repeating its words"—truly theological exegesis displays a "posture," or "a way of human thinking shaped by the Bible . . . in which those cultivated by its 'rule of thought' learn to think its thoughts and hear its message again and again."[37] Thus did Barth return to an earlier ecclesial mode of interpretation (e.g., Calvin's) in which there was a unity of biblical exegesis and theological reflection that derived ultimately from the unity of the subject matter itself: even within the distinction between *normans* and *normata*, the Bible and dogmatic theology were part of one dialectical theological conversation.

Rudolf Bultmann, probably Barth's only rival in influence, also interpreted scripture in light of its perceived subject matter and also believed that authentic interpretation was impossible apart from direct theological engagement with the witness of the Bible. In this way, Bultmann, too, returned to an earlier mode of interpretation in which biblical exegesis was believed to have "something to say to the present."[38]

In particular, Bultmann's reading of scripture in light of its subject matter resembled Luther's, in the sense that both interpreters moved to criticize portions of scripture as theologically deficient in light of their understanding of scripture's subject matter (*Sachkritik*). As Barth warned, "Those who throw stones at Bultmann should be careful lest they accidentally hit Luther, who is also hovering somewhere in the background."[39] For Bultmann, as for Luther, there was a deeply unified interpretation in which exegesis and theological reflection were brought into a synthetic relationship. On the basis of his exegesis of certain parts of the Bible (notably Paul and John)—and with considerable help from the early Heidegger—Bultmann developed a theological criterion (authentic believing self-understanding) with which he then returned to perform the exegetical task. If in reality Heidegger's existentialism provided the essential link between Bultmann's exegesis and his theology, in theory at least, Bultmann's highly sophisticated theology was exegetically shaped, even as his exegesis received its direction from his theological reflection.

37. Richard E. Burnett, *Karl Barth's Theological Exegesis: The Hermeneutical Principles of the* Römerbrief *Period* (Grand Rapids: Eerdmans, 2004), 58.

38. Bultmann, *Theology of the New Testament*, 2:251.

39. Karl Barth, "Rudolf Bultmann: An Attempt to Understand Him," in *Kerygma and Myth: A Theological Debate*, ed. H.-W. Bartsch (London: SPCK, 1962), 2:123.

(In this respect there is a strong, though rarely recognized, family resemblance between Bultmann's theology and the theologies of many feminist and liberationist theologians today who likewise discover within the Bible an anthropologically oriented theological criterion—whether a principle such as justice or freedom, or the divinely given dignity of marginalized groups—and then employ this criterion in critically interrogating the biblical texts. The work of Elisabeth Schüssler Fiorenza[40] is a particularly clear example of this method: a theologically grounded critical hermeneutics that thoroughly engages the historical exegetical task.)

Yet the conceptualization of the interface between exegesis and theology in Bultmann's interpretative vision was substantively different from Karl Barth's. Where Barth challenged the primacy of historical-critical investigation, Bultmann could write that "the one presupposition that cannot be dismissed is *the historical method* of interrogating the text. Indeed, exegesis as the interpretation of historical texts is a part of the science of history."[41] And though he could agree with Barth against Troeltsch that Christian faith is not a phenomenon of the history of religion, Bultmann could also characterize his *Theology of the New Testament* as one that stood within the history-of-religions tradition of investigation.[42]

Furthermore, where Bultmann differed from the history-of-religions school, he also differed from Barth in a way that drew significant criticism from the latter.[43] Bultmann accused the history-of-religions approach of tearing apart "the act of thinking" and "the act of living," by which he meant that Bousset, Wrede, and others failed to understand the theological thoughts in the NT as expressions of "believing self-understanding"—that is, the explication of "man's understanding of himself" from the perspective given by faith.[44] For Barth, however, to read the biblical texts as witnesses to human self-understanding—even if the change in one's self-understanding could be attributed to God—was to return to an anthropologically centered exegesis and, hence, to forfeit criticism of the history-of-religions paradigm at the place where it was most needed.

It is important to stress, however, that Barth and Bultmann were united in a common endeavor to read the Bible theologically in the face of a legacy

40. Elisabeth Schüssler Fiorenza, *In Memory of Her: A Feminist Theological Reconstruction of Christian Origins* (New York: Crossroad, 1983).

41. Rudolf Bultmann, "Is Exegesis without Presuppositions Possible?," in *Existence and Faith: Shorter Writings of Rudolf Bultmann* (New York: Meridian, 1960), 291.

42. Bultmann, *Theology of the New Testament*, 2:250.

43. Barth, "Rudolf Bultmann."

44. Bultmann, *Theology of the New Testament*, 2:249–51.

that, in large part, maintained the inappropriateness of such an endeavor. Despite the far-reaching differences between these two giants, in both Barth and Bultmann biblical studies and systematic theology were once again brought into dialogue. Though it is an oversimplification, it may not be too much to suggest that most, if not all, subsequent attempts to deal with the relationship between biblical studies and systematic theology swim with, or against, the wakes generated by Barth and Bultmann.

Despite its real differences from the theological scene in Germany, for example, the emphasis on the theological content of the Bible in the so-called biblical theology movement in America is practically inconceivable apart from Barth and Bultmann.[45] Further, when in 1962 Krister Stendahl famously advocated the necessity of a clear distinction in exegesis between "what it meant" and "what it means," Barth and Bultmann were the primary targets of his attack:[46] "[It] appears that the tension between 'what it meant' and 'what it means' is of a competitive nature, and that when the biblical theologian becomes primarily concerned with the present meaning, he implicitly (Barth) or explicitly (Bultmann) loses his enthusiasm or his ultimate respect for the descriptive task."[47] In its overall shape, Stendahl's own position was hardly a new one, even in North America.[48] Indeed, the sharp divide between "meant" and "means" was in essence a return through Wrede to Gabler, though Stendahl recognized in a way the others did not the difficulty in moving from the past to the present. He thus called for an intermediate stage in which attention would be given to the hermeneutical principles involved in rendering the past relevant for the present: "With the original in hand, and after due clarification of the hermeneutic principles involved, we may proceed toward tentative answers to the question of the meaning here and now."[49] Nonetheless, in conceptualizing the exegetical and systematic tasks as different modes of inquiry, sequentially ordered so that interpretation runs in one direction only—from the "original" to the "here and now"—Stendahl's program was Gabler's program *redivivus*.

45. Brevard S. Childs, *Biblical Theology in Crisis* (Philadelphia: Westminster, 1970), 18–22.

46. Oscar Cullmann was the third figure treated by Stendahl, but Cullmann came in for much less criticism than Barth and Bultmann. Indeed, Stendahl considered Cullmann's work to be largely accurate on the descriptive level.

47. Krister Stendahl, "Biblical Theology, Contemporary," in *The Interpreter's Dictionary of the Bible*, ed. George A. Buttrick (New York: Abingdon, 1962), 1:421; repr. as "Biblical Theology: A Program," in *Meanings: The Bible as Document and as Guide* (Philadelphia: Fortress, 1984), 11–44.

48. H. J. Cadbury, "The Peril of Archaizing Ourselves," *Interpretation* 3 (1949): 331–37.

49. Stendahl, "Biblical Theology, Contemporary," 422.

The influence of Stendahl's proposals was such that almost twenty-five years later, in a critique of the meant/means division, Ben Ollenburger could write that "the distinctions for which Stendahl pleaded have come to be seen as virtually axiomatic, and self-evidently so, particularly for distinguishing biblical from systematic theology."[50] There was of course the occasional appreciation of Barth from a biblical scholar,[51] and, methodologically speaking, the historical-critical aspect of Bultmannian exegesis had legions of followers among NT scholars (in contrast to the theological or existential dimension of Bultmann's work). But Ollenburger's statement was not unfair: well into the 1980s biblical studies and systematic theology were thought of as two different disciplines. The former worked on a strictly "descriptive" level and dealt with the historical problems and literary diversity encountered in the exegesis of a text in its original context ("meant"). The latter worked on a "normative" level with the abstract conceptual and philosophical issues that arise in the attempt to reflect theologically upon the content of the Christian faith in its connection to contemporary life ("means").

In more recent years, Stendahl's programmatic suggestions have lost the virtually universal, if subconscious, acceptance within biblical studies they once enjoyed. The learned publications of OT scholar Brevard Childs, for example, have displayed sophistication in both biblical exegesis and systematic theology and relentlessly called into question the necessity of their separation, as have those of his former OT colleague Christopher Seitz.[52] In NT studies, Richard Hays's book on NT ethics[53] exhibits wide-ranging theological analysis and construction, while Francis Watson has in two successive works[54] mounted extensive arguments for "biblical interpretation in theological perspective." Stephen Fowl's book *Engaging Scripture: A Model for Theological*

50. Ben C. Ollenburger, "What Krister Stendahl 'Meant': A Normative Critique of 'Descriptive Biblical Theology,'" *HBT* 81 (1986): 61.

51. Paul S. Minear, "Barth's Commentary on the Romans, 1922–1972, or Karl Barth vs. the Exegetes," in *Footnotes to a Theology: The Karl Barth Colloquium of 1972*, ed. M. Rumscheidt (Waterloo, ON: Corporation for the Publication of Academic Studies in Religion in Canada, 1974), 8–29.

52. Christopher R. Seitz, *Word without End: The Old Testament as Abiding Theological Witness* (Grand Rapids: Eerdmans, 1998).

53. Richard B. Hays, *The Moral Vision of the New Testament: Community, Cross, New Creation; A Contemporary Introduction to New Testament Ethics* (San Francisco: HarperSanFrancisco, 1996).

54. Francis Watson, *Text, Church and World: Biblical Interpretation in Theological Perspective* (Edinburgh: T&T Clark, 1994); *Text and Truth: Redefining Biblical Theology* (Edinburgh: T&T Clark, 1997).

Interpretation[55] found its way to a panel review session at the Society of Biblical Literature's 1999 Annual Meeting. Perhaps most impressive in its scale is the ongoing, multivolume work of N. T. Wright on "Christian origins and the question of God."[56] As the overall title of the series suggests, Wright is pursuing historical exegesis of the NT with explicitly theological ends in view. The Roman Catholic NT scholars Luke Timothy Johnson and William S. Kurz, SJ, have called for biblical scholarship to "imagine the world that scripture imagines" in ongoing conversation with the Catholic Church's rich tradition of theological interpretation.[57] Moreover, an ecumenical and interdisciplinary consultation of scholars, under the name the Scripture Project, has likewise offered a programmatic summons to the practice of biblical interpretation as a seamlessly integrated theological activity that speaks directly to the needs of the church.[58] The appetite for such work is evidently considerable: two new commentary series have of late been launched with the express purpose of bringing biblical exegesis and theological reflection into close relation.[59] Finally, from the side of systematic theology, it is significant that one of the most important contemporary systematic theologies claims that its success should be measured by its achievement or failure "as a hermeneutical principle for scripture taken as a whole."[60]

A particularly noteworthy development within this resurgence of theological integration has been a newly intensified interest, among both systematic theologians and biblical scholars, in *narrative* as the distinctive medium for the articulation of the Christian message. As Robert Jenson explains, "The message of Jesus' resurrection, the gospel, is a message about an event and so

55. Stephen E. Fowl, *Engaging Scripture: A Model for Theological Interpretation* (Malden, MA: Blackwell, 1998).

56. N. T. Wright, *The New Testament and the People of God* (Minneapolis: Fortress, 1992); *Jesus and the Victory of God* (Minneapolis: Fortress, 1996); *The Resurrection of the Son of God* (Minneapolis: Fortress, 2003).

57. Luke Timothy Johnson, "Imagining the World That Scripture Imagines," in *The Future of Catholic Biblical Scholarship: A Constructive Conversation*, ed. Luke Timothy Johnson and William S. Kurz (Grand Rapids: Eerdmans, 2002), 119.

58. Ellen F. Davis and Richard B. Hays, eds., *The Art of Reading Scripture* (Grand Rapids: Eerdmans, 2003).

59. See the Two Horizons Commentary series (a prospectus of which can be found in the collection of essays in Joel B. Green and Max Turner, eds., *Between Two Horizons: Spanning New Testament Studies and Systematic Theology* [Grand Rapids: Eerdmans, 2000]) and the Brazos Theological Commentary on the Bible.

60. Robert W. Jenson, *Systematic Theology*, 2 vols. (New York: Oxford University Press, 1997–1999), 1:33.

itself has the form of a narrative. Therefore, when the church sets out to read scripture as a whole, the kind of unity by which she construes this whole is narrative unity. The church reads her scripture as a single plotted succession of events, stretching from creation to consummation, plotted around exodus and resurrection."[61] This approach to biblical interpretation, obviously consonant with ancient patristic tradition, received new impetus through the work of Karl Barth and the theologians influenced by him. Especially significant for more recent theology have been the contributions of Hans Frei[62] and George Lindbeck.[63] These theologians have advocated an understanding of theology as what Lindbeck calls an "intratextual" enterprise, through which the community of faith retells and interprets its foundational story.

So long as "theology" was conceived in terms of systematically ordered propositions, whether by Protestant scholasticism or by scholars pursuing the Enlightenment's ideal of pure, generalizable universal truth, the biblical narratives appeared as limited and limiting texts, inconvenient in their crude particularity. Even Paul's letters, perhaps the most apparently theological writings in the Bible, were in fact, as read by historical criticism, contingent pastoral advice for ancient readers, not systematically constructed theological treatises. Theology had to be somehow *distilled* from the raw material of these texts, and the relation between descriptive biblical study and systematic-theological discourse was a fairly distant one.

If, however, the task of theology is understood in the postliberal mode as the reflective renarration of the community's identity-defining story within a particular historical moment, then not only Paul but also the canonical evangelists were practicing "theology" in a way that is exemplary for theologians in the church at any time, including ours. Consequently, the gap between the biblical scholar's close descriptive reading of the text and the theologian's constructive reflection about the text becomes indistinct; both are engaged in imaginative construal of one and the same story.

In other circles, however, the basic disciplinary divide promoted by Gabler, Wrede, and Stendahl continues strongly in force, as some erudite biblical scholars insist—in the face of postmodernism's erosion of "objectivity" in the doing of history—on the independence and priority of descriptive, historical

61. Robert W. Jenson, "Scripture's Authority in the Church," in David and Hays, *The Art of Reading Scripture*, 29.

62. Frei, *The Eclipse of Biblical Narrative*; Frei, *The Identity of Jesus Christ: The Hermeneutical Bases of Dogmatic Theology* (Philadelphia: Fortress, 1975).

63. George A. Lindbeck, *The Nature of Doctrine: Religion and Theology in a Postliberal Age* (Philadelphia: Westminster, 1984).

exegesis in opposition to "dogmatic abstractions."[64] "Gabler," as Räisänen put it, "was basically right."[65] Exegesis and dogmatics "are to be kept apart." There is room, of course, within today's Gablerian approach, for broadly theological concerns—for example, the use to which historical exegesis of the Bible is put—but systematic theology itself is, at best, seen to be of little help for exegesis.

At the present moment, then, with respect to the question of the relation between biblical studies and systematic theology, there are competing tendencies within the field of biblical studies that arise naturally out of the history of this field's unity with and separation from systematic theology. On one side, there is a conscious push toward theologically interdisciplinary work, in which biblical exegesis is related positively to systematic or dogmatic theology and in which systematic theology is considered an indispensable tool for the exegetical task. This tendency corresponds to the hermeneutically integrated interpretation of earlier ecclesial exegesis and, in more recent history, to the Barthian endeavor as well as to certain aspects of the Bultmannian theological program. The rapprochement between biblical exegesis and theology has been aided particularly by systematic theology's renewed interest in the narrative character of Christian convictions.

On the other side, however, there is a rueful memory of the long history of dogmatic prooftexting in the modern period, a recognition of the reality of the historical situatedness and diversity of the biblical texts, and a resultant desire to steer exegesis clear of the threatening systematic rocks. This tendency corresponds to the rise of a particular form of academic historiography in the Enlightenment, to the efforts of Gabler, Wrede, and Stendahl to achieve methodological distinction and clarity, as well as to the history-of-religions tradition in Bultmannian exegesis.

Concluding Reflections

In light of the tension in the present situation, we offer some concluding reflections on the basis of the foregoing history. First, it would greatly aid discussion to dispense with the idea that exegesis can be done without dogmatic interests. On this point at least, biblical scholars should—with help from postmodern

64. E.g., Wayne A. Meeks, "Why Study the New Testament?," *NTS* 51 (2005): 155–70.

65. Heikki Räisänen, *Beyond New Testament Theology: A Story and a Programme* (London: SCM, 1990), 137.

criticism if necessary—be ready to grant Barth his point: every exegete has dogmatic interests and presuppositions. Or, as Adolf Schlatter put it: "The connection between historical science and dogmatics . . . cannot be set aside until historical work is complete. . . . The relationship between the two functions is there right from the beginning of historical work. . . . It does not simply come in at the end, but permeates the whole course of historical work."[66] The task, then, is to acknowledge and probe the theological (or anti-theological) interests involved in exegetical work and, hence, to ask whether some interests are more fruitful for biblical interpretation than others.

Second, to speak of various texts together as the "Bible" or "New Testament" is in fact to make a dogmatic judgment. As Heinrich Schlier once wrote with respect to NT theology, "From a purely 'historical' stand-point . . . there is no justification for restricting it to the collection of books in the New Testament. Such a restriction is *already* a piece of theology."[67] Inherent in the name "biblical studies," in other words, is the theological decision that the particular documents that constitute the Bible are in some way related to one another, as distinct from their relation to other pieces of literature, and are therefore to be treated together. "Outside the church, no such entity as the Christian Bible has any reason to exist."[68] This does not so much settle as raise the question of how the documents relate to one another, but to read at least sixty-six texts together is to make a dogmatic theological judgment.

Third, such a judgment is not merely ideational abstraction; rather, it locates us socially in a community of interpretation. Indeed, as Wrede saw clearly, to interpret the "Bible" is to situate oneself within a specific set of ecclesial decisions: "Anyone who accepts . . . the idea of the canon places himself under the authority of the bishops and theologians of [the second to fourth] centuries."[69] To admit that there is an interpretative arena called the Bible places the interpreter (whether self-consciously or not) within a community of interpretation that evaluates positively the theological decision to read these disparate documents together. Conversely, to reject the necessity of the "Bible" or, as did Wrede, the appropriateness of the name "New Testament," is to situate oneself within a different community of interpretation on the basis of a different but equally "dogmatic" judgment. Thus the question of social

66. Schlatter, "The Theology of the New Testament and Dogmatics," 126.

67. Heinrich Schlier, "The Meaning and Function of a Theology of the New Testament," in *The Relevance of the New Testament* (New York: Herder & Herder, 1968), 5.

68. Jenson, "Scripture's Authority in the Church," 27.

69. Wrede, "The Task and Methods of 'New Testament Theology,'" 71.

location, or community of interpretation, is raised by the name we give to what we interpret, and the name we give to what we interpret is inseparably bound with theological decisions of one kind or another. Let us at least be consistent: if we say we study the "New Testament" but desire to do so free of doctrinal or dogmatic decisions, we are involved in a contradiction at a basic level, since in fact dogmatic decisions constitute in a crucial way the very object we claim to study. And if we reject the notion of the Bible, let us say on what dogmatic grounds we do so and in which community of interpretation we are thereby located.

Fourth, however much the previous points press for a recognition of the implicit unity between biblical studies and systematic theology, they do not preclude an emphasis within biblical studies on the distinctiveness and particularity of the diverse texts. In fact, it may not be too much to suggest that the careful delineation of the manifold and richly varied emphases of the individual witnesses within scripture is one of the unique contributions of modern biblical studies to the overall reception of the gospel. In this light, the insistence of Gabler and Stendahl upon descriptive exegesis is indispensable, even if their view of a separation from dogmatics is untenable. Descriptive exegesis always involves theological decisions with respect to the object described, but the content of particular descriptions is not for that reason predetermined or rendered irrelevant for theological reflection. Indeed, even Karl Barth was quick to say that there was no "path to the whole gospel except the one through the comprehension of the particular, for no one has yet displayed all sides simultaneously."[70]

We thus come, finally, to the question with which the essay began: the relation of biblical studies to systematic theology. The history of the relationship outlined in this essay suggests that where the subject matter of biblical exegesis and of dogmatic theology is not taken to be the same, there exists no real ground for mutual interaction between the two disciplines. Indeed, such interdisciplinary interaction may even be logically precluded, and the point of a biblical studies essay for a handbook of systematic theology would then be to say "Hands off!" to the systematicians. At best, systematic theology could attempt to appropriate the "results" of biblical exegesis. Such an essay would consist of a simple summary of the most significant advances in biblical studies, which the systematicians could then put to use—a contemporary remnant of the older prooftexting approach.

70. Karl Barth, "Vorwort zur zweiten Auflage," in *Der Römerbrief* (Zurich: Evangelischer Verlag, 1947), xvi.

However, where the subject matter of biblical exegesis and of dogmatic theology is thought to be the same, the two disciplines are of necessity inseparable. In this respect, to refuse interdisciplinary work between biblical interpretation and constructive theology is to deny the coherence of the subject matter itself. Today, however, the complexity of the interpretative task may warrant a continued, though always provisional and cooperative, division of labor between biblical scholars and systematicians. The exegete concentrates upon the refraction of the subject matter through particular witnesses, thereby penetrating more deeply into the particular shape of the subject matter and helping to avoid banal theological generalities.[71] And the theologian concentrates more upon the whole of the subject matter as it is expressed through the understanding of scripture in the dogmatic tradition, thereby helping to avoid the tendency toward fragmentation in exegesis (the old problem of losing the forest for the individual trees).

Yet, in continuity with the ancient church, there is no final division between biblical interpretation and theological reflection, for they are united in the common task of attending to the subject matter of scripture. Their actual relationship is thus dialectical, in the sense that within their respective foci there exists a constant movement between the particulars of the biblical text and the whole of systematic reflection in an effort to do justice both to the exegetical thickness of doctrine and the theological coherence of biblical exegesis.

71. Brevard S. Childs, *The Struggle to Understand Isaiah as Christian Scripture* (Grand Rapids: Eerdmans, 2004), xi.

New Testament Theology

◆ THE REVIVAL OF A DISCIPLINE

> The New Testament theology will never be written. It can never be written, because in principle the discipline . . . New Testament theology is never a finally closed book but constitutes a task that continues with us all our days.[1]

It has often been thought that since Bultmann's monumental *Theology of the New Testament*, New Testament theology (NT theology) has become a sterile discipline. It is true that, despite periods of activity after Bultmann, a glance at the state of research over the past fifty years does raise the question of whether or not NT theology has ever left its cul-de-sac. In the last decade or so, however, there has been a determined attempt to move forward.[2] Thus it is the purpose of this essay to review the most significant current work in the field and, on this basis, to identify briefly several areas that offer a sense of the shape and movement of the discipline.

1. Gerhard Ebeling, "The Meaning of 'Biblical Theology,'" in *Word and Faith* (Philadelphia: Fortress, 1963), 94.

2. See recently Frank J. Matera, "New Testament Theology: History, Method, and Identity," *Catholic Biblical Quarterly* 67 (2005): 6–15.

This essay was originally published as "New Testament Theology: The Revival of a Discipline; A Review of Recent Contributions to the Field" in *Journal of Biblical Literature* 125, no. 2 (2006): 393–410. It is reproduced with permission.

Significant Current Work in New Testament Theology

Ferdinand Hahn

The grandest of the complete NT theologies is Ferdinand Hahn's nearly two-thousand-page *Theologie des Neuen Testaments*.[3] Indeed, in terms of its critical sophistication and attempt at theological synthesis, Hahn's work is the most significant *Theologie* to emerge since Bultmann's. Hahn begins by distinguishing the NT theological task from theology more broadly conceived: "Theology is reflection on faith and thus reflection on the truth claim of the Christian message, which is recognized as valid. *New Testament theology* focuses on the testimony of faith of early Christianity, which as such is the basis of all Christian preaching and theology."[4] In order best to encompass the scope of "the testimony of faith of early Christianity," Hahn divides his NT theology into two volumes. The first volume, *Die Vielfalt des Neuen Testaments: Theologiegeschichte des Urchristentums* (The diversity of the New Testament: theological history of early Christianity), represents a diachronic investigation of the manifold and theologically diverse layers of tradition within the NT. The second volume, *Die Einheit des Neuen Testaments: Thematische Darstellung* (The unity of the New Testament: thematic presentation), provides a systematic ordering and presentation of the contents of volume 1.

Volume 1 is structured around the Jesus tradition and its reception by the post-Easter community.[5] In contrast to Bultmann, Hahn argues that close attention to early NT traditions reveals the interpretive necessity of an inquiry into Jesus ("Rückfrage nach Jesus"): insofar as the NT texts themselves exhibit a deep concern to relate the proclamation of Christ ("Christusverkündigung") to the history of Jesus ("Geschichte Jesu"), a theology of the NT must take seriously this movement toward the Jesus of history.[6] Hahn thus sees the probing of the space between the Proclaimer and the Proclaimed as an essential task of NT theology. Indeed, it is only in light of the "Rückfrage" that the NT kerygma can be seen in its complexity and depth. The significance of Easter not only entails the outward

3. Ferdinand Hahn, *Theologie des Neuen Testaments*, 2nd ed., 2 vols. (Tübingen: Mohr Siebeck, 2005).

4. Hahn, *Theologie des Neuen Testaments*, 1:1. "Theologie ist Nachdenken über den Glauben und damit Nachdenken über den als gültig anerkannten Wahrheitsanspruch der christlichen Botschaft. Theologie des Neuen Testaments konzentriert sich auf das Glaubenszeugnis des Urchristentums, das als solches Grundlage aller christlichen Verkündigung und Theologie ist" (emphasis added in translation).

5. "Jesustradition und deren Rezeption seitens der nachösterlichen Gemeinde." Hahn, *Theologie des Neuen Testaments*, 1:vii.

6. Hahn, *Theologie des Neuen Testaments*, esp. 1:30–32, 40–43.

movement of the message about Jesus but also the backward movement toward his earthly life and preaching. Hence, the first volume moves in (fairly standard) chronological order from the preaching and ministry of Jesus ("Verkündigung und Wirken Jesu") through its multifaceted reception in the earliest Christian communities (Aramaic and Greek speaking), to Paul, the Pauline school, the non-Pauline Hellenistic-Jewish writings (James, 1 Peter, Hebrews, and Revelation), the Synoptics (Acts is treated with Luke), the Johannine literature, and, finally, the "transition to the second century" (Jude, 2 Peter, and the Apostolic Fathers).

The exegetical attempt with each of these textual groups is to discern the diversity in the theological concepts and ecclesial practices that are a response to the Christ-event. This investigation yields a vast variety within NT Christianity in both practice and belief, to the extent that the reader is reminded of—and ultimately referred to—Käsemann's famous thesis regarding the concomitance between the diversity in the NT canon and later church confessions: the "diversity definitely contains the tendency towards divergent development of Christian identity and could under the right circumstances lead to different denominational expressions."[7]

Methodologically speaking, the chronological orientation and conceptual telos of Hahn's *Theologiegeschichte* are hardly original, as displaying the diversity in the various branches of tradition ("Traditionslinien") has long played a vital role in the history of the discipline.[8] Yet for Hahn, what is significant is not the diversity per se but rather the constructive character of such diversity for the question of the NT's unity: "The unity of the New Testament certainly cannot simply be taken for granted; it must be worked out critically on the basis of the analysis of the different traditions."[9] That is, the diversity of the NT is inherent to its unity. Here Käsemann is reversed: the radical diversity of the NT does not preclude but instead discloses its unity. In this way, the thematic presentation and argument for unity in volume 2 arise out of the technical tradition-history work in volume 1 (e.g., esp. 1:27), as the diversity of the NT demonstrated in the first volume determines materially *the kind of unity* exhibited in the second. The overall arrangement of Hahn's *Theologie des Neuen Testaments* is thus hermeneutically significant in that it moves beyond a mere

7. "Vielfalt enthält durchaus die Tendenz zu divergierender Ausbildung christlicher Identität und konnte gegebenfalls zu unterschiedlichen konfessionelle Ausprägungen führen (vgl. Ernst Käsemann)." Hahn, *Theologie des Neuen Testaments*, 1:763.

8. See recently Klaus Berger, *Theologiegeschichte des Urchristentums: Theologie des Neuen Testaments* (Tübingen: Francke, 1994).

9. "Die Einheit des Neuen Testaments darf keinesfalls einfach vorausgesetzt werden; sie muß Kritisch erarbeitet werden aufgrund der Analyse der verschiedenen Traditionen." Hahn, *Theologie des Neuen Testaments*, 1:26.

juxtaposition of two separate projects toward the structural and logical interpenetration of a truly synthetic account.

Moreover, for Hahn the synthetic nature of the NT theological enterprise is necessary sensu stricto. An authentic NT theology must pursue the question of the unity of the NT: "If a theology of the New Testament wants to do justice to its theological claim, it must deal not only with the diversity of the scriptures but also with the question of the unity of the early Christian testimony."[10] But it is insufficient to address this complex question in the customary final chapter; rather, "one must show, in terms of the central themes, how unity can be determined."[11] Volume 2, therefore, offers a thematization of the unity of the NT.

The overarching rubric under which Hahn constructs volume 2 is the revelation-act of God ("Offenbarungshandeln Gottes"): in the light of volume 1, God's act of self-revelation emerges as that which constitutes the unity in the various lines of tradition in the NT and thus enables them to be organized into a coherent thematic presentation: "New Testament theology is theology of God's revelation."[12]

The NT's account of God's revelation, however, is unintelligible apart from the OT.[13] With respect to the God who reveals God's self in the OT, there is with the NT a "salvation-historical continuity, which is constitutive for the understanding of the Christian faith."[14] Thus does a discussion of "The Old Testament as the Bible of Early Christianity" ("Das Alte Testament als Bibel des Urchristentums," Teil I) precede the thematic ordering of the unity of God's revelation in the NT.

The center of God's revelation in the NT is, of course, the person of Jesus Christ (part 2). In this way "Christology" provides the particular unifying force for the rest of volume 2, for it allows the most significant aspects of God's self-revelation to be related coherently to one center.[15] The further traditional distinction between the person and work of Christ proves valuable descriptively

10. "Eine Theologie des Neuen Testaments muß sich, wenn sie ihrem theologischen Anspruch gerecht werden will, neben der Vielfalt der Schriften auch mit der Frage nach der Einheit des urchristlichen Zeugnisses befassen." Hahn, *Theologie des Neuen Testaments*, 1:xv.

11. "Es muß anhand der zentralen Themen aufgezeigt werden, wie sich die Einheit bestimmen läßt." Hahn, *Theologie des Neuen Testaments*, 1:xv.

12. "Neutestamentliche Theologie ist Theologie der Offenbarung Gottes." Hahn, *Theologie des Neuen Testaments*, 2:167; cf. 2:27, 161.

13. Contra Hans Hübner, *Biblische Theologie des Neuen Testaments*, 3 vols. (Göttingen: Vandenhoeck & Ruprecht, 1990–1993), per se and not simply *in novo receptum*.

14. "Heilsgeschichtliche Kontinuität, die für das Verständnis des christlichen Glaubens konstitutiv ist." Hahn, *Theologie des Neuen Testaments*, 2:85; cf. 2:86–87.

15. Cf. Hahn, *Theologie des Neuen Testaments*, 2:259.

in that the various exegetical data of volume 1 can be coordinated with "The Revelatory Action of God in Jesus Christ," on the one hand (part 2), and the effects of this revelation, on the other: "The Soteriological Dimension of God's Revelatory Action" (part 3), "The Ecclesiological Dimension of God's Revelatory Action" (part 4), and "The Eschatological Dimension of God's Revelatory Action" (part 5).[16] Thus, the unity of the NT is, strictly speaking, theological: the NT traditions point in all their variety to the reality of the God of Israel's self-revelation in Jesus Christ.

Unity, however, is not uniformity.[17] To affirm the former rather than the latter is to allow tensions and even basic contradictions to remain. The many views of the Torah, for example, are in extreme tension ("höchst spannungsreich"), and "the chasm between Paul's statements about the utterly lost knowledge of God and Luke's view that all people, despite their sin and godlessness, have access to a conditional knowledge of God is unbridgeable."[18] Even within NT eschatology—an area treated as a dimension of the unity of God's self-revelation—it may be said that the "eschatological statements of the New Testament are very different and cannot be reconciled in their horizon of expectation."[19] In Hahn's sense, then, unity is not to be mistaken for an easy harmonization of the NT's theological diversity. Rather, "the unity of the New Testament consists . . . in a multifaceted development of the early Christian message."[20] Thus "the unity . . . can only be unity in diversity."[21]

But let there be no mistake: "unity in diversity" is a real, substantive unity. Contra William Wrede, Heikki Räisänen, and other skeptics, Hahn affirms that the theological gauntlet thrown down by the collection of twenty-seven

16. "Das Offenbarungshandeln Gottes in Jesus Christus" (part 2), "Die soteriologische Dimension des Offenbarungshandelns Gottes" (part 3), "Die ekklesiologische Dimension des Offenbarungshandelns Gottes" (part 4), and "Die eschatologische Dimension des Offenbarungshandelns Gottes" (part 5).

17. Hahn, *Theologie des Neuen Testaments*, 2:805.

18. "Zwischen den Aussagen des Paulus über die total verlorene Gotteserkenntnis und der Auffassung des Lukas, daß alle Menschen trotz ihrer Sünde und Gottlosigkeit über eine bedingte Gotteserkenntnis verfügen, ist keine Brücke zu schlagen." Hahn, *Theologie des Neuen Testaments*, 2:364–65, 2:804.

19. Die "eschatologischen Aussagen des Neuen Testaments sind höchst unterschiedlich und in ihrem Erwartungshorizont nicht miteinander zu vereinen." Hahn, *Theologie des Neuen Testaments*, 2:804.

20. "Die Einheit des Neuen Testaments besteht . . . in einer vielgestaltigen Entfaltung der urchristlichen Botschaft." Hahn, *Theologie des Neuen Testaments*, 2:805.

21. "Die Einheit kann nur Einheit in der Vielfalt sein." Hahn, *Theologie des Neuen Testaments*, 1:770.

different documents has been taken up: one can write not only a *Theologiegeschichte* but also a *Theologie des Neuen Testaments.*

Ulrich Wilckens

Ulrich Wilckens would agree. Already in his retirement, Wilckens began a three-volume *Theologie des Neuen Testaments.*[22] Because it is presently incomplete, however, Wilckens's project is difficult to evaluate comprehensively.[23] On the basis of his work in volume 1, it is nevertheless worthwhile to note some of the leading themes and methodological decisions, not least of all because they represent substantive convergence with Hahn.

First, with respect to the overall structure of the work, volumes 1 and 2 of Wilckens's *Theologie des Neuen Testaments* deal with the "historical presentation of the history of Jesus and early Christianity" and the "systematic-theological presentation of the whole of this history," respectively.[24] Like Hahn, Wilckens avers that the diversity of the NT writings must be respected. To understand the theological unity of the NT is to work through, not against, the contingency of the individual compositions. "Every writing," argues Wilckens, "should first be heard as it arose at its respective place in the history of early Christianity and as it was meant to be heard by its addressees."[25] Thus, for example, with respect to the Gospels, the presentation in volume 1 follows a historical rather than a canonical order: gospel material is of course used in part 1 to reconstruct crucial moments in the early history, but the treatment of the Gospels as whole compositions is reserved until part 4. Moreover, Wil-

22. Ulrich Wilckens, *Theologie des Neuen Testaments*, vol. 1, *Geschichte der urchristlichen Theologie* (Neukirchener-Vluyn: Neukirchener Verlag, 2002–2005).

23. Vol. 1, *Geschichte der urchristlichen Theologie*, has appeared in four parts: Teilband 1: *Geschichte des Wirkens Jesu in Galiläa* (2002; 2nd ed. 2005); Teilband 2: *Jesu Tod und Auferstehung und die Entstehung der Kirche aus Juden und Heiden* (2003); Teilband 3: *Die Briefe des Urchristentums: Paulus und seine Schüler, Theologen aus dem Bereich judenchristlicher Heidenmission* (2005); Teilband 4: *Die Evangelien, die Apostelgeschichte, die Johannesbriefe, die Offenbarung und die Entstehung des Kanons* (2005).

24. "Historische Darstellung der Geschichte Jesu und des Urchristentums . . . systematisch-theologische Darstellung des Ganzen dieser Geschichte," Wilckens, *Theologie des Neuen Testaments*, 1:1.50–51; vol. 3 offers a "kritische Darstellung der Geschichte der historisch-kritischen Bibelwissenschaft" (1:1.51) and gives the methodological justification for the procedure in vols. 1 and 2.

25. "Jede Schrift soll zunächst so gehört werden, wie sie an je ihrem Ort in der Geschichte des Urchristentums entstanden ist und von ihren Adressaten gehört werden sollte." Wilckens, *Theologie des Neuen Testaments*, 1:3.v.

ckens takes "every writing" seriously: part 3, for example, treats individually every letter in the Pauline corpus (in "chronological" order), Hebrews, James, 1 Peter, Jude, and 2 Peter.

Yet Wilckens is careful to underscore the point that every historical presentation of the diversity or individuality of the NT writings involves a larger schematized perception of the overall history and development that surround the particular NT documents: "The historical part assumes crucial aspects that are not presented thematically until the systematic part. However, this rooting of the historical in the systematic already determines the method of Vol. I."[26] This critical awareness of method prevents one from taking volume 1 in isolation, as if it could be viewed simply as the "historical" component of the *Theologie des Neuen Testaments* (with volume 2 as the "theological" component). Instead, at least if it is carried through, there is a substantive interpenetration of volumes 1 and 2. For Wilckens as for Hahn, diachronic investigation and systematic presentation are not two separate ventures but rather two movements in one interpretive enterprise.

Second, Wilckens argues that the "historical Jesus" is integral to NT theology. Here, however, Wilckens labors to redefine critically the way in which the historical Jesus has been conceived. Rather than a figure who is best accessed in abstraction from his resurrection,[27] the historical Jesus is the Jesus known through an examination of the essential continuity between the pre- and post-Easter period. If initially one is not committed to an understanding of reality that precludes resurrection,[28] then "a fascinating possibility opens up of solving the central problem of historical-critical New Testament research—the gap between the historical Jesus and the proclaimed Christ—historically in such a way that a *theological* connection is revealed that is just as meaningful as the historical connection is plausible."[29] Wilckens admits that securing a theologically discerned *historical* continuity between Jesus's self-understanding and the

26. "Im historischen Teil [werden] entscheidende Aspekte vorausgesetzt, die erst im systematischen Teil thematisch Zusammenhängen dargestellt. Diese Verwurzelung des Historischen im Systematischen bestimmt aber bereits die Methode von Bd. I." Wilckens, *Theologie des Neuen Testaments*, 1:1.51.

27. Wilckens, *Theologie des Neuen Testaments*, 1:1.29.

28. Wilckens, *Theologie des Neuen Testaments*, 1:1.21–29.

29. "Eröffnet sich eine faszinierende Möglichkeit, das Zentralproblem der historisch-kritischen neutestamentlichen Forschung: die Kluft zwischen dem historischen Jesus und dem verkündigten Christus historisch so zu lösen, daß sich ein *theologischer* Zusammenhang zeigt, der ebenso sinnvoll wie der historische Zusammenhang plausibel ist." Wilckens, *Theologie des Neuen Testaments*, 1:1.35.

"earliest Christian proclamation of Christ" ("urchristlichen Christusverkündigung") will involve "the whole historical picture of historical-critical research in a historical and theological revision from the ground up."[30] But, in his view, such a christological revision of modern conceptuality is nothing less than the task of NT theology.

Third, the unity exhibited through the diversity of the NT is ultimately a profoundly theological one: "The unity and common ground of early Christian faith and early Christian theology has its real basis in the reality of God."[31] In contrast to the old "Lehrbegriff" model, Wilckens is at pains throughout volume 1 to make clear that it is not the *idea* or doctrine of God that unifies the testimonies of the NT but "God" in the sense of a reality outside the text. "The conception of the 'Theology of the New Testament' presented here . . . is based on the judgment that all writings of the New Testament canon presuppose and testify to the reality of the very living God who reveals himself in the history of his dealings with people."[32]

Lest the NT scholar fret over the encroachment of systematic theology, it is important to note that such an explicitly theological claim functions also to ground Wilckens's conviction that NT theology must engage in rigorous historical inquiry. Because "the reality of God is itself historical" ("die Wirklichkeit Gottes ist selbst geschichtlich"), the NT theologian who seeks to explore this reality must do so *historically.* Thus the theological character of the NT provides the necessity for historical investigation: "There are above all theological grounds for the necessity of historical exegesis of the biblical texts."[33] In this way, for Wilckens, the unity of the NT texts (the reality of God) commits the exegete simultaneously to the diversity of the NT (the revelation of God's reality in history).

Finally, to locate the unity of the NT in the identity of God is also to point to the importance of the OT for the NT: "That one and the same God is attested

30. "Das ganze Geschichtsbild der historisch-kritischen Forschung in einer historischen wie theologischen Revision von Grund auf." Wilckens, *Theologie des Neuen Testaments*, 1:1.35.

31. "Die Einheit und Gemeinsamkeit urchristlichen Glaubens und urchristlicher Theologie hat in der Wirklichkeit Gottes ihren eigentlichen Grund." Wilckens, *Theologie des Neuen Testaments*, 1:1.55.

32. "Der Konzeption der hier vorgelegten 'Theologie des Neuen Testaments' . . . liegt das Urteil zugrunde, daß alle Schriften des neutestamentlichen Kanons *die Wirklichkeit des lebendigen Gottes selbst* voraussetzen und bezeugen, der sich in der *Geschichte seines Handelns* mit den Menschen offenbart." Wilckens, *Theologie des Neuen Testaments*, 1:4.vi; cf. 1:1.11.

33. "Für die Notwendigkeit *historischer* Exegese biblischer Texte [gibt es] vor allem *theologische* Gründe." Wilckens, *Theologie des Neuen Testaments*, 1:1.23.

in the Old as in the New Testament is the fundamental presupposition of any theology of the New Testament that wants to do justice to its content."[34] Wilckens's "Einführung in das Gesamtwerk" in 1:1, therefore, begins not with the NT but with the OT. With Hahn, moreover, Wilckens rejects Hübner's more narrow focus on the OT's reception in the New and maintains that "the Old Testament *as a whole* [must always be] constantly in view."[35] The OT is not a set of prooftexts from which the NT writers draw carefully (or willy-nilly) to suit the occasion. To the contrary, the OT informs the theology of the NT in a far-reaching and significant sense. For example, both the Christology and ecclesiology "of early Christianity [have] their roots in Israel's history of salvation."[36] The NT's construction of the identity of Jesus and the church is inseparably bound to the history of Israel and its God. Thus, to come full circle, NT theology is embedded in the OT because of the continuity in divine identity and act: "*Christian communities live with the God of Israel.* Therefore, the Old Testament is their Holy Scripture."[37]

Peter Stuhlmacher

Even Peter Stuhlmacher could not have put it more strongly. Stuhlmacher's second volume of his much-discussed *Biblische Theologie des Neuen Testaments* appeared in 1999.[38] For the purposes of this review, Stuhlmacher's project need not be covered in full. It will instead suffice to note three cardinal areas of similarity with Hahn and Wilckens.

First, the title of Stuhlmacher's work makes the importance of the OT immediately clear. By situating his NT investigations within the larger framework

34. "Daß im Alten wie im Neuen Testament der eine und selbe Gott bezeugt wird, ist die Grundvoraussetzung jeder Theologie des Neuen Testaments, die dessen Inhalt gerecht werden will." Wilckens, *Theologie des Neuen Testaments*, 1:1.2.

35. "Das Alte Testament als ganzes ständig im Blick stehen [muß]." Wilckens, *Theologie des Neuen Testaments*, 1:1.13 (emphasis added).

36. ". . . des Urchristentums [haben] ihre Wurzel in der Heilsgeschichte Israels." Wilckens, *Theologie des Neuen Testaments*, 1:1.56.

37. "*Christliche Gemeinden leben mit dem Gott Israels.* Deswegen ist das Alte Testament ihre Heilige Schrift." Wilckens, *Theologie des Neuen Testaments*, 1:1.55.

38. Peter Stuhlmacher, *Biblical Theology of the New Testament*, trans. and ed. Daniel P. Bailey with the collaboration of Jostein Ådna (Grand Rapids: Eerdmans, 2018). The original German editions: Peter Stuhlmacher, *Biblische Theologie des Neuen Testaments*, Band 1: *Grundlegung: Von Jesus zu Paulus* (Göttingen: Vandenhoeck & Ruprecht, 1991); Band 2: *Von der Paulusschule bis zur Johannesoffenbarung: Der Kanon und seine Auslegung* (Göttingen: Vandenhoeck & Ruprecht, 1999).

of "biblical" theology, Stuhlmacher is able to characterize his NT theological endeavor as "a biblical theology of the New Testament" that is both derived from and "open to the Old Testament." NT theology itself, that is, does not exist as a self-contained discipline; it is instead always and only "a subdiscipline of a whole-Bible biblical theology encompassing both Testaments."[39] Like Hahn and Wilckens, Stuhlmacher affirms that the importance of the OT for the NT is far greater than the significance attached to citations and allusions alone.[40] Indeed, "the New Testament is unthinkable without the Old."[41]

Where Stuhlmacher differs somewhat from Hahn and Wilckens, however, is in the amount of weight he places upon the history of canonization (*Kanonsgeschichte*). Adopting the thesis of Hartmut Gese, Stuhlmacher grounds the unity of the OT with the NT in the (debatable) fact that the "closing" of the OT and NT canon was actually one historical process, not two separate events. Around the time of the NT, that is, the OT canon was not closed but remained open to further developments. In point of fact, the open OT went in two observable directions: that of rabbinic Judaism with the Mishnah, and that of early Christianity with the NT texts. Thus, in Stuhlmacher's account, neither the OT nor the NT existed in final form independently. In the historical trajectory of the Christian tradition, there is really only one book: "The Old and New Testaments can therefore be differentiated as the first and second parts of the biblical canon, but not separated. Whoever separates them understands at least the New Testament from the wrong perspective both *historically* and theologically."[42]

The primary way in which a separation of the OT from the NT is wrong *theologically* joins Stuhlmacher closely again with Hahn and Wilckens. The God who is revealed in the OT and the NT is one and the same God. At bottom, then, the historical-canonical process has its meaning in the revelation

39. Stuhlmacher, *Biblical Theology of the New Testament*, 6 = Stuhlmacher, *Biblische Theologie des Neuen Testaments*, 1:5 ("eine vom Alten Testament herkommende und zu ihm hin offene Biblische Theologie des Neuen Testaments . . . Teildisziplin einer Altes und Neues Testament gemeinsam betrachtenden Biblischen Theologie").

40. Stuhlmacher, *Biblical Theology of the New Testament*, 38–39 = Stuhlmacher, *Biblische Theologie des Neuen Testaments*, 1:36–38.

41. Stuhlmacher, *Biblical Theology of the New Testament*, 743 = Stuhlmacher, *Biblische Theologie des Neuen Testaments*, 2:288 ("Das Neue Testament ist ohne das Alte nicht zu denken").

42. Stuhlmacher, *Biblical Theology of the New Testament*, 6 (emphasis added) = Stuhlmacher, *Biblische Theologie des Neuen Testaments*, 1:5 ("Altes und Neues Testament lassen sich darum zwar als erster und zweiter Teil des biblischen Kanons unterscheiden, aber nicht trennen. Trennt man sie, versteht man das Neue Testament sowohl historisch als auch theologisch falsch").

of God: "The church's decision in favor of the two-part Christian canon was the consistent reaction to the history of tradition and revelation to which the church owes its existence."[43]

Second, Stuhlmacher affirms that NT theology must give an explanation for the unity of the NT—for why, that is, precisely the twenty-seven NT books could be combined to make the second part of the canon.[44] Rather than an entire volume of systematic presentation, however, Stuhlmacher structures his opus differently. The overall work is divided into two parts: (1) "The Origin and Character of the New Testament Proclamation" (*Entstehung und Eigenart der neutestamentlichen Verkündigung*), and (2) "The Problem of the Canon and the Center of Scripture" (*Das Problem des Kanons und die Mitte der Schrift*). But one should note that volumes 1 and 2 of the original German edition do not correspond exactly to these two parts. (Indeed, part 1 comprises the majority of volume 2 as well.) Instead, volume 1—*Von Jesus zu Paulus*—presents the "foundation" (*Grundlegung*) of a biblical theology of the NT. Stuhlmacher begins with the message and life of Jesus, moves to the preaching of primitive Christian community, and closes with Paul. Volume 2 presents the rest of the NT as the building upon this foundation (the Pauline school, the "catholic letters," the Synoptics with Acts, and the Johannine literature). In the final 62 pages (out of ca. 750 total text pages in the two volumes), Stuhlmacher turns to part 2 of his project and grapples with issues of canon and the center of scripture.

Stuhlmacher's attempt to establish the unity of the NT could be caricatured as the "final chapter" statement against which Hahn warns. Such a caricature, however, would not do justice to the conceptual significance of the work's structure or to Stuhlmacher's resolute effort throughout part 1 to locate the points of continuity that then fund the construal of the NT's unity in part 2.

The structure and approach of the project together make a strong argument for the unity of the NT in tradition-historical (*traditionsgeschichtliche*) terms. There is a continuity in history between Jesus's life and message and the response thereto: "The preaching in the early Christian churches and mission is a histor-

43. Stuhlmacher, *Biblical Theology of the New Testament*, 769 = Stuhlmacher, *Biblische Theologie des Neuen Testaments*, 2:303 ("Die Entscheidung der Kirche für den zweiteiligen christlichen Kanon war die konsequente Reaktion auf die Traditions- und Offenbarungsgeschichte, der sie sich verdankt").

44. Stuhlmacher, *Biblische Theologie des Neuen Testaments*, 1:34 ("Umgekehrt muss die Theologie des Neuen Testaments auch verständlich machen können, warum gerade die 27 neutestamentlichen Bücher zum zweiten Teil des Kanons zusammengefaßt werden konnten").

ically legitimate proclamation about Jesus as the Christ of God. Or to formulate it with A. Schlatter: *The earthly Jesus was none other than the Christ of faith*."[45] For Stuhlmacher, this continuity is understandable only within the larger theological context of God's relation to the world as narrated in the OT. Thus is the theology of the NT a *biblical* theology of the NT: "The biblical theology of the (Old and) New Testament is constituted by the Bible's kerygmatic witness to the one God who created the world, chose Israel as his own people, and sent Jesus as the Christ in order to provide for the salvation of Jews and Gentiles."[46]

Third, despite the "clear contours of a doctrine of the Christian faith that stands above the differences between the various individual witnesses of the New Testament tradition," the unity "did not force them into uniformity."[47] It is therefore incumbent upon the NT exegete to draw out the diversity of the writings under discussion and to treat them in their individual, historical contexts.[48] The logic that undergirds the collection of twenty-seven different documents does not posit a bland theological uniformity but instead, under the conviction of a theologically continuous history, moves freely through the manifest diversity of the individual texts.

Read together, the NT theologies of Hahn, Wilckens, and Stuhlmacher constitute a powerful voice in German NT theology today. In multiple and important ways—and regardless of their many differences—their theologies converge to provide a coherent alternative to the larger Bultmannian paradigm in NT theology. Where Bultmann famously sidestepped the significance of the OT, Hahn, Wilckens, and Stuhlmacher all affirm the inseparability of the Old from the New. Where Bultmann refused the historical Jesus a part in the theology of the NT, Hahn, Wilckens, and Stuhlmacher press for the necessity of

45. Stuhlmacher, *Biblical Theology of the New Testament*, 180 = Stuhlmacher, *Biblische Theologie des Neuen Testaments*, 1:157 ("Die christliche Missions- und Gemeinde-Predigt [ist] geschichtlich legitimerweise Predigt von Jesus als dem Christus Gottes, oder mit A. Schlatter formuliert: Der irdische Jesus war kein anderer als der Christus des Glaubens") (emphasis added in the English translation of the Schlatter expression).

46. Stuhlmacher, *Biblical Theology of the New Testament*, 43 = Stuhlmacher, *Biblische Theologie des Neuen Testaments*, 1:38; cf. 1:34, 2:311–13 ("Die Biblische Theologie des [Alten und] Neuen Testaments wird konstituiert durch das kerygmatische Zeugnis von dem einen Gott, der die Welt geschaffen, Israel zu seinem Eigentumsvolk erwählt und in der Sendung Jesu als Christus für das Heil von Juden und Heiden genug getan hat").

47. Stuhlmacher, *Biblical Theology of the New Testament*, 778 = Stuhlmacher, *Biblische Theologie des Neuen Testaments*, 2:311 ("klare Konturen für eine Glaubenslehre, die über den Differenzen der verschiedenen Traditionszeugen des Neuen Testaments steht . . . [hat] nicht zur Uniformität gezwungen").

48. Stuhlmacher, *Biblische Theologie des Neuen Testaments*, 1:10.

Jesus's earthly life as an essential ingredient of NT theology. Where Bultmann saw deep and irreconcilable theological contradiction within the NT (the radical divergences between Paul/John and "early catholicism" [*Frühkatholizismus*], for example), Hahn, Wilckens, and Stuhlmacher argue for a discernible theological unity amid the obvious and real diversity of the NT writings. And, finally, where Bultmann's existential interpretation clearly placed the accent on theological *anthropology* (human "self-understanding"), Hahn, Wilckens, and Stuhlmacher all insist on the centrality of theology proper: the NT is first of all about *God.*

Georg Strecker and Joachim Gnilka

Recent German NT theology, however, is not univocal. Georg Strecker's posthumously published *Theologie des Neuen Testaments* (German, 1996; English, 2000), for example, continues in the Bultmannian vein with an explicit focus upon the cognitive structures of religious experience, "believing comprehension."[49] Strecker, moreover, does not argue for the unity of the NT. Indeed, he explicitly sets the NT's diversity over against the possibility of its unity: "The theological unity . . . cannot be presupposed. It is rather the case that in the writings of the New Testament we are met with a multiplicity of theological conceptions. These are to be investigated and presented according to their own structures of thought, in relation to their own historical and literary contexts."[50]

Joachim Gnilka, too, has offered a recent *Theologie des Neuen Testaments* that differs significantly from Hahn, Wilckens, and Stuhlmacher.[51] The title of the work notwithstanding, Gnilka, like Strecker, makes no concerted attempt to address the question of the theological unity of the NT. In fact, where he identifies the element common to the various "particularities" ("Vorgaben") of the NT documents—the kerygma of the death and resurrection of Jesus—he concurrently precludes the unity of the NT by also asserting that this is the *source* of manifold diversity.[52] In addition, though he begins with Paul, Gnilka agrees with Bultmann with respect to the role of Jesus in an NT theology: "In a discussion of the origins and beginning of the Church, Jesus of Nazareth is an

49. Georg Strecker, *Theology of the New Testament*, ed. F. W. Horn, trans. E. Boring (Berlin: de Gruyter; Louisville: Westminster John Knox, 2000), 2.

50. Strecker, *Theology of the New Testament*, 2–3.

51. Joachim Gnilka, *Theologie des Neuen Testaments*, HThKNT Sup 5 (Freiburg: Herder, 1994).

52. Gnilka, *Theologie des Neuen Testaments*, esp. 454–64.

indispensable ingredient. If you are writing a theology of the New Testament, you could dispense with this chapter."[53]

Despite the uncontestable sophistication of these works, it is difficult to concede that Strecker and Gnilka have written successful *Theologies* of the NT.[54] Although their studies carry forth Bultmann's perspective in certain important ways and display numerous exegetical insights, in the end they seem not to amount to more than valuable sets of historical- or redaction-critical articles. Yet precisely in this way they are tradents of one side of the history of the discipline, the side in which the extensive diversity of the NT appears to render questionable its existence as a collection.

François Vouga

A more creative effort to deal constructively with the NT's diversity from within the Bultmannian existentialist framework is François Vouga's *Une théologie du Nouveau Testament*.[55] In contrast to the diachronic methodology of Strecker, for example, Vouga's work is arranged thematically. The attempt here is not to follow the traditional dogmatic loci or a history of theological development but to let the NT itself suggest the organizing topics (esp. 19–21): "the revelation of the new time ["temps"]," "the reality of the new existence," the three theological virtues (faith, hope, love), and so on (these larger themes are also further subdivided).

The fresh aspect of Vouga's treatment is the imaginative manner in which he structures debates around these matters from *within* the NT itself. The NT texts are not pressed or mixed together in order to speak with one voice on a particular topic. The emphasis, rather, is upon letting the relevant NT authors speak with their own voices to a variety of different issues. So, for example, when Vouga treats "the reality of the new existence," he organizes the dialogue

53. "In eine Erörterung über die Ursprünge und den Anfang der Kirche gehört Jesus von Nazaret unverzichtbar hinein. Schriebe man eine Theologie des Neuen Testaments, so konnte man auf dieses Kapitel verzichten." Joachim Gnilka, *Die Frühen Christen: Ursprünge und Anfang der Kirche*, HThKNT Sup 7 (Freiburg: Herder, 1999), 11–12, with reference to his own *Theologie des Neuen Testaments*.

54. So, rightly, Matera, "New Testament Theology," 8, though his remark that they have presented "reliable accounts of the theologies *in* the writings of the NT" undercuts his critical move.

55. François Vouga, *Une théologie du Nouveau Testament*, Monde de la Bible 43 (Geneva: Labor et Fides, 2001); see 439, 445, etc.; though Swiss-born, Vouga's institutional home is the Kirchliche Hochschule Bethel in Germany.

around four different ways in which the NT authors construe "new existence": Luke and John are employed to address new existence in light of their emphases upon salvation ("salut"), while Hebrews and John are allowed to speak about the images of deliverance and purification ("images de la délivrance et de la purification"); Paul, Matthew, and Luke discuss forgiveness ("pardon"), and, lastly, Paul reappears to reflect with the author of Ephesians upon new existence as reconciliation ("réconciliation"). In this way, Vouga is able to elaborate the distinctive perspectives of the various NT documents from multiple angles of vision.

In Vouga's judgment, the diversity that emerges from this method of reading the NT texts together excludes the kind of final theological unity for which Hahn and others have argued. The response to the revelation of God in Jesus Christ is deeply pluralistic and cannot be reduced to an overarching theological perspective. In view of this irreducible diversity, NT theology becomes dialogue, debate, or finally a conflict of interpretations.[56] This conflict, however, is fully in accord with earliest Christianity itself, in which there never was an original theological unity (F. C. Baur's influence is marked); thus does NT theology as a conflict of interpretation mirror well the nature of its source (Vouga is aware of course that Acts, e.g., presents a more unified picture of early Christian theology than he does. But this picture, in his view, is a fictive projection of later ecclesiastical authorities/wishes).[57]

In light of such radical disagreement within the NT, one might expect Vouga to abandon altogether any attempt at unity. Instead, he presents "the diversity of theologies as a principle of the unity of Christianity."[58] For Vouga, diversity and conflict result in conversation, and it is this dialogical mode of discourse that itself becomes the proper form of unity: "Christianity defines itself as conflicting interpretations of God's historical revelation in Jesus Christ, *such that* open dialogue is the proper form of Christian unity."[59] Or, to state positively the "unity" of NT Christianity in Vouga's sense: "Unity . . . necessarily consists of a conflict of interpretations."[60]

56. Vouga, *Une théologie du Nouveau Testament*, 442–43.

57. Vouga, *Une théologie du Nouveau Testament*, 400.

58. Vouga, *Une théologie du Nouveau Testament*, 21.

59. "Le christianisme se définit lui-même comme conflit des interprétations de la révélation historique de Dieu en Jésus-Christ, *de sorte que* le dialogue ouvert est la forme appropriée de l'unité du christianisme." Vouga, *Une théologie du Nouveau Testament*, 442 (emphasis altered).

60. "L'unité . . . consiste nécessairement en un conflit des interpretations." Vouga, *Une théologie du Nouveau Testament*, 443.

If there remain structural curiosities and organizational oddities (e.g., the treatment of the historical Jesus in the middle of the book does not evidence a logically necessary relationship to its surrounding material), the overall conceptual proposals in Vouga's *Theologie des Neuen Testaments* are remarkably consistent. It is, finally, no small wonder that the only two figures who receive significant discussion are F. C. Baur and Bultmann.[61] If one is convinced in Baur-like fashion that the level of theological conflict in the NT is as substantive as Vouga believes, then it is indubitably convenient to be convinced in Bultmann-like fashion that the thrust of the NT is essentially anthropological ("self-understanding"). This coordination allows Vouga to avoid positing directly an essential conflict in the identity of God (as would be the case if he construed the unity in ultimately theological terms), for God is no longer the primary horizon of the NT.

George B. Caird

Vouga's work recalls the unfinished *New Testament Theology* of George B. Caird, who, like Vouga, attempts to bring the NT authors together in conversation with one another.[62] Structurally speaking, Caird rejects the dogmatic loci approach, the developmental or chronological approach, the kerygmatic approach, and the author-by-author approach (5–18). In the place of these defective organizational schemata, Caird sets the "Conference Table Approach." The methodological presupposition "is simply stated: to write a New Testament theology is to preside at a conference of faith and order. Around the table sit the authors of the New Testament, and it is the presider's task to engage them in a colloquium about theological matters which they themselves have placed on the agenda" (18). In practice, Caird's NT theology then proceeds thematically, and the NT authors are employed to speak with their own voices to various aspects of "salvation"—the overarching theme to which all others are related. Indeed, six of the eight chapters that compose the body of the book are essentially about salvation. The eighth chapter concerns "the theology of Jesus." This reflects Caird's conviction that Bultmann put "the cart before the horse" (25). Because we have only "the message of Jesus according to Mark, or Luke, or Matthew, or John," we can only arrive at the "teaching of Jesus" after a thorough study of the NT documents (25–26). Such an approach presupposes

61. Vouga, *Une théologie du Nouveau Testament*, 380–90, in a digression.

62. George B. Caird, *New Testament Theology*, ed. L. D. Hurst (Oxford: Clarendon, 1994). Hereafter, page references appear in the text.

that the task of NT theology is "modern academic research into the ideas of the New Testament writers," rather than a reconstruction of the message of Jesus behind the Gospels. Of course, this is precisely Caird's point.

Unlike Vouga, however, Caird displays no postmodern hermeneutical tendencies, affirming resolutely the traditional Wrede/Stendahl line: "New Testament theology is a historical discipline. . . . Its purpose is descriptive" (1). Also in contrast to Vouga, Caird holds out for the theological unity of the NT. The model is given by the NT itself in the form of the Jerusalem council, in which there was presumably unity without homogeneity (23–24). By no means, that is to say, is the "music of the New Testament choir . . . written to be sung in unison" (24). The question is not whether the NT texts "all say the same thing, but whether they all bear witness to the same Jesus and through him to the many splendoured wisdom of the one God" (24). Thus, for Caird as for Hahn and others, the unity of the NT is finally a question about the unity of God.

Philip Esler

Philip Esler shares Caird's conviction that a proper NT theology ought to be historical and descriptive.[63] The "normative" role of NT theology is rejected in favor of "the valorization of what Stendahl called the descriptive task" (36). Yet for Esler such historical work is theological in scope. Esler begins his "entirely different model" for NT theology by stating that his "intention in writing is an avowedly theological one," by which he means that he intends "to promote a specifically Christian rationale for reading the New Testament" (1). Thus the whole of the descriptive, historical investigations is "set within a theologically and socially constructed framework of persons in communion" (276). These are the two sides of Esler's proposal: on the one hand, there is the adamant commitment to the historical-critical and social-scientific enterprise, and, on the other, there is the attempt to develop a theological account of personhood.

Historical, social-scientific investigation centers the interpreter's attention upon the oral/aural dynamic of author/audience communication in the ancient world. "Textuality" is largely a modern construct; "scriptality"—despite the awkward neologism—captures better the fact that the author was presumed to be present via his/her written communication (180–90). That is, communication through written documents was not merely a dispensing of information but was an "interpersonal" affair. In the face of difficulties with authorial

63. Philip Esler, *New Testament Theology: Communion and Community* (Minneapolis: Fortress, 2005). Hereafter, page references appear in the text.

intention, textual transmission, and canonical shaping, Esler focuses on Paul and maintains that present-day readers still have direct access to the real (not implied) author through reading his documents. Indeed, this is the purpose of NT theology: to commune interpersonally with the authors of the NT.

In order to establish this communion as a serious possibility, Esler develops an account of the human person that draws on the thought of systematic theologians ranging from Schleiermacher to John Zizioulas (Orthodox), as well as on current work in genetics, sociology, literary theory, and philosophy. Esler's theoretical melting pot yields the conclusion that the old ecclesial notion of communion with the saints wields sufficient explanatory power as that notion that best brings "the results of historical criticism of the New Testament into fruitful conjunction with the ongoing life and belief of contemporary Christians" (256).

In the present climate, Esler's "new approach" to NT theology is novel in the sense that few NT scholars would want to claim that we have "direct" access to the NT authors, and probably even fewer that such "interpersonal communication" is a direct result of historical research. Yet the overall concern to bring together exacting historical exegesis and contemporary Christian life is hardly new at all. In fact, such a concern is arguably embedded in the origins of the discipline itself, and one has only to look over to the University of Aberdeen to see massive evidence of precisely this larger program.

I. Howard Marshall

Howard Marshall's recent tome is the best example of what divinity students typically think of when they think of NT theology: an exegetical and theological map of the NT that shows how all the various lines fit together to make one picture.[64] There are "many witnesses" but only "one Gospel." In a sense, the question of the unity and diversity of the NT stands at the center of Marshall's project. In contrast to the separate, systematic treatments of Hahn and Wilckens, however, the methodological manner in which Marshall considers this problem is essentially via the accumulation of descriptive exegesis: the construction of the work is an author-by-author treatment that builds its synthetic case in brief comparative sketches at the end of major textual groups ("The Theology of the Synoptic Gospels and Acts," "Paul, the Synoptic Gospels

64. I. Howard Marshall, *New Testament Theology: Many Witnesses, One Gospel* (Downers Grove, IL: InterVarsity Press, 2004). Hereafter, page references appear in the text.

and Acts," "John, the Synoptic Gospels and Acts, and Paul," "Hebrews, James, 1–2 Peter and Jude in the New Testament").

This structure reflects Marshall's conviction that if there is to be a synthetic NT theology, "it must begin with seeing each writer in his own terms" (726). The investigation of the individual witnesses of the NT does not proceed chronologically but, by and large, according to modern canonical groupings (Synoptics and Acts, corpus Paulinum, Johannine literature, the rest of the NT). The "historical Jesus," however, is not thereby set aside. To the contrary, Marshall relies heavily on the synoptic traditions and argues that NT theology must include "jesusology as well as christology" (46). Here, like the views of Wilckens and Stuhlmacher, Marshall's view of the historical Jesus is essentially concomitant with that of the figure presented by the Synoptic Gospels. In this way the theological continuity for which Marshall argues is also a historical one, in that the message of the NT (naturally) has its origin in the life and ministry of Jesus.

Unity and continuity do not mean, however, that the NT documents are simply identical in theological expression. Indeed, there are significant differences in the way the various NT authors develop the central theme of the gospel: "the unity is expressed in diversity" (726; see also 21, 731, etc.). Yet, as he candidly admits, Marshall's construal is weighted heavily toward the side of unity: "I have to admit that I am probably the kind of person whose bias or temptation is to see the likenesses and play down or not notice the differences, and therefore my observations may tend to be one-sided" (185).[65] Adopting J. C. Beker's "coherent/contingent" pattern of analysis for Pauline thought, Marshall argues that the coherence or "core" of the NT is its message of redemption (717). There are four discernible stages to this "religion of redemption . . . common to all the writers": (1) "a situation of human need . . . understood as sin that places sinners under divine judgment"; (2) "a saving act by God that is accomplished through Jesus Christ . . . whose death and resurrection constitute the saving act that must be proclaimed to the world"; (3) "a new life for those who show faith in God and Jesus Christ"; and (4) the act of God to "bring his redemptive action to consummation with the parousia of Christ, final judgment . . . and the establishment of the new world" (717–18).[66]

65. See esp. the evaluation of the list on 589–90 that compares the Synoptic Gospels with John. Of the nine listed items, four exhibit rather considerable differences between the Synoptics and John (nos. 1, 3, 4, and 5). But Marshall concludes that the list as a whole indicates "a basic agreement between the Synoptic Gospels and John" (Marshall, *New Testament Theology*, 590).

66. Marshall's formulations are purposefully reminiscent of Kümmel's articulation of

Further, in addition to the "main theme" of redemption, all the NT writers share the same larger conceptual structure, or "framework of thought," which is fundamentally Jewish in shape. The basic importance of the OT, for example, is presupposed (a "divinely authorized and inspired account of God's dealings with his people"), as are the doctrine of creation and the theological significance of history (718). Finally, though they do so in various ways, all the NT writers develop the main theme of redemption with an emphasis upon what Marshall broadly terms "mission" (the "context of mission," "center of mission," "community of mission," and "consummation of mission"). For Marshall, this is true historically no less than noetically. Not only is the existence of the NT dependent upon the "mission of Jesus"; it is also "worth remembering that people were believers only if they had become believers. . . . Inevitably, therefore, the church was active in mission, or else there would have been no church" (709). To the objection that Paul's letters, for example, are hardly tools of evangelism, Marshall has a ready reply. It is "a narrow view of evangelism that confines it to the activity whereby people are brought to faith; the nurture of converts and the establishment of the congregations they comprise are equally important as part of the task" (709). As Marshall defines it, the notion of mission thus encompasses the majority of the NT literature. "New Testament theology is essentially missionary theology" (34).

To his own question, then, of whether the diversity in the NT "amounts to significant difference or even contradiction" (726), Marshall has answered with a clear no. Paul and the Synoptics (with Acts) are "not identical, but they are recognizably the same" (483). The positions of Paul and James "on the issue of faith and works . . . are harmonious" (691). Though the NT authors may sing different parts, they "are all singing from the same hymnbook" (484); there is "a harmony between the different writers" (483). They all "bear testimony to what is palpably the same complex reality" (726).

In contrast to Vouga and Strecker, but like Hahn, Wilckens, and Stuhlmacher, Marshall obviously posits a substantial level of unity between the various NT documents. Yet, in contrast to Wilckens and others, this unity is not derived from the identity of God as much as it is located in the thought of the particular NT writers (esp., e.g., 28–30). In this sense, Marshall's version of unity is perhaps best read as a counterpoint to Vouga: where Vouga argues for permanent diversity on the basis of the perspectival differences between the authors of the NT, Marshall maintains that "a descriptive account of the

---

the message of Jesus, Paul, and John: "What Kümmel established for three witnesses can be extended to cover all of them" (Marshall, *New Testament Theology*, 715).

theological thinking of the early Christians" yields an essentially harmonious NT theology (45).

The Shape and Movement of the Discipline

It is impossible to evaluate individually each of the NT theologies treated above. It is also exceedingly difficult to draw together many thousands of pages from conceptually diverse works without reduction and oversimplification. Nevertheless, we may identify several areas of the foregoing discussion that help to sketch the development and present contour of the discipline.

1. The Old Testament

In marked contrast to a strong tendency in past scholarship (e.g., Harnack, Bultmann, Baumgärtel, Hirsch), recent work in NT theology has reached the point of consensus on the importance of the OT for NT theology: readings of the NT that downplay or even erase the fundamental historical and theological significance of the Old for the New contradict the NT itself to such a degree that they cease to be NT theology. Whether "soft" or "hard," Marcionite hermeneutics radically distort the constructive role of the OT in the NT. With varying interpretive strategies, the authors of the NT documents all seek to understand and explicate the meaning of the Christ-event in intimate connection with the OT. Moreover, contra Hübner, there is widespread agreement that the import of the OT extends far beyond citations and allusions; the entirety of the OT must be taken into account.

2. The Historical Jesus

There has also been a significant shift in NT theological research with respect to Jesus. Despite his otherwise enthusiastic acceptance of the Bultmannian program, even Vouga maintains that Jesus should occupy a place within NT theology. Gnilka demurs, but Hahn, Wilckens, Stuhlmacher, and Marshall all attempt to incorporate the question of continuity between the NT and the figure whose life and teaching generated its documents. By attempting to show that the unity of the NT has its basic origin in Jesus, these scholars argue for a unity that operates at a deeper level than an interpretation of the NT that would avoid asking the historical question. In their view, NT theology encompasses rather than brackets out the pre-NT period: there is in fact a *sachliche* continuity between Jesus's proclamation/life and its reception.

However, the question remains as to the definition of the "historical Jesus" and the consequences such definition has for the overall argument. As Martin Kähler might caution, there is a considerable difference between speaking of the "historical Jesus" in the sense of a critically reconstructed figure behind the Gospels, on the one hand, and in the sense of the figure presented by the Gospels, on the other. Where Stuhlmacher, for example, speaks of the "earthly Jesus," one would do well to interpret this expression primarily in the latter sense, for a "reconstructed Jesus" plays little to no part in his *Biblische Theologie des Neuen Testaments.* And where Gnilka objects to the place of the "historical Jesus" in an NT theology, one should interpret the expression in the former sense.

The critical point pertains to the theses of the scholars who locate the "historical Jesus" within their NT theologies and thereby argue for continuity between Jesus and the theology of the NT. If by historical or earthly Jesus one means in practice the figure presented by the gospel narratives, then it is of little wonder—and also of little historical, argumentative value—that this figure is basically continuous with the theology of the NT. Leander Keck's criticism of Alan Richardson is far overdone for the authors considered here, but it is not without a certain bite: "The Jesus who teaches everything Richardson attributes to him has been pasted together with New Testament texts; he is not a flesh and blood, first century, north Palestinian, Aramaic-speaking Jew. [Richardson's] Jesus is a Christian theologian, probably an Anglican."[67] That is to say, regardless of the perpetual methodological problems in so doing, if the attempt is to trace a historical continuity between the life of the Jesus who gave rise to the Gospels and the theology of the NT itself, then one will have to work with a historically reconstructed Jesus—the "historian's Jesus."[68] In my judgment, current research has not demonstrated that this particular task belongs properly to the discipline of NT theology. Bultmann's methodological manifesto is thus still on the table.

3. *NT Theology and* Theologiegeschichte

Stuhlmacher's response to the repristination of Wrede's vision by Heikki Räisänen captures well the larger contour of NT theology in the present: Räisänen's project should not bear the name *New Testament* theology, for the NT "has come to us as the *church's book*."[69] To commit oneself to a collection

67. Leander Keck, "Problems of a New Testament Theology," *Novum Testamentum* 7 (1964): 237.

68. Joachim Jeremias, *New Testament Theology: The Proclamation of Jesus* (New York: Charles Scribner's Sons, 1971).

69. "ist . . . als Buch der Kirche auf uns gekommen." Stuhlmacher, *Biblische Theologie des Neuen Testaments*, 1:34.

of (at least!) twenty-seven different documents is therefore to position oneself within a particular, ecclesial construal of these texts. Restricting one's analysis, that is, to the interpretation of the NT is *already* to adopt a theological posture, as Wrede himself understood well.[70] Conversely, to reject the demarcation of the NT as an interpretive field is to engage in a different task than that of NT theology. Pure (*rein*) or neutral NT theology is a fiction, as is the neutrality of an interpretation that rejects the NT (so Wilckens in particular).

Yet the basic Gablerian conviction that NT theology must deal with the NT historically continues fundamentally to shape the work of NT theologians. Thus the structure of both Hahn's and Wilckens's projects impressively makes the point that diachronic *Theologiegeschichte* (history of theology) is integral to NT theology. And Stuhlmacher's *traditionsgeschichtliche* method is shaped by a historical reconstruction of biblical tradition history. Still, the type of *Theologiegeschichte* advocated by these scholars is different in kind from that of the history-of-religions school or even Klaus Berger, for example. For the former, the NT itself was an obstacle to be overcome on the way to broader historical insight; for the latter, it is a quarry to be mined for a reconstruction of early Christian theology in toto (*Theologiegeschichte*, v: "die Geschichte der frühchristlicher Theologie im Ganzen . . ."). By contrast, the type of *Theologiegeschichte* that is associated with the NT theologies covered in this review is methodologically interwoven into the NT theological task itself. *Theologiegeschichte* in this sense is oriented teleologically toward the understanding of the *New Testament*, as a distinct textual entity. It is, understood methodologically, *Neutestamentliche Theologiegeschichte.* In point of fact, the particular emphasis within this kind of reconstructive task is the elucidation of the diversity of the NT. Such diversity, however, is not emphasized for its own sake, but rather for the purpose of working toward unity. Precisely in this way the larger integrative possibilities for NT theology proffered by Hahn, Wilckens, and Stuhlmacher move beyond Bultmann's methodological hybrid (where Wredian *Religionsgeschichte* and Heideggerian *Sachkritik* hardly converse).

4. *The Unity of the NT*

There is complete consensus in terms of the scholarly necessity to respect the diversity and individuality of the NT compositions. It would also not be an overstatement, however, to say that there is an emerging consensus that for a work to count as an actual NT theology it must address the problem of the

70. William Wrede, "The Task and Methods of 'New Testament Theology,'" in *The Nature of New Testament Theology*, ed. Robert Morgan (Naperville, IL: Allenson, 1973), 71.

NT's unity. Just how much unity is needed to retain the NT as one book, however, is unresolved. On one side, there is Vouga, who constructs his entire NT theology around the idea of theological or interpretive conflict *within* the NT. Yet Vouga's attempt is to present a way of taking the NT together as a whole. The form, to be sure, is a highly contentious debate, but the intent is to make it a *New Testament* debate. On the other side, there is Marshall, who does not shy away from difference within the NT, but clearly thinks that such difference does not amount to actual contradiction. Indeed, it is unclear in Marshall's NT theology whether or not there exists even serious tension within the NT. In the middle of Vouga and Marshall stands Hahn, inter alios, whose entire second volume argues forcefully for the unity of the NT. As we have seen, however, Hahn's is the kind of unity that allows contradictions to remain (e.g., in the realm of eschatology).

Such thorough differences in the accounts of the NT's unity should give one pause and encourage a more delicate probing of the intersection between the concept of unity, the view of the NT's subject matter, and the presuppositions about the nature of the biblical text itself. Such an investigation is impossible here. Suffice it to note that if one ultimately sees God as the subject matter of the NT and has a rather "high" view of the Bible, it will be difficult to admit to basic theological contradictions within the biblical texts (e.g., Marshall). If, however, one sees humanity in its self-understanding as the primary subject matter of the NT and views the biblical texts as various expressions of this attempt at religious self-understanding, then one can easily embrace significant contradictions (e.g., Vouga). For scholars such as Hahn or Stuhlmacher, however, the interconnection is not as easy to discern, due primarily to what presents itself as a suppleness in thought. At least on a prima facie account, it appears that the entire process of writing an NT theology that argues for unity as Hahn or Stuhlmacher understand it is intrinsically dialectical in that it involves a subtle movement between guiding principles of thought and their confirmation or disconfirmation by the NT itself.

At any rate, the *status quaestionis* in the present makes clear that, against detractors from various quarters, it is possible to make a robust case for the unity of the NT, both historically and theologically. At the same time, the divergent ways in which the case has been made—not to mention the varying outcomes—suggest that the unity of the NT cannot be read off the surface of the texts, as if any scholar who happened to ask the question would receive a clear affirmative answer. Thus does the entire issue need more reflection with respect to theological/philosophical questions (What exactly constitutes the unity?), epistemological questions (How does one know this?), and, for lack of a better term, quantitative/qualitative questions (What is the bar under which the NT cannot pass without forfeiting its unity?).

5. *Neglected Factors*

Though undoubtedly more could be brought forward, I will close with two issues that should provoke further thought about the discipline of NT theology, particularly as they pertain to its future. First, in relation to the problem of unity and diversity, there is a notable absence of reflection on narrative as a possible way to consider the problem. Stuhlmacher's "*regula fidei*" construal of the center or unity of the NT is perhaps the closest contemporary analogy in that it is stated in a narrative form, and there is probably an overarching narrative inherent in Hahn's systematic structure in volume 2.[71] Yet neither Stuhlmacher nor Hahn actually works on a sophisticated level with the narratives the NT texts "tell or presuppose."[72] Rather, discerning narrative at the heart of their construals of unity has far more to do with the irreducibly narrative shape of the grammar used to speak about unity. It is precisely this aspect of the problem that remains submerged in the "consciousness" of the discipline and needs to be brought to the surface. This absence of narrative is particularly regrettable since narrative has the inherent structural ability to exhibit considerable diversity and discontinuity within the unity and continuity of one story. In a word, narrative is flexible. The same kerygmatic story can be interpreted and reinterpreted in numerous ways without the abrogation of that which makes the story intelligibly the same story. As a medium for NT theology, narrative seems well suited to the task.

Second, there remains the remarkable lack of non-European contributions to NT theology. Prior to Frank Thielman's *Theology of the New Testament: A Canonical and Synthetic Approach*,[73] which reached me too late to be considered for this review (it is a cousin to Marshall's effort), the only substantive North American NT theology was written over thirty years ago.[74] More specifically, as Hahn repeatedly notes, NT theology has been primarily a

71. Cf. Matera, "New Testament Theology," 15.

72. Matera, "New Testament Theology," 16; Matera's suggestions here have much promise.

73. Frank Thielman, *Theology of the New Testament: A Canonical and Synthetic Approach* (Grand Rapids: Zondervan, 2005).

74. George Eldon Ladd, *A Theology of the New Testament*, ed. D. Hagner, rev. ed. (Grand Rapids: Eerdmans, 1993). The major exception here is by a non-NT specialist and spans both testaments: Brevard S. Childs, *Biblical Theology of the Old and New Testaments: Theological Reflection on the Christian Bible* (Minneapolis: Fortress, 1992).

German affair.[75] As it stands, a vast amount of significant work in NT scholarship is largely ignored. From the treatments of Pauline theology, for example, one would hardly know that there exist counterproposals to the traditional Lutheran debates over Paul's doctrine of justification (*Rechtfertigungslehre*). Though the names are occasionally mentioned, the signal contributions of E. P. Sanders, J. Louis Martyn, Richard Hays, and others have no substantive impact on the discussion. The problem is more than simply parochialism in German scholarship. It is indicative of a larger phrenic circumscription, in which the shape of human thinking is determined in important ways by deep-seated cultural and intellectual patterns (e.g., the *Wirkungsgeschichte* of biblical interpretation in Europe), the criticism of which is difficult—if not impossible—from the inside. Indeed, if Hans Frei is correct,[76] it is telling that the lack of attention given to narrative and the fact that NT theology "ist in der deutschen evangelischen Exegese beheimatet" are far from coincidental.[77]

Though it has been said that "writing a theology of the Old or New Testament . . . is no longer the ultimate aspiration of most biblical scholars," this survey offers some European evidence to the contrary.[78] In fact, given the recent surge of important works in NT theology, we may even be justified in speaking of a revival of the discipline. Nonetheless, if this resurgence is to be of more than passing significance, it must also arouse the interest and response of new communities of thought. Inasmuch as particular construals of NT theology involve larger—even universalizing—claims, they call for critical testing and reformulation by those who occupy culturally and intellectually different spaces of historical and theological inquiry.

75. Hahn, *Theologie des Neuen Testaments*, 1:xiii, xvii, 11, which is also an attempt to justify his almost exclusive concentration on German exegesis.

76. Hans W. Frei, *The Eclipse of Biblical Narrative: A Study in Eighteenth and Nineteenth Century Hermeneutics* (New Haven: Yale University Press, 1974).

77. Hahn, *Theologie des Neuen Testaments*, 1:11. The quoted phrase means "is native to, or at home in, German Protestant exegesis."

78. Leander Keck, "The Premodern Bible in Postmodern World," *Interpretation* 50 (1996): 132.

The Doctrine of God Is a Hermeneutic

◆ THE *BIBLICAL THEOLOGY* OF BREVARD S. CHILDS

One of the advantages of writing an invited essay is the chance it affords to explore new ways of thinking without worrying too much about the "field" for which the piece should be written.[1] This is particularly welcome in the case of an essay about the thought of Brevard Childs, who did not really have a "field" in which he worked. It is true, of course, that he was an OT scholar. But it is no less true that he was a scholar of the NT, of the history of interpretation, of dogmatic theology, of theological ethics, and so on. This is not to say that he was equally learned in every one of these modes of inquiry. It is rather simply to make the point that the fecundity of Childs's thought is due as much to his integrated way of working and refusal to remain within a single field as it is to anything else.

As a way of honoring his commitment to the integration of theological thought, the following essay will attempt to sketch the theological underlay of the whole of his *Biblical Theology of the Old and New Testaments* (*BTONT*).[2]

1. The typical audience for the *Journal for the Study of the New Testament* differs, for example, from that of *Modern Theology.* Reflecting on the target audiences of various publication outlets illustrates how frequently these venues determine what we write (at least with respect to genre, scholarly apparatus, and so forth). Precisely because many of these outlets result in practice from disciplinary separation, we have good reason to be thankful for the many new ventures that are seeking to overcome a separation long repugnant to Childs: the division between biblical studies and dogmatic theology. We may think, for example, of the new *Journal for Theological Interpretation* and of the various groups at SBL that provide space for constructive efforts to bring the theological disciplines together (e.g., Christian Theology and the Bible; Theological Hermeneutics).

2. Brevard S. Childs, *Biblical Theology of the Old and New Testaments: Theological Re-*

"The Doctrine of God Is a Hermeneutic: The *Biblical Theology* of Brevard S. Childs" was originally published in *The Bible as Christian Scripture: The Work of Brevard S. Childs*, ed. Kent Richards and Christopher Seitz (Atlanta: Society of Biblical Literature, 2013), 155–70. It is reproduced with permission.

The hope in so doing is threefold: to help readers of this work to understand it better than they have; to correct some misapprehensions about Childs's hermeneutical proposals as a whole; and to illustrate how the doctrine of God is inextricably tied to a particular way of thinking about the interpretation of scripture.[3]

The Misapprehension

To many scholars the constructive proposals in Childs's *Biblical Theology* about how to read the Christian Bible remain a mystery. The reasons for this are probably many. For example, Childs may not have conceptualized his audience clearly enough, and hence may have overlooked the fact that a great many (all?) of his readers would not share his learning in all the areas in which he makes detailed argument.[4] Thus would the amount of "background" knowledge needed to track precisely the movement of his various arguments exceed what could be expected from lesser mortals. Or, to mention another bibliographical matter, Childs works considerably in both past and contemporary German research, and his arguments thus frequently reflect an academic context that is known to many North Americans only via mediation (or not at all). Or perhaps it is simply his admittedly clunky writing.

Such problems notwithstanding, I think there is a deeper reason that Childs's proposals have not found proper consideration, at least among biblical scholars:

flections on the Christian Bible (Minneapolis: Fortress, 1992). Hereafter, page references appear in the text.

3. On the one hand, the essay's primary aim is not to introduce Childs's thought to those who have never studied it. I will assume familiarity with Childs's publications and main lines of thought, and will therefore make direct citations of his work only where they are obviously needed or particularly illuminating for the point under discussion. On the other hand, insofar as the essay is a "sketch" that helps to explain some of the larger matters that are at stake in reading Childs's most comprehensive book, it will simultaneously facilitate a better understanding of his work for all who care to read it carefully.

4. Cf. Christopher R. Seitz, *Word without End: The Old Testament as Abiding Theological Witness* (Grand Rapids: Eerdmans, 1998), 108–9: "The question is: is there an alternative either to rationalism on the right or left or to an experientialism of the pious, but also modern consumerist, sort? Childs's *Biblical Theology* may prove to be a book in search of an audience, and for that reason it will be judged by the widest variety of readers as learned but unsatisfactory and by an even smaller audience as the most brilliant proposal for theological exegesis offered in recent memory, but one unlikely to gain the sort of foothold necessary to transform the church in its use of scripture."

we have failed to grasp the dogmatic theological moves that fund the entirety of his conceptions about how to read the Bible. If, however, we think carefully along with Childs about reading scripture, we will discover that his thinking presupposes and articulates a particular doctrine of God. Like his theological mentors John Calvin and Karl Barth, Childs knew that to think about the Bible was to think primarily about God.[5] In order to see how reflection on the doctrine of God illumines Childs's interpretive project, however, we must first say clearly what Childs's project is not, and then, briefly, what it is.

Childs's Project

Of all the things that could be said wrongly about Childs's work, the one that is probably the most common is that Childs is an advocate of a particular method called *canonical criticism*, a method that can be placed alongside form criticism, redaction criticism, literary criticism, and so on. After all the diachronic digging and textual comparison has been done, so a common reading of his work runs, we can then—as a kind of supplemental or final move—consider our exegetical results in light of the so-called final form or canon. Or, in another common version, we can simply leave off the initial historical and comparative work and begin straightaway with the final form. In both cases the assumption is that canonical criticism is one method among many others that we may choose to use. Let it be said emphatically: *this is not Childs's project.*[6]

For Childs, the entire project of canonical interpretation hinges in its intellectual suppositions, not so much on a literary phenomenon, the final form of a text, as it does on the divine referent of scripture. The reason we read all these different and disparate documents together as one book, that is, is not because there is something ipso facto literarily pristine or exegetically satisfying about

5. Of course, in that he begins the constructive sections of *BTONT* with the "identity of God," the structure of the book illustrates Childs's commitment to the priority of God. Cf., e.g., Childs, *BTONT*, 82, on the "primary" reality of God.

6. This fact could be realized from a simple glance at the table of contents. For example, the *Tetraevangelium* is treated in an order we find only in a twelfth-century manuscript in West Saxon (Mark, Matthew, Luke, and John). The logic that makes intelligible the order of this presentation is that which lies behind a particular view of the "synoptic problem" (Mark is earliest; Matthew and Luke use Mark, etc.). If nothing else, the treatment of the four Gospels should alert the sensitive reader to a more complex agenda than that of a simple focus on the "final form." For a list of the orders in which the Gospels occur, see Bruce M. Metzger, *The Canon of the New Testament: Its Origin, Development, and Significance* (Oxford: Clarendon, 1997), 296–97.

final forms—his two *Introductions* might even suggest otherwise—but because together all these various texts constitute Israel's and the church's witness to the one God.[7] Indeed, it is not only that the texts are the human witness to God but also that, in a frequent Childsean phrase, God is the reality that "*evokes* the witness" (379; emphasis added).

Because it is ultimately God who holds the documents of the canon together in one book—it is not merely a decision by Jewish and Christian communities—to reject the normative claim or hermeneutically distinctive boundary of the canon is actually to fragment the divine reality, and thus ultimately to sever our connection to God. It is also implicitly—whether we intend this or not—to offer a counterproposal about the way in which divine reality is rendered, and thus to offer a counterproposal about our connection to God, or lack of it. In Childs's way of thinking, therefore, reading canonically is not a general "solve-all-problems" exegetical program,[8] or a simple application of one type of literary criticism, or a new critical methodology. Rather, it is the necessary anthropological and ecclesial correlate to the God of Israel's self-revelation in Jesus Christ. Canonical interpretation, that is, is a positive response to the normative claim to render God inherent in the notion of Christian canon. Or, to move a little closer to Childs's own language, it is a response to the pressure exerted by God upon the interpreter of this particular book.

The Identity of God and the Unity of Scripture

Childs's insistence upon the necessary link between God and the Christian canon raises numerous important questions, but for this essay we shall deal with only two: (1) the identity of God, and (2) the relation of this identity to the two testaments of the Bible.

Identity of God

Childs speaks about the God of the Bible in numerous ways: "the subject matter," "substance," "reality," "*res*," and so forth. Yet, in contrast to the lin-

7. See, e.g., his remarks in Brevard S. Childs, *Introduction to the Old Testament as Scripture* (Philadelphia: Fortress, 1979), 76.

8. This seems to be another frequent misunderstanding, even among sophisticated OT interpreters. See, e.g., Walter Brueggemann, "Against the Stream: Brevard Childs's Biblical Theology," *ThTo* 50 (1993): 279–84; and of course James Barr, *The Concept of Biblical Theology: An Old Testament Perspective* (Minneapolis: Fortress, 1999). See Childs, *BTONT*, 670.

guistic habits of many modern biblical scholars, "God" is not spoken of in such general terms alone. Rather, Childs specifies at point after point that the God about whom the Bible speaks in its canonical shape is the God known in the Christian church as the triune God, Father, Son, and Holy Spirit. Thus, for example, Childs can speak of the Bible's "full divine reality in its Triunity," and can entitle the final section of his chapter on the identity of God "From Biblical Theology to Dogmatics: Trinitarian Theology" (380, 375).

Childs is careful not to confuse the triune reality of God with the biblical text itself or with the historical dynamics involved in the epistemic realization of the one God's triunity. He knows, for example, that "the Bible does not contain a fully developed doctrine of the Trinity," and that "historically, the doctrine of the Trinity developed from a christological center" (374–75; see esp. 364–66). But he is equally clear that God cannot be spoken of in general precisely because the Bible pressures its readers to answer the question of God's identity in triune terms. To speak of the God of the Christian canon is necessarily to employ Trinitarian grammar.

In speaking clearly of God as triune, Childs recognizes what many theologians have long said—namely, that Trinitarian doctrine is what actually makes the Christian doctrine of God Christian (375). But he also recognizes what many theologians—and biblical scholars—in the modern world have not: the Trinitarian doctrine of God is also what makes the Christian doctrine of God *biblical*.

It is true, of course, that the renewed interest in Trinitarian doctrine in the twentieth century helped to fund various exegetical studies of the relation between the NT and the Trinity. As a whole, however, such studies were textually selective—focusing primarily on Paul or John—and built methodologically around "functional Christology" or predication (e.g., Where is Jesus actually called God?). In midcentury, Arthur Wainwright, Reginald Fuller, and Oscar Cullmann, among others, asked how Jesus and God overlapped in their function (e.g., as "Judge"), and in the 1990s Murray Harris and Raymond Brown, for example, offered careful exegetical discussion of the few cases in the NT where *theos* is potentially predicated of Jesus. Such studies are far from unneeded; indeed, they can illuminate well particular features of the biblical portrait of God.[9] But considered as a whole, they display a rather limited range of questions and methods. Rarely did the exegetes interested in the NT's doctrine of God, that is, carry their studies further and pose the broader, more difficult

9. See my earlier argument in C. Kavin Rowe, "Luke and the Trinity: An Essay in Ecclesial Biblical Theology," *SJT* 56 (2003): 1–26.

question about how the Trinity might relate to the Bible as a whole.[10] Stated otherwise, if the achievement of the work of Wainwright, Harris, and others is to have put at least something of the exegetical shape of the NT's view of God back on table, their failure is in not having done this in a hermeneutically constructive manner, or in not having connected some of their findings with an overarching conception of the God about whom they were reading. In this way, the contrast with Brevard Childs could scarcely be more striking. Unlike these earlier studies, Childs's *BTONT* not only exhibits a careful attention to a Trinitarian conception of God but also demonstrates considerable reflection on what difference such a conception makes for biblical interpretation.

In what is one of the most revealing passages in the book—which is therefore worth citing almost in its entirety—Childs writes:

> It is constitutive of Biblical Theology that it takes seriously the historical forms of the biblical witnesses which are registered in the two testaments. Yet it was a fatal mistake of some forms of Biblical Theology when dealing with the identity of God to feel that it could reflect on the subject only in terms of its historical sequence. This appeal to the so-called "economic Trinity" would restrict the doctrine of God to the divine workings within a historical trajectory of past, present, and future: God, Christ, Spirit. . . . However, the attempt to describe God's identity merely in terms of his acts, apart from his being, is not a serious theological option for either Biblical or Dogmatic theology. The subject matter itself requires that proper theological understanding move from the biblical witness to the reality itself which called forth the witness. In terms of the aforementioned division of labor, those scholars trained in dogmatic theology are often better equipped to pursue in detail the nature of God's being, especially in the light of the modern challenges to the biblical witness from various forms of philosophy. Yet it is an equally important responsibility of Biblical Theology to assure that the reflection on the being of God remains integrally related to his redemptive action within human history for the sake of Israel, the church, and the world. (370)

Leaving aside questions of the proper "division of labor" (if for no other reason than that Childs himself does not really observe it), we can discern in this passage several theologically intertwined commitments that help to structure Childs's interpretive project as a whole.

10. An exception of sorts is Karl L. Schmidt, "Le problème du Christianisme primitive," *Revue d'histoire et de philosophie religieuses* 18 (1938): 126–73.

First, though he objects to a modalist historical schema (God, Christ, Spirit) as a legitimate way to talk about the "economic Trinity," Childs clearly affirms the correspondence between God's economy and "the biblical witness." Second, he affirms that this correspondence entails an obligation to take seriously the integral relation between God and "human history," or "historical sequence."[11] Third, he argues that attending to the biblical display of God's economy is not theologically sufficient in and of itself, as if we could restrict our speech about the identity of God solely to his "acts." We must instead seek to speak also of God's "being," and thus move "from the biblical witness to the reality itself which called forth the witness." Fourth, the necessity of such a move toward reflection on God's being is not simply for the sake of philosophical clarity about the challenges posed to scripture in modernity, but is, more importantly, a response to the call of the "subject matter"—which is to say nothing less than that the God who reveals himself in scripture requires reflection on who he is.

Taken together, these intertwined theological commitments reveal the attempt to work carefully with the dogmatic distinction between the economic and immanent Trinity.[12] Childs's larger point is that the identity of God is known on the basis of a biblical text that displays an undeniable historical sequence, even as this identity exceeds in "being" the witness that makes it known. Or to put it formulaically: we know from the witness of the Bible to God's acts in history that God himself exceeds ontologically the human history in which he acts redemptively; yet these two aspects of God, economic revelation and immanent reality, are not ultimately two different things, but are two ways we must think in order to speak with the requisite breadth and sophistication about the identity of the one God of the Bible.[13]

11. One could speak here about the doctrine of providence that accompanies the theological meaning of "historical sequence"—that is, in God's providence, he chose to create human time in such a way as to ensure that it had a linear dimension: he chose Israel before sending the messiah, became incarnate before the church worked out the doctrine of the immanent Trinity, etc. That modern thinkers have characteristically reduced time to its linear dimension and forgotten its fullness, as it were, is well explored by Matthew Levering's stimulating book *Participatory Biblical Exegesis: A Theology of Biblical Interpretation* (Notre Dame, IN: University of Notre Dame Press, 2008). Levering's point is not that time does not have a linear dimension but rather that this dimension is only one "horizontal" aspect of how we should think about time (creation). There is also the "vertical" dimension to time, in which we are always and constantly participating in God's life as creator and sustainer.

12. See the remark cited on p. 93 below from Childs, *BTONT*, 378.

13. This is also why Childs speaks of a "division of labor" between biblical and dogmatic theology rather than of two fundamentally different tasks: they are both concerned with the same subject matter. If the former focuses more on the economic Trinity and the latter on the immanent Trinity, they are nevertheless both reflecting on the one triune God.

Childs's condensed articulation of the necessity to think both about God's immanent reality and his economic expression raises critical questions for scriptural hermeneutics. In relation to Childs's work, such questions can be focused rather simply: How should we read scripture so that we do justice both to "God's being" and to the "historical sequence" in which his being was made known? And, more specifically, how should we speak of the triunity of God in relation to the Old and New Testaments?

The Triune God and the Two Testament Bible

Nowhere is Childs's programmatic commitment to the historical sequence of God's self-revelation more strikingly evident than in the structure of his *BTONT* as a whole. From the table of contents alone, we can learn that one must pass through the "discrete witness" of the OT to the "discrete witness" of the NT before arriving at the substantive matters treated in the section entitled "Theological Reflection on the Christian Bible."

By "discrete witness," Childs means in practice a historically contextualized reading of the various canonical texts, which is itself the theological attempt to hear the voice of Israel and of the church in their own time and space.[14] To attend to the time and space of the voice of Israel, to stay with the importance of historical sequence, is not to deny that its voice may sound the note of promise—which of course is a notion that is concretely intelligible on the basis of a fulfillment—but it is to reject a mode of reading that would "fuse promise with fulfillment" (379).

Childs's objection to such fusion, however, is not predicated on a blind endorsement of historical criticism, or a kind of "historical consciousness" that one sees in such figures as Ernst Troeltsch or William Wrede, for example, but upon a deeper theological claim that the vertical dimension of God's self-revelation is to be taken seriously. "There is no legitimate way," writes

14. Cf. among many other statements to the same effect: "It is incumbent on the interpreter, especially of the Old Testament, not to confuse the biblical witness with the reality itself. In order to hear the voice of each biblical witness in its own right, it is absolutely necessary to interpret each passage within its historical, literary, and canonical context" (Childs, *BTONT*, 379). Whether this interpretive moment is to be identified with historical criticism depends more on the conceptual commitments one associates with the term than it does on a common commitment to historical depth. That is, if one of the intellectual principles of historical criticism is that theological concerns should be excised from the interpretive endeavor, then obviously Childs does not favor historical criticism. If, however, such anti-theological prejudice is not taken as constitutive for rigorous historical work on the Bible, then obviously Childs would be more sympathetic. And so forth.

Childs, "of removing the Old Testament's witness from its historical confrontation with the people of Israel" (379). The OT testifies to the real revelation of God to Israel in time and space precisely in its function as the historical and literary reception of that revelation. To lose the voice of Israel, therefore, is not so much to violate a supposed set of the "laws of history" or the "philosophical principles" that underwrite historical-critical investigation as it is to lose the historical and literary contour of the vertical dimension of God's self-revelation in the concrete life of the Jews. The particular shape of biblical history is itself the intersection between God's self-revelation and its reception. For Childs, the economic Trinity thus functions not as a dogmatic construct with little interpretive weight—as if God's economy somehow hovered above the historically deep texture of the Bible—but as a way to speak about the God who is made known through the biblical text in just the way we have it.

Yet in consonance with his insistence upon the requirement to reflect on God's being, Childs also affirms that the interpreter is to read scripture in light of "the full-blown reality of God" (380). For all its truth, the interpretive direction entailed by an emphasis on the economic Trinity "remains one-sided and prone to error without attention to the 'immanent Trinity,' that is, to the nature of God's being" (378). Although it is true, for example, that the servant in Isaiah 53 "addresses the suffering community of Israel within the context of the old covenant" and proclaims "the message of salvation through the vicarious suffering of a divinely appointed servant," it would be theologically insufficient not to relate this figure to the divine reality toward which the biblical text aims as a whole. Thus, knowing "the will of God in Jesus Christ [opens] up a profoundly new vista on this prophetic testimony to God. . . . For those who confess the Lordship of Jesus Christ there is an immediate morphological fit" (382).

Childs's overall attempt to deal constructively with the economic and immanent distinction in Trinitarian theology thus correlates with a dual emphasis that marks the entirety of *BTONT*: first, upon the discrete voice of each Testament (thus preserving the integrity of their historical sequence), and, second, upon their fundamental theological unity (thus preserving the integrity of their unified subject matter). To see how this dual emphasis leads directly to more specific hermeneutical proposals, we turn to Childs's language of interpretive "levels."

Levels of Interpretation

When Childs asks, "If [after a careful reading of the biblical text] we now understand the triunity of God, must not the grasp of this reality affect how we now interpret both testaments?" readers new to his work would likely—and reasonably—expect a direct answer: yes (379). But of course, as seasoned readers of his work would know, direct answers seldom follow Childs's rhetorical questions. In this case, his "answer" is a complex discussion about the various hermeneutical levels required to interpret scripture well in light of the two more basic emphases mentioned in the previous section.

Childs is "naturally aware of the serious problems which arose when the church opted for a fourfold hermeneutic." But ecclesial misuse of the fourfold method no more obviates the need for a "multiple-level reading of scripture" than the misuse of a hammer makes it the wrong tool for driving nails. Childs does not, however, simply adopt the four different modes of reading and redescribe their respective foci in modern terms, but instead develops an interpretive grammar built around three different "levels" or "avenues" (esp. 379–80).

The first level is that at which the interpreter hears "the voice of each biblical witness in its own right." At this level, "to read back into the [OT] story the person of Jesus Christ, or to interpret the various theophanies as the manifestation of the second person of the Trinity, is to distort the witness and to drown out the Old Testament's own voice" (379). There is a "historical voice" to each Testament to which we must listen if we are "to hear precisely the form of the witness as it entered into its concrete historical form" (381–82).

The second level is "another avenue into the Bible," in which the "literal/historical" reading of the first level is not contradicted but extended. At this level, the interpreter seeks to relate the two testaments to one another not only in terms of structural similarities and differences but also in terms of their common "content." "Comparison" is the central mode of analysis—indeed, in a way that is materially analogous to typological reading. In relation to the identity of God, for example, at this second level the interpreter asks, "What features do the two testaments hold in common respecting the mode, intention, and goal of God's self-manifestation?" (380).

Whereas the first two levels are most appropriately understood as a movement from witness to reality—that is, from text to God—the third level of scriptural interpretation involves the reverse movement from reality to witness: "Is the concern with the full divine reality in its Triunity only the subject matter of Biblical Theology? Does it have no place within the exegesis of the biblical text? Is the hermeneutical movement of biblical interpretation only from witness to reality or can one also proceed from reality to witness?" (380). Once again, a simple answer is eschewed. In its place is a description of this third level of reading in terms that can only really be adequately understood as an encounter with God. That is to say, while Childs affirms the movement from reality to text, he does not describe this third level as a particular method—allegory, for example—but more as "a response to a living God who graciously lets himself be known" (382). Indeed, "much of the success" of this third level of reading "depends on how well God's presence has been understood" (382).

Precisely because an encounter with God cannot be limited to one piece of an interpreter's overall noetic apparatus, it would be a gross mistake to think of this third level of reading as a "final step"; exegesis, says Childs in a provocative statement, does not "proceed in stages within a fixed sequence" (381).[15] "True interpretation" is more comprehensive in scope and "[moves] within a circle which encompasses both the movement from text to reality as well as from reality to text" (381). Let us make no mistake: for all the warning against the dangers of allegory and "retrojection," in Childs's logic all true interpretation is in fact spiritual reading: "If the church confesses that the spirit of God opens up the text to a perception of its true reality, it also follows that the Spirit also works in applying the reality of God in its fullness to an understanding of the text. The two movements cannot be separated" (382). The "reality of God testified to in the Bible, and experienced through the confirmation of God's Spirit, functions on a deeper level to instruct the reader toward an understanding of God that leads from faith to faith" (382). In short, for Childs, multileveled interpretation is but a contemporary rendition of ancient hermeneutical wisdom: all Bible reading is faith seeking understanding (esp. 86).

A New Proposal: Childs's Theological Hermeneutic

Childs's language of interpretive levels has proved difficult to understand.[16] I know of no accounts of his hermeneutical proposals by any biblical scholars, however, that interpret them explicitly within the framework of the Trinitarian doctrine of God. My contention is that it is this framework, more so or even rather than a single method, that renders Childs's constructive moves intelligible. That is to say, in contrast to those who pigeonhole him as an advocate of "canonical criticism" or believe his project is to bring the artificially distinct categories "history" and "theology" together under one roof, my reading of

15. The statement is provocative because of his language of "first, second, third."

16. In a somewhat startling comment, even Childs himself gestures toward the inevitable difficulty that will surround our attempts to engage in or describe "true" interpretation: "The very fact that the Christian church has continued to be drawn back to allegory in a way that is not the case for Judaism could well be an indication of a genuine search for a level of exegesis which has not been satisfactorily met" (Childs, *BTONT*, 381).

Childs forgoes the attempt to find his particular method in favor of construing his overall hermeneutical habits as the outworking of a view of God. To illustrate concisely the explanatory advantage this way of reading Childs's work has over the effort to formulate his method, we can focus on the apparently contradictory statements that the interpreter both is and is not to read the OT in light of the full divine reality—that is, the triune God.

As we saw in the previous section, at the first hermeneutical level, that of the discrete witness or historical voice of the testaments, christological interpretation of the OT is inappropriate: the second person of the Trinity is not to be identified with the manifestation of God in the various OT theophanies. By the third level, however, the entire Bible is to be read in light of the full reality of the triune God. If we attempt to hold these two interpretive moves together in a single or stepwise methodology, we shall—at least on the face of it—have to judge these contrary claims to be blatant contradictions. Put simply: On the one hand, if the God of the entire Bible is the triune God, then the manifestations of God in the OT are of *this* God, and the attempt to bracket out the Trinity from OT interpretation would sever the biblical text from the reality of God himself. On the other hand, if the God manifested in the OT is not the triune God in his full reality, then the triune God is not the God of the *entire* Bible, and the unity of the testaments at the level of their subject matter would be undone. Either way, Childs would seem to endorse incompatible theological claims.

If, however, we reread his language of levels with an interpretive framework that is cognizant of the theological importance of the distinction between the economic and immanent Trinity, then his project appears in a different light. This is not to say that such a distinction solves all the difficulties we might encounter in Childs's proposals, but it is to point out that to think from the economic side of God's triunity is to think in such a way as to take seriously the historical contour of the biblical text in which the triunity of God is not fully apparent in the life of Israel during the time of the OT—and that to think from the immanent side of God's triunity is to think in such a way as to take seriously the eternality of God's triunity required to sustain the testaments' unity at the level of their subject matter. In short, to move too quickly or simplistically to one side or the other would be to dissolve the tension necessary to speak rightly about the concrete salvific expression of God's eternal reality. The movement from text to *res* charted in levels one and two, therefore, just is the movement from the economic to the immanent Trinity. Insofar as interpreters follow this movement, they reproduce in their own reading the epistemic path of the church from scripture to doctrine. And the movement from *res* to text spoken of in level three just is the movement from the immanent to the economic Trinity. Insofar as interpreters follow this movement, they reproduce in their own reading the ontologically grounded path of the church from doctrine to scripture.

If this way of interpreting Childs is accurate, the tension in his proposals turns out to mirror the tension between epistemology and ontology that accompanies the distinction between the economic and immanent Trinity—which is to say that the economic and immanent Trinity can be distinguished in thought and speech (hence Childs's reticence to adopt a blatant christological reading of the OT), but in reality can never be separated or apportioned to different departments of theological study (hence Childs's reticence to rule out a christological reading of the OT). This tension, therefore, is not a final one, as if God were consigned to appear ever as economic or immanent and not simply as himself; indeed, the unity of the economic/immanent tension is nothing less than the reality of God himself. So, too, for Childs the tension between the different levels of interpretation is not final, as if one had always to choose between reading at the first or third levels. And so, too, it is God himself, rather than a particular methodological construct, who provides the final unity of the different interpretive levels: "The true expositor of the Christian scriptures is the one who awaits in anticipation toward becoming the interpreted rather than the interpreter. The very divine reality which the interpreter serves to grasp, is the very One who grasps the interpreter. The Christian doctrine of the role of the Holy Spirit is not a hermeneutical principle, but that divine reality itself who makes understanding of God possible" (86–87).

Thus, rather than a contradiction or an ultimate failure to unify "historical criticism" with "theological interpretation," Childs's project displays the attempt to work hermeneutically on the basis of the inescapable complexity involved in describing the unity of the triune God. His claim for the theological importance of the "historical voice" may not, at the end of the day, fully satisfy those whose interpretive tendencies lean more heavily toward the immanent Trinity, just as his insistence that the OT must be read in the direction from *res* to witness may not satisfy those whose interpretive tendencies lean more heavily toward the economic Trinity. But perhaps that is just Childs's point with the imagery of the circle: to describe fully the identity of the God to whom the Bible points, we must be on the move, speaking now about the historical voice (economic) and now about the total *res* (immanent), all the while keeping in mind that these different modes of exegetical speech are in fact about the *same* reality, the One whose patient self-revelation and redemptive acts in concrete human history (economic) are always and ever the saving disclosure of the being of the triune God (immanent).

Conclusion

In this brief essay I have suggested that in order to understand the depth of the argumentative moves in Brevard Childs's *Biblical Theology of the Old and New Testaments*, we need to read the book as the hermeneutical outworking of a Trinitarian doctrine of God. Doing so allows us to see that many of the central interpretive proposals depend for their viability—and, indeed, their intellectual sense—on the constructive tension that exists when one inhabits the economic/immanent distinction as a way to work with the relation between the biblical text and the reality to which it points. Whether or not Childs has ultimately succeeded in this attempt, it is undeniable that his effort to think clearly about the intersection between the triune God and the biblical text by which we know this God creates the right space in which theological thinking about the interpretation of scripture should be done. Childs's work, that is, is not about hermeneutics in general but about the particular kind of hermeneutics required in light of the complex texture of God's self-revelation.[17] Biblical scholars who are not accustomed to reflecting on dogmatic distinctions for help with their exegesis may be somewhat puzzled at all the talk about the Trinity and the Bible. But then again, as Childs himself knew well, to read the Bible well is to read it in light of the God to whom it points.

17. An interesting corollary of the interconnection between the doctrine of God and biblical hermeneutics is that where our hermeneutics differ from Childs's, we may reasonably expect to find differences in how we conceive of the doctrine of God. Conversely, if we disagree with Childs about the way to frame the Trinitarian doctrine of God, we should reasonably expect to disagree with him about how to read the Bible. To say it bluntly, the idea that we could simply analyze Childs's hermeneutical proposals without simultaneously grappling with a Trinitarian notion of God is an error: but it is just this error that characterizes so much of the work on Childs's thought ("canonical criticism" and the like).

What Is a Theological Commentary?

◆ WITH RICHARD B. HAYS

Jaroslav Pelikan, the longtime Sterling Professor of History at Yale University, will be well known to readers of *Pro Ecclesia* for his many scholarly contributions, including his magisterial five-volume work *The Christian Tradition: A History of the Development of Doctrine*. The editors of the new Brazos Theological Commentary on the Bible could not have found a more distinguished and erudite author for the initial volume in this ambitious new series. Alas, this first Brazos commentary was to be Pelikan's last work, as he succumbed to lung cancer in May 2006. In this final work, Pelikan seeks to heed the advice of Adolf von Harnack, that past master of *Dogmengeschichte*, who declared that a historian of the early church "must always be ready . . . to take on the exposition of a book of the New Testament."[1]

Pelikan's commentary exhibits several commendable features. We shall identify two. First, in the face of standard exegetical practice, Pelikan employs the Nicene-Chalcedonian faith as an "a posteriori organizing principle for the exegetical task" (28). Pelikan's admission that this interpretive procedure is "highly anachronistic" actually serves to illustrate well the point that all analytical exegesis uses interpretive schemata to organize and present the material under discussion (27). The indubitable strength of Pelikan's judgment about the hermeneutical helpfulness of later Christian formulations is that it puts forcefully the point that no interpreter of the Bible can evade the question of theological commitments. To be made aware of one's organizing scheme is to be forced to justify it as that which best facilitates good exegesis. Pelikan's

1. Jaroslav Pelikan, *Acts*, BTCB (Grand Rapids: Brazos, 2005), 17 (Adolf von Harnack to Karl Holl). Hereafter, page references appear in the text.

"What Is a Theological Commentary?" (with Richard B. Hays) was originally published in *Pro Ecclesia* 16, no. 1 (2007): 26–32. doi:10.1177/106385120701600104.

bold assertion, then, demands of the reader at the outset rigorous theological reflection about the basic premise of the commentary (and the Brazos series as a whole): that later doctrine can provide—not only de iure but also de facto—"structure and cogency to scriptural interpretation."[2]

Second, because of Pelikan's enormous erudition, simply reading the book is an education in Christian history. For example, where one might find contemporary commentaries that ruminate upon the Mt. Sinai typology evident in Jesus's forty days of instruction (Acts 1:2–3), Pelikan provides a fascinating discussion of the early church's practice of locating the origin of much of its teaching and ritual in this period of instruction (38–41). The "narrative of Acts, indeed the history of the early church in the following centuries, can be read as the process of making explicit what was implicit in the 'gospel of forty days,' of giving ritual form and eventually written form to a tradition, attributed to none less than the risen Lord himself, that was oral in its origins and in its transmission" (40). To take another example, where we (post)moderns might too easily conceive of finely wrought systematic theologies as the height of theological reflection, Pelikan teaches us that it has been otherwise throughout much of the history of the church: in actuality, the *commentary* was long considered to be the "primary means of theological reflection" (25). Or, to cite just one more of many examples, Pelikan takes Luke's account of the Apostolic Council in Acts 15 as the occasion to offer the reader an outline of the history of the seven great ecumenical councils, ranging from AD 325 to 787, accompanied by a reflective excursus on the authority of church councils (175–77). This example demonstrates nicely the way that Pelikan draws the full range of his learning into the commentary. At the same time, unfortunately, it leaves the reader with the slightly unsettling impression that the author may be less interested in the interpretation of Acts than in using the text as a springboard for his own synthetic reflections on church history. As readers, we are grateful to have such fascinating reflections—final reflections, as it has turned out—from an octogenarian scholar who was the twentieth century's greatest authority on the history of doctrine. Yet we find ourselves wishing for an exposition that stays more closely in contact with Acts and with the first-century issues that Luke actually addresses. We shall return to this problem below.

Our chief point in the present context is that the book is a treasure-house of learned overviews of church history, combined with fascinating tidbits of information ancient and modern. One of our favorite tidbits is the disclosure that the twentieth-century Masai Creed glosses Acts 2:24 with this confession:

2. R. R. Reno, introduction to Pelikan, *Acts*, 16.

"He lay buried in the grave, but the hyenas did not touch him, and on the third day he rose from the grave" (55). (John Dominic Crossan, take note.) Or again, how can we do otherwise than admire a book that contains incomparably phrased sentences such as the following: "It is another of the many historical ironies of the Christian message that of all the famous ancient Romans—Julius Caesar or Cicero or Vergil—none has achieved even nearly the universal name recognition of an otherwise obscure provincial gauleiter named Pontius Pilate, who has the distinction—which he shares with, of all people, the Blessed Virgin Mary, and with no other human creature—of having his name recited every day all over the world in the Nicene Creed (as well as in the Apostles' Creed)" (266). With its numerous artfully crafted mini-essays on doctrinal history, the commentary is best savored if taken in small, nourishing bites.

Despite its several excellences, however, the volume also exhibits some weaknesses. First, we question Pelikan's decision to privilege what amounts to the Western text of Acts where the readings offered by this tradition "are not altogether trivial or theologically insignificant" (34). The Greek text of Acts exists in essentially two, sometimes very different, forms: a Western and a non-Western text, the former of which is nearly 10 percent longer than the latter. Modern critical editions of the NT, as well as most contemporary translations, are weighted heavily toward non-Western readings. Consequently, Pelikan's decision to favor the Western text represents a de facto rejection of the consensus findings of NT textual criticism.

Pelikan's procedure has some partial justification on reception-historical grounds. Western readings are reflected in Tertullian and Cyprian, for example. On the other hand, Clement of Alexandria, whose text for the Gospels is primarily Western, cites Acts primarily in its non-Western (Alexandrian) form, while Eusebius of Caesarea offers a mixture of Western and non-Western textual traditions. Athanasius, as we might expect, reflects Alexandrian readings, and Origen, whom Pelikan seems to link with the Western text,[3] actually reads Acts in its non-Western form. Thus, Pelikan's designation of the Western text as the *textus a patribus receptus* (TPR) is a misleading generalization. A more careful examination of the evidence undermines historically the logic of his hermeneutical choice to read the Western text.

Moreover, it should be noted that Pelikan's privileging frequently occurs at just the places where NT scholars would naturally be inclined toward suspi-

3. Here Pelikan (*Acts*, 33) cites out of context a paragraph from Eldon Jay Epp, "Western Text," in *Anchor Bible Dictionary*, ed. David Noel Freedman (New York: Doubleday, 1992), 6:910. At this point, Epp is speaking of the entire NT rather than of Acts alone.

cion—readings that are theologically significant—thus casting aside a hard-won canon of text criticism (i.e., later scribes regularly amplify their texts theologically) and assimilating Luke's distinctive witness into a later tendency of one stream of tradition. At other times, however, Pelikan seems to admit a reading, even if against the Western text, simply because it raises significant theological questions (see, e.g., the discussion of Acts 15:29, 16:4a, and 16:4b). The point here is not so much that Pelikan errs in text-critical matters. It is rather that, on the one hand, the "TPR" text that he interprets is less the text of Acts than it is a later interpretation of the text of Acts, and, on the other, that the commentary lacks a consistent, critically grounded sense of exactly what text needs to be interpreted. That is, at certain points at least, Pelikan is selectively reading (part of) the tradition's reading of Acts. Whether such interpretations are theological commentary on Acts itself or on the history of the interpretation of Acts then becomes an important question. This question points, in turn, to a significant issue in theologically interdisciplinary exegesis.

Certainly, Pelikan's type of *Rezeptionsgeschichte* is itself theological exegesis. After all, one would scarcely want to claim that Western text readers such as Tertullian and Cyprian were *not* engaged in an analogous practice. Still, today the difference does seem to remain between a theological exegesis that begins with a (critically established) text of Acts and one that begins with a text of Acts already in midflight, as it were, in the history of reception. If it is part of the Brazos project to blur such a distinction between text and reception—and, philosophically/theologically speaking, this may well be justifiable (the *text* we receive is always *received*)—then it cannot be done well without careful attention to the "technical" matters of biblical scholarship.

Second, Pelikan's commentary as a whole places surprisingly little emphasis on the historical setting of the Acts of the Apostles in relation to first-century Judaism and Jewish traditions. By focusing chiefly on a reading of Acts through the lens of the church's later dogmatic traditions, Pelikan overlooks the numerous crucial theological issues that emerge when we see Luke as a theological interpreter seeking a hermeneutical transformation of Jewish tradition in light of the story of Jesus. For example, the commentary has relatively little to say about the revisionary interpretations of Israel's scripture that play such a prominent role in the apostolic speeches throughout the first half of the book. What does it signify that in Acts 15:16–18 the decisive scripture quotation in James's speech to the council is based on the LXX, which here differs dramatically from the Hebrew text of Amos 9:11–12? This issue—which obviously has substantial historical and theological implications—is the sort of problem that barely surfaces in Pelikan's treatment.

Third, one might offer a similar regret about Pelikan's lack of sustained attention to the politics of Luke's story in its first-century Roman imperial context. How does the portrayal in Acts of Jesus's followers as a divinely ordained, Spirit-empowered community pose a challenge to the Roman Empire's claims of sovereignty and authority? Does the lordship of Jesus pose a threat to the rule of Caesar and other political authorities (see, e.g., Acts 4:23–31; 17:6–7)? The question has been intensely debated in NT scholarship, but it appears only on the periphery of Pelikan's treatment. Even where he addresses it briefly (e.g., 88–90, 266–68), his interest lies more in the later *Wirkungsgeschichte* of the text than in the book's own historical setting and Luke's own treatment of the problem. As a result we miss in Pelikan's commentary a distinct sense of Luke *as a theologian* or *as a theological interpreter of the tradition that he received*; hence, the possibility of learning from Luke how we, too, might engage the world with the gospel is forfeited.

The final weakness of the commentary is that it bears a distinctive resemblance to the *Scholia* tradition. Pelikan has decided to compose a series of discrete cameo essays on various *loci communes*, theological issues that have proven significant nodal points for the development of the dogmatic tradition. He has distributed these mini-essays, at the rate of precisely three per chapter (thus eighty-four in all), throughout the commentary where he finds some point of contact in the language of the text. (So, for example, he attaches an essay on the distinction between *fides qua creditur* and *fides quae creditur* to Acts 26:18, where he finds a reference to "those who are sanctified by faith in me" [271–73].) In principle, such a form of interpretation may well be legitimate (as of course it long was). In practice, however, the effect in Pelikan's volume is to produce a series of rather random notes upon the text. The notes are theological to be sure, but—as far as the shape of Acts itself is concerned—they are random all the same. Missing from Pelikan's work is a sense that the theological reflection is driven by the text upon which Pelikan commentates. To cite one particularly egregious example: because the name of Mary is mentioned in passing in 1:14, we find in the commentary on Acts 1 a mini-essay on "Mary the Theotokos" and the problem of Mary's perpetual virginity (a topic on which Luke says nothing whatever); by contrast, Pelikan fails to mention the important fact that Acts 1:8 provides a preview of the overall narrative program of Acts. In this instance—as in many others throughout the commentary—the theological concerns that give Acts its shape are occluded, not illuminated, by the history of interpretation that Pelikan so elegantly details. Though indubitably complex, the book of Acts is nevertheless a single coherent story, a narrative whole. One might expect a commentator to display this unity or coherence regardless of the form in which the comments are given. One does of course find numerous cross-references throughout the work, but it remains unclear how Pelikan's notes form a unified whole. As a consequence, the unity of the story in Acts is obscured by these scattered *Scholia* rather than illuminated.

The foregoing observations cause us to ask a fundamental question about the aims of a book such as this: *What is a theological commentary?* Since Pelikan's is the initial volume of a much-anticipated and needed series, it warrants a few closing remarks that could be more widely discussed and applied. While we affirm the importance of freedom in method—"No reading strategies are proscribed, no interpretive methods foresworn"[4]—we would nevertheless argue that a theological commentary should take account of the basic fact that the church canonized *texts*. This fact is itself theologically significant. Even given the indisputable and inseparable role of doctrine in the canonical process, the church did not simply draw up lists of crucial beliefs but actually canonized particular texts with particular shapes. The implication would seem to be that the particular *form* of the writings is constitutive of, rather than incidental to, the theological construal of the whole. Against numerous attempts at a harmony of the Gospels from Tatian to Augustine and beyond, the church as a whole insisted that it could do with no fewer (or more) than four gospels. For the church, despite the fact that the tensions between these different accounts were clearly felt, doctrine and textual particularity were not ultimately opposed.[5] Rather, faith and text exhibited an interconnection that led both to precise doctrinal formulation and to the canonization of particular documents. The theological insight embedded in this canonical judgment is that the gospel is rendered through, not in spite of, textual particularity. To invoke an old ecclesial distinction: canonically viewed, textual particularity belongs to the *esse* of the gospel, not the *bene esse*.

With respect to the Brazos series, there is of course a sense in which this particularity is acknowledged: the commentaries are commentaries on discrete biblical books (Acts, Matthew, and so on). In the case of Pelikan's volume, there is a deeper sense, however, in which the particular form of Acts imparts

4. Reno, introduction, 16.

5. See, e.g., Oscar Cullmann, "The Plurality of the Gospels as a Theological Problem in Antiquity," in *The Early Church: Studies in Early Christian History and Theology* (Philadelphia: Westminster, 1956), 39–54; and Nils A. Dahl, "The Particularity of the Pauline Epistles as a Problem in the Ancient Church," in *Neotestamentica et Patristica: Eine Freundesgabe, Herrn Professor Dr. Oscar Cullmann, zu seinem 60. Geburtstag überreicht*, Novum Testamentum Supplement 6 (Leiden: Brill, 1962), 261–71.

scant theological substance to Pelikan's interpretation. Those committed to the Nicene-Chalcedonian faith will want to affirm, with Pelikan, the fruitfulness of that faith for the interpretation of scripture. Yet a better way actually to display how such an "a posteriori organizing principle" elucidates the particular texts of scripture would be to follow more closely the moves of the text itself. In this way, the theological interpreter would reflect in doctrinal perspective but through the lens of a particular text: the larger doctrinal pattern would constitute the wider horizon within which biblical interpretation takes place, but the precise texture of the theological commentary would be that of the biblical book in focus. To take the present book in question, if it is nothing else, a *theological commentary* on Acts ought at least to be a theological commentary on *Acts*.

Finally, we may ask whether a truly theological commentary may remain content with discourse in a secondary, descriptive mode. In this book, Pelikan writes chiefly as a historian, not a theologian. His learned disquisitions on the *loci communes* that he has identified generally take the form of summaries of the history of interpretation on particular questions, but rarely does Pelikan venture to put forward his own judgments or to speak the primary language of Christian proclamation. For example, in a section on "the ministry of women" (204–6), Pelikan records Luke's special emphasis on "celebrating the ministry of women and of hearing and recording also treble voices." He sets in opposition to this the observation that the twelve chosen by Jesus were all male and that when the time came to replace Judas, only male candidates for the office were considered (Acts 1:15–24). In view of this evidence, he concludes that responsible interpretation of the ministry of women must "find a way to encompass and to come to terms with both—not one but both—of these theological realities in the book of Acts" (206). And there the chapter ends! A similar ambiguity is left hanging in the air at the end of Pelikan's treatment of resurrection of the body (248–50). In both cases Pelikan has framed the background and led the reader to the brink of theological reflection, but there he stops. Surely a theological commentary owes its readers something more than that. *How* are we to come to terms with the realities Pelikan has described? He gives us no indication.

Perhaps it is ungenerous of us to expect a distinguished historian at the end of his career to cast off the historian's hat and write theology. Perhaps we should be content with receiving the edifying historical instruction he has in fact offered us. But the issue here, we reiterate, is what should be expected from a "*theological* commentary." Theologians have often complained that commentaries written by biblical scholars have been mere repositories of historical information that fail to illuminate the theological message of the text. Pelikan's commentary shows that it may be only a marginal improvement to produce a descriptive compendium of the history of interpretation if the commentary stays safely under the cover of reporting what others have said. Seen critically, the church's great theological commentators—Chrysostom, Augustine, Luther, Calvin, Barth—did not write histories of interpretation. Instead they employed the history of scriptural interpretation in the context of a primary engagement with the biblical texts; their chief aim was not to collect significant statements from the past but to hear the word of God in the text and to articulate it freshly for their own time. That is precisely what this first volume in the Brazos series signally fails to do. In that sense, Pelikan's learned and helpful work remains propaedeutic to the proper task of theological commentary.

For Future Generations

◆ WORSHIPING JESUS AND THE INTEGRATION OF THE THEOLOGICAL DISCIPLINES

To anyone acquainted with the history and development of the theological disciplines, it should be evident that, outside of certain religious studies departments, the long-standing and thick wall of separation between biblical exegesis and constructive theological reflection has begun to crumble.[1] As Brian Daley has recently observed, there is "a growing sense among biblical scholars and theologians—especially those under forty—that the dominant post-Enlightenment approach to identifying the meaning of scriptural texts has begun to lose some of its energy, that it has less that is new and substantial to say than once it did to those who want to spend their time reading the Christian Bible: the members, by and large, of the Christian churches."[2]

Indeed, if one measures simply by the number of new publication ventures, the interest in interweaving reflective theology and biblical studies is not only growing but growing rapidly.[3] Whether we attribute this growth to a

1. For a survey of the original unity and subsequent separation of biblical studies and systematic theology (as well as the *status quaestionis* today), see C. Kavin Rowe and Richard B. Hays, "Biblical Studies," in part 1 of this volume.

2. Brian Daley, "Is Patristic Exegesis Still Usable?," in *The Art of Reading Scripture*, ed. Ellen F. Davis and Richard B. Hays (Grand Rapids: Eerdmans, 2003), 69.

3. We may think immediately, for instance, of the *Dictionary for Theological Interpretation*, the Two Horizons Commentary series, the Brazos Theological Commentary on the

"For Future Generations: Worshiping Jesus and the Integration of the Theological Disciplines" was originally published in *Pro Ecclesia* 17, no. 2 (2008): 186–209. doi:10.1177/106385120801700204. I would like especially to thank my colleagues in theology and ethics who read an earlier draft of this essay: Stanley Hauerwas, Reinhard Hütter, and Geoffrey Wainwright. My seminar on the Bible and Christian doctrine (Fall 2006, Duke University Divinity School) also read and discussed a version of the essay; thanks are due to them as well.

desire for deeply rooted traditions in the face of the intellectual and spiritual homelessness of postmodern experience, or to a recognition that scripture cannot be read profitably merely on historicist terms (or to some combination thereof), the point for this essay remains the same: we stand now at an important moment in which there exists substantial potential for the integration of the theological disciplines.

And yet, without educational training ground for theological integration, movement toward this goal can come only from individuals whose "interests" happen to be conducive to the task. With the waning of such interests and the disappearance of these individuals, the potential for genuine theological integration will have gone unrealized, and the current growth will appear in hindsight as little more than a fad.

In an academic culture that rewards individual intellectual achievement and insight—the capitalist counterpart to the Cartesian cogito—it is all too easy to forget that "I can only think adequately by and for myself insofar as I do so in the company of others."[4] Our habits and abilities as particular thinkers, that is, are fundamentally dependent upon the kinds of communities in which we are trained. Indeed, as MacIntyre would remind us, there is no such thing as theology apart from human community. Theology, no less than morality, is "nowhere to be found except as embodied in the historical lives of particular social groups." The work of theological integration cannot, therefore, take place in abstraction from its "expression in institutionalized practice [and] discourse."[5] Unless and until institutional space is devoted to this task, our divinity schools and seminaries—Protestant and Catholic alike—will continue to produce at best the *need* for theological integration, not its practice. My larger concern in this article is thus to point toward the kind of interpretive communities we need to develop for training and sustaining theologically integrated interpreters.[6]

Bible, and Studies in Theological Interpretation. We might also mention the relevant sections at the annual meeting of the Society of Biblical Literature as indicative of the climate change (e.g., Christian Theology and the Bible, and Theological Hermeneutics of Christian Scripture), as well as the newly launched *Journal of Theological Interpretation*. There are of course ongoing objections. See, e.g., the polemic against "biblical theology" in Wayne A. Meeks, "Why Study the New Testament?," *NTS* 51 (2005): 155–70.

4. Alasdair MacIntyre, *Three Rival Versions of Moral Enquiry: Encyclopaedia, Genealogy, and Tradition* (Notre Dame, IN: University of Notre Dame Press, 1990), 64.

5. Alasdair MacIntyre, *After Virtue*, 2nd ed. (Notre Dame, IN: University of Notre Dame Press, 1984), 265.

6. Werner Jeanrond, "After Hermeneutics: The Relationship between Theology and Biblical Studies," in *The Open Text*, ed. Francis Watson (London: SCM, 1993), esp. 98–99, has

However, I intend to get at this issue indirectly rather than directly. Implicit in this essay, that is, is a vision for training students that runs counter to the disciplinary separation of much institutionalized practice and discourse; yet to make this vision overly explicit would probably amount to little more than (im)plausible suggestions or exhortations ("we should do this, we should do that . . ."). Thus, instead of arguing for a particular curricular design relevant to all institutions (an impossibility in my view),[7] I shall offer a model of theological integration that will compel us to recognize the inseparability of doctrinal reflection and biblical interpretation. Actually specifying the interconnection between exegesis and doctrine—the constructive task of the piece—will disclose a demand for disciplinary integration that issues from the unity of the theological subject matter itself. The immediately relevant corollary of this demand is simple but far-reaching: to refuse theological integration is to opt for incoherence at the deepest level possible, that of the subject matter. To the extent, therefore, that theological institutions continue to embody a rigid separation of the disciplines, they call into question and even undermine their identity and vocation. Theological integration, as it turns out, is not one choice among other legitimate ways of doing theology. It is an obligation.

To proceed with our task, we shall focus upon the possible connections between the Christology of Revelation and the *homoousios* doctrine. In this way, the argument will make a contribution to a growing support for a post-Enlightenment reconnection of the *homoousios* doctrine to scripture[8] on the

---

perceived the problem here. Yet it is very difficult to see how his proposed solution cuts deep enough, particularly because it seems to subsume the doctrinal question into that of a general hermeneutics: "I would strongly suggest that we try to organize university positions and seminars in biblical theology and require from the occupants and participants a thorough knowledge of interpretative theory, theological method and the pluralism of biblical theologies as well as a readiness to transcend their confessional theological heritage and constraints" (99). For an account of the beginnings of the institutionalized separation, see Edward Farley, *Theologia: The Fragmentation and Unity of Theological Education* (Philadelphia: Fortress, 1983).

7. It is prima facie impossible to give a universal prescription for educational reorganization. To be effective such movement will need to be worked out "on the ground," in close coordination with the strengths of particular faculties and institutions.

8. See David S. Yeago's well-known and astute analysis of *homoousios* in relation to Pauline theology, "The New Testament and Nicene Dogma: A Contribution to the Recovery of Theological Exegesis," *ProEccl* 3 (1994): 152–64. Yeago argues that "the Nicene *homoousion* is neither imposed *on* the New Testament texts, nor distantly deduced *from* the texts, but rather describes a pattern of judgements present *in* the texts, in the texture of scriptural discourse concerning Jesus and the God of Israel" (153).

way toward an illustration of the coherence and necessity of theological integration.[9] This essay, therefore, commences with the attempt to speak with precision about the relationship between text and doctrine ("Biblical Pressure" and "The Analogy of Language"), and, on the basis of the character of this relation, moves to consider critically the configuration of the theological disciplines ("The Dialectical Unity of the Disciplines"). We will begin with the notion of pressure.

Biblical Pressure

In an earlier publication I developed the notion of pressure—derived ultimately from the usage of Brevard Childs—as a way to explicate the movement between text and doctrine.[10] On the one hand, the concept of pressure was employed critically to argue against the prevailing tendency of modern exegesis to view doctrine as an alien, merely ideational, mode of reflection that was superimposed upon the biblical texts. In contrast to this position, I argued that the biblical text "pressures" its interpreters toward doctrinal formulation. To perceive exegetically the pressure of the text is simultaneously to begin the search for a range of terms—indeed, a language—that can receive interpretively this aspect of the biblical text. The need to speak in the language of doctrine is not due primarily to the metaphysical predilections of the Greek world but rather arises out of a dynamic that is internal to the biblical text itself.[11]

9. Obviously the way in which I tell the story, so to speak, bears the marks of my particular ecclesial tradition. Despite the (now) clear theological problems with their work, for example, I still think John Calvin and Adolf Schlatter to be exemplary scriptural interpreters from whom we can learn much worth knowing. What we should learn from them about reading scripture, however, should in our own time push us toward an ecumenically generous ecclesiology. Indeed, I would like to think this essay provides a Protestant counterpart to Pope John Paul II's formulation in *Ut Unum Sint*, 79, in which "Sacred Scripture" is "the highest authority in matters of faith" with "Sacred Tradition as indispensable to the interpretation of the Word of God." But addressing this subject directly is of necessity for another day.

10. C. Kavin Rowe, "Biblical Pressure and Trinitarian Hermeneutics," *ProEccl* 11, no. 3 (2002): 295–312, now in part 1 of this volume. In a similar manner, I employed the term "pressure" to speak about Lukan exegesis in "Luke and the Trinity: An Essay in Ecclesial Biblical Theology," *SJT* 56 (2003): 1–26. Geoffrey Wainwright, "Trinity," in *Dictionary for Theological Interpretation of the Bible*, ed. Kevin J. Vanhoozer (Grand Rapids: Baker Academic, 2005), 815–18, is correct to see my use of pressure at the heart of the former article's thesis. Childs himself has not sought to elucidate his notion of pressure, but his interpretive approach is consistently informed by attention to the pressure or "coercion" of the biblical text.

11. The point here is not to deny the importance of Greek metaphysics for the outworking

On the other hand, the concept of pressure was employed constructively to argue for the appropriateness of a mode of reading that would interpret the Bible in light of later dogmatic formulations. In the face of the (simplistic) charge of anachronism, recognizing that the biblical texts call for an interpretive language to make sense of their pressure allows us to affirm the hermeneutical worth of doctrine. There is a "fit" or correspondence between the pressure of the biblical text and later creedal statements such that the latter can serve as a guide to the interpretation of the former. The hermeneutical guidance of doctrine formulated in terms of the pressure of the text points to the horizon of thought within which one can perceive the larger connections that render intelligible the particular moves of the biblical text.

An example may serve to clarify both the critical and constructive aspects of biblical pressure. The book of Revelation has long puzzled its would-be interpreters. Fortunately, we may leave aside almost all of the bedeviling conundrums to focus upon one significant aspect of the book's theology—namely, that Jesus is worshiped with the God of Israel.

Revelation 4 and 5 exhibit a pattern of worship that is noteworthy for its inclusion of Jesus—the Lamb—in the heavenly worship of God. After a description of heavenly creatures, the surroundings of God's throne, and the cry of the four creatures ("Holy, holy, holy"), the visionary speaks of the worship (προσκυνέω) of the twenty-four elders who will fall down before (πεσοῦνται . . . ἐνώπιον) God and sing, "You are worthy (ἄξιος), our Lord and God, to receive (λαβεῖν) glory (τὴν δόξαν) and honor (τὴν τιμήν) and power (τὴν δύναμιν), because you created all things and by your will they existed and were created" (4:11). This dramatic portrayal of the elders' worship grounds their action in the identity of God as Creator. Because (ὅτι) he has created all things, God is worthy of worship. Worship is in this way coordinated with the distinction between Creator and creature.

It is therefore remarkable that the scene immediately following describes a vision in which the twenty-four elders fall down before (ἔπεσαν ἐνώπιον, 5:8) the *Lamb* and cry out, "Worthy (ἄξιος) is the slain-Lamb to receive (λαβεῖν) power (τὴν δύναμιν) and wealth and wisdom and strength and honor (τὴν τι-

of Christian doctrine but instead to make a critical move against earlier accounts of the relationship between doctrine and scripture that would see the former as Greek philosophical distortions of the latter (see, e.g., Adolf Harnack, *Das Wesen des Christentums* [Gütersloh: Kaiser/Gütersloher Verlaghaus, 1999]). Cf. Robert Louis Wilken, *The Spirit of Early Christian Thought: Seeking the Face of God* (New Haven: Yale University Press, 2003), xvi: "The notion that the development of early Christian thought represented a hellenization of Christianity has outlived its usefulness."

μήν) and glory (τὴν δόξαν) and blessing" (5:12). Moreover, the following praise is formulated in the universal terms of all creation: All creation—"every creature which is in heaven and on the earth and under the earth and in the sea and all therein"—extols simultaneously God and the Lamb: "to him who sits upon the throne and to the Lamb be blessing and honor (τὴν τιμήν) and glory (τὴν δόξαν) and might for ever and ever!" (5:13). With this last doxological phrase, Revelation locates the Lamb on God's side of the Creator/creature distinction. All creation worships the Lord God and the Lamb together. The crucified Jesus is thus placed within the ambit of what it means for God to be God.

The significant theological move in these two chapters is not an isolated phenomenon within Revelation.[12] Indeed, it is arguable that the entirety of the book is bracketed by the concern to include Jesus in the identity of God and, thus, to locate the coming of the former as the coming of the latter.[13] The first spoken words of Revelation belong to God and introduce John's divine commission to record his vision: "'I am the Alpha and the Omega,' says the Lord God, 'the one who is and who was and who is coming, the Almighty'" (1:8).[14] Then in 21:6–7 God says again, "I am the Alpha and the Omega, the beginning and the end." God's identity as the Alpha and Omega, the universal scope of his status as Creator, is here unambiguously proclaimed for the second time by God himself, much in the same way as in the resounding declarations of Second Isaiah: "I am before and after all things (Ἐγὼ πρῶτος καὶ ἐγὼ μετὰ ταῦτα). Besides me there is no god!" (Isa. 44:6). Yet the final use of this type of phrase in Revelation occurs in the mouth of Jesus and is spoken with reference to himself: "I am the Alpha and the Omega, the first and the last, the beginning and the end" (22:13; cf. 1:17).[15] The theological point evidenced by the juxta-

12. Nor is devotion to Jesus an isolated or merely "late" phenomenon in early Christianity as a whole. See, for instance, Larry W. Hurtado, *Lord Jesus Christ: Devotion to Jesus in Earliest Christianity* (Grand Rapids: Eerdmans, 2003).

13. As a whole, my reading of Revelation is in substantial agreement with that of Richard Bauckham. See esp. *The Theology of the Book of Revelation* (Cambridge: Cambridge University Press, 1993). To mention but one of several possible examples, we may draw attention to the intertextual significance of the titles κύριος κυρίων καὶ βασιλεὺς βασιλέων (17:4; 19:16). For a consideration of some of the relevant OT and early Jewish texts, see David E. Aune, *Revelation 17–22*, WBC 52C (Nashville: Thomas Nelson, 1998), 953–55. Aune also provides material for reflection upon the critical-political edge of the titles.

14. For a thorough historical analysis of the phrase ὁ ὢν καὶ ὁ ἦν καὶ ὁ ἐρχόμενος in Rev. 1:8, see Sean M. McDonough, *YHWH at Patmos: Rev. 1:4 in Its Hellenistic and Early Jewish Setting*, WUNT 2/107 (Tübingen: Mohr Siebeck, 1999).

15. Though it may at first appear that there is some ambiguity as to the speaker's identity, 22:16 makes this identity explicit (Ἐγὼ Ἰησοῦς). On the matter of the "abrupt" shift between

position of these texts could hardly be clearer: Jesus shares in the identity of God. To the question, Who is the Alpha and Omega, the beginning and the end?, Revelation presents a twofold answer: God/Jesus.

Given this picture of worship, it is also highly important to note the author's clear differentiation between Jesus and other heavenly beings, on the one hand, and God and other heavenly beings, on the other. Immediately prior to Jesus's reference to himself as the Alpha and Omega, the author writes: "When I heard and saw these things, I fell down to worship at the feet of the angel who showed them to me. And he said to me, 'Do not do that! I am your fellow servant and that of your brothers the prophets and those who keep the words of this book. Worship God'" (22:8–9).[16] Revelation 22:8–9 thus makes clear, for the second time (see 19:10), both the distinction between God and angels (explicitly) and the distinction between the Lamb and angels (implicitly).[17] The overall logic is rather simple, if startling: angels cannot be worshiped because they are not placed on God's side of the Creator/creature divide; Jesus, however, can be worshiped because he does stand on God's side of the Creator/creature divide.

The book of Revelation, then, operates within a traditionally Jewish theological framework—God is the Lord God of Israel, the Creator of all that is—but simultaneously tells of God's identity in such a way as to include a crucified human being within it. This construction of divine identity is, in turn, the ground of the worship that is offered to God and Jesus.

It is not that the author of Revelation consciously writes with a determined attempt to formulate doctrine or even that the text itself speaks in doctrinal terms. To the contrary, Revelation is the apocalyptic vision of a seer whose theological form is primarily liturgical confession. Yet the coordination of Jesus—a crucified human being—and the God of Israel *within* the divine identity requires the sensitive reader to reflect upon the theological presuppositions that fund this particular picture of God's identity. The dynamic of the text

---

22:11 and 22:12 (the speaker changes from the angel to Jesus), see the astute discussion in Aune, *Revelation 17–22*, 1217–18.

16. On the angelic refusal of worship as a motif within Jewish literature, see Richard Bauckham, *The Climax of Prophecy: Studies on the Book of Revelation* (Edinburgh: T&T Clark, 1993), 120–49. Within Revelation at least, this refusal is important to note for the explication of Revelation's Christology. Put simply, "angelology" is explicitly ruled out as the hermeneutical matrix for Revelation's Christology.

17. Cf. Bauckham's remark that the repetition of these scenes speaks for the "strategic effect" and theological importance of the differentiation (*The Theology of the Book of Revelation*, 59).

itself, that is, pressures its interpreters to work out the precise way in which such a seemingly contradictory confession can stand.

It is prima facie obvious, despite a considerable openness within Jewish monotheistic theology around the time of the NT, that the worship of a crucified human being alongside the God of Israel threatens the OT to the point of breaking with it altogether.[18] "I will not give my glory (τὴν δόξαν) to another!" declares the Lord (Isa. 42:8; 48:11; Ezek. 28:1–2; etc.).[19] Yet all creation does precisely this in the book of Revelation when the Lamb who was slain is given glory and worshiped together with God. The exact place at which the pressure occurs, then, is the question "how?"—how is it, theologically speaking, that the pattern of worship displayed in the text can say what it seems to say? To this question the text itself provides no answer, in the sense that the theological warrant needed to justify this practice of worship is not articulated (the liturgical confession is simply made).[20] To seek after an answer to this "how"

18. The discussion in Hurtado, *Lord Jesus Christ*, 32–53, is concise. For our purposes, Hurtado's criticisms of Crispin H. T. Fletcher-Louis, "The Worship of Divine Humanity as God's Image and the Worship of Jesus," in *The Jewish Roots of Christological Monotheism*, ed. Carey C. Newman, James R. Davila, and Gladys S. Lewis, Supplements to the Journal for the Study of Judaism 63 (Leiden: Brill, 1999), 112–28, are important to note. To those correctly adduced by Hurtado, one may also add that Fletcher-Louis's interpretations seem methodologically to presuppose a subtle Christianizing of the texts in question (along the lines of the doctrine of the incarnation). But this is to confuse epistemology with history. Not cited in Hurtado's book is Daniel Boyarin's important piece, "The Gospel of the *Memra*: Jewish Binitarianism and the Prologue to John," *Harvard Theological Review* 94, no. 3 (2001): 243–84.

19. This is not to deny the "openness" in Second Temple Jewish monotheism demonstrated in the work of scholars such as Bauckham, Hengel, Hurtado, Newman, Stuckenbruck, et al. The crucial epistemological point is actually quite simple: to affirm that Jewish monotheism is in fact open to a practice such as we see here in Revelation is *already* to have situated oneself—whether willingly or not—*within* the Christian construal of the practice. Conversely, to deny the openness of Jewish monotheism to such a practice is to situate oneself over against its specifically Christian justification. That is to say, finally, that this practice forces one away from the question of openness in general and toward the worship of Jesus in particular: Was Jewish theology open to the worship of *this* man? It is difficult to conceive of an answer to this question that does not simultaneously contain a judgment about Jesus's identity (and especially, we may say, his ignominious execution). On the entire issue of idolatry, see the stimulating book by Moshe Halbertal and Avishai Margalit, *Idolatry*, trans. Naomi Goldblum (Cambridge, MA: Harvard University Press, 1992), who note in relation to the present topic that "the heads of the great powers in the geopolitical arena of the Bible are described as people who have dared to cross the boundary between the human and the divine" (216–17, citing Deuteronomy, Isaiah, Jeremiah, Ezekiel, various Midrashim, etc.).

20. There is no evidence of a theological struggle within Revelation to predicate "di-

question is to formulate the theological intelligibility of the text. In just this way, to attend to the "how" question is to reflect doctrinally. Thus, rather than a superimposition upon the book of Revelation, theological inquiry is required by the direction internal to the text and the ecclesial practice it presupposes: there is an exegetical necessity to doctrinal reasoning.

However, reflecting doctrinally in light of this perceived necessity bears no resemblance to the old prooftexting methods of the Protestant scholastics. Instead of employing collections of texts—extracted from their primary context—to "prove" a specific dogmatic position, the move here involves a thorough conversation with doctrinal history toward an interpretive language that can best explicate the reality of the text.[21]

With respect to the present exegesis, it becomes immediately obvious that the text will not consent to an explanation of the worship of Jesus along docetic lines. It is true, of course, that within a docetic framework of thought "Jesus" could conceivably be worshiped as *theos*, but only because he is no longer *anthrōpos*. Yet above all else in Revelation, Jesus is the *Lamb*, an image and emphasis completely unintelligible apart from the inexorably human event of the cross.[22]

Further, there is no move to guard the Jewish God's uniqueness by qualifying the identity of Jesus as, for example, a *deuteros theos*, such as we see in Philo's effort to speak of the *logos*.[23] Nor is there any other exegetical data that

---

vinity" of the "Son of God" in such a way as to clarify the relationship to "his God and Father" (Rev. 1:6; cf. 2:28; 3:5; 3:21; 14:1) in order to justify their joint worship. Of course, the categories and images employed to characterize the Lamb in divine terms (the throne, etc.) show the author's awareness of how to paint the picture of worship in terms of the Lamb's identity, but the text obviously does not offer a reasoned theological justification for the use of the categories or images themselves.

21. Robert Louis Wilken, "Interpreting the New Testament," *ProEccl* 14 (2005): 15–25, writes eloquently of the different "contexts" in which scripture can be interpreted (location within a particular biblical book, the entire canon, the liturgy, etc.). Yet, while it may be true that "we are so accustomed to think of context as literary or historical that we forget that the words of the Bible have a life that transcends their original setting" (22), we should also not forget that embedding words in new contexts transforms their meaning (as interpretive context changes, so does word meaning): to know that such transformations are faithful reinterpretations—rather than simply wishful theological creations, for example—we need to know first their situatedness in their original literary context. Thus, there is a certain philosophical (word meaning) and theological (issue of faithfulness) primacy to the particularities of the biblical texts.

22. More than anything else, of course, the admission of a real crucifixion signals the end of docetism (in a docetic construal Jesus could possibly be worshiped but never crucified).

23. The most interesting passage is probably *Quis rerum divinarum heres sit* [*Her.*] 205–6:

would evidence an attempt to differentiate Jesus from God by means of their location on a continuum of being. Whatever complex use Philo attempted to make of such an ontological continuum, the text of Revelation makes none.[24]

"To his *logos* the Father of all has given the special prerogative to stand on the border and separate the creature from the Creator. . . . [The *logos*] glories in this prerogative and proudly describes it in these words, 'and I stood between the Lord and you' (Deut. 5:5), that is, neither uncreated by God nor created as you, but midway between the two extremes, a surety to both sides." Boyarin, "The Gospel of the *Memra*," 251, comments provocatively: "Philo oscillates on the point of the ambiguity between separate existence of the Logos, God's Son [citing *De agricultura* 51], and its total incorporation within the godhead. If Philo is not on the road to Damascus here, he is surely on a way that leads to Nicaea and the controversies over the second person of the Trinity." There is a sense in which this is profoundly correct (cf. Justin Martyr, as Boyarin also correctly notes). Yet it is also important to point out that the coherence of Philo's point here is extremely difficult to grant outside of the metaphysical framework of Middle Platonism. That is to say, for a metaphysic that would distinguish clearly between God and everything else, the possibilities for sufficient christological articulation present themselves quite differently. Thus, without the intention of drafting Philo further into Christian debate, it would be more accurate to say that in the manner of his reflection he may be on the road to the Trinitarian controversies, but in the substance of his articulation he is on his way not so much to Nicaea as to the metaphysic of the Arians. On the possible contradictions in Philo's statements in *Her.* 205–6, Darrell D. Hannah, *Michael and Christ: Michael Traditions and Angel Christology in Early Christianity*, WUNT 2/109 (Tübingen: Mohr Siebeck, 1999), 82–83, is concise.

24. The "great chain of being" is of course a remarkably flexible metaphysic and is particularly attractive to those who worry about the "suffering" of God because they can attempt to speak of the Son's real suffering (immanence) without impugning the impassibility of the Father (transcendence). The Middle or Neoplatonic metaphysic can also be used to characterize the Christian life, as Augustine does so effectively in the *Confessions*; indeed, this metaphysic is likely the larger template upon which he writes Christian autobiography (i.e., his procession away from and return to God). For the relation of Philo in particular to the NT's picture of devotion to Jesus, Larry W. Hurtado, "Does Philo Help Explain Early Christianity?," in *Philo und das Neue Testament: Wechselseitige Wahrnehmungen*, ed. Roland Deines and Karl-Wilhelm Niebuhr, WUNT 172 (Tübingen: Mohr Siebeck, 2004), is brief and lucid (esp. 90–92). Contra those who would caution strongly against the novelty of "christological monotheism" (e.g., Horbury), Hurtado's judgment regarding Philo's treatment of Moses is also pertinent to the evaluation of the status of other "intermediaries": Moses is not a "god" in the sense of a "divinized being" because "Moses receives no cultic worship in the devotional practice advocated and observed by Philo" (90); both the MT and the LXX seem to require the simile "like/as" a god to Pharaoh as the meaning of "I have given [נְתַתִּיךָ/δέδωκα, Exod. 7:1] you a god to Pharaoh." It is manifestly otherwise with the Revelation texts. One should, however, see the interesting, and predominately later, evidence adduced by Wayne A. Meeks, "Moses as God and King," in *Religions in Antiquity: Essays in Memory of Erwin Ramsdell Goodenough*, ed. Jacob Neusner (Leiden: Brill, 1968), 354–71. The oft-noted possible exception of the Son of Man figure in the Similitudes of Enoch (1 En. 37–71)

Its theological expression is instead more clearly determined by the OT, in which the line between God and creature remains distinct. Moreover, the way in which this line remains "ontologically" unblurred—indeed, the way in which one sees it clearly in the first place—is through Revelation's depiction of the practice of worship. Even angels, which in modern biblical studies have been viewed more generally as a theological attempt to speak about the transcendent God's immanent activity, are plainly differentiated from God not by Neoplatonic nuance but by the prohibition against worship. A mode of explanation for the inclusion of Jesus within the worship of God that would introduce an ontological differentiation between God and the Lamb is foreign to the dynamic of the text.

To the contrary, by virtue of the theological perspective generated by the practice of worship, Revelation pushes one's thought in the opposite direction, toward an account of Jesus's identity that would exclude ontological differentiation from God and, hence, allow their mutual worship.[25] Mutual worship, to put it still more simply, creates the angle of vision from which it can be seen that to embrace an ontological differentiation between the OT God and the Lamb is simultaneously to name Revelation's vision of worship as idolatry.

When couched in these terms, it thus becomes apparent that the "how" of the text cannot be answered adequately with the language of Arian or ultimately subordinationist Christology,[26] in which a crisp—if at times slight (cf. *homoiousios*)—ontological differentiation between the Father and the Son

is obviously fraught with numerous and major interpretive problems due to the absence of the Similitudes from the Judaean Desert manuscripts of 1 Enoch, their unknown date of composition, and, correspondingly, the possible Christian influence upon them.

25. Thus it is not ontology per se that is "foreign" to the text but rather a particular kind of ontology.

26. By "Arian" and "ultimately subordinationist" I intend to refer to all theological positions that would differentiate the one God in his identity from Jesus Christ regardless of their specific differences (e.g., perhaps by Eunomius's time Arianism was more "radical" than it was with Arius himself, but such differences as there were do not affect the issue at stake here). For instance, Origen's insight into the eternal generation of the Son was of monumental import, but—in that it finally could not account for the worship of Jesus—it still did not go far enough and, hence, is not yet a position sufficient to receive interpretively Revelation's worship of the Lamb. Cf. the remark of Robert C. Gregg and Dennis E. Groh, *Early Arianism—a View of Salvation* (Philadelphia: Fortress, 1981), 1: "Everyone familiar with the early Arian writings knows the large claim made by them for the redeemer. . . . But if all the criticism leveled at the Arian representation of Christ . . . could be reduced to a single line, it would read like this: no matter how the Arians huff and puff, what they preach is a creature promoted to the status of a god. The Alexandrian bishops had it exactly right." For a highly sophisticated account of the theologies involved in the "Nicene controversy," broadly

was posited as a way to defend the uniqueness of the one God.[27] On broadly Arian grounds, one is forced either to judge Revelation's vision of worship as itself idolatrous or to deny the worship of Jesus that the text clearly grants.

Over against these (and other) exegetical impossibilities, the dogmatic specifications opened by the Athanasian use of *homoousios* allow for the possibility of the text.[28] Indeed, they articulate its intelligibility—its "how"—and, in precisely this way, receive interpretively the questions posed by the text's pressure. This is not to imply that the author of Revelation was thinking in fourth-century terms or that the "real" telos of Revelation was, after all, the Nicene-Constantinopolitan Creed.[29] On the contrary, it is to say that *homoousios*, as a cipher for a larger mode of discourse about proper worship, displays the logic inherent to the inclusion of a fully human being within the identity of the God of Israel. *Homoousios*, as Athanasius and the Cappadocians rightly pressed, coordinates symmetrically divine identity with the practice of the worship of Jesus and thus best captures the range of convictions that makes possible the pattern of worship in Revelation.

For this reason we can speak of the hermeneutical worth of doctrine. The Athanasian *homoousios* gives us a linguistic lens through which to perceive the theological coherence of Revelation, the noncontradiction of seemingly contradictory claims. Because he shares with God what it means to "be" God, Jesus the Lamb can be located within the God of Israel's identity and, hence, worshiped as that God is worshiped.[30] As Robert Jenson puts it in a slightly

considered, see now Lewis Ayres, *Nicaea and Its Legacy: An Approach to Fourth-Century Trinitarian Theology* (Oxford: Oxford University Press, 2004).

27. By "uniqueness" I mean to draw the circle wide enough to encompass the various concerns involved in such a distinction without suggesting that they were of the same import for all parties involved (God cannot suffer; God is immune to change; God cannot be differentiated within himself, be diffuse, etc.).

28. For an excellent, concise discussion of both the historical and systematic significance of *homoousios*, see Robert W. Jenson, *Systematic Theology*, 2 vols. (New York: Oxford University Press, 1999), 1:90–114. On the relation of the Council of Antioch (which condemned *homoousios*) to Nicaea, John Behr, *The Formation of Christian Theology*, vol. 1, *The Way to Nicaea* (Crestwood, NY: St. Vladimir's Seminary Press, 2001), 218–19, is concise; for a more extended account, see Ayres, *Nicaea and Its Legacy*, 11–121.

29. This distinction is crucial: the continuity for which I argue does not rest at the noetic level—the authors of Revelation and Athanasius obviously thought differently—but at the ontic level. Despite the differences in their conceptual structure and articulation, the object of which Revelation and Athanasius speak is the same. If I may indulge in a self-quotation: "To suggest that the biblical writers were consciously thinking in later creedal terms is in fact a major anachronistic mistake" ("Biblical Pressure," 297). On this point, see further below.

30. It is of course of more than passing interest to the question of the Bible's relation

different context, "The Crucifixion's sort of God is indeed the one God."[31] This, too, is the text of Revelation and the language of the *homoousios*.

As the discussion of Revelation has sought to elucidate, "pressure" as I have employed it is the word that attempts to speak about both the exegetical necessity of doctrinal formulation and the hermeneutical advantages of reading with doctrinal acuity.[32] In this way, pressure is essentially an attempt to describe in shorthand the dialectical nature of an interpretive procedure that attends concurrently to the particulars of the biblical text and to the larger Christian theological tradition. To develop this notion with more precision, we turn now to an analogy of language.

The Analogy of Language

It is well-known that the intense philosophical scrutiny of language is a hallmark of late/postmodern thought. As Charles Taylor notes, "The language debate itself reverberates through a number of hotly debated questions in aesthetics, poetics, literary criticism, philosophy, [and] human sciences."[33] Theologians, too, have made much good use of the explanatory potential of the various aspects involved in the analysis of language (grammar, syntax, and so on).[34] For our purposes it is not necessary to rehearse the substantial

to Christian doctrine to observe that the argument for the *homoousios* "judgment" (David Yeago's terminology) works not only for Paul but also for Revelation.

31. Jenson, *Systematic Theology*, 1:189.

32. There are naturally many more examples that could illustrate the idea of pressure equally well. In terms of the doctrine of God, for example, I note with considerable interest the remark of Ulrich Wilckens, *Theologie des Neuen Testaments* 1/4 (Neukirchen-Vluyn: Neukirchener Verlag, 2005), 139, that there is a "trinitarische Struktur der von Lukas erzählten Heilsgeschichte." Wilckens is quick to point out that this "structure" is given in the narrative, not worked out in typical systematic fashion: "Hier finden sich bei näherem Zusehen erstaunlich viele trinitarische Hinweise. Nirgendwo aber werden diese theologisch zusammengedacht" (139). The crucial question of course is how to articulate exegetically and theologically this narrative structure. Though the manuscript was at the publisher prior to the appearance of Wilckens's *Teilhand* 4, I attempted something like an answer to this question in C. Kavin Rowe, *Early Narrative Christology: The Lord in the Gospel of Luke*, BZNW 139 (Berlin: de Gruyter, 2006; repr., Grand Rapids: Baker Academic, 2009).

33. Charles Taylor, *Philosophical Arguments* (Cambridge, MA: Harvard University Press, 1995), ix.

34. The best-known of which is probably George A. Lindbeck, *The Nature of Doctrine: Religion and Theology in a Postliberal Age* (Philadelphia: Westminster, 1984). Rowan Williams, however, is perhaps the most elegant. See, for instance, his essays in *On Christian*

theological gains that have been made by attending closely to language. We may instead begin immediately to construct our analogy with a brief recapitulation of the influential distinction between *parole* and *langue* introduced by Saussure.[35]

For Saussure, language as a whole is to be understood as a deeply dialogical interaction between its two component parts, parole and langue. Individual acts of speech (*actes de parole*) presuppose for their intelligibility a larger linguistic system (langue) upon which they draw. While parole is what we actually encounter, we could not make sense of the particular forms of speech without the existence of language. We know what others' speech means because we are sufficiently able to fit it into a larger linguistic pattern. Once raised to the level of conscious reflection, we may thus see that, in a significant sense, parole discloses langue.

Langue itself, however, is not static or frozen, as if the linguistic system informing the speech in Elizabethan English were simply identical with that of the contemporary American scene. Rather, *actes de parole* impact the linguistic system from which they are drawn such that it shifts in light of actual speech.[36] Grammar books, dictionaries, and the like, to make the matter obvious, are in need of frequent adjustment and reform. Viewed in toto, then, language is best described as a mutually constitutive dialectical process that involves both radical particularity and wider patterns of thought, the latter of which both inform and—at the end of the day—are constituted by verbal particularity.

The point here is hardly to endorse the various forms of intellectual mania that stem from Saussure's semiotics.[37] Nor is it, contra Bultmann, to say that we

Theology (Oxford: Blackwell, 2000). From a somewhat different angle, the importance of language in Stanley Hauerwas's Gifford Lectures can hardly be overestimated; indeed, taken as a whole, the lectures can be read as a sophisticated and grand attempt to teach the church how to speak truthfully about God (*With the Grain of the Universe: The Church's Witness and Natural Theology* [Grand Rapids: Brazos, 2001]). The explanatory power of language has not gone unnoticed by biblical and patristic scholars. See, for example, the important work of Stephen B. Chapman, *The Law and the Prophets: A Study in Old Testament Canon Formation*, Forschungen zum Alten Testament 27 (Tübingen: Mohr Siebeck, 2000), esp. chap. 2; and Ayres, *Nicaea and Its Legacy*, esp. 14–15 on "grammar."

35. Ferdinand de Saussure, *Course in General Linguistics* (New York: Philosophical Library, 1950), esp. chs. 1–4.

36. As Taylor sees, even "deviant usage" can "gradually become standard" (*Philosophical Arguments*, 134).

37. I take it as self-evident that the notion—repeated in multiple ways with varying sophistication—that language refers *only* to itself is for Christians untenable on theological grounds and to be rejected a priori. I would also highly question the exegetical usefulness

can simply translate biblical and theological issues into philosophical terms.[38] It is, instead, to note how the general contour of Saussure's parole/langue distinction proves descriptively advantageous in the effort to give a constructively coherent account of contemporary theological exegesis.[39]

Initially, of course, what would likely come to mind is the potentially fruitful analogy with the necessity for historical investigation: to understand the discrete *actes de parole* within the biblical documents, one must investigate the langue they presuppose, meaning in this case their cultural environment. While this is indubitably true—indeed, it is essentially the philosophical insight that lies behind Umberto Eco's notion of a cultural encyclopedia—it is not the primary concern of this essay. Moreover, there is an important, though frequently overlooked, sense in which the kinds of questions raised by the pressure of the biblical text cannot be settled from within the noetic resources of the text's historical surroundings.[40] The focus here is thus upon langue as the larger doctrinal pattern disclosed by the particular forms of biblical parole and the resultant implications for the necessary relationship between biblical exegesis and systematic theology.

For Christians who affirm the primacy of the Bible in theological reflection, the thrust is as much epistemological as it is historical (the criterion of "apostolicity" in traditional parlance).[41] This conviction makes the point powerfully

---

of the attempt to strain the NT texts through a semiotic sieve. For this trend in biblical studies, one may consult any number of the articles in the early issues of the journal *Semeia*. In particular, see esp. issues 1–6 (1974–1976) and 10 (1978).

38. Or, to take an ancient example, Eunomius. For a concise discussion of this problem in relation to the theological disputes of the ancient church, see Robert L. Wilken, "Not a Solitary God: The Triune God of the Bible," *ProEccl* 3 (1994): esp. 52–54; or, from a different angle, Frances M. Young, "The God of the Greeks and the Nature of Religious Language," in *Early Christian Literature and the Classical Intellectual Tradition: In Honorem Robert M. Grant*, ed. William R. Schoedel and Robert L. Wilken, Théologie historique 53 (Paris: Éditions Beauchesne, 1979), 45–74.

39. There are obviously limitations to the analogy developed here. But such is the case with any analogy. The important question is whether the similarities are significant enough to make the analogy descriptively useful or whether the dissimilarities render it pointless.

40. To stay with our example from Revelation: A thorough investigation into the historical possibilities of worshiping a human being within a Jewish religious framework helps substantially to show *what* the text is doing (including Jesus within God's identity; see the studies in notes 12, 18, 23, and 24 above), but it still does not produce an articulation of precisely *how* such worship is theologically possible. Still less does it account for the judgment about the crucified Jesus in particular. On this point, see further the remarks in note 19 above.

41. Regrettably, the way in which the Reformation slogan *norma normans non normata*

that we do not simply have access to "doctrine" in abstraction from scripture, as if it were possible to know God's revelatory act in Jesus Christ without the story told in the NT.[42] Whatever else doctrine is, it is not a set of the eternal truths of reason that can be known independently of the particulars of the biblical texts, however critically they may be sifted. To put it into linguistic terms: The possibility of the knowledge of langue is dependent upon the concrete occurrences of parole. There is no immediate or independent knowledge of langue. Speech is thus, in this epistemological sense, primary; it actually reveals the linguistic system. To inquire into the grammatical structure of langue is to do so on the basis of parole.

Hence, embedded within the distinction between particular forms of speech and the linguistic system they presuppose is an original and identifiable epistemological movement from the former to the latter. Insofar as it becomes aware of the pressure of the biblical texts toward a larger doctrinal langue, the exegesis of the individual *actes de parole* brings to expression this original movement. Exegesis, in this sense, is primary.[43]

Yet once the movement from parole to langue has been made—the recognition that the particular forms of speech both constitute and require a

---

has been put to use has often obscured the fact that, dogmatically speaking, there is nothing in the theological affirmation of the primacy of scripture that would require the abandonment of the Christian theological tradition as the interpretive context in which it makes sense to speak of a biblical "norm" in the first place. At least from our vantage point today, such an emphasis is, indeed, fundamentally consonant with John Paul II's formulation in note 9 above.

42. Even advocates for the possibility of natural theology should be able to give their assent here under the traditional distinction between general and special revelation. For disputants of natural theology, the point is obvious. Cf., for instance, the implications of Wolfhart Pannenberg, *Systematic Theology*, 3 vols. (Grand Rapids: Eerdmans, 1991–1998), 1:107–8: "By nature, i.e., from creation, God, the God of the apostolic gospel (Rom. 1:19–20), is known to all people. This is not a statement of natural theology. It is a statement that is made about us in the light of the revelation of God in Jesus Christ"; or, Hauerwas, *With the Grain*, 142: "I assume that 'natural theology' simply names how Christian convictions work to describe all that is as God's good creation."

43. At least in part, this is the insight that accompanies the provocative statements to the effect that dogmatic/systematic theology is, after all, but commentary upon scripture. See, for instance, the preface to Barth's first volume of the *Church Dogmatics*: The Bible is "the basic text upon which all the rest and everything of our own can only wait and comment" (Karl Barth, *Church Dogmatics* I/1, 2nd ed. [Edinburgh: T&T Clark, 1975], xii); and, Jenson, *Systematic Theology*, 1:33, who notes, in relation to his own systematic project, that it should be "tested against Scripture by its success or failure as a hermeneutical principle for Scripture taken as a whole."

larger frame of reference for their intelligibility—the subsequent dialectical character of the relation can be seen. On this side of the analogy, the wider doctrinal pattern of langue can inform substantially the exegete's understanding of specific *actes de parole* by explicating the logic necessary to the text's theological moves and ultimate intelligibility. In this way the hermeneutical key to questions posed by particular forms of biblical speech rests in the contemporary interpreter's ability to engage those questions within a prior context of understanding—Christian doctrinal tradition.[44]

The practice of theological exegesis is thus one dialectical interpretive act. Parole and langue are mutually constitutive and mutually presupposing. They cannot, therefore, exist independently from one another but rather constitute something of a whole. Yet there is a certain order to the dialectic. Doctrine, when rightly fitted to the particulars of the biblical parole, is logically prior to exegesis, even as exegesis is both theologically—that is to say, dogmatically—and epistemologically prior to doctrine.[45]

There are at least three further descriptive advantages to this analogy. First, the articulation of the difference between parole and langue allows for considerable movement of and flexibility within a linguistic system on the basis of its actual engendering speech. Parole thus displays a decisive ability to reform and reshape langue through actual usage and over time. There is in this sense a "givenness"—or, perhaps, solidity—in particular forms of speech to which the construction of a linguistic framework must be accountable for its coherence and persuasiveness. In view of the topic considered in this essay, it is important then to emphasize that the doctrinal langue that is logically prior to the biblical parole is itself to be based upon—revealed by—the biblical parole. To employ hermeneutically this logically prior context of understanding (langue) is not at all, therefore, to force the particulars of the biblical texts into doctrinal straitjackets.[46] To the contrary, the flexibility inherent to the relation between

44. In my judgment, it is precisely this aspect of Brevard Childs's *The Struggle to Understand Isaiah as Christian Scripture* (Grand Rapids: Eerdmans, 2004) that makes this book a fascinating study in the theological understanding of history.

45. Cf. Richard E. Burnett, *Karl Barth's Theological Exegesis: The Hermeneutical Principles of the* Römerbrief *Period* (Grand Rapids: Eerdmans, 2004), 87: "Those who accuse Barth of imposing a dogmatic *a priori* on the Bible are wrong . . . not because he does not read the Bible with dogmatic presuppositions, but because his dogmatic presuppositions, at least as he saw it, were established not in *a priori* fashion but in an *a posteriori* fashion."

46. This way of putting it is obviously to point to the reality of doctrinal error and the necessity of "fit" between biblical speech and doctrinal language. To state it rather crudely: For various reasons (poor exegesis, lack of self-criticism, intellectually distorting sin, etc.) we may construct the incorrect doctrinal langue on the basis of the biblical parole. Inasmuch as

parole and langue points to the genuineness of the dialectical movement between text and doctrine.

We may briefly clarify this matter by putting it into narrative terms, for the distinction between parole and langue helps to elucidate what it means theologically to receive and retell a comprehensive story. The particular biblical texts presuppose a foundational story for their intelligibility.[47] Doctrine provides the grammatical rules necessary for the story to be well told; in this way, it illuminates the particularities of the texts themselves (much in the same way as the entirety of a novel helps to explain the significance of its individual chapters). Yet to interpret this story at all is to read it through its particular embodiment in the biblical texts (to stay with the metaphor: there is no novel without the actual chapters that create the book). Thus, the biblical texts generate the story that they presuppose. The movement between the generation of this story and its reflective articulation is the movement between biblical exegesis and Christian doctrine.

Second, the parole/langue distinction provides a way to illuminate the necessary correlation between the biblical text and later Christian doctrine without simultaneously involving crude anachronism and a cavalier dismissal of human situatedness within history (theologically said, our status as creatures).[48] Although a person's particular manner of speech presupposes a larger

---

langue is constituted (disclosed) by parole, doctrine is always subject to the corrective witness of scripture. To tell faithfully the story of scripture in a doctrinal idiom is to articulate the *correct* langue in light of the biblical parole. One of the more interesting—and perhaps compelling—contemporary examples of the reassertion of biblical speech in relation to doctrinal language is the rethinking of the metaphysical assumptions that informed the classical accounts of God's impassibility and immutability. Of course, this way of framing the issue is to raise, rather than settle, the important question of the difference between "irreversible" dogmatic truths and doctrinal articulation. On this point, Jenson, *Systematic Theology*, 1:35–39, is concise. See also note 66 below (on Barth's remarks in *Church Dogmatics* IV/4).

47. This is true in two senses: first, in the sense that the individual documents themselves presuppose an underlying narrative (see in relation to Pauline theology, for example, Bruce Longenecker, ed., *The Narrative Dynamics of Pauline Theology: A Critical Assessment* [Louisville: Westminster John Knox, 2002]), and, second, in the sense that the canonical collection of the biblical documents is comprehensible only upon the presupposition of an overarching unity. That this unity is to be construed narratively can be debated, but that the canonical structure itself—however sprawling and complex its contents—presents its unity narratively seems indisputable (to mention only the obvious example: Genesis tells of the beginning of all things and Revelation the end of all things; the plot, as it were, is from creation through new creation to consummation).

48. See MacIntyre, *Three Rival Versions of Moral Enquiry*, for an account of our "historically situated rationality" (65).

linguistic pattern, it is hardly necessary noetically to posit reflective awareness of this larger pattern as the basis for correct or intelligible speech.[49] If doctrine is a case in point, working out the necessarily presupposed linguistic pattern may in fact take many lifetimes and countless different efforts from numerous subtle thinkers.[50] Thus, the revelatory aspect of parole for langue is to be located in the text rather than in strictly cognitive or epistemological possibilities—that is, in the author's mind.[51] Positively put, Saussure's distinction allows us to account for the multiple and profound noetic differences between the biblical authors and later interpreters while simultaneously preserving the equally profound ontic unity in the object of our thinking.[52]

49. Anyone who has ever been with young children in a foreign country where a different language is spoken will know this upon a moment's reflection. Despite assiduous grammatical study, the adults inevitably and regularly blunder. By contrast, the children, who have no formal knowledge of the grammar of the foreign tongue, simply "pick up" the language and speak it correctly. Indeed, theologically or philosophically speaking, it may well happen that the complex langue that shapes our parole remains hidden from us and—for critical leverage to be gained—needs to be exposed. For example, one way to understand Charles Taylor's influential *Sources of the Self: The Making of the Modern Identity* (Cambridge, MA: Harvard University Press, 1989) is to read it as a massive attempt to do the conceptually arduous work of making explicit the long and well-hidden langue of modern moral parole. See especially chapter 1, "Inescapable Frameworks," and Taylor's discussion of Saussure's distinction in relation to his own project in Taylor, *Philosophical Arguments*, 134, 178.

50. Here I am dependent upon the insight of Frances Young and David F. Ford, *Meaning and Truth in 2 Corinthians* (Grand Rapids: Eerdmans, 1987), esp. 255–60. Though they do not mention the distinction between langue and parole, their basic point is similar and, in my judgment, exactly on target: "We do need to ask about the relation of 2 Corinthians to later doctrine, but . . . we are not looking for a deduction of the Trinity from Paul's words. . . . The analogy of grammar is helpful here. It is possible for someone to speak perfectly grammatically without ever consciously knowing any grammar. Grammatical terms and systems are a late development in any language. So it is conceivable that the 'grammar' of Paul's talk of God might have been correctly understood by later doctrine even if their terminology seems alien" (256).

51. The formulation above is not intended to neglect the role of the interpretive community but rather simply has a different focus (presumably, the church is the "place" where it makes any sense at all to offer an account of the interrelation between the biblical texts, their human authors, and later Christian doctrine). For a treatment of "inspiration" that is weighted heavily toward the text, I cite again the work of my OT colleague Stephen B. Chapman, "Reclaiming Inspiration for the Bible," in *Canon and Biblical Interpretation*, ed. Craig Bartholomew et al., Scripture and Hermeneutics Series 7 (Grand Rapids: Zondervan, 2006), 167–206.

52. Another possible way to hold to continuity in the object of inquiry while allowing for substantial differences in the nature of the inquiry itself would be to adopt the threefold schematic analysis of the history of human understanding given by Edward Schillebeeckx, *Jesus: An Experiment in Christology*, trans. Hubert Hoskins (New York: Seabury, 1979),

Third, this ontic unity in the object of reflection is precisely that which is required by the mutually constitutive relation between parole and langue. Parole and langue, therefore, are not two ultimately separate entities but two aspects of the same reality—language. Despite their different areas of descriptive reach, the subject matter with which they deal is the same: the totality of linguistic life. By now the point should be clear. Doctrinal reflection and biblical exegesis are bound together theologically by the coherence and unity of their common subject matter. The different areas of focus, to put the issue again in narrative terms, represent not two different stories but the requisite amount of breadth and sophistication needed to speak faithfully the language of the same comprehensive story. They are, as it were, different moments in the overall attempt to listen to and retell the story told in scripture.

Finally, then, we may come full circle and complete our analogy: to attend to the necessary interrelationship between parole and langue is to perceive the pressure of the biblical text both critically and constructively. It is, in this way, to specify the connection between text and doctrine in terms of the unity of the subject matter to which scripture testifies and, hence, in terms of the final unity of the different interpretive practices needed to engage that subject matter.

The Dialectical Unity of the Disciplines

Sixteen years ago Brevard Childs prefaced his magnum opus with what was then an expression of hope: "Church history bears eloquent testimony to

---

576–79. Using the metaphor of concentric circles in a kind of inverted cone, Schillebeeckx envisions the history of human understanding in a threefold simultaneous movement in which each of the circles turns at a different speed. The first is labeled "ephemeral history" (or "fact-constituted history") and, with its "brief and rapidly expiring rhythm," corresponds to the coming and going of "the events of every day." The middle circle is labeled "conjunctural history"; its tempo is considerably slower and thus corresponds to more prolonged periods of change. Finally, at an even deeper level there is "structural history," the circle whose turning is exceedingly slow and whose "time-span [is] centuries." Structural history, which "almost borders on the central point between what moves and what does not," appears between ephemeral and conjunctural history "as a kind of invariable." They move around it "like concentric orbs about a slow-moving axis." These three circles "together constitute the one history of humankind." Geoffrey Wainwright, to whom I owe the reference to Schillebeeckx, puts well the crucial point: the intellectual and cultural tensions that we experience "on account of the different rhythms of change in the different areas of understanding" help to explain why the "language of the New Testament and of the early creeds . . . can strike us as *both* meaningful *and* strange" (*Doxology: The Praise of God in Worship, Doctrine, and Life; A Systematic Theology* [New York: Oxford University Press, 1980], 194; emphasis added).

a few glorious periods when suddenly unexpected interest in the Bible exploded within the life of the church, and biblical scholars and theologians found themselves engaged in a common enterprise."[53] Childs's evaluation of the potential for fashioning such a common enterprise in his lifetime was rather negative, but he did note that "many of the younger generation were hard at work in trying."[54]

In light of the formulations given in the previous two sections of this essay, we may say that the "common enterprise" of which Childs speaks is in fact required by the unity of the subject matter and, further, that those of us in the younger generation(s) have the theological responsibility to see it through. If our thinking and interpretation is to derive from rather than create (à la Feuerbach) its object—if, that is, the shape of *all* theological reflection should be determined by the subject matter to which it is accountable—then at bottom our work ought necessarily to reflect the fact that "theology . . . is an undivided whole, in which biblical and systematic elements are inextricably intertwined."[55]

Thus, the kind of unity in interpretive practice upon which we want to insist is not a unity of two independent tasks, as if in good Gablerian fashion biblical scholars could simply hand their descriptive work over to the systematic theologians for contemporary construction, thereby "linking" the two separate projects together. Rather, the unity envisaged here operates at a much deeper level in that it calls for a subtle permeation or interpenetration of exegesis and dogmatics in the act of interpretation. In this way—to take two examples from my own ecclesial tradition—the unity of the interpretive enterprise is akin to what one senses in the prefaces to Calvin's *Institutes of the Christian Religion* (*ICR*) or in the programmatic criticisms expressed over three centuries later in Adolf Schlatter's brilliant essay "The Theology of the New Testament and Dogmatics."[56]

53. Brevard S. Childs, *Biblical Theology of the Old and New Testaments: Theological Reflection on the Christian Bible* (Minneapolis: Fortress, 1992), xvi.

54. Childs, *Biblical Theology*, xvi. Cf. the remark by Joseph Cardinal Ratzinger, "Biblical Interpretation in Crisis: On the Question of the Foundations and Approaches of Exegesis Today," in *Biblical Interpretation in Crisis: The Ratzinger Conference on Bible and Church*, ed. Richard John Neuhaus (Grand Rapids: Eerdmans, 1989), 1–23, that a theologically satisfactory approach to biblical interpretation "will demand . . . the attentive and critical commitment of an entire generation" (16). Would that it take only one generation.

55. Avery Dulles, "Response to Krister Stendahl's 'Method in the Study of Biblical Theology,'" in *The Bible and Modern Scholarship*, ed. J. Philip Hyatt (Nashville: Abingdon, 1965), 216.

56. Schlatter's essay appears in English translation in *The Nature of New Testament Theology*, ed. Robert Morgan (Naperville, IL: Allenson, 1973), 117–66. The German text of the essay "Die Theologie des Neuen Testaments und die Dogmatik" can be found conveniently

Despite much superficial understanding of the *ICR*, Calvin did not intend the work to be a self-contained systematic theology, a body of divine revelation that functioned independently of its connection to scripture and could, paradoxically, simply attract prooftexts with the gravitational force of its truth.[57] On the contrary, Calvin characterized his work as a hermeneutical guide to scripture—a propaedeutic for the right understanding of the Bible—which was itself to be tested by its conformity to scripture: "Above all, I must urge [the reader] to have recourse to scripture in order to weigh the testimonies that I adduce from it."[58] And Schlatter, while displaying the deep respect for historical *Wissenschaft* typical for his time, contended vigorously—perhaps even prophetically—for the impossibility of a historical approach to scripture that was not at the same time theologically determined.[59] Historical research and dogmatics are inextricably intertwined: "Neither is simply independent;

in *Das Problem der Theologie des Neuen Testaments*, ed. Georg Strecker (Darmstadt: Wissenschaftliche Buchgesellschaft, 1975), 155–214.

57. On the difference between the "formal" and "material biblicism" of the early and later Protestants, see the insightful remarks of Burnett, *Karl Barth's Theological Exegesis*, 57–58.

58. John Calvin, "Subject Matter of the Present Work," in *Institutes of the Christian Religion*, ed. John T. McNeill, trans. Ford Lewis Battles, 2 vols. (Philadelphia: Westminster, 1960), 8; hereafter *ICR*. In point of fact, the remarkable conceptual interweaving of the *ICR* and Calvin's biblical commentaries was such that, in the latter, he felt "no need for long [doctrinal] digressions" since in the *ICR* he had expounded "almost all the articles pertaining to Christianity" (7). Taking the commentaries together with the *ICR*, we can see that Calvin's primary literary work forms a unified theological project. He was, moreover, open to significant correction, at least in theory; for instance, after a brief citation/interpretation of a few passages pertinent to the question of whether or not forgiveness removes the "penalty" of sin, Calvin concludes the section with startling humility: "Here I must adjure my readers not to heed my glosses, but only to yield some place to the Word of God" (*ICR*, III.4.29, p. 657). Cf. Jenson's remark mentioned in note 43 above.

59. See also, for example, Schlatter's response to the provocative criticism by Wrede et al. who would dismantle canonical boundaries in the name of "historical research": "The distinction between New Testament writings and later literature is not based upon arbitrary fiat. It has historical reasons. By canonizing these writings, the generations following the apostles expressed where they found that word through which the church emerged and receives for all time its connection with the Christ. They found it not in the utterances of contemporary teachers and leaders, but in the writings of these men who speak to us in the New Testament. If we obscure this fact, we come into serious conflict not with a dogma but with history. . . . Mixing up . . . ecclesiastical and apostolic writings . . . corrects the historical facts of the matter by reference to the historian's own dogmatic judgment" (Schlatter, "Theology of the New Testament and Dogmatics," 146–47). Schlatter's argument here is a great deal more nuanced than this limited quotation can suggest and merits careful consideration for questions of canon today.

neither is merely the basis of the other. And neither is merely derivative or conditioned. Historical research has its independent foundation in the completeness of the past. Similarly . . . dogmatics is something primary (*ein Erstes*) which influences all our looking back to what has happened."[60] Thus, for both Calvin and Schlatter, to interpret scripture theologically is to foster critically the interplay between the possibility of exegetical perception created by the dogmatic tradition and the prior scriptural basis for such theology.

For modern biblical scholars, it is perhaps less startling to ponder the issue of a scriptural basis for later theological reflection than it is to think that the Christian doctrinal tradition can actually create exegetical perception, to shift, that is, from seeing the major points on the dogmatic compass as a bizarre form of schematization to comprehending them as directives for biblical interpretation. Yet, over against our modernist objections, what is so clear for Calvin and Schlatter—despite all the differences of time and emphasis[61]—is that the theological tradition is not something that precludes genuine "critical research," the freedom to hear in scripture a corrective to an interpretively preexistent theological framework. Rather, the tradition frees the interpreter for rigorous and ultimately more profound exegetical work by establishing a connection to scripture's subject matter at the level of an overarching inter-

60. Schlatter, "Theology of the New Testament and Dogmatics," 126 (Morgan's emphasis upon "primary" does not appear in the original text and is thus here removed). Indeed, though he energetically eschewed theological biblicism (117–18), Schlatter went even further and argued that "as dogmatics gets from history content and justification for its statements, so too the emergence and growth of dogmatic knowledge has a verifying and purifying effect on historical judgments. Then the possibility and even relative necessity of a variety of historical efforts can be understood" (155).

61. And there are naturally many differences. By using Schlatter and Calvin as examples, I do not intend to lend support to either of their theological programs in their entirety. Instead I mean simply to indicate that there exists a quality of interpretation in both of these scholars that is worthy of emulation regardless of the many exegetical or theological quarrels we may have with them. For example, looking back through the history of the discipline, it is difficult to imagine that the pressing task of NT theology is to divide itself "into as many theologies as there are New Testament authors" (Schlatter, "Theology of the New Testament and Dogmatics," 140). To the contrary, such work is essentially groundwork for the actual NT theological task: the attempt to say in what the theology of the NT consists. Lest we leave out Calvin: Whatever one thinks of Barth's reconstruction of the doctrine of election (*Church Dogmatics* II/2 [Edinburgh: T&T Clark, 1957]), he was almost certainly correct that Calvin erred when the latter articulated his doctrine of election in abstraction from Jesus Christ, and, therefore, in a sense non-Christianly. This error has grave exegetical consequences, for example, in Calvin's treatment of Rom. 9–11.

pretive perspective.[62] This perspectival connection with the subject matter of scripture facilitates the work of exegesis in that it enables a more refined grappling with the subject matter as it resonates within its particular incarnation in the distinct biblical texts.[63] To put it in the terms of our earlier analogy: Knowing the langue of the biblical parole does in fact enable one to work better inside the theological logic of the *actes de parole*, and precisely in this way, knowledge of the theological tradition engenders an otherwise unavailable form of interpretive perception.[64]

Such perception, however, does not predetermine the shape of the exegetical connection to scripture's subject matter. Indeed, what the young Barth wryly called the "unexplained historical crumbs"[65] of exegetical research may in fact contain the potential to reconfigure fundamentally the shape of doctrinal perception.[66] In this way, the recognition of the epistemologically and dog-

62. In explicitly theological terms, one might speak here of the essential identity between the Word and the Spirit.

63. A brief example here is Jesus's "Cry of Dereliction" in the Gospel of Mark (Mark 15:34, citing Ps. 22). Exegesis that is unaware of the doctrinal tradition can obviously perceive the profound Godforsakenness of this apocalyptic event simply by attending to the contours of Mark's Gospel. Yet a reading that is open to the resonance created by the unity of the theological subject matter is able to hear the Cry of Dereliction not as an event between two totally separate parties (God forsaking Jesus) but as an event within the life of God himself (involving the Father and the Son). Not only is this latter reading a more profound explication of a *theologia crucis*, but it is also, I would argue, truer to the animating convictions of Markan theology. In this way the doctrinal tradition deepens or, perhaps, extends theologically the exegesis of Mark rather than obstructing it. For a reading that pursues this line of theological interpretation, see Stanley Hauerwas, *Cross-Shattered Christ: Meditations on the Seven Last Words* (Grand Rapids: Brazos, 2004), 59–66.

64. Whereas the typical historical scholar of the nineteenth century saw doctrine as corrupting exegetical judgment, it can also be seen to have a critical effect upon the proclivity of interpreters to orbit about the circle created by unacknowledged presuppositions that conflict with the aim of the biblical texts. Bultmann held this to be true of the historical method (Rudolf Bultmann, "Is Exegesis without Presuppositions Possible?," in *Existence and Faith: Shorter Writings of Rudolf Bultmann* [New York: Meridian, 1960], 289–96, 314–15), but it is certainly no less true for doctrine's ability to dismantle—and reconstruct—hermeneutically defective schemata.

65. Burnett's translation of "unerklärte historische Brocken" (*Der Römerbrief*, xv). This is one place at least where staying close to the letter stays close also to the spirit (in a way that Hoskyns's translation does not: "fragments of past history," 12).

66. See, e.g., the important section in Barth's preface to the fragment on baptism in which he writes, with reference to Markus Barth's 1951 exegetical study of baptism, that "in the face of the exegetical conclusions in my son's book, I have had to abandon the 'sacramental' understanding of baptism, which I still maintained in 1943" (Karl Barth, *Church*

matically prior nature of scripture requires the interpreter to work through, rather than against, the particularity of the biblical texts to test the precision of the doctrinal langue against the exegesis of the concrete expressions of parole.[67] Insofar as the interpretive perception created by the dogmatic tradition is true to its subject matter, it will be so on the basis of its congruence with the subject matter rendered in the particulars of the biblical texts.

As the reader will by now have noticed, the vision of unity in interpretive practice offered here is complex precisely because it is dialectical. A separation of biblical studies from doctrinal reflection shatters our perception of the unity between scripture's subject matter and the church's reflective encounter with scripture through time; it is therefore to be resisted and rejected. Yet such unity in interpretive practice does not preclude a differentiation in the intensity of one's working focus, as it were, that would correspond somewhat to the traditional distinctions between biblical studies and systematic/dogmatic theology (the use of the langue and parole terminology says as much).[68] Let there be no mistake, however; the vision here is more than simply a plea for genuine conversation between mutually concerned parties. To be sure, conversation is a sine qua non for decent theological work. But if the above articulation of the necessity of theological exegesis has any merit to it, we will need to go significantly beyond that and begin to train and encourage scholars (the future generation) in a more self-consciously interdisciplinary manner. To do this well will require the overcoming not only of the fear of ignorance that accompanies the reality of increasing specialization within the traditional fields of study but also the inevitable inertia that accompanies the structure of educational institutions. With respect to the former, we will—let's face it—simply have to read more widely outside our own particular field of expertise, let some things go, and do the hard

---

Dogmatics IV/4 [Edinburgh: T&T Clark, 1960], x). I am not suggesting, of course, that Barth reversed his criticism of Jülicher, Wernle, et al. ("historische Brocken") but rather—and crucially—that technical, exegetical detail did actually matter doctrinally for Barth (though the antisacramental direction of Markus's book is to be regretted).

67. For a remarkable attempt, see recently Ferdinand Hahn, *Theologie des Neuen Testaments*, 2nd ed., 2 vols. (Tübingen: Mohr Siebeck, 2005). Further, as Childs notes, such close reading prevents the "retreat into generalities" and the "drawing [of] only a few broad lines" (*The Struggle to Understand Isaiah*, xi).

68. Cf., for instance, Barth's remarks about his *Römerbrief* commentary in an early draft of the preface to that work: "Because this book is not my dogmatic but an exegetical work, I was not able to say everything about each of the topics touched upon, but only about that which lies directly in the path of Paul's words. One is not allowed, therefore, to read its statements as a treatise but should rather be interested, first of all, in the understanding of the text itself" (Preface Draft III, trans. by Burnett, *Karl Barth's Theological Exegesis*, 289).

work of separating the wheat from the chaff. Mutatis mutandis, we probably should ignore "the thousandth article or book on the true meanings of *Hamlet* [or John 3:16] and the article immediately following in rebuttal, qualification or augment."[69] With respect to the latter, we will have to have vigorous discussion about and imaginative attempts to reshape the institutionalized separation of the theological disciplines. There are obvious and manifold objections to such restructuring (many of which are sound), but schools and programs that simply repeat what has been done—let us say it again—will lead once more to the need for theological integration, not to its practice.[70]

In the introduction to *The Art of Reading Scripture*, the authors write that the aim of the various scholars who produced the book was "to overcome the fragmentation of the theological disciplines by reading Scripture together."[71] Taken as a whole, one scholar noted, the group of different specialists could thus be considered a "Complete Theologian." It is true, of course, that it will be incredibly difficult to recover the form of a complete theologian in particular scholars, but it is this point on the horizon toward which we should move: the task of theological integration demands not only that we converse with other specialists but also that we begin to develop communities of interpretation that can train and sustain a more integrated kind of theologian.

69. George Steiner, *Real Presences* (Chicago: University of Chicago Press, 1989), 5. Steiner's imaginative vision of a "politics of the primary" is obviously an ideal of which we will fall short. Yet the value of its critical attack upon the "dominance of the secondary and parasitic" is hardly for that reason diminished (even as it clearly pins the genre of this essay—an irony of which I am all too aware).

70. We will naturally still need to think hard about the appropriate divisions of labor (not everyone will need to learn Coptic or become an expert in the issues of the eucharistic debate surrounding Radbertus and Ratramnus, for example). At the very least, we can say with Ferdinand Hahn that "der Vertreter einer Teildisziplin [ist] für das Ganze der theologischen Arbeit verantwortlich und [muß] insofern auch ein Mitspracherecht in den anderen Arbeitsbereichen haben" ("Exegese, Theologie und Kirche," in *Studien zum Neuen Testament. Band I. Grundsatzfragen, Jesusforschung, Evangelien*, ed. Jörg Frey and Juliane Schlegel, WUNT 191 [Tübingen: Mohr Siebeck, 2006], 22).

71. Ellen F. Davis and Richard B. Hays, eds., *The Art of Reading Scripture* (Grand Rapids: Eerdmans, 2003), xv.

Biblical Pressure and Trinitarian Hermeneutics

In life and in death we belong to God. . . . We trust in one triune God, the Holy One of Israel whom alone we worship and serve.[1]

—Presybterian Church (USA)

The question of the relation of the persons of the Trinity to one another, and the question of the divinity and humanity in the person of Christ as a question of ontological relations could only arise when the Old Testament had lost its meaning for the early Christian church.[2]

—Claus Westermann

The church's struggle with the Trinity was not a battle *against* the Old Testament, but rather a battle *for* the Old Testament.[3]

—Brevard Childs

1. "The Brief Statement of Faith—Presbyterian Church (USA)," in *The Constitution of the Presbyterian Church (USA) Part 1: The Book of Confessions* (Louisville: The Office of the General Assembly, 1994), 275.

2. Claus Westermann, "Das Alte Testament und die Theologie," in *Theologie—was ist das?*, ed. Georg Picht and Enno Rudolph (Stuttgart: Kreuz Verlag, 1977), 49–66: "Die Frage nach dem Verhältnis der Personen der Trinität zueinander und die Frage nach Gottheit und Menschheit in der Person Christi als Frage nach Seinsverhältnissen konnte erst aufkommen, als das Alte Testament seine Bedeutung für die frühchristliche Kirche verloren hatte" (50).

3. Brevard Childs, *Biblical Theology of the Old and New Testaments: Theological Reflection on the Christian Bible* (Minneapolis: Fortress, 1992), 376.

"Biblical Pressure and Trinitarian Hermeneutics" was originally published in *Pro Ecclesia* 11, no. 3 (2002): 295–312. doi:10.1177/106385120201100303.

In the present day, the church would be hard pressed to find more significant questions than the question of the relation of the God of the OT, the "Holy One of Israel," to the God of the NT and the corresponding question of the doctrine of the triune God and biblical interpretation. Put simply: Who is the God of the whole Bible? and How do we read the Bible in light of this God?

It is not my intention to relate the history of the development of the doctrine of the Trinity, nor do I intend to chart in detail the later exclusion of this doctrine from biblical exegesis with the rise of historical criticism in the modern period. Instead, this essay will seek to explore what I take to be the internal logic and connection of the two questions above and, on that basis, make a few constructive proposals about how and in what direction ecclesial biblical exegesis is to proceed in light of our present state of affairs. But first we need briefly to appreciate some dynamics of the problem that confronts us.

A Sketch of the Problem

The juxtaposition of the statements the "one triune God" and "the Holy One of Israel whom alone we worship and serve" in the confession of the Presbyterian Church (USA) sets the problem in sharpest relief. The continuity posited here is that of identity between the God who revealed himself to Israel by name as YHWH and the later church doctrine of the Trinity. It is this point that is ultimately at issue in the antithetical statements of the OT scholars Claus Westermann and Brevard Childs.

That Westermann does not stand alone in his denial of the necessary relation of the OT to the later ecclesial formulations should be obvious to anyone familiar with the present state of critical exegesis. This view turns primarily on the understanding of history that arose underneath and alongside the historical-critical method wherein history came to be seen as a strictly linear development. Church dogma with its watchwords (*homoousios*, *hypostaseis*, etc.) was clearly later than the biblical texts in the chronological sequence of events. Therefore to understand and interpret the Bible in light of the Trinity was of logical necessity to pervert the truth of historical development and damage beyond repair the historical sense of the text.[4] Further, the later creedal

4. On the matter of the "historical" and "literal" sense of scripture, see esp. Brevard Childs, "The Sensus Literalis of Scripture: An Ancient and Modern Problem," in *Beiträge zur Alttestamentlichen Theologie*, ed. Herbert Donner et al. (Göttingen: Vandenhoeck & Ruprecht, 1977), 80–93, and the exchange between James Barr and Childs on the basis of Childs's article: James Barr, "The Literal, the Allegorical, and Modern Biblical Scholarship,"

formulations were deemed products of Greek philosophical thinking that lay entirely outside the biblical horizon, so that to affirm a positive connection between church dogma and the biblical testimony was to impose an alien conceptual coating on the texts and lapse into fanciful allegory under a form of thought fundamentally adverse to the living religion of the Bible. Under such assumptions, the worship and practice of the church, which confessed one God as Father, Son, and Holy Spirit, were divorced from a historical, biblical exegesis that resisted such understanding and interpretation as anachronistic distortions. When pressed these assumptions disclose the propagation of a theology (!) that would destroy the connection between the reality to whom the Bible testifies and the reality whom the church worships. That is, at bottom, the question of Trinitarian interpretation of scripture turns out to be essentially bound up with the divine referent of scripture.

Such a brief sketch hardly does justice to the complexity involved in the course of historical-critical interpretation, but it is needed nonetheless to feel at least somewhat the weight of the problem. The historical-critical approach is correct in a crucial and far-reaching aspect: the doctrine of the Trinity is later than the biblical texts and to suggest that the biblical writers were consciously thinking in later creedal terms is in fact a major anachronistic mistake. Thus if we are to respect this basic insight into the movement of external history, we will have to pursue the relation of the triune God to the Bible in a different manner.

Perhaps some would simply want to dispute the way historical critics such as Westermann put the question and affirm on different theological grounds the legitimacy of Trinitarian interpretation of the Bible in light of the church's confession: we stand within the church that has confessed the God of the Bible to be triune and therefore read the Bible, including the OT, accordingly. However, this argument affords no easy escape; problems arise even from within the strictly dogmatic side of things, especially in light of the incarnation and the doctrine of the Trinity itself.

The case can be made, in analogous form to the charges leveled against Wilhelm Vischer's *Christuszeugnis*,[5] that to engage in full-fledged Trinitarian

---

JSOT 44 (1989): 3–17; Childs, "Critical Reflections on James Barr's Understanding of the Literal and Allegorical," *JSOT* 46 (1990): 3–9; and Barr, "Wilhelm Vischer and Allegory," in *Understanding the Poets and Prophets: Essays in Honour of George Wishart Anderson*, ed. A. Graeme Auld (Sheffield: JSOT Press, 1993), 38–60.

5. Wilhelm Vischer, *The Witness of the Old Testament to Christ*, vol. 1, *The Pentateuch* (London: Lutterworth, 1949). Volume 1 of the German original, *Das Christuszeugnis des Alten Testaments: Das Gesetz*, was first published in 1934. See esp. Barr, "Wilhelm Vischer," 55–58, and Brevard Childs, "Old Testament in Germany 1920–1940: The Search for a New

interpretation of the OT is not to take seriously enough the incarnation.[6] Such a charge would find its strongest support in two primary forms. First, the most historically obvious thing about Jesus of Nazareth is that he was a first-century Jewish male. That is to say, to interpret the OT without regard to this basic fact is to deny the particularity, and thus reality, of the incarnation. Jesus the first-century Jew is, of course, not to be separated from his self-same identity as the eternal Son of the Father, but to have Jesus parading about during the time of the OT is to dehistoricize the scandalous claim of the incarnation captured explicitly in the biblical "became" (ἐγένετο) of John 1:14 (such a move could also lead to an anti-Judaism wherein Jesus's Jewishness ceases to be important in any substantive way—which itself leads to serious difficulties in terms of a positive relation between the Old and New Testaments). Second, such dehistoricization could be said to open the door to a theological docetism wherein Jesus's flesh and historical situatedness within the first century as a real person would not make any significant difference for theology and, indeed, would even run counter to some of the most basic ecclesial affirmations about the importance of Jesus's full humanity (as well as the corresponding implications for the doctrine of atonement, etc.).

Within much recent Christian understanding of the doctrine of the Trinity is the important point that we know the immanent Trinity (God is triune in himself) on the basis of the economic Trinity (the activity of God in history);[7] thus it is that God's act is revelatory (and some would say constitutive) of his identity.[8] It follows that God's act and identity cannot be separated but are to be held together. The difficulty for our present topic is, of course, how to respect

---

Paradigm," in *Altes Testament: Forschung und Wirkung*, ed. Peter Mommer and Winfried Thiel (Frankfurt am Main: Lang, 1994), 233–46.

6. Stephen Chapman in particular deserves thanks for directing my attention in a more detailed fashion to the issue of the incarnation in relation to Vischer's *Christuszeugnis*.

7. Of course, there are those who would reject the immanent and economic distinction, but there is not room here to discuss the issue systematically. The rest of the essay will indicate some of the lines that could be taken. Colin Gunton, "The God of Jesus Christ," *ThTo* 54, no. 3 (1997): esp. 328–30, helpfully condenses what is at stake in the debate without lapsing into substanceless generalities. For sophisticated and nuanced arguments against our ability to speak meaningfully about God in himself apart from his creation, see Friedrich Mildenberger, *Biblische Dogmatik: Eine Biblische Theologie in dogmatischer Perspektive*, 3 vols. (Stuttgart: Kohlhammer, 1991–1993), esp. §§22, 23, 24, who coordinates his dogmatic position with profound exegesis of the biblical texts.

8. See the concise survey by Christoph Schwöbel, "The Renaissance of Trinitarian Theology: Reasons, Problems and Tasks," in *Trinitarian Theology Today*, ed. Christoph Schwöbel (Edinburgh: T&T Clark, 1995), 1–30.

the economy of God in light of his immanent reality. The problem is acute in connection with Trinitarian interpretation of the OT. In other words, if we interpret the OT in light of God as Trinity, is this not to let the immanent Trinity overrun the economic expression? Does not such a complete fusion actually dissolve any meaningful understanding of the course of biblical history and, resultantly, of God's divine economy? Does it not matter for interpretation that God in his good pleasure and sovereign freedom did not choose to reveal himself fully as Trinity until "the fullness of time," and even then only in a latent sense in comparison with the later creedal affirmations? Thus the doctrine of the Trinity itself in seeking to preserve the economy of the Bible does justice to certain aspects of the insights of the historical critics regarding the movement of history and, hence, should caution us against an easy, immediate Trinitarian interpretation of the biblical texts, or, indeed, any interpretation of the Bible that runs roughshod over the course of "external" history.

The Battle for the Old Testament

Keeping before us the historical and theological questions of the preceding section with respect to the divine referent of the biblical text, we can appreciate the far-reaching significance of Childs's claim with which we began this essay: "The church's struggle with the Trinity was not a battle *against* the Old Testament, but rather a battle *for* the Old Testament." Those who know well volume I/1 of Karl Barth's *Church Dogmatics* will recognize in Childs's assertion Barth's statement to the same effect: the doctrine of the Trinity (which proceeded from the reality of God in Jesus Christ and the implications thereof) was "not a battle against the Old Testament, but . . . was a battle for the Old Testament, i.e., for the one eternal covenant of God with men sealed in time, for acknowledgment of the perfect self-unveiling of God."[9]

Such claims strike to the heart of the problem in opposite fashion from Westermann and others in that they argue for a necessary and essential connection between the OT (and, by implication, the entire Christian Bible) and the doctrine of the Trinity. In light of the objections raised in section one and the opposition of the Barth/Childs position noted in this brief section, three questions will shape the remainder of this essay as one that hopes to contribute to the crucial task of theological exegesis: (1) Is there a necessary and essential connection between the OT and Trinitarian doctrine, or has this doctrine left

9. Karl Barth, *Church Dogmatics* I/1, 2nd ed. (Edinburgh: T&T Clark, 1975), 319.

the OT behind? (2) What is the specific nature of the relation of the Old and New Testaments to the doctrine of the Trinity? (3) What do the answers to questions one and two mean for Trinitarian interpretation of the Bible?

The Bible and the Trinity: Biblical Pressure

The question of the necessary connection between the OT and the Trinity immediately involves the New Testament and its relation to the Old. That is to say, our question really concerns the point of connection between the Old and New Testaments. It is safe to say that the doctrine of the Trinity would never have arisen on the basis of the Old or the New Testament taken in isolation. The problematic emerges precisely because the writers of the NT presupposed the authority of the OT and made explicit use of the theological grammar that undergirds the OT's language about the one God. Simply stated, the Lord and Redeemer of Israel was the one and only God of the world.[10] He was not part of the world in any way but instead was totally other than the world. As its sole creator, the Lord God required absolute allegiance from his people and would not tolerate the worship of any other thing other than himself: the Lord is a jealous God. Thus there exists in the OT a qualitative distinction between God the Creator and everything else, creation.[11] This distinction corresponds to the directives for Israel's worship: true worship was worship of the Creator, and worship of any part of creation was idolatry (for Paul's view on this matter, see especially Rom. 1:18–25). Such "monotheistic" affirmations with respect to reality and to worship are seen in thetic form in the Shema of Deuteronomy:

> Hear O Israel: The Lord [YHWH/κύριος] our God, the Lord [YHWH/κύριος] is one [εἷς]. You shall love the Lord [YHWH/κύριος] your God with all your heart, and with all your soul, and with all your might. (Deut. 6:4–5 LXX)

10. The confession "*heis theos*" (one God) and its equivalent "*monos theos*" (only God) were foundational for Second Temple Judaism. See esp. Gerhard Delling, "*MONOS THEOS*," in *Studien zum Neuen Testament und zum hellenistischen Judentum: Gesammelte Aufsätze*, ed. Ferdinand Hahn et al. (Göttingen: Vandenhoeck & Ruprecht, 1970), 391–400, and Ulrich Mauser, "*Heis Theos* und *Monos Theos* in Biblischer Theologie," *Jahrbuch für Biblische Theologie* 1 (1986): 71–87.

11. Such a qualitative distinction in no way implies the denial of God's immanence or relation to his creation, in particular as expressed through Wisdom, the *Shekinah*, etc. For a helpful introduction, see esp. Richard Bauckham, *God Crucified: Monotheism and Christology in the New Testament* (Grand Rapids: Eerdmans, 1998).

The negative implication of the positive command of Deuteronomy 6:5 is found a few verses later and follows from the utter singularity of the Lord God expressed in Deuteronomy 6:4:

> You shall fear the Lord your God; you shall worship/serve [λατρεύσεις] him; you shall cleave to him; and you shall swear by his name. Do not follow any other gods . . . because the Lord your God, who is present with you, is a jealous God. The anger of the Lord your God would be kindled against you and he would destroy you from the face of the earth. (Deut. 6:13–15 LXX)[12]

The intertextual dependence upon the first two commandments of the Decalogue is clear:

> I am the Lord your God. . . . You shall have no other gods before me.
>
> You shall not make for yourself idols in the likeness of anything, whether in the heavens above, or on the earth beneath, or in the waters under the earth. You shall not worship them or serve them because I am the Lord your God, a jealous God who punishes the sins of the fathers upon the children to the third and fourth generation of those who hate me. (Deut. 5:6–9 LXX)

A further and crucial point to be made is that the Creator of the world and Redeemer of Israel had a proper name and had revealed this name to Israel. In Hebrew the name is YHWH. How this name was conveyed in Greek is debated, but it is safe to say that the writers of the NT understood this name in Greek as *kyrios*. In almost every single instance where the NT cites the Greek Old Testament (LXX) as it corresponds to the Hebrew Old Testament YHWH, the NT authors wrote *kyrios* for the divine name.[13]

That the Creator of the world was the only true God, that this God demanded total and exclusive worship, and that this God's proper name YHWH was rendered in Greek in the NT by *kyrios* assume tremendous importance precisely at the point of the OT's relation to Trinitarian doctrine. Obviously in this essay there is not space for extensive commentary, but we must nevertheless note a few texts whose representative significance is of paramount importance.[14]

12. In the temptation scene in Matthew and Luke, Jesus cites the form of Deut. 6:13 found in MS A (Codex Alexandrinus), but the order of dependence here is unclear. The Gospels read: "You shall worship [*proskynēseis*] the Lord your God and him only [*monō*] you shall serve [*latreuseis*]."

13. *Theos* is very infrequent.

14. Three points are in order: (a) I make no claim to comprehensive coverage of impor-

Exegesis

1. *Joel 3:5 (English version 2:32); Romans 10:13; Acts 2:21*: Nearly half a century ago, C. H. Dodd argued on the basis of the use of Joel 3:1–5 in Romans 10 and Acts 2 that this OT text was an important *testimonium* for the early church.[15] There is debate about the *testimonia* hypothesis, but suffice it to say here that there is strong support for Dodd's point in that both Paul and Luke draw upon this Joel text and use it in a christologically transforming fashion. We will look briefly only at Romans 10:13.[16]

Joel 3:5 is essentially the same in the Masoretic Text and the LXX, as well as in Romans 10:13. The key phrase reads: "All who call on the name of the Lord [τὸ ὄνομα κυρίου] will be saved." Through the verbatim citation of Joel 3:5 in Romans 10:13, Paul's christologically explicit use of *to onoma kyriou* here issues in a dialectical identity of subject. The theological medium is that of overlap and resonance such that the conjunction of the text of Joel 3:5 with Romans 10:13 produces the conceptual space wherein the resonating identification between YHWH and Jesus occurs. The name that *is* the God of Israel alone (κύριος)[17] is now the name that *is* Jesus (κύριος). The salvific name in its original context was YHWH; now the salvific name is Jesus. In Joel the Israelites would have called out "YHWH" to be saved, and now in Romans all would call out "Jesus." "The name of the Lord" = YHWH has become, by virtue of the intersection between Joel and Romans, "the name of the Lord" = Jesus.

2. *John 20:28*: Doubting Thomas's confession of Jesus as "my Lord and my God!" (Ὁ κύριός μου καὶ ὁ θεός μου) does not cite directly any particular

---

tant texts—such texts are far too numerous (1 Cor. 8:4–6; 12:4–6; Phil. 2:5–11; Eph. 2:18–22; John 1:1; Matt. 28:19; Luke 1–2; etc.). (b) The selection of texts was made in accordance with their representative significance and, as such, is indicative of much larger patterns within the thought of the writers of the NT. (c) Trinitarian dogma is obviously not directly in the Bible. No one thinks that it is. The dogma rests, rather, on a reading of scripture as a whole such that representative text selection is not at all to be identified with a "prooftexting" approach that seeks to extract phrases from their context and use them polemically to support an already existing belief.

15. C. H. Dodd, *According to the Scriptures: The Sub-structure of New Testament Theology* (London: Nisbet, 1952), 28–29.

16. For an extended exegetical treatment of Rom. 10:13 and its implications for later theology, see C. Kavin Rowe, "Romans 10:13: What Is the Name of the Lord?," *HBT* 22, no. 2 (2000): 135–73.

17. See Gerhard von Rad, *Old Testament Theology*, vol. 1 (New York: Harper & Row, 1962), 179–87, for a theologically penetrating discussion of the revelation and significance of God's name in the OT.

OT passage. This homologia, however, invokes language fundamental to OT "God-talk," both in terms of identity and in terms of worship. Psalm 34:23–24 LXX, to cite only one of many pertinent examples, reads:[18]

> Rise up, O Lord [κύριος], and give heed to my judgment!
> My God and my Lord [Ὁ κύριός μου καὶ ὁ θεός μου],
>   to my cause . . .
> O Lord my God [κύριε ὁ θεός μου]!
> Do not let them exult over me!

Reading John 20:28 in conjunction with the divine grammar of the OT brings forth a claim of ontological identity between YHWH, the God of Israel (ὁ κύριος ὁ θεός), and the risen Jesus Christ (ὁ κύριος ὁ θεός). Thomas's address does not, however, fuse or confuse the differentiation between Jesus and the Father. Rather, throughout the Gospel of John the evangelist maintains the differentiation of Father and Son. The logic of John 20:28 read with the *inclusio* of John 1:1 and in the context of the gospel as a whole allows for a differentiation of YHWH into Father (the Sender, the One who is revealed, etc.) and Son (the One who was sent, the Revealer, etc.), while simultaneously maintaining that the Father and Jesus the Son are in fact "one" (ἕν, John 10:30). They are together "the Lord God" (ὁ κύριος ὁ θεός), even as the Father is "greater" than the Son in the way that the sender is greater than the one who is sent.

We must now pause briefly to take note of a crucial implication of Romans 10:13 and John 20:28.[19] Among both Protestant and Roman Catholic exegetes and systematic theologians[20] there is a common (and in many ways understandable) assumption that YHWH, the God of the OT, is the Father *only*.[21]

18. See, e.g., Pss. 29:3 LXX; 85:15 LXX; 87:2 LXX; 2 Kgdms. 7:28; 3 Kgdms. 18:39; Jer. 38:18 LXX; Zech. 13:9. So, too, in Rev. 4:11 the worshipers address God as "O Lord our God" (ὁ κύριος καὶ ὁ θεὸς ἡμῶν).

19. Cf., e.g., Luke 3:4–6; Acts 2:25–28; etc.

20. On the Protestant side, see, e.g., Paul Meyer's stimulating essay "'The Father': The Presentation of God in the Fourth Gospel," in *Exploring the Gospel of John: In Honor of D. Moody Smith*, ed. R. Alan Culpepper and C. Clifton Black (Louisville: Westminster John Knox, 1996), esp. 256, and Wolfhart Pannenberg, who gives this impression in chapter 5 of his *Systematic Theology*, vol. 1 (Grand Rapids: Eerdmans, 1998). On the Roman Catholic side, see esp. Karl Rahner's classic *The Trinity* (New York: Crossroad, 1997) and Joseph Fitzmyer's technical and learned article "The Semitic Background of the New Testament *Kyrios*-Title," in *The Semitic Background to the New Testament* (Grand Rapids: Eerdmans, 1997), esp. 130 and nn. 36 and 90.

21. For still excellent theological exegesis to the contrary, see John Calvin, *Institutes of the*

This assumption, however, will not stand under exegetical scrutiny. The NT texts never identify the Father as the Son or vice versa, but they do give the divine name *kyrios* (= YHWH) to both the Father and the Son. The word *kyrios* (and less frequently *theos*) and the way in which it is used in the NT in OT citations, hymns of worship, prayers, soteriological statements, and so on exert a unitive pressure in two directions with respect to its referent, toward the Father and toward Jesus. This pressure moves us to the conclusion that YHWH is not the Father alone. There is a differentiation into Father and Son within the unity of the one Lord (κύριος εἷς in Deut. 6:4).

3. *2 Corinthians 3:17a*: However isolated an occurrence it may be,[22] 2 Corinthians 3:17a is not a liability for Trinitarian theology (as has often been thought) but instead is an asset. The simplest and most straightforward way to translate the Greek is as follows: "the Lord (ὁ κύριος) is the Spirit (τὸ πνεῦμα)." Contrary to first impressions, this statement is not an identification of the person of Jesus with that of the Spirit. It is, rather, a gloss on the *kyrios* of what is a fairly loose citation of Exodus 34:34 in the previous verse:[23]

> And whenever Moses went in before the Lord [ἔναντι κυρίου] to speak to him, he removed the veil until he went out. (Exod. 34:34 LXX)
>
> But whenever he turns to the Lord [πρὸς κύριον], the veil is removed. (2 Cor. 3:16)
>
> The Lord [ὁ κύριος] is the Spirit [τὸ πνεῦμα]. (2 Cor. 3:17a)

Paul's Spirit-identifying gloss on *kyrios* subsumes the Spirit under the divine name *kyrios*, which is used both of the Father and of Jesus the Son. Richard Hays rightly notes the helpful translation of the New English Bible: "However, as Scripture says of Moses, 'whenever he turns to the Lord the veil is removed.' Now the Lord of whom this passage [Exod. 34:34] speaks is the Spirit."[24] Here,

---

Christian Religion 1.13.9–20, 24–29. Contrast also Vladimir Lossky, *The Mystical Theology of the Eastern Church* (Crestwood, NY: St. Vladimir's Seminary Press, 1976), 64: "If one speaks of God it is always, for the Eastern Church, in the concrete: 'The God of Abraham, of Isaac and of Jacob; the God of Jesus Christ.' It is always the Trinity: Father, Son and Holy Ghost."

22. See, however, Richard B. Hays, *Echoes of Scripture in the Letters of Paul* (New Haven: Yale University Press, 1989), 125–53, who shows the basic importance of this entire unit (2 Cor. 3:1–4:6) for Pauline hermeneutics.

23. See Hays, *Echoes*, 143–49, for an extended treatment.

24. Hays, *Echoes*, 143.

then, the Spirit is not Jesus, nor is Jesus the Spirit, but both are "the Lord" (ὁ κύριος). The very next phrase confirms such a differentiation within the identity of the Lord: "and where the Spirit of the Lord [τὸ πνεῦμα κυρίου]—freedom!" (2 Cor. 3:17b). Read canonically, then, the full unity of God as expressed through his name *kyrios* is that of Father, Son, and Spirit: the one Lord (κύριος εἷς) of Deuteronomy 6:4 is in the NT differentiated into Father (κύριος πατήρ), Son (κύριος Ἰησοῦς), and Spirit (κύριος πνεῦμα). Thus the oneness and unity of God is not impaired but is dynamically upheld through the use of his name *kyrios* for the Father, Son, and Spirit, the one Lord God.[25]

4. *Galatians 4:4–6*: In Galatians 4:1–7 Paul expands his earlier point with regard to Abraham (3:23–29) and assures the Galatian believers of their status as children and heirs of God. The principal appeal of the argument is to the presence of the Spirit. Within this larger unit with its emphasis upon the Spirit, verses 4–6 display Paul's view of the economy of God *in nuce*. It should be mentioned that the divine economy, by definition, entails God's relation to his creation ("redeem those under the law," etc.), but for our present topic we need only to look at the logic and implications of Paul's language about God:

> But when the fullness of time came:
> God sent forth (ἐξαπέστειλεν)
> his Son,
> born of a woman, born under the law . . .
> God sent forth (ἐξαπέστειλεν)
> the Spirit of his Son . . .
> crying "Abba Father."

This expression of the divine economy reveals a fundamentally Trinitarian pattern. God the Father—*theos* is always the Father in Galatians—exists in relation to his Son as well as in relation to the Spirit of his Son. The Spirit of the Father's Son, in turn, testifies (in the hearts of believers) to the Father of the Son. This relationship between the Father, his Son, and the Spirit of the Father's Son is mutually constitutive, which is to say that the economy of the one God, the Creator of the world, is here spoken of in a way in which each of the three "persons" are immediately interrelated: the Father is the Father of his Son; the Son is, obviously, the Son of his Father; and the Spirit is the Spirit of the Son of the Father. This relationship has two further dimensions. First, the

25. Cf. the interesting essay of R. Kendall Soulen, "YHWH the Triune God," *Modern Theology* 15, no. 1 (1999): 25–54.

relationship between the Father, Son, and Spirit is eternal.[26] Paul's emphasis in "born of a woman . . . ," following from the apocalyptic phrase "when the fullness of time came" (4:4), may rest upon the birth of Jesus or upon his entire life, death, and resurrection or upon its redeeming effects, or upon all three, inseparable as they are. Regardless, there can be no question that the "fullness of time" read in conjunction with "born of a woman . . ." *assumes* a relationship of prior existence between the Father, Son, and Spirit and a doctrine of incarnation, however nascent. Second, the relationship implies some type of movement in the life of God himself. This movement can be characterized, at least in some sense, as outward in nature, a sending out (ἐξ-αποστέλλω), and is in fact the inseparable events of the incarnation and giving of the Holy Spirit. Taking these two points together allows and even requires us to affirm an intrinsic incarnationality within the life of the eternal God realized, as it were, in the fullness of time. The incarnation and the gift of the Holy Spirit make a difference for our understanding of the triunity of God.

5. *Romans 8:9–11*: Though the particular points of emphasis are somewhat different, Romans 8:9–17 contains similar affirmations to those of Galatians 4:1–7 regarding the believers' status as children of God (cf. esp. 8:15–17). So, too, there is a marked focus upon the Spirit. For our purposes we will take note of the strictly theological implications of Paul's language about the Spirit. The crucial point is the interchangeability between "of Christ" and "of God" (the Father) with reference to the Spirit. Hence, "the Spirit" in verse 9a is the "Spirit of God" (πνεῦμα θεοῦ) in verse 9b, and the "Spirit of Christ" (πνεῦμα χριστοῦ) in verse 9c. "Christ in you" in verse 10, as Gordon Fee rightly observes, is not an identification of Christ and the Spirit but rather is "simply Pauline shorthand for 'the Spirit of Christ in you.'"[27] In verse 11 Paul then switches back to speaking about "the Spirit [who] is life" (v. 10) as "the Spirit of the One who raised Jesus from the dead," that is, the Spirit of God the Father:

26. So, rightly, Richard B. Hays, *The Letter to the Galatians*, in *The New Interpreter's Bible*, vol. 9, ed. Leander E. Keck (Nashville: Abingdon, 2000), 283, in light of Phil. 2:5–11; 1 Cor. 8:4–6; etc. Contra James D. G. Dunn, *Christology in the Making: A New Testament Inquiry into the Origins of the Doctrine of the Incarnation*, 2nd ed. (Grand Rapids: Eerdmans, 1996), 38–44. For a succinct discussion, see Richard N. Longenecker, *Galatians*, WBC 41 (Dallas: Word, 1990), 166–75.

27. Gordon D. Fee, *God's Empowering Presence: The Holy Spirit in the Letters of Paul* (Peabody, MA: Hendrickson, 1994), 548. See also Fee's article "Christology and Pneumatology in Romans 8:9–11—and Elsewhere: Some Reflections on Paul as a Trinitarian," in *Jesus of Nazareth: Lord and Christ; Essays on the Historical Jesus and New Testament Christology*, ed. Joel B. Green and Max Turner (Grand Rapids: Eerdmans, 1994), 312–31.

The Spirit (8:9a):
Spirit of God the Father (8:9b)
    Spirit of Christ (8:9c)
    [Spirit of] Christ (8:10)
Spirit of God the Father (8:11)

This linguistic flexibility carries tremendous significance when we remember that for Paul the Spirit of whom he speaks is none other than the Spirit of the God of Israel. That is to say, Paul's reflexive interchanges call forth an understanding of the one Spirit of the Creator God that exhibits the awareness of the Spirit of this God precisely as the Spirit of Christ, experienced as the presence of God, Christ, God in Christ, and so on. The connection, then, is of an inseparable nature such that the Spirit of the God of the OT is now indissolubly bound up with the human figure of the risen Jesus Christ—the Spirit of Christ. It is such inseparability that allows for the reflexive interchange present here in Paul's pneumatological grammar.

Implications

The theological logic of the texts above forces us to reject the widespread position represented by Westermann at its general level and to conclude that there is a necessary and essential connection between the OT and, at least, economic Trinitarian doctrine. This connection is mediated most explicitly through the NT's presupposition and use of the OT—that is, at the point of the unity of the testaments in their testimony to the self-same God in the one divine economy.

The overlapping use of the divine name *kyrios* for the God of Israel and for the human person Jesus Christ within the citations and theological grammar of the OT presses for an identity of subject matter, as does the use of *kyrios* for the Spirit in 2 Corinthians 3:17a (cf. the third article of the Creed of Constantinople). Further, the inseparability of the Spirit's identity as the Spirit "of God" (the Father) and the Spirit "of Christ" (the Son) requires an understanding of the dynamism of the one God of the OT as essentially and formally related to the Spirit of God as the Spirit of the risen Jesus. Thus at the point of the unity of the testaments there is a foundational Trinitarian syntax that informs the pattern of language about the identity of the one Lord God of the OT as the Father, the Son, and the Spirit revealed in the fullness of time in the single divine economy.

Westermann's criticism, however, reaches further than the economic Trinity by specifying the break with the OT in terms of "the question of the relation of the persons of the Trinity to one another, and the question of the divinity and humanity in the person of Christ as a question of ontological relations." Such questions of "being," it is presumed, lie at the heart of Greek philosophical thinking, and the attempt to relate them to the Bible is misleading and distorting (see above). That the Bible is not as explicitly concerned with questions of ontology as is Greek philosophy can be readily observed. It does not necessarily follow, though, that the ontological questions of the relation of the Father, the Son, and the Spirit to each other or the divinity and humanity of the person of Christ leave the Bible, especially the OT, behind. In fact, the exact opposite is the case: *the continuing authority and use of the OT forced such questions to be addressed.*

The NT and early church made claims about the human person Jesus of Nazareth and about the Spirit (see above texts) that required *specification in terms of ontology.* It would not do simply to state the claims (YHWH is somehow both Father and Jesus Christ; the Spirit is somehow inseparably the Spirit of God the Father and of the human person Jesus Christ; there is a Trinitarian pattern of salvation; etc.). The relation of God the Father, Jesus Christ, and the Spirit as well as the relation of Jesus's divinity and humanity had to be specified in terms consistent with the most fundamental theological thrust of the OT, that of the unity and singularity of the one Creator God and the directives for exclusive worship that were inextricably bound with this God's identity. That YHWH (κύριος) is both God the Father and Jesus Christ leads of necessity to the question of "essence," or "being," most acutely at the point of the Christian worship of Jesus Christ. If the OT counts for anything, we cannot worship a mere human (one who is created) instead of, in conjunction with, or over against the one God of the OT. Such worship would mean rank and obvious idolatry, the total denial and destruction of OT monotheism. The early church had to find a way to account for its claims and practice, and such an accounting was necessary along ontological lines because of the continuing authority of the OT. Athanasius saw to the heart of the matter most clearly in terms of the person of Jesus Christ, and Basil the Great in terms of the Holy Spirit: Jesus Christ and the Spirit must be of the same "essence" as God the Father. Then and only then do the claims of the NT make any sense within the framework of an authoritative OT theology.[28] Thus it can be seen that instead of breaking with the OT, the questions of the relation of the persons of the Trinity to one another and of the divinity and humanity of Christ could

28. See, e.g., Athanasius's *Four Discourses against the Arians* and Basil's *On the Holy Spirit*. Geoffrey Wainwright, "The Holy Spirit," in *The Cambridge Companion to Christian Doctrine*, ed. Colin Gunton (Cambridge: Cambridge University Press, 1997), 273–96, sets forth the basic systematic issues with clarity and brevity.

only properly emerge by taking the OT with utmost seriousness in relating the person of Christ and the role of the Spirit to its central theological thrust regarding the identity of the one God. To put it into dogmatic terms: we cannot simply confess an economic Trinity but must also move to specification with respect to the immanent Trinity if the OT is to retain its authoritative witness. Conversely, the OT's affirmations about God and the worship of God force us to make statements about divine ontology in light of the claims of the NT.

We may go one step further yet and assert that the ontological judgments of the early ecumenical creeds were the only satisfying and indeed logical outcome of the claims of the NT read together with the Old. That is to say, for a Christian faith that upholds the unity of the Bible and the continuing authority of the OT, the one God is Trinity in himself, affirmed on the basis of his economic expression. There is no other way to justify the claims about and worship of the fully human Jesus Christ within an OT framework. It is likewise with the Spirit: given the authority of the OT, to recognize the "personhood" of the Spirit in coordination with the claims of the NT regarding the Spirit's inseparability from Jesus Christ in worship and in presence is to affirm that the Spirit, too, is of the "same essence" as the Father and the Son. For the church to turn its back upon the creeds is to turn its back upon the OT. So, too, to turn its back upon the OT is to loosen entirely the restraints that operate in the creedal formulations of the Trinitarian nature of the one Lord God. To speak about the one Lord God of the OT as Father, Son, and Spirit requires that this one God is in fact triune and, conversely, that the Father, the Son, and the Spirit are of one and the same essence with respect to their reality, which, in turn, is the ground of worship.

The Bible and the Trinity: Nature of the Relation

A central point in the argument above has to do with the word "pressure." The pressure language itself is Childs's and, in my view, is one of the most important contributions of his *Biblical Theology* taken as a whole. The biblical text is not inert but instead exerts a pressure ("coercion") upon its interpreters and asserts itself within theological reflection and discourse such that there is (or can be) a profound continuity, grounded in the subject matter itself, between the biblical text and traditional Christian exegesis and theological formulation.[29] Thus, in terms of this essay, the two-testament canon read as one book pressures its interpreters to make ontological judgments about the

29. The pressure of the biblical text can also break apart existing systematic structures,

Trinitarian nature of the one God *ad intra* on the basis of its narration of the act and identity of the biblical God *ad extra*.[30]

Childs speaks about the nature of such pressure from the text in various and suggestive ways (e.g., "reality," "*res*," "subject matter," etc.), but, to my knowledge, he has not formulated the nature of this pressure theologically with precision. My own attempt at such formulation is a first and brief working out of this crucial point of the relation of biblical exegesis and Christian theological tradition.

While the preceding section sought to argue for a substantive and essential connection between the OT and, by necessity, the whole of the Christian Bible with later Trinitarian doctrine, this continuity is not sufficiently understood if we rest content with its demonstration. What exactly is continuous? That is, what specifically is the nature of the relation of the Old and New Testaments to the doctrine of the Trinity? In order to get at these questions, our discussion must assume the posture of explicit theological confession and reflection wherein the biblical text is understood as God's Word to us in which God himself is present.

Within the purview of such a posture the nature of the pressure of the biblical text can be coordinated with the divine will. As Ernst Käsemann wrote in his classic article on the righteousness of God: "God's power . . . is not silent but bound up with the Word. It speaks . . . so that we experience the pressure of its will, and, by means of the Gospel, sets us in the posture . . . 'before the face of Christ.'"[31] Thus the textual pressure we perceive can be theologically formulated in terms of the actuating influence of the divine will through the divine Word. It is in fact the divine will mediated through God's own Word that compels us to speak in Trinitarian terms about God. We may even say that it is the presence of God himself in his Word that wills and moves us to speak in this way about God. "What God speaks . . . is known and true in and through the fact that He Himself says it, that He is present in person in and with what is said by Him."[32] So, finally, Trinitarian language about God on the basis of the pressure of the biblical text is, perhaps mysteriously, God's own

---

but that is a subject for another essay. See Brevard S. Childs, "Toward Recovering Theological Exegesis," *ProEccl* 6, no. 1 (1997): 16–26, esp. 17.

30. The systematic implications are evident at this point: God is as he has revealed himself to be; there is no god lying behind or beyond the God we know in Jesus Christ as attested in scripture, etc.

31. Ernst Käsemann, "'The Righteousness of God' in Paul," in *New Testament Questions of Today* (Philadelphia: Fortress, 1979), esp. 176–77.

32. Barth, *Church Dogmatics* I/1, 137.

testimony to himself as Trinity.[33] Thus the continuity is rooted in God himself, which is to say that the economic expression of God's triunity proceeds from the prior reality of his immanent triunity.

The Bible and the Trinity: Implications for Hermeneutics

In light of the previous two sections of the essay it may seem that the implications for Trinitarian interpretation of the Bible are rather obvious. They are not. At this point I can only add my voice to the summons of Childs and others[34] and affirm that this entire area needs more and deeper reflection, especially from the biblical and exegetical wing of the church. What follows below is an attempt to draw together the implications from the above arguments and thereby indicate a particular path of fruitful theological exegesis.

Perhaps the reader will have realized by now that the central issue in the topic of the Trinity and the Bible requires us to think in two different directions. The question of whether or not there exists a necessary and essential relation between the Old and New Testaments and Trinitarian doctrine focuses our attention in the direction that moves from the Bible to the later Trinitarian formulations. The question of whether or not we can interpret the Bible in light of the later dogma focuses our attention in the reverse direction that moves from the Trinitarian formulations to the Bible. A positive answer to the first question, such as we have given in this essay,[35] does not necessitate a sweeping and unconditional "yes" to the second question. The matter is much more complex.

There are several problems associated with Trinitarian interpretation of the Bible. First, as mentioned above, the historical critics are simply correct that to read the Trinity back into the Old or even into the New Testament as concomitant with the original sense of the text is highly problematic and smooths over the manifest differences in the movement of external historical development. Neither the Priestly writer, nor Isaiah, nor Paul, nor even John

33. Cf. Eberhard Jüngel, *The Doctrine of the Trinity: God's Being Is in Becoming* (Grand Rapids: Eerdmans, 1976), 15, who, in discussing Barth's exposition of the doctrine of the Trinity along the lines of revelation, writes: "The doctrine of the Trinity is the interpretation of God's self-interpretation."

34. See, e.g., the excellent article of David S. Yeago, "The New Testament and Nicene Dogma: A Contribution to the Recovery of Theological Exegesis," *ProEccl* 3 (1994): 152–64.

35. I have sought to explore exegetically this positive connection in relation to Luke's Gospel in "Luke and the Trinity: An Essay in Ecclesial Biblical Theology," *SJT* 56 (2003): 1–26.

thought explicitly in terms of later creedal dogma (we need not even mention the countless literary and textual traditions and developments within scripture that took place over time). Second, the incarnation (and death and resurrection) must actually make a difference for our doctrine of God. This assertion does not introduce any kind of polarity or separation between the Son and the person of Jesus of Nazareth[36] but rather affirms the movement of the biblical narrative and the reality of the two-testament canon wherein the Son of God the Father actually took flesh in a manner not inconsistent but thoroughly self-consistent with his nature and identity, yet in a way that was essentially "new." The unity of the Old and New Testaments is grounded in God himself, the self-same reality to which both testaments bear witness, but the very divine reality himself takes form in a "new" way, and this reality should, then, make a difference for our interpretation of the witness that points to him. Third, such an affirmation regarding the incarnation is at the same time an affirmation of the epistemic priority of the economic Trinity even as it preserves the ontological priority of the immanent Trinity. And herein lies the crux of the issue, dogmatically formulated, in that we must seek to do justice to God's eternal immanent triunity precisely on the basis of his economic expression.

How, then, can we justify Trinitarian interpretation of the Bible? In my judgment, the crucial points are tied to the nature of the pressure of the biblical text and the corresponding question of the divine referent of the words of scripture. On the basis of the exegesis of the biblical texts above, I have argued that scripture exerts a pressure upon its interpreters to understand the God of the entire Bible as the Trinity and that this pressure is felt most acutely at the point of the intersection of the Old and New Testaments. This pressure in every instance relates to the reality of God, which is to say that the claims move from the original sense to the level of ontology. The NT in all its manifold diversity, while affirming its eschatological newness, so to speak, also claims that in the person of Jesus Christ there is none other than the God of the OT, the Creator of the world. Such continuity can be expressed in terms of promise and fulfillment as it relates to the historical sense (cf. Childs) and movement of the testaments from Old to New, but the claims of the New Testament in light of the Old extend to that of God's reality and argue for the other side of a dialectic wherein theology discloses the nature of internal history (cf. the implications of John 1:1–18 as a commentary on Gen. 1–3) so that the interpreter must move also from New to Old. It is the continuity of God's

36. I would affirm that we cannot think of God in abstraction from Jesus Christ and that it is precisely such a truth that requires us to think of an actual incarnation (and vice versa).

reality that not only justifies but necessitates Trinitarian interpretation of the Bible such that the reality to whom the words "YHWH," "Elohim," "Kyrios," "Theos," and so on point is in fact the triune God. Our question, that is, has to do with the *God outside of the text* to whom these words direct us. Thus the historical movement of the Old to New Testaments captured in the terms "promise" and "fulfillment" corresponds to the reverse movement entailed in Trinitarian interpretation, both of which find their ground in the claim of the incarnation regarding the ontological reality of the self-same eternal God as he "became" flesh in the person of the first-century Jew Jesus of Nazareth.

That the pressure of the Bible operates at an ontological level within history corresponds to the nature of this pressure as formulated above in terms of the pressure of the divine will through God's presence in his Word. To interpret the Bible in light of the doctrine of the Trinity does not, therefore, distort its basic content but penetrates to its core with respect to the reality of the divine identity, the living God outside of the text known truly by Israel and fully in Jesus Christ. Such interpretative liberty does not entail a dismissal of the original sense of the text but instead seeks to illuminate the full breadth of ontological reality about which the biblical text, Old and New Testaments together, speaks in its entirety. In this way Trinitarian interpretation of scripture expands the original sense to include questions of ontology in view of the divine referent of the words of scripture and addresses such questions according to scripture's own testimonial pressure, ultimately understood as the *viva vox evangelii*. Thus, to read the Bible in light of later Trinitarian dogma is to read the Bible in light of the reality of God himself as he has pressured us through his Word—that is, his speaking—to speak about him.

Part 2

THE NEW TESTAMENT, GRAMMARS OF LIFE, AND RELIGIOUS COMPARISON

Making Friends and Comparing Lives

What he sees of the human condition, what unseats his reason, is converted into and treated as an intellectual difficulty.[1]

Can rivals over truth be friends? Paul and Seneca, so it was once imagined, became friends.[2] But at least on that imagining they did not see eye to eye and did not resolve their differences. The short letters are replete with personal affection, but looking for philosophical agreement or even substantive exchange will produce only disappointment. Evidently, the author of their correspondence did not think theoretical agreement or even discussion was necessary for friendship. Friendship has affective possibilities, a set of virtues, fruit to bear—and all this in a way that does not finally depend on the dissolution of difference.[3]

1. Cora Diamond, "The Difficulty of Reality and the Difficulty of Philosophy," *Partial Answers: Journal of Literature and the History of Ideas* 1 (2003): 19. She is discussing Stanley Cavell's notion of deflection. Diamond's topic in this essay is not comparison, but her sense of the world's otherness and the corresponding opacity that is part of human knowing/speaking is germane to the questions I raise in this chapter. The essay as a whole has to do with Cavell, his notion of deflection, the novelist J. M. Coetzee, the ability of ordinary language to render (or not) the strangeness and hardness of the world, and how this (im)possibility is connected to our ability to stand and take what frightens us, what shames us, what turns us away, what horrifies us as a species, and so forth.

2. The correspondence is not taken as authentic by any modern scholar. And, in fact, it reads neither like Paul nor like Seneca. But before we are too quick to think the ancients so clumsy, we should remember that it was taken as authentic by no less a textual scholar than Jerome.

3. On the Paul-Seneca correspondence, see Alfons Fürst et al., *Der apokryphe Briefwech-*

"Making Friends and Comparing Lives" was originally published in *The New Testament in Comparison: Validity, Method, and Purpose in Comparing Traditions*, ed. John M. G. Barclay and B. G. White (London: T&T Clark, 2020), 23–40. It is reproduced with permission.

I begin with the imagined friendship between Seneca and Paul because I think we too easily forget that comparison between strong traditions of life asks us what we make of the truth claims of others. It requires us, therefore, to specify what posture of reasoning we take toward them and what the consequences are of our rejection/acceptance. Comparison is finally a question of truth, of relationships, of politics, and thus of practical reason. Which is to say that comparison questions the shape of our existence, both what we've been and what we will become.

The trouble is that the very phenomena that give rise to our projects of comparison can in fact be our undoing. As Cora Diamond puts it in an essay on the "otherness" of reality (quoted earlier), "What [we see] of the human condition, what unseats [our] reason, is converted into and treated as an intellectual difficulty." As we ourselves know, and as the history of scholarship shows, it is all too easy to take claims about existence—this is how to be truly in the world as a human being—and turn them into thoughts about thoughts (this is what to think if you are interested in questions that interest intellectuals). Our reason shows that it has been unseated not because we cease to think about comparison but because we deflect the questioning of philosophy and cease to think about the truth of our lives.

What follows is a theory-light version of what I take to be essential points in any comparative project that deals with traditions of life that claim truth for their way of being in the world. I obviously do not say everything that could be said; indeed, I do not even try. I focus instead on four things you must think about if you are to think well about comparison between traditions that rule each other out in one human life. These four things are: the narrative determination of texts, traditions, and the meaning of words; the significance of incommensurable and non-compossible forms of life; the relation between understanding and opacity; and the posture of reasoning we call friendship and the virtue learned through scholarly study that makes friendship possible through time.[4] The ensuing sections unfold logically in order, but they should be thought dialogically in relation to one another or, in fact, all at once. It is only by taking them whole that one can see why comparison

sel zwischen Seneca und Paulus—Zusammen mit dem Brief des Mordechai an Alexander und dem Brief des Annaeus Seneca über Hochmut und Götterbilder, Sapere 11 (Tübingen: Mohr Siebeck, 2006).

4. Perhaps it goes without saying: you do not necessarily have to think what I think about these points, but if you are interested in "comparison," you will in fact have positions on them and would thus do well to think about them.

is a problem of practical reason and why this matters for what we make of comparative inquiry.[5]

Narrative

In what is arguably one of the great books in twentieth-century ethics, Alasdair MacIntyre enjoins his readers to imagine the following situation:

> I am standing waiting for a bus and the young man standing next to me suddenly says, "The name of the common wild duck is *Histrionicus histrionicus histrionicus*." There is no problem as to the meaning of the sentence he uttered: the problem is, how to answer the question, what was he doing in uttering it? Suppose he just uttered such sentences at random intervals; this would be one possible form of madness. We would render his action of utterance intelligible if one of the following turned out to be true. He has mistaken me for someone who yesterday had approached him in the library and asked: "Do you by any chance know the Latin name of the common wild duck?" *Or* he has just come from a session with his psychotherapist who has urged him to break down his shyness by talking to strangers. "But what shall I say?" "Oh, anything at all." *Or* he is a Soviet spy waiting at a prearranged rendez-vous and uttering the ill-chosen code sentence which will identify him to his contact. In each case the act of utterance becomes intelligible by finding its place in a narrative.[6]

There are, of course, virtually countless other situations one could imagine that would make the man's *histrionicus* utterance make sense. The crucial point for all of them is this: every possible sense-making scenario presupposes a narrative.

To the objection that the action (say) of a man throwing clear liquid on a fire is intelligible without a narrative as the discrete action "putting out fire," MacIntyre could reply with a series of questions that would unearth the narrative(s) we took for granted in reading the action as intelligible: How do you

5. A part of what I will say has strong resonance with the larger argument of *One True Life: The Stoics and Early Christians as Rival Traditions* (New Haven: Yale University Press, 2016), and the rest is either presupposed by that book or follows from it.

6. Alasdair MacIntyre, *After Virtue*, 3rd ed. (Notre Dame, IN: University of Notre Dame Press, 2007), 210.

know that the liquid is water? How do you know that he is putting it out rather than simply controlling the rate of its burn? Answering these and other like questions would immediately show that the action's interpretation depended upon a sequence that gave the action its intelligibility. "I know it's water because I saw the man run to the garden hose and fill his bucket"; "I know he's putting it out because he yelled, 'I have got to put this fire out before it spreads to the dry grass!'" *Or* "I know he's actually not putting the fire out because he told me just now that he wants only to reduce its heat so he can roast some hotdogs for his children." In each case (and others like them), the justification for the intelligibility of the action involves telling a story about how one knows what sort of action the action is. The intelligibility-delivering sequence is inescapably a narrative. Try all we like to find the action's intelligibility elsewhere—in this or that isolated context—and we still will wind up with story.[7] As MacIntyre states, "An action is a moment in a possible or actual history or in a number of such histories."[8]

What MacIntyre's example also shows is that the meaning of the words uttered is tied to the history (and therefore narrative)[9] that makes them make a particular sense. On the face of it, the simple meaning of "the common name . . . *histrionicus*" is clear. But on closer inspection the clarity is only because we have a sense of how to talk that way at all. It may be that we now talk that way for X or Y purpose (if we speak as, e.g., a spy or an ornithologist), but utter that sentence prior to the development of modern scientific classification, and the priority of "meaning-in-light-of-a-particular-history" to "meaning" is immediately evident. Insert it into a first-century text, and the point is even clearer. *Histrionicus histrionicus histrionicus* means no more and no less than what it means in the narrative(s) that tells one what it means.[10]

7. Another way to put this point is to say that one cannot refer back behind story to some other more basic unit of intelligibility. The story just is the thing in itself. "The characterization of actions allegedly prior to any narrative form being imposed upon them will always turn out to be the presentation of what are plainly the disjointed parts of some possible narrative" (MacIntyre, *After Virtue*, 215). This has been recognized in other disciplines as well. See, e.g., the discussion in Lee Hester and Jim Cheney, "Truth and Native American Epistemology," *Social Epistemology* 15 (2001): 319–34. They conclude, "The narrative is as close to the truth as you can get" (332).

8. MacIntyre, *After Virtue*, 214.

9. Recounting the history of scientific classification is narrating—i.e., giving the story of its origins, use, etc.

10. MacIntyre says that there is no problem in the meaning of the sentence; I disagree: there is all the problem in the world with the meaning. Intelligible action and the meaning of the word(s) cannot be divorced. They go together. If while lighting a fire someone says,

Why does this discussion about actions and words matter for thinking about comparison? There are three chief reasons that, when taken together, point toward a crucial feature of all comparative projects.

First, attending carefully to the conceptual order MacIntyre elucidates helps us to understand something crucial about reading (e.g.) Christian and Stoic texts; namely, the very identification of these texts (or fragments thereof) as Christian or Stoic presupposes a narrative that makes a text intelligible as *this* kind of text rather than *that* kind or *that* kind. We use the description "Christian" et cetera because we find the text intelligible in terms of the history/narrative that is the way we think about Christian, Stoic, and so on. Treating the Gospel of Luke or 1 Corinthians as an instance of Christian literature means precisely that we take it to exemplify the Christian narrative that we use to name it as "Christian" in the first place. Arguments about what sort of text an ancient text is—what exactly the Gospel of Philip is, for example—are arguments about the extent to which a text exemplifies the conceptually prior narrative of what it is that we seek instances of. Of course, the narrative we presuppose in locating a text or texts is itself partly dependent on the texts that we try to identify; but just to the extent that we find any particular text to contribute to or be an instance of a tradition of life we read it in light of the narrative that locates it in that tradition.

What this means for comparison is all but obvious: the fact that the identification of this text as a Christian text precedes our comparison—indeed, our interest in comparison rests on this prior identification—means that what is already presumed in the comparison is the narratives that make the comparison make sense as something to do in the first place. At a more comprehensive hermeneutical level, then, when we compare texts, we are not simply comparing Christian text A with Stoic text B (or C, D, etc.) but comparing in light of the narrative that makes text A show up to us as "this specific sort of thing to be compared" with the narrative that makes text B appear to us as "this

"I'm putting out a fire," the understanding is either that the person doesn't know the meaning of "putting out" and wants "lighting" instead or that the action is unintelligible as the action "putting out a fire." I think his comment that we "allocate *conversations* to *genres*, just as we do literary narratives" actually speaks for my point (*After Virtue*, 211; emphasis added). This problem applies to "propositions" of every sort (see Troels Engberg-Pedersen, "The Past Is a Foreign Country: On the Shape and Purposes of Comparison in New Testament Scholarship," in *The New Testament in Comparison: Validity, Method, and Purpose in Comparing Traditions*, ed. John M. G. Barclay and B. G. White, LNTS [London: T&T Clark, 2020], 41–61, and my comment in n. 30 in my response, "Response to Friend-Critics," in part 2 of the present volume).

specific sort of thing to be compared." And what *this* means is that we cannot get to actual comparison without dealing with the narratives that make this particular comparative project or that particular comparative project make sense in the first place.[11]

It is critical to understand that the foregoing discussion about narrative should not be confused with an assumption that traditions are "pure."[12] I do not deny and do not think we should deny that human beings who live in roughly the same time and place share all sorts of things in common, can work together against this or for that or on this and on that, can assent to similar claims (we should render unto Caesar what is his), can read the same books, can play music together, can understand each other in a regular and important way at the bank or supermarket or pagan festival, and so on. As Bernard Williams observes, "Cultures, subcultures, fragments of cultures, constantly meet one another and exchange and modify practices and attitudes. Social practices could never come forward with a certificate saying that they belonged to a genuinely different culture, so that they were guaranteed immunity to alien judgements and reactions."[13] The point is simply that no matter how diverse a tradition, no matter how rich and deep the contestation over what the tradition entails and does not, no matter how much any tradition has in common with the wider culture in which it is embedded, to name a text (e.g.) Christian is to presuppose a narrative about a tradition of which this text is an exemplar. One may, as some scholars were once wont to do, speak of Christianities as

11. This is quite a different thing from the comparison of "motifs" or "myths" that Jonathan Smith works with in the chapter "On Comparing Stories" in his *Drudgery Divine: On the Comparison of Early Christianities and the Religions of Late Antiquity* (Chicago: University of Chicago Press, 1990). Smith's "stories" are really more like extractions and abstractions, the creation of connections that make a story that occurs in the "space of the scholar's mind" (115). They are not the elucidation of the narrative(s) that makes the words make the sense they do in a text under discussion or the narrative that allows us to locate a text in a particular tradition.

12. See, e.g., Elizabeth Agnew Cochran's reply to my criticism of her use of Stoicism, "Bricolage and the Purity of Traditions: Engaging the Stoics for Contemporary Christian Ethics," *JRE* 40 (2012): 720–29.

13. Bernard Williams, *Ethics and the Limits of Philosophy* (Cambridge, MA: Harvard University Press, 1985), 158. From a Christian theological perspective, there are some significant qualifications to at least one part of Williams's point, viz., the church does claim that it is in some way a genuinely new "culture." Obviously, its newness takes shape in time and space and is therefore bound up with the social realities of which it was and is a part. But the claim is that its inception—as with the election of the people of Israel—is based on God's prior, founding act.

an attempt to avoid notions of pure traditions (or "orthodoxy"). But this only reinforces the point: at least as the grammar—and therefore thought—runs, Christianities are diverse instances of some larger and presupposed tradition called Christianity. If this were not so, you would not know what to call them or would call them something else. Speaking of Christianities means that you evaluate them in light of a narrative that tells you what to call them. Without the narrative, you would not have the language to use that you actually use.[14] The question of purity is a distraction; nothing human is pure. The question is whether there is a tradition or not. If there is, you have a narrative.[15]

Second, and relatedly, understanding the narrative conditions for intelligible actions and sentence meaning means that focusing on what we might call weight-bearing words—words that are meant to be productive points of thought in comparative projects—is but another way of asking what narrative it is that enables us to know how to understand them and relate them to their occurrence in other texts. The occurrence of *pneuma*, *sōma*, *psychē*, *sarx*, *theos*, *autarkē*, *prohairesis*, and so forth in multiple texts from different traditions tells us nothing about either similarity or difference but only that we need to think about the way the words figure in the narrative that gives their sense within the tradition to which the text belongs. Professional biblical scholars, of course, have known at least since James Barr's withering critique of Kittel's *Wörterbuch* that words do not mean anything in themselves but mean only in the context of other words.[16] The point at this juncture goes well beyond Barr: "context" is not simply an immediate textual phenomenon—though it is doubtless that—but is finally the narrative we presuppose in understanding

14. Of course, this does not mean that any given scholar is aware of the narrative presupposition of the classification of texts. The point, rather, is that it is there whether one is aware of it or not. Another way to put it is this: the singular is conceptually prior to the plural (this would be true also for those who wish to speak of multiple narratives rather than a singular story).

15. There will always be the question of the boundaries of a tradition—when, e.g., a text or group ceases to be or never was a part of a specific tradition. My assumption about this question is rather simple: by and large, this sort of thing is a matter of ongoing dispute, disagreement, and discovery. But none of the fuzziness about boundaries erases the basic fact that a tradition itself can be seen. Wittgenstein puts the point in relation to the elasticity of word meaning. It is not a defect, he says, that many words don't have a strict meaning. To "think it is would be like saying that the light of my reading lamp is no real light at all because it has no sharp boundary" (*The Blue and Brown Books* [New York: Harper & Row, 1958], 27). On tradition as a "singular" thing, see my comments in my response, "Response to Friend-Critics," in part 2 of this volume.

16. James Barr, *The Semantics of Biblical Language* (Oxford: Oxford University Press, 1961).

a word's history and use. Words, no less than actions, are moments in a narrative or a history. When we say things such as "this is a Stoic word" or "that is a specifically Christian word," we mean that "this word finds its meaning in the Stoic/Christian narrative or history." And when we discern similarity or difference or both, what we discern is not most fundamentally similarity/difference in the "concepts" that go with the words but similarity or difference in the way the stories tell what the words mean.

Third, precisely because of the connection between intelligible actions and the sense that words make, the meaning of words is finally a lived meaning. Which is to say something like this: it is one thing to say that 4 is the answer to 2 + 2 for each and every human being who adds 2 to 2;[17] it quite another to say that your life will be transformed if you live certain words. "If you confess with your mouth and believe in your heart that Jesus is Lord," *sōtēria* will be yours (Rom. 10:9). "Practise the truth," says Seneca, and "despise death" (*Epistles* 98.17; 78.5). Words such as these are intelligible not in abstraction from the actions that show forth what they mean but in the context of a human life whose actions make these words intelligible in human existence. "Knowledge" of the meaning of words is finally, then, a "narrative of a life lived in the world."[18]

In sum, attending to the role that narrative plays in the connection between actions, words, and human life leads to the rather pedestrian but crucial insight that projects of comparison are simply swimming in narrative. Comparative work that attempts to get away from or ignores the narrative structure of its work is always self-deceived. When we engage in comparing ancient texts, we engage in narrative reasoning. Indeed, as MacIntyre puts it, "Narrative is not the work of poets, dramatists and novelists reflecting upon events which had no narrative order before one was imposed by the singer or the writer." He continues: "Narrative form is neither disguise nor decoration. Barbara Hardy has written that 'we dream in narrative, day-dream in narrative, remember, anticipate, hope, despair, believe, doubt, plan, revise, criticize, construct, gos-

17. Although this truth does not tell us why anyone would be counting in particular. For that, we need a narrative; i.e., to understand the action "counting" or "adding" we need the same sort of thick narrative understanding as we do to understand *Histrionicus histrionicus histrionicus*.

18. Lee and Cheney, "Truth and Native American Epistemology," 331. Many writers have long known this, of course, even in the "bestseller" genre. Among recent ones from that class, see James Rebanks's remarkable book about life as a shepherd in the valleys of the Lake District, *The Shepherd's Life: Modern Dispatches from an Ancient Landscape* (New York: Flatiron Books, 2015): "We are, I guess, all of us, built out of stories" (80).

sip, learn, hate and love by narrative.'"[19] If MacIntyre and Hardy are right—and they are—the question for comparative projects whose modus operandi is the discernment of similarity/difference is: How do we agree and/or disagree in narrative? What is (dis)agreement?

Disagreement and Difference

One of the more obvious features of comparative projects is the focus on the potential agreement/disagreement and on similarity/difference between the things being compared. What is less obvious is the way in which we might actually know agreement/disagreement and similarity/difference when we see it. What is it to agree/disagree? What is it to differ?

For our purposes, we shall focus on only three of the many dimensions of this question. First, as Donald Davidson, Jeffrey Stout, and others argued, there are the sorts of disagreements that presuppose a set of shared agreements. It is these agreements that form the background against which the disagreements make sense. When in US government Democrats and Republicans bitterly disagree over the precise political meaning of democracy, they nevertheless share a complex cluster of agreements that make their disagreements intelligible as disagreements (e.g., a nonviolent transfer of the presidency every four to eight years, the right to vote members of Congress in or out every few years, the electoral system as a whole, the bicameral nature of Congress, the process for appointing Supreme Court justices, and so on). Or when Paul and the apostles and elders in Jerusalem attempted to work out a way for Christian Jews and Christian Gentiles to worship and eat together, Paul may well have differed from Peter, James, and others on many things, but their disagreements were disagreements within a shared commitment to Jesus of Nazareth as God's Messiah, to the authoritative role of Israel's scriptures, to the rejection of pagan idolatry, to the importance of public witness, and to many other things besides.

In short, there is a sort of disagreement where something(s) must be shared in order for *disagreement* to characterize what it is that is occurring. Having an argument, on this view, is actually a remarkable achievement. An argument means that you share enough to recognize on similar or the same terms as your disputant what the disagreement entails. One may or may not be able to resolve

19. MacIntyre, *After Virtue*, 211. Cf. Bernard Williams, "Life as Narrative," *European Journal of Philosophy* 17 (2007): 305–14.

the disagreement to each party's satisfaction, but in principle the disagreement is grounded in a deeper (set of) agreement(s). Without such agreements, there is no disagreement; you are simply talking about something else.

Of course, sometimes one actually is talking about something else. So, second, there is a sort of difference that on the face of it appears to be a disagreement but on closer inspection requires a more nuanced and difficult description. Such differences are commonly characterized as incommensurable. There is no shared agreement or standard of evaluation such that the difference could be dissolved or resolved as it (in principle) could be with a straightforward disagreement. There are many ways to illustrate incommensurability. The most helpful for thinking about comparison for the thrust of this essay, however, is the sort that Bernard Williams calls incommensurable "forms of life" (or "cultures").[20]

To get at the incommensurability of different forms of life, Williams draws an analogy with scientific theories.

> Some philosophers of science hold that scientific theories may be incommensurable with one another because they differ in the concepts they use, the reference they give to various terms, and what they count as evidence. These theories will not straightforwardly contradict one another. Yet they do exclude one another. If they did not, there would be no difficulty in combining them, as one can combine the topography of separate places. They cannot be combined. . . . Some radical philosophers of science will say that you cannot combine the two theories merely because you cannot combine accepting both theories: the research activities characteristic of each theory, the direction of attention appropriate to each, and so on, cannot be combined. You cannot work within both of them.[21]

Williams actually thinks this is a "wild exaggeration" when it comes to the history of science, but "a story of this kind may be appropriate to what really are different cultures or forms of life" (157). The outlook and lived possibilities of one "society might to an important extent be incommensurable with that of another, but they would still exclude one another. The conflict would lie in what was involved in living within them" (158–59). The different forms

20. The immediate connection between Williams's language of form of life or culture and the term "tradition of life" should be self-evident.

21. Williams, *Ethics and the Limits of Philosophy*, 157. Hereafter, page references appear in the text.

of life, as he puts it earlier, would each "track the truth" but in different and incommensurable ways (143). But how, we might wonder, could different, incommensurable forms of life each track the truth?

Truth here for Williams does not mean what an analytical observer would find true according to the standards of his philosophical investigations. It is, rather, tied directly to the form of life that determines how inquiry is conducted and what the thick concepts are that enable people to "find their way around in a social world." "Granted the way that the people [in a certain form of life] have gone about their inquiries, it must be no accident that the belief they have acquired is a true one, and if the truth on the subject had been otherwise, they would have acquired a different belief, true in those different circumstances" (142–43). Assuming one has the cultural and numerical sense relative to the example, a rolled die that comes up 6 would be taken as a 6 and not something else, a 4 as a 4 and not something else, a 2 as a 2 and not something else, and so on.[22] To track the truth is thus to think and live what is true within the form of life whose patterns make truth what it is and comes to be for those who live it.[23]

If, then, there are forms of life that are incommensurable—and there were and are—and there is difference over what truth is—and there was and is—that difference is irresolvable. One cannot decide what is really true. There is no shared standard of measurement, as it were, that would enable each form of life's truth to be measured, evaluated, decided upon.[24] (The notion that one

22. The assumption this sentence names is indispensable to this "rough" illustration, as Williams notes: "Perhaps I cannot read four dots as 4, though I can read six dots as 6. What if I can only read six dots as 6, and everything else as not 6?" (218, n. 10). One could, moreover, think a die any number of things other than an object whose rolls turn up numbers. The point is that tracking the truth in this example depends not only on an accurate reading of the number that comes up but also on the whole complex cluster of things that goes into interpreting the roll of a die as a roll of a die at all. One tracks the truth of the number but only because one knows how the whole thing works, as it were.

23. Williams's description of tracking the truth bears striking resemblance to Lee Hester and Jim Cheney's conception of "responsible truth" as the sort of truth that *just is* truth in some Native American epistemology. See their "Truth and Native American Epistemology."

24. This obviously raises all kinds of difficult questions about knowledge vis-à-vis scientific truth, etc. Williams deals with these matters fairly well. Most thinkers would see some sort of significant difference between scientific knowledge and strong traditions that claim truth for their way of life. It's true, e.g., that the sun is a giant ball of hydrogen gas (more or less) whether a certain group of "traditional" people think this or not. It may equally be true that the sun is an integral part of God's way of creating a life-sustaining planet in our solar system. But this second truth is of a different sort than the first. It does not, e.g., entail a particular position on the sun's chemical composition.

could stand outside a form of life and judge its truth is simply a *reductio*: the standard of truth by which you judge the other's truth is the truth of your own form of life—and so on ad infinitum . . .) As Williams explains with reference to particular actions, however, for confrontation, collision, and even rejection to occur between incommensurable forms of life it is not necessary that the "parties conceptualize in the same way the actions in question . . . [indeed] they will not do so." One culture's religious truth takes it, say, that human sacrifice is a necessary part of maintaining the balance of cosmic power and practices accordingly; another culture has no such truth and sees this practice as a "deliberate killing of a captive" (158). There is no way to debate or negotiate the meaning of the action on culturally independent grounds. To understand the meaning of the action is to understand the culture; to change the meaning of the action is to change the culture. And yet they conflict.

Williams's example characterizes well this central feature of incommensurable ways of being true: confrontation, collision, clash. Note, too, the way in which Williams's example illustrates MacIntyre's point about intelligible action: there is no such thing as human "sacrifice" per se; for one, this is the practice that tracks religious truth; for another, it is murder. The practice itself is the enactment of a religious or ethical narrative that goes with a form of life, a culture, a tradition. Reading Williams and MacIntyre together, that is, helps us to see how incommensurability in the living of life is inseparably tied to the stories that make sense of the lives that we live.[25]

Taking seriously confrontation and collision as a way to describe the encounter of incommensurable difference(s) leads to the third important feature of difference or disagreement—namely, whether the collision is primarily notional or lived. Williams once again: a lived confrontation between two outlooks "occurs at a given time if there is a group of people for whom each of the outlooks is a real option." By "real option" Williams means primarily a socially dense possibility whereby one could "go over" to the confronting outlook and "live inside it in their actual historical circumstances and retain their hold on reality, not engage in extensive self-deception, and so on" (160–61). A "notional confrontation, by contrast, occurs when some people know about two divergent outlooks, but at least one of those outlooks does not present a real option" (160). The lives, for example, of a "Bronze Age chief or a medieval samurai are not real options for us: there is no way of living them" (160). A notionally divergent outlook may call into question all sorts of current commitments,

25. Incommensurability is not reducible to story but is tied inseparably to it.

practices, arguments, and so forth, but the result of such questioning could never be to inhabit the outlook that produced the questioning.

Taking note of the difference between notional and lived confrontation helps underline the difficult and dramatic nature of a confrontation that demands a decision about the truth of the sort of life that can and will be lived from the point of confrontation.[26] When this sort of confrontation is rooted in disagreement, the decision can in principle be made on the basis of the resolution of disagreement. When, however, the confrontation over a true life is rooted in incommensurable difference, the decision cannot be made on the basis of resolution. There is no ground on which the resolution could happen. Roman Stoicism and early Christianity, for example, do rule each other out as life options, but they do not straightforwardly contradict each other as they would if they shared enough agreements about the words *theos*, *cosmos*, and so forth to differ only in their explication. Their difference over the true life is incommensurable difference. It is the difference of different stories by which life is lived, or—in reverse—it is the difference of the lives by which the stories are existentially told.[27]

Irresolvable existential confrontations over truth—those confrontations that simply by posing the question demand a judgment one way or the other with the life you live—are in my view the sort that are the most interesting for the question of "comparison." This is precisely because it is unclear how you could really compare them. How, then, might we understand existentially confrontational difference?

Opacity and Understanding

"Understanding" has of course been a subject of perennial philosophical interest. I cannot claim to understand the history of understanding or of understanding understanding. Nevertheless, there is a critical point about understanding irresolvable confrontations over true lives that bears directly on our thinking about comparison.

At first glance, of course, understanding does not appear all that difficult: if you understand this sentence, you know what understanding is even if you

26. For MacIntyre, this sort of confrontation has the possibility of an "epistemological crisis." For a description and evaluation of his notion, see Rowe, *One True Life*, 249–58.

27. There isn't a way to join the two stories or to go behind them to tell one story that encompasses them both.

do not have a rich theory of human understanding in general. Reading ancient texts, in this simplified sense, is not much different from reading this sentence. If there is enough of a context, and if you have some general working knowledge of the assumptions that the text makes use of, you can, if the words are clear enough, understand it. Pick up and read. Or at least: study, pick up, and read.

But what if upon studying, picking up, and reading one discovers that one does not understand what one is reading? This experience, too, presumes some understanding: you understand that you do not understand. But what exactly is it that you understand that you do not understand?

There are of course multiple and often interpenetrating answers to such questions (e.g., you do not know the original language of the text you're reading and therefore cannot see how the words run; or you are unfamiliar with the key weight-bearing terms of the text). But the principal scholarly answer we tend to give today is rooted in what is "implicit in the work of all scholars in the humanities"—namely, the correlation between the belief in the translucifying power of universal reason and the practice of study. The "faith that such understanding is, in principle, possible is a normative assumption as well as a hopeful one." The scholar's "daily business is to make strange goings-on—the historically or culturally distant traces of human activities—more familiar."[28] Which is to say that we don't understand because we don't yet know enough to understand. Understanding is what we increase by acquiring knowledge. Learn a little more, and we understand a little more. Understanding, in this way of looking at things, is not an either/or but a more and a less, a spectrum along which one is positioned relative to the knowledge one has acquired through training and study. More and less, well and poorly; this is the grammar of scholarly understanding.[29]

28. These citations are from Jeffrey Stout, "Commitments and Traditions in the Study of Religious Ethics," *JRE* 25 (1997): 23–56. In "Beyond Compare: or: Some Recent Strategies for Not Comparing Early Christianity with Other Things," in Barclay and White, *New Testament in Comparison*, 79–94, Matthew V. Novenson borrows this citation to agree with Stout, but Novenson's actual argument does not make clear why he does, nor does he appear to recognize that Stout's position here is taken in relation to his pragmatic sense of what we're up to (not because it must be metaphysically the case that understanding works like this).

29. One could perhaps speak of "the comparative enterprise in modes appropriate to the academy's self-understanding," though in truth there is no such thing as the academy's self-understanding, as if the academy is a thinking thing with a self or as if there is an intellectual-employment context whose rules are known and accepted by all who work there. There are only academicians, and these have a wide range of different understandings of their comparative work. The cited phrase is from Smith, *Drudgery Divine*, vii.

The problem with this way of thinking about understanding is not that it does not apply to many things we seek to understand; indeed, it clearly and demonstrably does. The problem is that it leaves out a whole range of the experience of being human.

Gadamer once wrote that the "finite nature of one's own understanding is the manner in which reality, resistance, the absurd, and the unintelligible assert themselves. If one takes this finitude seriously, one must take the reality of history seriously as well."[30] Hermeneutics was for Gadamer the science not only of understanding but of opacity, particularly as opacity was rooted in the pre-reflective condition that is the human being's finitude and in the unconquerable otherness of life.[31] It seems to me that much that is assumed in the premise of the humanist understanding is in the nature of the thing committed to denying what Gadamer asserts. But it is Gadamer who makes the deeper and better point. Finitude, historicity, opacity: these are the necessary experience of human thought and understanding. There is no rule—metaphysical, logical, hermeneutical, or otherwise—that entails or implies the intelligibility of all forms or traditions of human life. By contrast, finitude is a fact. In at least one utterly stunning and profoundly significant way, it offers permanent, recalcitrant resistance to humanist claims about the translucifying power of universal reason: where we encounter traditions or forms of life that claim "living" is necessary to "understanding," we at once discover the boundary—and concomitant opacity—placed on reason and study by time and death. To understand we must live; to live we must have time; but we cannot live different "understanding lives" at the same time.[32] In Diamond's way of putting it, reality resists and exceeds our ability to think it; we cannot get our lives across and over into another life to think it without taking ourselves with us.[33] Or, to

30. Hans-Georg Gadamer, *Truth and Method*, 2nd ed. (New York: Continuum, 1996), xxxv.

31. Hermeneutics thus names not so much a "methodology but a theory of the real experience that thinking is" (Gadamer, *Truth and Method*, xxxvi).

32. We do not have the time before we die to live more than one life. Indeed, you might say that at least one of the most important things death does is to call you to account for, or at least provide closure-like commentary on, the one life you've lived.

33. See her "The Difficulty of Reality and the Difficulty of Philosophy." An example: one of the participants at the conference (I cannot now recall which one) said that the Stoics have "God" as their companion. For this, I can think of Seneca's "God in/with you" language or Epictetus's pious language (prayer, etc.) or Cleanthes's hymn—or many other statements—and "understand" what is meant. But when I read Epictetus and think that I understand what he, too, means, I then realize that I don't know what he really means by "pray to God," for example, because I cannot pray like he can. The way he uses *theos* is closest to what I

make this same point differently, we could say that our bodies are necessary to understanding. The understanding intellect qua intellect is an abstraction; there is only the I that reasons as long as it is bodily alive. Denying the limits that time and death place on reason involves a corresponding denial of bodily life.[34] In short, the historicity of understanding is connected most deeply to the humanity of understanding: not only to when and where we live but also and always to the time it takes to live from birth to death.[35]

If the premise of understanding in the humanities is "study something long enough and you will understand it," my question in light of the humanity of understanding is thus: What if the longer you study something, the more you understand that you do not understand it because you discover that it is calling you to live in a certain way of life, to become a different sort of person—that understanding in this deeper sense would mean becoming what you are being summoned to become—and you say *no*? The door to that becoming is then closed, and you are shut out. How do you take people seriously who live on the other side of a door that is closed to you? If you're shut out, why read their texts? If you nevertheless do read, what are you doing when you try to read what they have written?[36]

---

think of with *kosmos* or *ktisis*, and, in my understanding, this makes no sense to pray to. I have not ever prayed to the world/creation and do not believe in its inherent sublimity or the divine grain of nature (etc.); so I finally think that I do not really "understand" in a thick sense what "pray to God" means in a thick sense for Epictetus. Does pray mean think hard about? Concentrate on the idea of? Talk to? To what? Expect an answer from? From what? and so on and on. In my view, this sort of dynamic is often left out of scholarly discourse, but it is critically important for how we think about understanding other traditions, about the ancient world, and about the use of words in texts.

34. See also Stanley Hauerwas, "Bearing Reality: A Christian Meditation," *Journal of the Society of Christian Ethics* 33 (2013): esp. 6–10.

35. The attempt to transcend existential unintelligibility (we cannot understand with our lives, *in* our lives, another strong tradition of life that claims that understanding is a sort of becoming, or is inextricably bound with a becoming) is an attempt to transcend finitude, or to transcend reflection's inevitable and inexpungable historicity. I think, to say it slightly differently, that the hermeneutic assumptions of certain modes of scholarly discourse entail a denial of a significant part of the experience of being human, a denial of the limits of animated dust.

36. The language of summoning, of becoming, of saying no or yes, of being shut out, and so on raises the question of "conversion." The wager—in the Pascalian and Kierkegaardian sense—of the convert is the existential correlate of human finitude. Try as you might, you cannot find criteria "outside" your life or "before" your living of it that can or will justify your life as the right, rational—indeed, true—one to live (especially vis-à-vis the remarkably wide range, diverse, and different sets of criteria that allegedly exist). MacIntyre et al. worry about

A Scholarly Work: Friendship and Patience

What are we doing if we are reading things that require for their "understanding" a life that we will not or cannot live—if the kind of conflict or incommensurability between traditions of life is existentially thick? My argument is that we are not doing what we typically think but something much more important, and, further, that to treat comparative inquiry as a predominantly theoretical question is to make a fundamental mistake, that of thinking of comparison as something other than the work of practical reason.

In a generous review of *One True Life*, Professor Teresa Morgan notes that the limitations placed on our knowledge of strong traditions by the fact that we do not or will not live them raise serious questions:

> [Rowe's] conclusion, that the possibilities of comparative scholarship are severely limited, articulates one of the central paradoxes of research in the humanities and social sciences. He might have gone further and shown why, given the inevitable limits of empathy, researchers (including himself) continue to investigate cultures and systems of thought not their own. No scholarly account of another culture is perfect, but there is no reason to think that reaching an understanding of other world views is impossible. One might argue that it is essential. If we cannot at least try to understand other philosophies, societies or religions, what point is there in research? What hope is there for the world?[37]

this as a "criterionless choice" in the face of reason's workings. But his worry, rather than his argument against it, is the right position: there is no reason or pattern of reasoning that can justify your life from your thought. Of the various conversions that have been written about, one of the more interesting ones for my purpose here is that of Georg Lukács to Marxism (see the treatment in Alasdair MacIntyre, *Edith Stein: A Philosophical Prologue 1913–1922* [New York: Rowman & Littlefield, 2006], esp. 153–61). Lukács was initially persuaded that Weber's account of the modern world as "disenchanted" was right and the consequences for work and life inescapable (the severing of soul and work, the reduction of "value" to the smallness of private life, and so on). When he began to wonder if Weber's account was of things only as they seem but not as they truly are, Lukács discovered that he could not actually answer this question without becoming a different type of person. He, like other inhabitants of modernity, was imprisoned within Weber's picture and could not think his way out. So he became something else, a Marxist (of a particular type). It was only from a different existential vantage point that he could understand how Weber was wrong. On the case for Marxism as a "religion"—or at least what we moderns usually mean by this term—see Paul Griffiths, *Problems of Religious Diversity* (Oxford: Blackwell, 2001).

37. Teresa Morgan, "Becoming Christian," review of *One True Life*, by C. Kavin Rowe, *Tablet*, September 15, 2016.

The connection between research and hope for the world is explicit in Professor Morgan's questions. The unarticulated assumption, I think, is that understanding other cultures or "world views" will somehow lead to a better world. The full thought, then, is something like this: academics contribute to a better world through their research because such research enables us to understand others better and such understanding, in turn, leads to—or is a condition of, or productive of—more harmonious relations between people (presumably in the sense of less violence, less bigotry, less barbaric treatment of people whom we now understand to be something other than barbarians and thus worthy of humane treatment, conversation, and so forth).

Professor Morgan's commitment to the human good of research gets to the heart of what comparison of religious traditions might be for—the wider purpose of scholarly work within the human lives that even the most absent-minded scholars actually have to live. For this she is to be commended and her thought welcomed. In contrast to Professor Morgan, however, I see no essential connection between academic study of other traditions (or anything else) and more humane relations. Indeed, there is no reason in principle to rule out the possibility that the more you study another form of life, the more you may come to dislike it, find it completely odious, wish it had never existed, and want it to go away.[38] More and better research does not intrinsically mean more and better human sympathies and consequent action. Research on others may, of course, play some role in a much wider ethical stance toward those others, but it may not, and it may even deepen or increase the problems of alienation it allegedly addresses. Grasping this point is critical because it helps to expose the enormous hope we academics place in the work of understanding itself.[39] If we can understand, we have hope.

38. Examples where academic study is said to lead to more humane relations are exactly and only cases where this is alleged to have happened. The actual causal link between study and behavior is impossible to demonstrate. It could easily be rather that the scholar was really nice and the adherents of the tradition being studied happened to have among their current number some very kind and generous people—and the two sides, as it were, were able to get along in the plain human sense of getting along well together. Had the academic and the tradition's representatives been of different temperaments, it could have gone otherwise. But let us grant that somehow we could establish a causal relation between research and hope for the world in the form of better human action in any (or, in fact, every) case: simply because it has gone this way one time, or multiple times, or even always in the past does not mean it would go that way tomorrow or the next day or, indeed, ever again. It is always possible for things to go differently.

39. Reading Prof. Morgan's statement suggests the thought that without being able to place our hope for more humane relations in the work of understanding, it is pointless to

Alas, the work of understanding cannot bear this hope. Indeed, as I argued earlier, when it comes to lived traditions of truth, the work of understanding is better described as a becoming, and we cannot become something we will not or cannot become or do not have time to become. I thus think of the purpose of comparative inquiry quite differently.

Charles Taylor's view that "the great challenge of this century [twenty-first] is understanding the other" sounds about right.[40] But it is not. The greatest challenge is how to understand our lack of understanding another—since this lack will not go away, since we cannot simply overcome it with more and more and more understanding—and, further, how in the face of such lack we can allow others to remain truly other, others whose lives of truth we challenge or reject simply by the fact that we go another, quite different way in the world and locate our lives by stories that are not theirs. What practices and habits do we need, say, to take the pagan as the pagan and not, say, as an implicit Christian or anonymous liberal democrat who just does not yet know his true desire to live in light of the common good or to protect the inalienable rights he has yet to discover exist—or whatever set of character traits we would most like to assign to the people we would most like to have in the world with us?[41]

Rather than continuing to hope that we can escape the barriers placed on understanding by our bodily existence in time and death, I suggest that friendship is the best reasonable answer to hermeneutical and existential opacity.[42] In his book on the role and importance of practical reason for public dispute and common life, Eugene Garver notes, with Aristotle, that treating a practical problem as a purely technical one can be an ethical error.[43] Virtues and vices are at work in our understanding of and judgments about others' reasoning. To neglect the ethics of reasoning is not, so Garver argues, to attain clearer or

do research on other traditions at all. This kind of "hope in or don't do it" is understandable but also unnecessary.

40. Charles Taylor, "Understanding the Other: A Gadamerian View of Conceptual Schemes," in *Dilemmas and Connections* (Cambridge, MA: Belknap Press of Harvard University Press, 2011), 24–38.

41. I am very suspicious of attempts at dialogue, etc., that wind up meaning that other people are not as serious about their lives—and the claim to truth that goes with their lives—as they seem to believe that they are. And so I am interested to think as well as possible about questions of otherness in ways that preserve a certain amount of opacity or resistance to cosmopolitan understanding.

42. The word "reasonable" in the sentence to which this note is attached is meant literally: friendship is a posture of practical reason.

43. Eugene Garver, *For the Sake of Argument: Practical Reasoning, Character, and the Ethics of Belief* (Chicago: University of Chicago Press, 2004), 10ff.

purer reasoning about others' reasoning but is instead to neglect the basic way we reason at all—thus essentially distorting not only what is going on in the reasoning of those whom we seek to understand but also our own. By contrast, paying attention to the habits and dispositions that form part of what reasoning is requires us to specify what we need to become in order to engage richly with those with whom we do not or cannot agree or those whose lives we do not or will not live. What we need to become, says Garver, is friends. Friendship is the human relational pattern of sustained, intellectually productive conflict—especially, one might say, when the conflict is rationally irresolvable.[44]

Friendship, after all, does not require theoretical understanding for its practice. Moreover, it aims at truth[45]—not the sort of shared truth that is a product of agreement about "content-full morality" or anything so grand, but the sort of relational, friendly truth that emerges from truth-telling about the conditions that make our lives. We might speak here of a kind of understanding: we understand one another as friends do, even if the grammars of our traditions remain grammars of conflict and summons. Paul and Seneca could, after all, write letters to each other, or so someone who understood friendship across traditions knew how to imagine.

As the reference to Paul and Seneca should remind us, friendship was of course a topic of extensive discussion in the ancient world, too.[46] What is

44. Garver argues that modern democracies are insufficiently "ambitious" in their attempt to make the right sort of space for human flourishing precisely because they too easily abandon friendship for justice (passim). Aiming for justice does not ipso facto require the virtues and practices that go with friendship—trust, for example, and truth telling. But, according to Garver, it is precisely these kinds of things that politics needs for human beings to flourish. Attention to virtues and vices is what is missing in Prof. Barclay's suggestion that comparison of the sort he outlines might just be the critical prompting of the Spirit. It is true that it might work that way. After all, as Barth famously said, God can speak even through a dead dog (*Church Dogmatics* I/1, 2nd ed. [Edinburgh: T&T Clark, 1975], 55: "Russian Communism, a flute concerto, a blossoming shrub, or a dead dog"). But the point is that it *might* or might *not*. How would we know? Situating comparative work within a wider context of virtue and vice makes clear that the effort to put scholarly comparison to work in certain ways—prompting self-criticism, ameliorating hostility between religious traditions, etc.—is often merely *assertion* or wishful thinking about its good. It certainly does not ipso facto "*create* the capacity for self-criticism, and thus the ability for a tradition to change" (John M. G. Barclay, "'O Wad som Pow'r the giftie gie us, To see oursels as others see us!': Method and Purpose in Comparing the New Testament," in Barclay and White, *New Testament in Comparison*, 21; emphasis added). I take comparison to be a good, but I'm able to specify it as a good only within a wider context of virtue and vice, viz., as a way practical reason deals with human difference (friendship).

45. Garver, *For the Sake of Argument*, 43 et passim.

46. For an excellent study that traces "friendship" from Homeric Greece to the Chris-

missing from the discussion as a whole is an emphasis on patience as a (the?) central practice that makes friendship possible through time.[47] Indeed, patience is the requisite virtue for becoming and being friends with those who are and will remain opaque to you precisely because it is what enables you to take the time it requires to become friends with strangers.[48] You can, I think, learn to be friends with people who have different schemes of life—and when

---

tians in the fourth and fifth centuries and argues that ancient friendships were much more like modern ones than has been thought in recent scholarship, see David Konstan, *Friendship in the Classical World* (Cambridge: Cambridge University Press, 1997). For studies that relate friendship to NT texts, see the essays in John Fitzgerald, ed., *Friendship, Flattery, and Frankness of Speech: Studies in the New Testament World* (Leiden: Brill, 1996); and Fitzgerald, ed., *Greco-Roman Perspectives on Friendship* (Atlanta: Scholars Press, 1997).

47. From the world of late antiquity, St. Augustine is the outstanding exception. See his remarkable little work *On Patience.*

48. And, for Christians, to love your enemies. Of course, we need a whole lot more than patience to love our enemies. For example, a commitment not to kill them. If we are patient and if we refuse to kill when things would suggest killing is the best (or even least bad) option, then we have all the time we need to work on being friends—even in and through times of great antipathy. Friendship then turns out to resist and substitute for violence. In her essay "On Comparing, and Calling the Question," in Barclay and White, *New Testament in Comparison*, Margaret Mitchell faults me for not saying enough in *One True Life* about Christian violence (n. 109). I did deal with this question in much more detail in *World Upside Down*, but one cannot cover everything satisfactorily in each book. Here is the main suggestion for Christians to realize their vocation not to kill: become nonviolent. A second suggestion: embrace just war. In my view, there is no other Christian option than these two. To the extent that we have practiced otherwise, we have betrayed Jesus and our vocation. Mitchell's implicit suggestion—that there is a traceable connection between the commitment to traditioned reason and military action and its cousins—is a common feature, of course, of a certain modern narrative about politics and religion, and it often goes with an appeal to the purported pax-making capacities of liberal democracies. That narrative, however, is best understood not as a demonstrable truth about the political effect of serious religious commitment but as the legitimation of modern nation-states and their "right" to use force to ensure that no one outside their sphere of justified force can legitimately use force. For a helpful introduction to the larger question of narratives about politics and religion in modernity and the way in which they bear on this particular point, see William T. Cavanaugh, *The Myth of Religious Violence* (New York: Oxford University Press, 2009). For sophisticated arguments that include robust religious commitments within the practices of liberal democracy—rather than pitting them against one another, as Rorty did, for example—see Jeffrey Stout's *Democracy and Tradition* (Princeton: Princeton University Press, 2004) and *Blessed Are the Organized: Grassroots Democracy in America* (Princeton: Princeton University Press, 2010). Stout himself is not religious, of course, but he recognizes, among many other crucial things, the indispensability of tradition for thought and practice and sees clearly that religious sensibilities often work to counter the oppression and violence that are endemic to political life within even the best of liberal democracies.

the conflict between you is existential and irresolvable—but to be true friends with them you have to learn to be patient. How can you learn patience if you are an academic? You take the time and effort it requires to study extensively a strong tradition of truth that you do not understand and cannot or will not live, and you grant to that concomitant existential opacity a certain kind of integrity—that is, that lives that are not yours are still as serious about their lives as you are about yours.[49]

"Textual friendships," as we might call them in our particular area of inquiry, with people/texts who think the human story runs another way are thus a "spiritual exercise" (as the ancient philosophers would have said), or a means "to work on oneself" (as Wittgenstein would have said), an academic's manner of developing the patience needed to be(come) a friend.[50] Textual friendships is the name of a hermeneutics that refuses to deflect the truth of reason's rootedness in the life of the reasoner.

Lest someone object that developing patience is an underwhelming product of comparative academic work, it should be rejoined that without patience friendship is impossible. Lest someone object that friendship is not really an academic-enough way to think about comparison, it should be rejoined that friendship is a posture of reasoning—and a posture of reasoning about the reasoning of others and how best to engage it. Reason that reasons apart from postures of this or that sort is an abstraction; there is no such reason. Friendship names the posture of reasoning that best befits irresolvable existential conflict.[51]

49. One of the more difficult dangers of scholarly work is the temptation to study other human beings or their artifacts (texts, etc.) in a way that denies them the seriousness with which they take their own lives, their own traditions, their own claims to truth—as if scholarly seriousness is somehow a higher, better, truer, or more comprehensive seriousness than that of the adherents of the traditions we study. Cf. Garver, *For the Sake of Argument*, 45: "Ultimate orientations or modes of thinking are ways of looking and acting; they are not objects to look at, and so judging between them makes them into something they are not. To judge between incommensurable modes of thought is not a good way to make friends."

50. Anthropologists who conduct fieldwork are being trained in patience, too, but in a different, perhaps more direct, way than those scholars who study ancient texts.

51. One may wish to argue for a different posture, but in so arguing the point about postured reasoning would simply be reinforced. Though it has now been over a quarter of a century since publication, I continue to think Charles Taylor's essay on the types of argument that can be made via practical reason and Martha Nussbaum's reply stand out among concise treatments for their insight into the argumentative power of ad hominem reasoning, biography, passion/emotion, and human relationships. See Taylor, "Explanation

To put this personally: I do not know how much I understand Seneca, but I do now think of him as a friend. Of course, inasmuch as Seneca is long dead, my friendship is "imagined" or "textual." But that in a sense is exactly the point of the study: I hope that I have practiced patience in trying to be friends with Seneca through his texts.[52] If so, I will have learned something of what is required to be friends with someone who thinks the human story goes another way. My reason will have acquired something of the posture it needs to be in a world with people whose lives imply that mine is false (and vice versa) and who may remain opaque to me, and I to them, until we die.

This is a practical suggestion for a practical problem, which is to say that it is practical reason's answer to the questions it cannot escape when faced with incompatible and incommensurable claims to existential truth and the ineliminable fact that we can live only one true life. As should now be obvious, this way of thinking is an overall attempt to reframe comparison of traditions of truth/life as a practical problem. Insofar as comparison is repeatedly conceived as a theoretical problem, we should expect only more theories, some of which will be clearer than others, some of which will have more promise than others, some of which will raise better questions than others, but none of which will get down to the real business of comparing lives.[53] That is what comparison of traditions has always been and still is—the attempt to see why other people live the lives that they do.

---

and Practical Reason," and Nussbaum's reply in *The Quality of Life*, ed. Martha Nussbaum and Amartya Sen (New York: Oxford University Press, 1993).

52. I found it harder to become friends with Epictetus. Whether this is because of his rough pedagogy, his particular expressions, the subjects Arrian selected to publish from his notes, or something else altogether, I'm not sure. But I know I have to be more patient in becoming friends with him than with Seneca (or Marcus, for that matter). The challenge, then, is to continue reading Arrian's records with the understanding that I am learning how to be a friend.

53. For an attempt to think of the "other" in comparison as an explicitly theoretical question, see Jonathan Z. Smith, "What a Difference a Difference Makes," in *To See Ourselves as Others See Us: Christians, Jews, "Others" in Late Antiquity*, ed. Jacob Neusner and Ernest Frerichs (Chico, CA: Scholars Press, 1985), 3–48. Smith's essay is of considerable interest because, on the one hand, he recognizes that the question of "otherness" or "others" is an inescapably relational and therefore political question, and, on the other, he continues to talk as if theorizing otherness is the way to come to terms with it. Smith also recognizes that opacity is a necessary part of any thinking about the other, but only up to a point. The otherness of a housefly, e.g., is impenetrable and thus "of no theoretical interest" (47). I would rather say that the interest in the housefly lies precisely in the fact that it is impenetrable.

Conclusion

Looking back through the sections of this chapter, the logic is this: irresolvable existential conflict (of which there is plenty in the world) is entangled in the narratives that make sense of the truths that we claim for our lives, the words we use to claim them, the texts we use to inscribe them; the way to be intellectually productive in the face of such conflicts is to become friends. To be friends with those with whom you conflict over truth requires you to be patient. To study alternative traditions as an academic is to learn patience. As a whole, this is what it is to treat comparison of strong traditions of life or truth—what looks on first glance like a theoretical problem—as a problem of practical reason.

A Response to Friend-Critics

Wittgenstein once remarked, "An honest religious thinker is like a tightrope walker. He almost looks as though he were walking on nothing but air. His support is the slenderest imaginable. And yet it really is possible to walk on it."[1] I wrote *One True Life* as an attempt to display what an honest religious thinker looks like. To some, it may look like I have walked on air. But it is not so. The support may be slender, indeed *almost* imperceptible, but it is nevertheless there, real, can be seen, touched, and even walked on.

I take "honest religious thinker" to be a way of naming what scholarship is that works with the questions that question us. To encounter ancient Christianity and Stoic philosophy is, if nothing else, to encounter questions that question us. Read the old texts well, and we will find ourselves exposed. We may, of course, then choose to hide. Or we may not. *One True Life* argues by structure and discourse that intellectual and existential judgments are not two decisions but one. It is an attempt not to hide, especially not behind the veil of learning.

Some Direct Replies

I am honored by the attention given to *One True Life* both at the conference and in these essays.[2] Although I may have put some of the cookies a little high

1. Ludwig Wittgenstein, *Culture and Value* (London: Wiley-Blackwell, 1995), 7.

2. It is important for readers of the essays to know that even though the arguments can

"A Response to Friends/Critics" was originally published in *The New Testament in Comparison: Validity, Method, and Purpose in Comparing Traditions*, ed. John M. G. Barclay and B. G. White (London: T&T Clark, 2020), 125–41. It is reproduced with permission. Unless otherwise specified, all references in the essay and its footnotes to Mitchell, Engberg-Pedersen, Martin, Novenson, and Watson refer to those authors' essays in *The New Testament in Comparison* (hereafter *NTC*).

on the shelf, I did not write the book so that it would "automatically separate those who understand it from those who do not."[3] Nevertheless, apart from a passing reference in Jonathan Linebaugh's treatment of Hamann's hermeneutics, *One True Life* has been misunderstood and misrepresented in some materially significant ways.

Because I obviously cannot go point by point for each of the essays that engage *One True Life*, I will respond by focusing on six substantive issues and leave lesser matters for another occasion.[4] The following issues are indispensable for an intelligent reading of the book, whether one agrees with its central claims or not.

Do We Compare Things?

Several of the essayists insist that we humans really do compare things. And the essayists insist or imply further that this truth somehow runs against the

---

be sharp (especially between Mitchell and me), there is plenty of room for conversation, discussion, and even genuine friendship and warmth. But the issues are complicated, serious, and evoke all kinds of reactions from all of us. That is, I think, to be expected.

3. Wittgenstein, *Culture and Value*. Besides, as he says shortly thereafter, "telling someone something he does not understand is pointless, even if you add that he will not be able to understand it" (7).

4. For example, in *NTC*, 123 n. 164, Mitchell misreads my sentences about the Loeb series translations and confuses the question of philology with that of philosophical "translation" that I discuss later in *One True Life* (224–26). What I said about the Loeb series was, I thought, rather clear: for the sake of the reader's convenience, I cite the Loeb whenever possible, adjusting as I see fit. The fact that many citations of Seneca et al. correspond to the Loeb is thus entirely unsurprising since that is (a) what I intended, and (b) what consistent practice in line with such an intention would reveal. That is, "as close to the base" means "as close to what you'll regularly find in this book," not "the Loeb series is *the* critical edition; I know about no others, and no others were consulted." I actually wrote not only with various texts open but also, when applicable, while reading multiple "translations" in English, German, and French. So I very much believe in the importance of philology, and the conference version of her essay "demonstrated" no such thing as she claims ("dismissive attitude"—yet another attempt to divine my psychological/emotional posture, something about which I say more later in this response). In fact, one of the major points of my book is that language and thought are inseparable. But I also believe—correctly, as it turns out—that many readers of *One True Life* are not as interested in the "minutiae" of extensive philological analysis as they are in being able to go read through some of the texts that I treat. Since not all readers of my book can do philological analysis or read Greek or Latin, I preferred to aid them in reading the editions that are widely available. I did not imagine it would be controversial to say that it is possible to get too far down in the weeds in a book that is aiming to do something else.

argument of *One True Life*, in which I am alleged to have severely problematized or rejected comparison of all kinds. To be blunt: I find this reading of the book bizarre. Of course human beings compare things and cannot not compare and contrast. But *One True Life* is about lived religious/philosophical traditions. I do not think we have trouble comparing apples to apples, or even to oranges or mangoes, or fruit to vegetables or to trees or trains—and countless other things—but I do think traditions of life cannot be conceptualized in the way that modern comparative inquiry requires us to assume that they can be. Whether they can or not is the only issue worth talking about.

I would be foolish indeed if what I thought was "we cannot compare" and then actually forgot that and wrote parts 1 and 2 of the book, placed them next to each other on purpose, and went on to argue against myself in part 3. What I think is this: comparison is of course unavoidable, but comparison of traditions of life under the philosophical conditions I describe is best conceived as juxtaposition. Juxtaposition turns out to be the way difference/similarity is construed; language the way we think through the construal; narrative the way we know how language games work; existential truth the way narratives are lived and life made sense of; incommensurability the name for the lack of a common measurement that would allow rational evaluation of difference over life; and Kierkegaard the best thought I know of that corresponds to the condition we humans find ourselves in, in which we cannot rationally adjudicate between different lived claims to existential truth.

I argue further that there is no intellectually more fundamental place outside of the traditions that can hold them at bay, set them up side by side, and evaluate them in comparative inquiry. There is a position that says that this larger place of knowing exists, and this epistemic possibility inescapably entails philosophical positions on the human being (what sort of self we are or have that can know in this way, the significance of historical conditioning for what we know and what we take ourselves to be as knowing subjects, the importance of time and death for the limits of knowledge, and so on). In both its original Enlightenment and updated forms, it is the encyclopedia. I deny that this is a true account of the way we can know or compare traditions of life. I maintain instead that summons and conflict, or invitation and conversation, or display and critique, are the way incommensurable religious/philosophical traditions interface with each other. The "come now, we really do compare things" objection is a serious distraction from the main issue involving traditions of life. One can argue for a reinstantiation of the encyclopedic mode of knowing—in more contemporary dress, of course—or one can go another direction. But insisting that we compare things is akin to insisting on the wetness of water. Who would deny it?

Incommensurability and Invitation

There is, next, the question of incommensurability and how it relates to the book as a whole. Followed by Novenson, Mitchell maintains that *One True Life* is a *protreptikos*. Like Clement (an honor, really), I use learning not to compare things as I should but to preach to the already converted about the superiority of Christianity. My argument is less an argument about how traditions of life relate to one another than it is an altar call.

There are many replies to such an astounding reading, but I focus here on two in particular. First, to say that traditions are incommensurable is automatically and necessarily to say that you cannot argue for the superiority of one over another. Why? Because there is no shared standard of measurement by which such superiority could be shown to exist. That is what incommensurable means. The conceptual arrangement and entire argument of Mitchell's essay presuppose that this most basic point has been missed.[5]

The structure of my book, the repeated affirmations throughout, and the Kierkegaardian conclusion make clear that the two traditions of life stand face to face, that they both exist inseparably with grammars of invitation and commitment, of claim and conflict, that they both insist on living the *philosophia* to know what true knowledge is, and so on—and that there is no way rationally to resolve the rivalry.

I suppose Mitchell's misreading may result partly from my straightforward admission that I am a Christian. But, of course, that I admit this and that I take it to be indispensably significant for how I reason is part of the overarching claim about traditioned rationality in the first place. Mitchell misunderstands what is a philosophical claim about the possibility and subsequent shape of human reason vis-à-vis traditions and confuses the matter by (unintentionally, I assume) relocating this question within guesswork about a sort of quasi-personal piety as that which underlies the book's purported exhortative genre.[6]

5. It is also interesting to note that none of the essayists actually give an account of incommensurability as a feature of traditions. Perhaps they think such a thing does not exist, that it is simply a figment of the imagination. But, if so, they would need to give the narrative that allows the traditions' narratives to be subsumed.

6. A key example is her reading of Wittgenstein as me (*NTC*, 111 n. 107, "seizing on a way of life believingly, lovingly, through thick and thin"); she also thinks I'm "nostalgic." This turn to see into my mind or my spiritual disposition ("fundamentalist"; Engberg-Pedersen) or political leanings (possible "conservative"; Martin) or psychological state ("anxious"; Novenson) is characteristic of the essays that miss large parts of the philosophically constructive moves of *One True Life*. Since I am skeptical of the ability to know the things about other

I take it to be constitutive of rationality that we reason from within the traditions that turn out to make rationality what it is. It is thus rather basic to the understanding of *One True Life* that arguing rationally in the absence of a shared standard will not—because it cannot—produce a defeat of a tradition since rationality itself will be traditioned. There is no rationality to which we can appeal that exists above or lies beyond what rationality is in the traditions; if we could appeal to it (either as a formal capacity or as a set of principles/beliefs or whatever), we would of necessity invoke a shared standard.[7]

Informing readers that I am a Christian is thus nothing more, but also nothing less, than a naming of the shape of rationality that I take to be possible. This is so both historically (the language we have been given that is the antecedent condition of our thought) and anthropologically (the only thinking self that exists is the self that is embedded in the traditions that make the thinking self what it becomes through time). Incommensurability is a way of saying that there is no self and no history that can take you back behind the human condition of your knowing to something purer, more pristine, more thought as thought. Your knowing life is the only place from which you can know. All this—and much of what it might entail—has also been missed.

Second, the language of these religious/philosophical traditions is both proclaiming and invitational, which is to say that the Stoics and the early Christians took themselves seriously enough as possessors of the truth that they fashioned their speech accordingly. The grammar of their texts displays not the existential indifference of much current academic discourse but an intensity of purpose; they have something to offer the world. Indeed, it is

---

people through their writings that the essayists claim to know about me, I do not know exactly why they turn to things they cannot know about me (and, as it turns out in fact, are incorrect). But it is guesswork, a little run at mystical telepathy to go with some arguments. The conceptual lines to follow are those that could be traced primarily between MacIntyre, Wittgenstein, Kierkegaard, and Gadamer. Tracing some of these lines would not necessarily result in agreement, of course, but it could aid in a better reading.

7. Mitchell seems to think that because Stoicism is no longer alive in the way that Christianity still is, I ipso facto present Christianity as superior. But I nowhere say anything like this. Moreover, *One True Life* is focused on the Christianity of Paul, Luke, and Justin, which is quite different from ours today (contra Engberg-Pedersen's assertion that I see no difference). Stoicism is a permanent possibility of sorts, runs deep in the modern world, and always lies close at hand. Will it re-form with teachers, schools, etc.? Who's to say? There is no reason—metaphysical, logical, historical—that it cannot (as if there were something written into the structure of the universe that prevented Stoics from existing). There are of course dedicated Stoics today (see, e.g., modernstoicism.com), but they are not really a school or a scheme in the sense that the ancients were.

virtually inconceivable that these traditions could ever have gotten off the ground without this sense about their claims. I say explicitly that I am trying to write in something akin to Ricoeur's second-naïveté, that I am attempting to think with the sources and reproduce this sense rather than simply reporting on them. Contrary to Mitchell's assertion, this style does not entail a denigration of academic reporting.[8] If I have re-displayed the grammatical nature of these traditions of life—their claim and conflict, their proclamation and invitation—I count that as a success. It is what an interpretation looks like that allows the questions of the sources to mingle, linger, and reside within our own questions—which, I still maintain, is historically closer to the animating moves of the texts of both the Roman Stoics and the early Christians.[9] To miss this point about the grammar of traditions of life and replace it with psychological gestures about my intentions in writing is once again to confuse a philosophic claim about the working-end of a tradition's language with what might have been going on in my mind or heart or wherever it is we come up with intentions (which, of course, we do not know, cannot know, and therefore cannot assess in another person).

Non-compossibilty and One Life to Live

Several of the essayists question whether we actually live only one life. Dale Martin, for example, notes that he is an amateur musician, philosopher, and so forth, and believes this means that he lives more than one life. Frankly, this is baffling.

8. Mitchell also suggests I denigrate regular scholarship. But this is untrue. I have often written the "regular" scholarly way. The hermeneutical point is something else entirely. To my mind, there are many other puzzling features in her essay. For example, she takes my remarks about Paul's influence on Western tradition to be an argument about spiritual/religious superiority. But I took them to be simply a matter of the historical record. The remarks are descriptive, not jubilant exaltation, and, as far as I can see, historically incontestable.

9. I don't think the way the grammar works is the same for everything in the world—choreography, baseball, swimming, say—but I do think this would be the case for religious/philosophical traditions of the sort that are under discussion to begin with. Claiming truth is ingredient to their identity as particular traditions. My understanding of hermeneutics also owes much to what George Steiner has called "answerable understanding" or "answerability" or "responding responsibility" wherein we become "answerable" to the texts we read. Reading well means we become "answerers in action." Too often academic work avoids exactly this critical, more fully human dimension of hermeneutics. The ancient Stoics and Christians were interested precisely in "answerers in action." See George Steiner, *Real Presences* (Chicago: University of Chicago Press, 1989).

It is Dale Martin who is/does these things, and exactly to the degree that he can name them as his activities, he presupposes the unity across, in, and between them that is he himself.[10] These are things that Professor Martin does/is. "Dale Martin" picks out the one who is/does these various things through time.

If we change the example to sickness and death, say, the anthropological point emerges more sharply. Who is it that gets sick? Who dies? Imagine this brief exchange: "John Doe is sick. Is he at home?" "No, he is in the hospital." "Will he make it?" "Alas, likely not . . ." [then later] "John died this afternoon." The unity presupposed in the exchange is Mr. Doe's life and death. Whose life can you live but your own? Whose death can you die but your own? As it applies to the existence of individual human beings, I find the notion of living only one life so basic that I cannot fathom Professor Martin's form of denial.[11] Kavin Rowe lives the life that only—and precisely only—Kavin Rowe can live. And when Kavin Rowe dies, it is only—and precisely only—Kavin Rowe who dies. "Kavin Rowe" names in shorthand the life and death that I am through time in all the various things I have done, do, will do, and permanently cease doing.[12] It is this sort of human life, the only one that we can live along the trajectory from birth to death, that rival traditions attempt to claim and for which they compete.

What I can better understand, I think, is the question about the unity of life as it pertains not to individual identity in a stricter sense but to the ability to live the pattern of more than one tradition of life at a time. Engberg-Pedersen, for example, "personally doubts very much" whether "any human being *just* 'lives' in accordance with a single worldview."[13] And Mitchell speaks of Paul's "bi-cultural" identity.[14] But the point in *One True Life* was not to deny that we all

10. Both the *idem* and the *ipse* in Ricoeur's language (see his *Oneself as Another* [Chicago: University of Chicago Press, 1995]).

11. There is a sophisticated form of denial: genealogists who would deny inherent identity between the masks that we choose to wear for whatever reasons we choose to wear them. The mask is the thing itself, as it were, and there is nothing—no human, no continuous life—behind it. But, again, just to the extent that genealogists employ language that requires a subject who *is* (not who *wears*) the mask, they presuppose a person that subsists through time, and they therefore undermine the attempt to get free of a unified life.

12. The connection to narrative here is indissoluble. Even to begin to answer the question "Who is [Kavin Rowe]?" one will necessarily begin to tell a story or, perhaps if the situation already provides some initial clarity, to point to pieces of a human identity (e.g., "the first violinist") that derive their specific intelligibility from the narrative that is the background answer to the question "who?"

13. *NTC*, 46.

14. *NTC*, 95.

inhabit complex cultures, that we draw from this piece here and that piece there in our daily activities, and so on. It was rather to insist on non-compossibility as an essential way these particular traditions of life exist and what they claim for those who would join them. Can one, for example, worship the God of Israel and not worship the God of Israel, or take Jesus of Nazareth to be God's Messiah and take him to be not the Messiah but a pretentious Galilean Jew, and cultivate love as the rightly ordered wellspring of virtue and endeavor to eliminate love in a self-risking way, and dozens of other things besides—all at the same time in the same pattern of one human life? I think not.[15]

One of the outstanding strengths of Martha Nussbaum's *Therapy of Desire* is her depiction of Nikidion's philosophical journey as change through existential formation and re-formation: Niki does not simply learn to think differently when she changes philosophical schools; her very self is actually constituted and reconstituted by the new life she learns she must begin to live as she moves from school to school.[16] Her life-shape is the way she acquires the knowledge she must gain. And Pierre Hadot, though often known only for his description of "spiritual exercises," also compellingly depicted philosophical life as one of attraction and lived response.[17] Earliest Christianity is

15. Even successive stages display the existentially exclusive shifts that must take place, say, for example, from the lived affirmation that Jesus is the Lord, to the realization that Pliny's coercive pressure is too much, to a subsequent denial and sacrifice and return to pagan life (Jesus is not the Messiah after all).

16. Martha Nussbaum, *The Therapy of Desire* (Princeton: Princeton University Press, 1996). Bernard Williams notices this in his review of Nussbaum, though Williams thinks it is a detriment to Nussbaum's style. By contrast, I think it is an advantage and that Williams missed a chance to see how the "not much remains constant" with Nikidion relates to Nussbaum's depiction of the re-formation of the self. Mitchell also notes that I do not mention Nussbaum's work on toleration, etc., and—perhaps—suggests that I do not know of it or for some inexplicable reason choose not to refer to it. I do know it, but the reason I do not mention it is simple: I do not find it particularly helpful. There are several reasons for this, but the principal one to name is that despite the elegance and passion of her work, Nussbaum appears to me to presuppose a philosophically liberal notion of the human person, and I take that anthropology to be self-defeating in attempts to argue for toleration/tolerance. Though I could write only several pages about toleration/tolerance, I worked extensively through this question in both the Greco-Roman world and the modern period for my book *World Upside Down: Reading Acts in the Graeco-Roman Age* (New York: Oxford University Press, 2009).

17. Hadot's project can be seen most clearly in four books: a brief study of Plotinus called *Plotinus, or, The Simplicity of Vision* (Chicago: University of Chicago Press, 1994), a more detailed work on Marcus Aurelius named *The Inner Citadel: The Meditations of Marcus Aurelius* (Cambridge, MA: Harvard University Press, 1998), a collection of essays entitled *Philosophy as a Way of Life* (New York: Blackwell, 1995), and the programmatic history *What*

unintelligible apart from the sense that it, too, "called" people of all stripes to be transformed in the patterns of their lives. Even to acknowledge these most basic matters is *already* to have granted the point that traditions of life were schemes into which adherents were inducted and taught to live. To argue that the Christian scheme and the Stoic scheme were compatible in one human life is then to erase the anthropological limitations of induction, transformation, and time, and, implicitly at least, to argue for a fantasy: an elastic view of the self undetermined by body, time, and death; indeed, one that finally abstracts the self from the life lived by the person whose self it is. These traditions involve the sort of existentially thick claims to truth that mean one has to choose a life that turns out to make truth what it comes to be for the self that also itself comes to be;[18] and this choice will, moreover, simultaneously involve choosing against—again, in an existentially thick sense—other forms of life that claim their own truth. One simply cannot live in the cluster of things that make for a Christianly patterned existence and the cluster of things that make for a

Is Ancient Philosophy? (Cambridge, MA: Harvard University Press, 2002). Taken together, these books display not only deep historical knowledge but also a systematic philosophical interpretation of ancient philosophy itself. This is not, of course, to say that Hadot treats every twist and turn of each ancient thinker or his school, but rather that Hadot's historical readings aim at something much more difficult and philosophically significant: he attempts to grasp the whole of what ancient philosophy actually was and, subsequently, to reintegrate ancient wisdom into modern intellectual life. (In *The Veil of Isis*, which is more about the history of the idea of "nature" than about ancient philosophy, and in *The Present Alone*, which is a series of conversations and statements of his views, Hadot presents his own philosophy/ideas through the testimony of the ancients, but he does not offer the kind of interpretations present in the other books.) Mitchell suggests that I "harden" Hadot and turn his insights about philosophy and life into a "rigid epistemological prescription that the condition for all knowing, and any knowing worth achieving must come from 'living its way of life'" (*NTC*, 112 n. 111). Again, I say nothing of the kind. The book treats religious/philosophical traditions, not all kinds of knowing. I imagine that people from various traditions of life or who position themselves outside any tradition could agree on any number of things worth knowing (whether prednisone helps asthmatic flares, or when the French Revolution occurred given conventional dating schemes, or the significance of resilin in a flea's legs for its jumping ability, or when the Cubs last won the World Series . . .) but would require a different, existentially engaged sort of posture vis-à-vis such questions as raised by the Christian and Stoic traditions: Was Jesus of Nazareth the Messiah of the Jews? Should one strive to extirpate passion? Is the cosmos eternal? Can death finally be overcome? and so on. As Hadot himself put it, the problem that animates religious/philosophical traditions is "not the problem of knowing this or that, but of *being* in this or that way" (*What Is Ancient Philosophy?*, 29).

18. See the discussion of understanding as "a becoming" in my "Making Friends and Comparing Lives" in part 2 of this volume.

Stoically patterned existence at one and the same time. Non-compossibility is thus finally less a theory about the exclusivity of traditions and human finitude than it is an acknowledgment of phenomenological fact.[19]

Words, Stories, and More Words

It is quite surprising that not one of the critics of *One True Life* really addresses the question of the interdependence of words, narrative, and translation in the philosophical sense in which I discuss it.[20] In fact, the essayists proceed almost as if this question does not exist or could be bypassed in the discussion of how we think comparatively.

19. I take it to be a phenomenological fact of both past and present that there are competing ways to live and that many of these ways force choices. There may well be no metaphysical necessity to this reality: it could, insofar as we know, have gone differently. One may have theories about why such a phenomenon is not *really* the way things *are*, that the choices amount to the absence of difference in God's eyes (e.g., John Hick's pluralism) or do not matter that much as long as we can get along in the public square. But who would deny that this is the way the world appears to us? In my view, the phenomenon is rooted in the finitude of the creature. We really do have to live just one life. The schemes are instances of the way this life is ordered toward its perceived end.

20. On this point, see my essay "Making Friends and Comparing Lives" in this volume. Martin mentions *pneuma* but his discussion illustrates the *problem* I describe: the Stoics and the Christians do not mean the same thing with the word. Martin also wonders why I do not employ Wittgenstein's notion of family resemblance. The reason is uncomplicated. Wittgenstein thought of family resemblance in relation to the meaning of words: he wondered why words that do not have the exact same meaning all the time—they do not have a core or an essence—can nevertheless be seen to have something like a similar meaning from context to context. They have a family resemblance. This is manifestly not the case with words such as *theos*, *cosmos*, etc., when looking at the Christian and Stoic use. Family resemblance works best within traditions (the theological grammar of the NT documents, e.g., has a family resemblance). Francis Watson's paper in this volume (i.e., *The New Testament in Comparison*), e.g., may work with a notion of family resemblance inasmuch as Watson treats Christian texts that can be read profitably together. In short, family resemblance is an excellent way to think, but it is precisely the sort of language that illustrates the real difference between the sort of comparison Watson engages in and what I am talking about with the language of rival traditions. The Gospel of Peter and the canonical gospels may be part of the same family—at least it's debatable who belongs to this family, who's a brother or sister, who's an extended relative, or long-lost cousin and so on—but Stoicism and Christianity are not part of the same family in any real sense. If we personalize the image a bit, Seneca and Paul are not brothers or first cousins or distant relatives from the same family; they are friends. Martin's discussion of *pneuma* is *not* family resemblance in Wittgenstein's sense.

But the truth is that we cannot think without words. The words that we think with are the thoughts we have.[21] Paying close attention to the way words work, therefore, is a sine qua non for thinking about what comparison entails. *One True Life* argues by way of repeated case-by-case demonstration that words work in particular ways in the language games in which they are played (i.e., the texts and narratives of the traditions in which they play their roles).[22] Let this point sink in: in order to counter these arguments, one would have to show that the words work differently from how I say they do, that in fact the same words (or those closely clustered with them) work the same way in different traditions, and that there is thus the same narrative that allows the words to work the same way. One cannot simply *assert* that incommensurability or untranslatability is not the way traditions relate to each other. One must show that the words work the same way for the instances—and eventually the totality—of the things one is trying to align. That is, one would have to display the complicated interconnection of words, lived traditions, and narrative, and all in a way that meant same-saying—and therefore the possibility of translation in the philosophical sense—was what had been discovered.

Once one understands the connection between words, language games/texts, narrative, and traditions, one will see that this "word-study" section is the one place in *One True Life* where case-by-case counterarguments would complicate or even potentially defeat my sense of comparison. But no one took up the challenge. Not a single argument of this sort has been forthcoming. I can assume only that this is because the significance of the linguistic/narrative point was not grasped, or perhaps the language-game demonstration was completely persuasive (though if so, the significance of such persuasiveness was missed).[23] If I were to write against myself, I would start here.

21. If you disagree with this, tell me the thoughts you have with the words you need to tell me the thoughts you have without words. You will be telling me your thoughts with words—i.e., the words that are your thoughts. Or: try telling me the thoughts you have without the words you need to tell me the thoughts you have without words. This, of course, you can't do. The words are your thoughts.

22. See *One True Life*, 226–35, on *theos, cosmos, anthropos*, etc.

23. Mitchell drastically misunderstands the final sentence of the book, and accuses me of arrogance, inexplicably suggesting that the Yale Press readers were ignored (they were not since they raised other matters than the ones that bother Mitchell). The point—once again, philosophical—is about the unity of words and life; it encapsulates, in fact, my criticism of MacIntyre in light of how I read Wittgenstein. One wishes that this type of philosophical scrutiny had been possible at several points. I did not expect all the right echoes to be heard, but somehow Mitchell seems to have heard many of the wrong ones. How exactly this hap-

A clarifying way to put the whole question of words/narrative and theological/philosophical knowledge is in relation to natural theology.[24] In the appendix to *One True Life*, I say that I reject natural theology. I would rather have said that I prefer to rename natural theology as "the reader's knowledge of how the story really goes." This way of putting it acknowledges the importance of narrative and plays on dramatic irony and the difference in knowledge between the characters in the story and the readers of the story. I do not, that is, deny that the words in pagan texts were and can be read to express Christian truth ("the father and maker of all"; "we are his offspring"; "God is near you"; and countless other phrases): that is the reader hearing the words in light of how the larger story really runs. But I do deny that the authors of those pagan texts would have meant what Christians mean, and that they would agree with the Christian extraction and transformation of their lines (the meaning of the words in the context of the texts in which we originally find them is different from the meaning of the same words in the Christian texts). So arguments that run "if they [authors/words] speak truly, they speak truly of the one God since there is no other of whom they could truly speak and be true" strike me as exactly correct; it is simply that the truth that the words speak is not according to character but according to reader. Casual understandings to the contrary, this is not the same thing as affirming "insights" or granting the order of being/order of knowledge division as it has historically been used. "Insights" are what the Christians read in the words. The order of being/knowledge distinction says that while the statements of a Seneca, for example, are true according to being, Seneca himself does not know this. In my judgment, this distinction assumes something false—namely, that there is a univocal meaning of the words; that is, that the words mean in Seneca's text what they mean to the order-of-being reader. While I see that words can mean Christian things (used for true statements about the order of being in light of Christian theological knowledge), I think that there are two meanings of the words, and these meanings are not the same at all. There is the Stoic meaning and the Christian meaning, and no amount of order of being/knowledge distinction can make the same words say the same thing.[25]

---

pens is complicated: some of it may be my direct way of writing, some a lack of philosophical analysis, and some a genuinely perplexing misfire on both parts. We are working on it.

24. I wince even as I write "natural theology," for the term is itself equivocal, of course, as is its close cousin, natural law. Among others, see Russell Hittinger, *A Critique of the New Natural Law Theory* (Notre Dame, IN: University of Notre Dame Press, 1987).

25. There are or can be of course many more than "two meanings." I simply use two to make the difference apparent. Noticing this difference in word meaning problematizes the

So, yes, of course there is extensive borrowing, use, quotation, and so forth.[26] There is a Philo, and a Clement, and dozens of others. But all the piling up of cross-references in the world will still show the same basic hermeneutical difference: the words mean different things in the different texts/traditions.[27]

---

use of "concepts" to describe what the Christian readers found in the pagan texts. What they found were words. When these words were resituated within Christian discourse, they expressed the concept needed for the discourse to work. That is, you can't know what the concepts are apart from the words that are used, and when you look at the words used in the pagan texts you see that they don't have the thought that you count as an insight since their words do not work the way the same words work in what you mean by "insight."

26. Augustine's famous image is finding gold among the Egyptians (*De doctrina Christiana* 2.40, 60–61). The words are the gold.

27. An example from the Stoic material is Seneca, who frequently recommends something from Epicurus for Lucilius to meditate on: Seneca clearly says, I think, that it is the comprehensiveness of the Stoic take on the world that allows him to borrow the maxims from others (e.g., *Epistles* 6; 8.7ff.; 9.19ff.; 33; 90; 95). The Stoic tradition assimilates to itself whatever it wants/needs/finds useful. It does not simply "agree with" what it finds in other philosophical traditions. It "makes use of" what it finds in ways that fit the purpose at hand. Mitchell notes the occurrence of other philosophical material in the Stoics but cannot get past a kind of "citation-means-same-meaning-of-words-and-therefore-agreement" hermeneutic. It is as if merely finding the words of tradition A in a text from tradition B indicates conceptual overlap, agreement, and so on, when in fact it does no such thing at all. The accumulation of examples of cross-tradition citation is thus philosophically useless. It simply means that one has more of what one already knows exists. It is like getting more and more and more blood tests with the same reading. The question is what to make of them. And for this, one will have to make something of the interpretative register that makes the particular interpretation make the sense it makes. Here is, I suppose, as good a place as any to address briefly the questions raised in her comments on A. A. Long's essay (*NTC*, 118–19 n. 146). First, I remember the question-and-answer at the time of the conference somewhat differently, and we did have a productive exchange about the texts and Long's essay afterward in which I attempted to say a good deal more than what is reported in her footnote. Second, what I say about Long is not that he is my source for what I think about all things Stoic—indeed, Pohlenz and Veyne and others have made similar points to the one I took Long to make—but that Long's comment about philosophical unity should apply to the Roman Stoics. I cannot read them as a dilution of Chrysippus, though there is a strain in the scholarly literature that sees them that way. I read Long's essay differently from Mitchell, but for the sake of the main point, let it be said: if Long thinks the Roman Stoics cannot be read as examples of the philosophical comprehensiveness of Stoicism, then I disagree with him. There are too many texts that speak against the dilution thesis on this point: to point only to Epictetus, see *Discourses* 1.16.17; 2.12.3; 2.20; 4.1.131; 4.4.39, all of which speak of and/or presuppose Stoicism's philosophical comprehensiveness and its truth as the "one way" to life (*mia hodos*). By attempting to recruit Long's essay to her side of the argument, Mitchell pays admirable attention to an important essay but misses the larger hermeneutical question altogether.

What makes the difference in meaning? The narrative that makes "Christian" and "Stoic" make sense as particular religious/philosophical traditions in the first place. Words, narratives, knowledges: these must be seriously tackled if there is to be advanced discussion on the question of rival traditions. But these matters, too, have, alas, been missed.

Traditions of Life, Rival Traditions, and Judaism

Several of the essayists raise questions in one way or another about the interdependent matters of my understanding of tradition, my use of Alasdair MacIntyre, and my view of early Christianity vis-à-vis Judaism. Four larger points are in order. First, my understanding of tradition is obviously and heavily MacIntyrean. But it is not MacIntyre *simpliciter* for reasons that are critical to understand. The "of life" is my attempt both to extend and criticize MacIntyre's understanding of traditions specifically in light of the ancient insistence on the indispensability of living for what we make of how we think. Of course, MacIntyre is well known for his insistence on the inseparable connection between social practice and thought, but when it comes to his analysis of the epistemological conditions of incommensurable traditions and their rivalries, he retreats to his basic views about nature, the clear division between theology/philosophy, and so forth, and resorts to quasi-metaphorical descriptions of the resolution of rivalry by natural reasoning ("imagination" or "sympathy"). The best reason he offers for this move is that the inability rationally to resolve conflict between traditions would require us to assume criterionless choice as our only option in the face of rivalry.[28] Which is to say that MacIntyre realizes quite clearly that his explanation of rival traditions could lead to Kierkegaardian conclusions. But MacIntyre himself, at least on this matter, recoils from Kierkegaard. I do not.

I think, instead, that if you follow MacIntyre's basic account of traditions, and if you embed thought as fundamentally in the human being's finitude—its

28. This somewhat depends on what we mean by criterion. I can, for example, find something attractive in the life of another and simply desire to do it too, or be like that too, without being able to articulate rationally why his life is superior to mine and thus makes a better choice. After the change, reasons may be given. But that means that the rivalry has been resolved in the life of the "convert" before rational resolution is possible; moreover, the "ratio" with which the convert works post-conversion is the traditioned ratio of the new way of life. For the way our life experience conditions genuine ignorance/knowledge in relation to "major" decisions of life, see also philosopher L. A. Paul, *Transformative Experience* (New York: Oxford University Press, 2014).

actual living and dying—as the ancients would have us to do, you must embrace Kierkegaard as the best articulation of the impossibility of a rational resolution between incommensurable traditions.[29] In short, the "of life" is the Kierkegaardian side of my departure from and disagreement with MacIntyre about nature, theology/philosophy, the limits of traditioned rationality in the life of the knower, and so on.[30] It is this attempt to hold MacIntyre and Kierkegaard together in a dialectical move about traditions/living/rationality that generates the complexity of my position and its conclusions. I may be wrong that Kierkegaard and MacIntyre can be dialectically held together, but if so, it is certainly not because of simplistic reassertions of Stout's view of scholarship or yet another, though thoroughly thoughtful, insistence on "propositions" as a way to get at the essence of human reasoning.[31] It would be instead because I am wrong about the inescapable weight of time and death upon human thought (I think it is heavier and more limiting than it is) and the Thomists more or less right in their claims about the natural potential and tendencies of human thought qua thought.[32]

29. This entails the judgment that MacIntyre himself is inconsistent. I think in order to avoid Kierkegaard he has to soften his account of rivalry, traditioned rationality, and translation. Novenson's claim that I out-MacIntyre MacIntyre is puzzling for these reasons among others and, at the least, suggests the need for a more thorough exposure to philosophical options.

30. Engberg-Pedersen quotes MacIntyre's earlier work (*NTC*, 48–54). Though it is not its purpose in Engberg-Pedersen's essay, this citation foreshadows MacIntyre's problem, or at least the place where I think differently from him. Engberg-Pedersen thinks my departure from MacIntyre is strange and unsupported. Is what is meant that he does not like it? It has plenty of support, as MacIntyre himself recognizes (see his response essay, "Once More on Kierkegaard," in *Kierkegaard after MacIntyre: Essays on Freedom, Narrative, and Virtue*, ed. John J. Davenport and Anthony Rudd [Chicago: Open Court, 2001], 339–56). I grant that if you think "reason" (*histrionicus*) is what Engberg-Perdersen thinks it is, traditioned rationality may appear strange.

31. Engberg-Pedersen's slippage between "a set of faculties," a "capacity," a "faculty," "faculties" of "rationality" and "imagination" is typical, perhaps inevitable, when one ties rationality to propositions (see 48 and esp. n. 10). Engberg-Pedersen treats propositions (belief assertions, etc.) as if one can know what they mean without the narrative that tells one how the words work. One can, for example, "entertain" and "assent" to propositional content "on its own." But in fact propositions, no less than individual words, simply say *histrionicus histrionicus histrionicus* until you know the narrative that interprets the words. If one grants this, and one should, one grants, linguistically/hermeneutically speaking, the whole ball of wax.

32. Perhaps I should say that there are plenty of days where I go back on myself and think the Thomists are essentially right about reason. Of course, to say Thomist is already to say traditioned reason, but it is traditioned in a way that gives an account of different possibilities.

Second, Professors Barclay and Mitchell note that the ancients did talk about morality and query my rejection of "morality" as an abstraction. The point, however, is not that the terms *mores* or *ethē* are absent in ancient literature, since of course they are not, but that the sense of *mores* or *ethē* is not what "morality" has come to be in modern ethics. Morality in the modern sense is what MacIntyre and Bernard Williams both reject as a philosophical option and what Kantians and utilitarians believe in and try to argue about. It is a domain of action with its own discernible rules in which we all equally share and to which we contribute by our conduct and views about such conduct. Ethics is the directive logic of morality. One can see this conception at work clearly in current discussions in bioethics, for example, where we behave as if we can get content-full or content-rich agreements;[33] we behave this way because we assume that there is a realm of inquiry/behavior that is detachable in some significant sense from religious convictions or knotty metaphysical puzzles or quantum physics or botany or emotional commitments to important people in our lives (or whatever). *Ethē*, whatever else it means in ancient traditions, does not mean morality in this modern sense. My point is simply, but importantly, that there is no larger arena than the traditions themselves, no isolatable sphere with behavioral norms in which all humans participate equally irrespective of the traditions in which they otherwise live.[34] The norms generated by the traditions are not instances of some larger universal human ethics. Scholars who make it look like there is such an arena in which all ancients work philosophically, pastorally, etc., reproduce a modern way of avoiding the depth of traditioned inquiry for what human action should entail. In this way, they create both historical and philosophical problems. Morality is tradition all the way down.

Third, Mitchell in particular asserts that I "operate with a single, unitary conception of Christianity."[35] But in the conceptual sense so does every person who thinks Christianity is an identifiable tradition. Conceptually speaking,

33. See H. Tristan Englehardt's work, for example, *The Foundations of Bioethics*, 2nd ed. (New York: Oxford University Press, 1996).

34. When Malherbe, for example, writes about morality in the ancient world, he constructs a spectrum that makes it look like the various traditions/texts he discusses are participants in a larger arena called the moral. In case one wonders: neither for MacIntyre nor for Williams (nor for the pragmatist Stout) does negating the modern sense of morality rule out the pursuit of common goods. We can simply pursue common goods without the background notion that it is something called Morality that binds us together with specific obligations, norms, etc.

35. *NTC*, 114.

the plural *Christianities* is given its intelligibility by the narrative that allows one to see pluriform instances of some specific thing. In the very nature of the case, one cannot answer "how specific?" because the pluriformity is ingredient to the tradition itself; following MacIntyre, I say explicitly that traditions are in part constituted by their different instantiations, arguments, contests, and so on through time. But if one did not presuppose a Christian tradition, one would not be able to speak of its variations. The variations would, that is, simply be different traditions or different forms of life and one would need different words for them. If one calls variations of Christian life *Christian* variations, one has already invoked the narrative presupposition that tells one that these are *variations* rather than something else.[36] I have no quarrel with Mitchell in thinking that there are internal complications, contestations, and developments

36. This, of course, is the conceptual answer to Mitchell's pointed question about whether or not I would take Liberal/liberal Protestants to be Christians (!). By speaking of a part of the Christian tradition as L/liberal Protestants, I have *already* named them as Christians. Perhaps I am too hard on them, but I do not at all mean "liberal" in today's American culture-war sense. I mean it in relation to philosophical commitments within certain forms of Protestantism that stem from notions of the self that go back at least to Locke and are underwritten by convictions about the existence and subsequent importance of autonomous individuals and their voluntary participation within certain democratic practices. That such commitments can lead to more fully developed "liberal" positions that I reject as good options—not "weak," something I nowhere say—should be no more surprising than the realization that there are conflicting options in any *inner*-tradition philosophical negotiations. (On the origins of the various conceptions of the self that are still with us, I am unaware of any better account than Charles Taylor's now classic work, *Sources of the Self: The Making of the Modern Identity* [Cambridge, MA: Harvard University Press, 1989]). So, too, Mitchell seems to confuse questions of "in and out" with that of being able to speak of a tradition at all and labels my willingness to speak of Christianity as a tradition as "exclusivist" (*NTC*, 112 nn. 109, 111). Mitchell may not mean it this way in the least, but I regard such contemporary jargon as part of a wider moralizing grammar that substitutes implicit accusations for a description of more serious positions. We could talk about "in and out" in many different ways, but any discussion that would touch on what I think about this question would have to include, among other things, the central theological importance of the NT's claim about Jesus as the Second Adam (i.e., all humans are "in"); Karl Barth's reconstruction of the doctrine of election, which I take as a dogmatic development consonant with an Adam/Christ typology; the implications of being "in" for nonviolence (and/or just war) vis-à-vis friends, strangers, and enemies; the work done by the distinction between the visible and invisible church; the importance of the virtues, and so forth. The question of how to locate a tradition so you can speak of it and the question of who is in and out of a tradition are of course linked, but they are not the same question. I am quite willing to speak of Christianity as a tradition since, conceptually speaking, one has to do so if one thinks there is such a thing as "Christian" anything, but reasoning theologically about in and out must range much more widely.

of almost unimaginable variety within Christianity. But, to put it simply now, if you do not have a singular conception of a religious/philosophical tradition, you would not know what you were looking at and would not have the word for it. This is not "essentializing" but simply the way that concepts work.

Fourth, some of the essayists assert that *One True Life* problematizes Judaism as a possible conversation partner for the early (and contemporary?) Christians. This is very odd for two different but related reasons. First, *One True Life* is not about Judaism and Christianity but Roman Stoicism and early Christianity; and, second, I explicitly deny that the relation between the Stoics and the Christians is the same as that between Christians and Jews. Had I written a book about Christians and Jews, I would not have conceived the question in terms of rival traditions. Why? Because I do not take them to be rival traditions.

In contrast to Mitchell's attempt to force me to dissolve the differences I see and say that Jews and Stoics stand in the same relation to Christians, I maintain that the Christian-Jewish relation constitutes a very complex, complicated, and chronologically continuous argument about how to carry Israel's story forward from the advent of Jesus of Nazareth.[37] Not only Jesus but the earliest Christians were themselves Jews and claimed that they were continuing God's purpose in the election of Israel by following his Messiah. Whether they were right about this or not was initially an ongoing argument between Jews who thought not and Jews who thought so; in short, what was contested was where Israel's history was now to go. There was a shared history, texts, theological grammar, and so forth. A "yes, Messiah" or "no, not Messiah" judgment about the significance of Jesus for Israel's history obviously had and has massive consequences for hermeneutics, doctrine, practice, and many other critical matters. But it is precisely in the tension of the yes and the no that the ongoing argument about the true trajectory of Israel's election subsists.[38]

37. Mitchell's arguments here are puzzling for the chief reason that she acknowledges that I do not say what she thinks I should say but then goes on to argue that I really mean what she says I should have said.

38. The question of non-compossibility is also different in the Christian-Jewish relation. Obviously you cannot eat pork and not eat pork at exactly the same time, but it is possible to be a Messianist Jew, as Messianist Jews themselves attest. The early church also had Torah-observant "Christians," whose pattern of life is reflected in one way or another in most of the NT texts. The arguments about whether Torah observance was/is necessary simply amplifies my point. For an excellent analysis of these matters in relation to John's Gospel, see Christopher Blumhofer, *The Gospel of John and the Future of Israel*, Society for New Testament Studies Monograph Series (Cambridge: Cambridge University Press, 2019). Blumhofer's book should reopen the question of how best to interpret John vis-à-vis Judaism.

To say it this way is, I think, both historically defensible and a specifically Christian way of framing the issue. A Christianity that does not see itself as a continuation of Israel—an ongoing, historically dense argument about that very history and its telos—is a Marcionite Christianity and one that I regard as both historically and theologically indefensible. It was hardly, therefore, an oversight or a mistake not to write about choosing between Judaism and Christianity but a particular theological commitment to seeing at the heart of the Jewish-Christian relation an argument about Israel's history rather than incommensurable difference.

I speak of *eschatological* resolution of this difference because I follow Paul's reasoning in Romans 9–11, because both Jewish and Christian traditions look toward eschatological disclosure of God's final truth about the world to come, and because it maintains indefinitely the *connection*—not the dissolution—of Christian and Jewish history.[39] Speaking of eschatology is a way of naming the specific character of the argument as a real argument: there are shared agreements about a great many things (especially over against any form of pagan life about which we know much of anything at all and over against many of the more powerful currents of modernity). But these agreements are exactly the sort that make the discussion incapable of resolution apart from the disclosure from God's side of things of the true identity of the Messiah.

Traditions of Life, Cosmopolitanism, Conversation, and Education

Because Mitchell thinks I "wish" to "dismantle" the humanities, because it was a topic much discussed at the conference, and because I was regularly asked about it thereafter, and still am so asked, it is important to point out that certain critical features of the Kierkegaardian either/or are intrinsic to the humanities and cannot be dismissed simply as extreme or as if they have been overcome or as if they bring humanistic study to an end. They exist at the heart of serious humanistic education.[40] The either/ors are now hidden, however,

39. On this point, see Bruce Marshall, "Christ and Israel: An Unsolved Problem in Catholic Theology," in *The Call of Abraham: Essays on the Election of Israel in Honor of Jon D. Levenson*, ed. Gary A. Anderson and Joel S. Kaminsky (Notre Dame, IN: University of Notre Dame Press, 2013), 330–50.

40. My point was not that the humanities should come to an end but that they should be conceived more closely in line with the human being itself and the choices we have to make based on the knowledges that expose us as choice-bound creatures. Mitchell cannot

by the sense that the real life-shape of the human being is not what is at stake in philosophical or religious (etc.) education. (What is at stake may be hard to specify, but it is not cynical to say a good job.) The profound differences of religious/philosophical traditions that one learns about are subsumed by the structure in which the larger sense that thinking and study are all equally the same thing is generated and subsists.[41] Students are not educated to choose between a Nietzsche, an Augustine, a Kant, an Epictetus, or any of the others—which are existential as much as intellectual choices, not possibilities of combination. One can live either as Kant or as Nietzsche declare you should or can, but not both. This absorption of difference by combination is cosmopolitanism writ large—a universal, untraditioned rationality written into the institutional structure that delivers the sense of what education is or should be. Students can simply move from course to course mentally absorbing information as they go (hopefully on the way toward a successful career). Cosmopolitanism in this instance is the implicit understanding that makes intelligible the sense that all these differences can be taken in without having to make choices that would impinge on the trajectory of a life.[42]

Traditioned reason, on the other hand, displays that there are massive, existentially determining choices that all humans have to make simply to get through life as human beings—whether they know it or not, like it or not, want it or not, and so on. One decides, implicitly or explicitly but always by practice, whether to keep Kosher or not. One cannot *not* go one way or the

---

seem to take philosophical objections as objections about thinking/existence and continues to refer to what I "wish" to do. Her quotation of me illustrates the problem, not what she claims I wish to do.

41. Individual teachers may think differently, of course, and doubtless many do; the point is about the structure of departments, universities, etc. That is, insofar as teachers who think differently about what they are doing are themselves absorbed by the larger pattern of students-consuming-information-as-they-go, the teachers, too, are absorbed by the effect of the cosmopolitan.

42. Cosmopolitan is not a cheap shot at the Enlightenment way of knowing (there are many obvious gains) but the best word I know that gestures toward the narrative that delivers a philosophical anthropology that says persons can overcome incommensurable but conflicting claims of religious traditions in their knowing and non-compossible claims in their being/becoming. Obviously I have in mind certain kinds of modern research universities and not, for example, specifically religious colleges that may well have a normative vision that transcends the departments. Of course, "cosmopolitan" modernity hardly explains everything about current university educational structure. But I do think it is what renders the sense that it makes to take courses in everything and come out of all of them with information. Education is the acquisition of lots of information—important to be sure, but information all the same.

other. Traditioned reason thus allows for—indeed, insists on—the human in the humanities. The Kierkegaardian either/or cuts to the heart of the promise and risk of education: send your children to the university, and they might just choose to change their lives.

The question then often comes: If traditioned reason shapes our thinking, how do you justify conversation between different traditions of life or existential choices? Why talk to others? My view is that you do not need a theory for talking with other people. You simply talk with them. (Perhaps only academics would require a theory for conversation.) Why would you talk to people from other traditions if comparison works in the ways you have suggested? My view is: why wouldn't you? Again, human existence is simply denser and more complicated than any theoretical account that would purportedly grant permission for us to say why we would be interested in talking to people from other traditions of life. Perhaps you share an office, play tennis together, or like the same fried chicken, slaw, and hush puppies. Or maybe your kids play middle infield together on the same baseball team and you watch them turn double plays. Or maybe you have always been interested in things foreign, like the way foreign-accents sound, or hope to learn about something new to eat. Or maybe for reasons you cannot articulate to yourself you simply like another person's company. Or maybe you really do *not* like his company and think to yourself that you need to grow out of your dislike and mature. Or maybe you are friends because you have joined a diverse group that works against poverty. Or maybe . . . a thousand other things. What theory can account for conversation that comes from life?[43]

There is also the assumption, implicit perhaps, that the only way you can criticize your own tradition—or that anyone else can criticize your tradition—is if you ascribe to a certain modern strain of epistemic criteria and then in this vein study another tradition. Well, maybe that helps, maybe it does not. There's no necessary connection, no metaphysical or intellectual law that makes it help. What is a necessary and perceivable connection, however, is the "fit" between claim and life, which is to say that hypocrisy is always a critique and self-critique. "You say we are to have all things in common, but you yourself have a private bank account from which you buy all sorts of things when you think no one is looking." "You claim to get free of passion. We see your life is wildly otherwise." This is both public and internal critique.

43. If the question is "Why *study* other traditions?" there are again many answers. Some of them would be as simple as: one enjoys reading Seneca. A more important one is given in my essay in this volume "Making Friends and Comparing Lives."

A Final Statement

By now it should be clear: I take comparative inquiry to be less of a question about specific method than it is about being human in a world with competing accounts of what that is.[44] Comparative inquiry is a way that we try to take seriously the seriousness of the competition between divergent accounts and to get at their significance for the lives that we have to live. Several of the essayists believe that the essence of comparative practice is best grasped by boiling it down into some laws (three), some operations (three), some theses (twelve). Perhaps. But I rather doubt it. Techniques of this and that sort are simply a part of thinking—about the ancient world and a great many other things besides. Moreover, the most important question—some might think the most obvious one—has been left out, that of truth.

In a brilliant book on being human, Robert Sokolowski writes, "We cannot help but take ourselves and one another as involved in truth, but what it means to be so implicated remains obscure to us."[45] *One True Life* tries to make explicit what it means to be implicated in certain kinds of truth—namely, traditions that claim that our implication in truth requires our commitment, and, even more pointedly, that tie truth and commitment together in a way that necessitates either/or choices. Intellectual, existential, incommensurable, non-compossible truth. How do we compare *that*?

Drawing on Feuerbach's well-known critique of religion, Bernard Williams coined the term "Feuerbach's axiom": if religion is not true, it cannot explain anything and is itself in need of explanation.[46] How right he was. What the

44. Mitchell's triumphal declaration that *One True Life* should "not be taken as a contribution to method in comparison in the New Testament and ancient Christianity" is thus unproblematical for me: I am not trying to make a contribution to an established method but to reshape the question. Once again: the reaction to the book shows, I think, that at least some of its arguments struck home. Exactly to the degree that my arguments cannot simply be absorbed by Mitchell, Engberg-Pedersen, et al. and turned into yet one more instance of contemporary methodological discussion do they illustrate the inability of encyclopedic reasoning to capture that which rejects it.

45. Robert Sokolowski, *Phenomenology of the Human Person* (Cambridge: Cambridge University Press, 2008), 1. Some of Sokolowski's formulations run toward "nature" in a more Thomistic sense than I would take them. But I take his phenomenology—that we appear in the world like this to ourselves and to others—to be fundamentally correct.

46. By other things: psychological projections, social dynamics, etc., Williams often discussed religion, Feuerbach, etc., but he coined this phrase in his review of Charles Taylor's *Sources of the Self*, in *Essays and Reviews 1959–2002* (Princeton: Princeton University Press, 2014), 308, 310.

traditions of life invite us to discover is whether fundamentally they explain or must themselves be explained, which is the same thing, these traditions might have said, as discovering in our lives whether they are true or not. That we cannot discover the truth merely by reflection, or through a collection of like terms, or by the making of scholarly models, is endemic to the claim. To recognize this is already to engage in historically rich comparative inquiry *and* to make far-reaching decisions about the kind of thinking-thing the human being is. Come and live, they say, and you will know the truth. Or not.

The Art of Retrieval: Stoicism?

"Parallels" and the Retrieval of a Tradition

Many regular readers of the *Journal of Religious Ethics* may not have heard the term "parallelomania," but it is worth learning. The word was first used a half century ago by the Jewish biblical scholar Samuel Sandmel in his 1961 presidential address to the Society of Biblical Literature (1962). Sandmel coined this word to describe what was then a prevailing tendency in much scholarship on both the Old and New Testaments: researchers would find "parallels" to biblical texts in nonbiblical texts and make two subsequent moves. First, they would move from similar-sounding words to an attribution of similarity in meaning; second, they would move from similarity of meaning to lines of influence. Sandmel's disarmingly simple point was far-reaching in its critical implications: texts mean different things in different contexts, even when they may appear to sound alike, and if they mean different things, it is prima facie unlikely that one materially influenced the other. The net effect of Sandmel's lecture (and its subsequent publication) was to require scholars of ancient texts to return to those texts with more care, to reduce the amount of "extraction for the sake of comparison," and to force upon the guild the necessity of patience in the face of difficult problems of comparison.

The recent article by Elizabeth Agnew Cochran on the Stoics and Jonathan Edwards is not an instance of parallelomania in another field.[1] Indeed, Cochran's attempt to "retrieve" certain features of Stoic tradition for Christian

1. Cochran does use the language of parallels and eventually speaks of "the Stoic logic undergirding Edwards's moral thought" (Elizabeth Agnew Cochran, "Consent, Conversion, and Moral Formation: Stoic Elements in Jonathan Edwards's Ethics," *JRE* 39, no. 4 [2011]: 645). But her analysis is clearly much more subtle than the targets of Sandmel's address.

"The Art of Retrieval: Stoicism?" was originally published in *Journal of Religious Ethics* 40 (2012): 706–19.

virtue ethics is both far more interesting and more important than the lists of alleged parallels produced by biblical scholars in the mid-twentieth century. She does not simply try to show a similarity between certain aspects of texts A and B but presses us to think more deeply about the nature of their relation, about the material substructure of Christian reasoning, and about the sort of ethics that are embedded in the way we do comparative work. Yet there is a certain "echo"—to use one of Cochran's own favored words—of the comparison-by-extraction method that underlay much of the parallelomania of the mid-twentieth century. If we are going to read the Roman Stoics for our own sake, we need to see them more clearly. In what follows, therefore, I will use Cochran's essay to make four points about the difficulties and promise of returning to the Roman Stoics to retrieve a moral discourse that can inform contemporary Christian ethics. Grasping the importance of these four points will allow us to conclude with some brief suggestions about the ethics of retrieval in the case of the Stoics.

Roman Stoicism

The leading Roman Stoic was Musonius Rufus, the Roman version of Socrates, as was sometimes thought in antiquity and is still thought today. Musonius, however, left us only some fragments to read.[2] To form a decent picture of the Stoic philosophical tradition during the Imperial period, we have to read the primary witnesses to the tradition: Seneca, Epictetus, and Marcus Aurelius.[3] And we must read them whole. For reasons that will become clear below, the philosophical claims that are internally and strictly necessary to Stoic reasoning render it exceedingly difficult to read the Stoics well through the lens of a modern anthology.[4] Taking them whole, however, allows us to create a picture of the tradition that we must have in view if we are to wrestle with the ancient Stoics. It would obviously be impossible to deal with each important feature

2. See the fragments in Cora Lutz, "Musonius Rufus: 'The Roman Socrates,'" *Yale Classical Studies* 10 (1947): 3–147. See 3–30 for her discussion of the association with Socrates.

3. Cochran, "Consent," 625. Cochran cites Norman Fiering, who includes *Plutarch* in his list of Stoics. Plutarch was not a Stoic. He was a Platonist of sorts (and a priest at Delphi). He even wrote a work against the Stoics. This citation is somewhat puzzling given that Cochran does seem aware of Plutarchian polemics; she cites him later in the essay (633).

4. The anthology *The Hellenistic Philosophers*, ed. A. A. Long and D. N. Sedley, 2 vols. (New York: Cambridge University Press, 1987), remains indispensable for quick consultation on a wide range of ancient philosophic matters.

that emerges from a reading of the Stoic works. We will thus focus on four crucial points that intersect Cochran's essay and are particularly important vis-à-vis the attempt to retrieve the Stoics for Christian ethics.

Sense Impressions

Cochran suggests that for the Stoics "sense impressions" are epistemologically primary; they constitute the place from which Stoic knowledge begins and are the "foundation for the pursuit of virtue."[5] In one way this is correct: the Stoics thought that we encounter the world through what they called *phantasiai*. *Phantasiai* are not limited to sense impressions—they include things that arise from within, as it were—but the three Stoics under consideration do speak frequently about *phantasiai* as impressions that come upon us from without, from the world's side of things.

In another way, however, Cochran's claim is problematic as an understanding of the Stoics' point. Epictetus, for example, repeatedly exhorts his students to discriminate between impressions, to sort them on the basis of a prior scheme. The first statement of his *Manual* captures well what one hears over and over again in the *Discourses*: "Some things are under our control, and some things are not."[6] "Under our control," he immediately continues, "are conception, choice, desire, aversion, and, in a word, everything that is our own doing." By contrast, things that are not under our control are "our body, our property, reputation, office, and, in a word, everything that is not our own doing."[7]

The importance of this basic scheme of sorting to the larger Roman Stoic tradition would be hard to overestimate.[8] Its significance is paramount: yes,

5. Cochran, "Consent," 641.

6. Epictetus, *Manual*, trans. W. A. Oldfather, LCL (Cambridge, MA: Harvard University Press, 1925), 1.1. The translations in this article are generally my own. Interested readers can consult the Greek/Latin texts in any number of places, as well as the many different translations currently in existence. The standard place for the philologically curious to begin, however, is still the Loeb Classical Library (Marcus Aurelius, *Meditations*, trans. C. R. Haines, LCL [Cambridge, MA: Harvard University Press, 1916]; Seneca, *Epistles*, trans. Richard M. Gummere, LCL [Cambridge, MA: Harvard University Press, 1917]; Epictetus, *Discourses, Books 1–2*, trans. W. A. Oldfather, LCL [Cambridge, MA: Harvard University Press, 1925]).

7. Epictetus, *Manual* 1.1.

8. The entire doctrine of assent, for example, depends upon the right application of the scheme. Our child is sick: it seems to us that we should worry and feel anxious on the basis of this circumstance (the *phantasia*). We should not, however, assent to the truth of this *phantasia* because this is a circumstance that falls on the side of things that are "not

phantasiai come upon us from without and give us the stuff to sort. In this way they are primary. But they are not themselves the foundation of Stoic knowledge. To make them so is to formulate a kind of abstract theory about the significance of *phantasiai* that the Stoics themselves would deny. The foundation of Stoic knowledge is actually the Stoic *dogmata*, the principles that allow the right sorting of *phantasiai*. Without the Stoic scheme of sorting impressions, that is, there is no Stoic knowledge. *Phantasiai* have no independent significance for a theory of human knowledge. What is most important for Stoics, epistemologically speaking, is thus not what is outside (stimuli for impressions) but what is inside (Stoic training of the mind). When Cochran says that, like Edwards, the Stoics think we need help from beyond ourselves, she thus misunderstands the role and significance of *phantasiai* in the Stoic tradition.[9] The Stoic point is that precisely because of the way the "outside" comes to us unsorted, we have to rely on what can be established inside us. In a somewhat paradoxical way, the Stoic focus on what comes to us from without turns us away from impressions themselves and toward what they called the "inner" part of the human being. This leads to the second point.

Anthropology and Self-Sufficiency

Edwards held that we needed help from the triune God who was Lord over the cosmos and was not contained either in or through it. Human beings could not achieve true knowledge or live according to the pattern of Christ apart from the help of this God. The Stoics believed nothing of the kind. Indeed, the keystone of Stoic anthropology—or at least what makes their epistemology both exquisitely intelligible and consistent—is the radical self-sufficiency of the human being. By radical self-sufficiency the Stoics did not mean that humans were undamaged or that we needed no repair. (Stoicism itself is a way of conceiving the relation between human damage and repair.) What they meant, rather, was that by nature human beings had the incorruptible and

---

in our control." Both Epictetus (*Manual* 3.1) and Marcus Aurelius (*Meditations* 8.49; 9.40) use the case of a sick child to make this point. This example was not necessarily only a pedagogical device. In the case of Marcus at least, we know from his correspondence with Fronto that both he and Faustina were much troubled by the illness of their first daughter (little Faustina), who was sickly and then died. They lost other children as well. On this point, see Anthony Birley, *Marcus Aurelius: A Biography* (New Haven: Yale University Press, 1987), 105–8.

9. Cochran's understanding is predominantly on display in section 4 of her article ("Consent," 638–43).

indestructible ability to discipline themselves through a regime of practical knowledge. Seneca, Epictetus, and Marcus Aurelius did not have a rigorously consistent tripartite (or bipartite) anthropology, either in their own thinking or taken together, but they did speak clearly about the human being's possession of all the power it needed for true knowledge and self-governance. Seneca frequently speaks of the *anima*, Epictetus uniquely of the *prohairesis*, and Marcus regularly of the *hēgemonikon.* Each term signified the same basic anthropological reality: there is a space, or a faculty, whose sovereign power over impressions—and therefore over the life that emerges out of our ability to sort them correctly—is intrinsic to its very existence. Where is this space? It is within. The part of us that remains free and able to form right judgments is not in any sense "out there," something beyond us on which we must rely for healing. It is "in here," a materially constitutive part of our humanity. We can rely entirely upon ourselves because the inviolable, unconquerable place to look for help is, in fact, within ourselves.

Of course neither Seneca nor Epictetus nor Marcus believed in Cartesian-like innate ideas. Looking within, for the Roman Stoics, was more complex than looking for something that already existed in clear and distinct logical form. Being naturally able and free to sort impressions correctly is not the same thing as actually doing the job. To exercise well the natural and untouchable freedom of our inner faculty, the Stoics thought—no surprise, really—that we needed to become Stoics. The big three both presupposed and affirmed the importance of training so that when we looked within, what we would find would be Stoically formed judgments. When Marcus Aurelius admonishes himself again and again to "look within" and to retreat to his "inner fortress," he expects to find there not Descartes but Epictetus (whose discourses he closely studied), Rusticus (his early teacher), and perhaps Diognetus (who first showed him the worth of philosophical asceticism, "the pallet and the cloak"). In short, Marcus expects to find that the Stoic tradition is that which has taken up residence and awaits him within his acropolis. For the Stoics, precisely because sense impressions do not come already sorted, we must not look for help outside ourselves but must instead look to the only safe place in which we can surely place our trust: our inner fortress.[10]

10. For this reason Cochran's worry about the tendency of virtue ethics to foster an excessive focus on the self appears odd in an essay devoted to the promise of Stoicism. A reading of Marcus Aurelius's *Meditations* should show that the focus on the self was intense (see, e.g., 8.40). Indeed, Cochran's point against an extreme focus on the self could be turned against the Stoics.

Cosmology

Cochran's article frequently uses the words "God/divine" and "providence," at times implying that Edwards and the Stoics meant the same thing by these words: "Edwards and the Stoics share a conviction that moral development depends upon our encounters with external evidence of God's moral excellence."[11] "Both the Stoics and Edwards," Cochran later concludes, "put forth a view of moral formation that an agent cannot pursue exclusively through her own efforts. Virtue and its achievement are radically dependent upon the divine being."[12] Cochran does, of course, make some allowance for theological differences.[13] But she vastly underestimates the extent of the differences and the significance of such difference. For the Stoics there is no room for a categorical, ontological distinction between the referent of the words "god" and "world." God and world are different words that refer to that which eternally exists. As Seneca puts it, "This whole universe that encompasses us is one and it is God."[14] "All that you behold," he later tells Lucilius, "both god and humanity, is one—we are the parts of one great body."[15]

11. Cochran, "Consent," 642. See, too, p. 640: "Although Edwards's account of moral formation differs from that of the Stoics, he shares with them a conception of humans as dependent on divine providence." In order for Edwards to share a conception of dependence on divine providence he would have to share a conception of divine providence. But "dependence" and "divine providence" are here abstractions. Edwards does not agree with the Stoics about abstractions if only because it would be impossible to do. There is no meaning of providence prior to its embeddedness within a wider account of what it is. Compare also, for example: "Edwards develops a view of virtue as love to God, and his account of this virtue draws upon a philosophical framework with evident Stoic roots. Stoic assent to providence involves both an intellectual recognition of divine goodness and a volitional desire. . . . Edwardsean virtue likewise arises from 'spiritual knowledge' of God's goodness" (632).

12. Cochran, "Consent," 643. In this sentence, for example, the word "dependent" has drastically different connotations for the Stoics and Edwards. Edwards believes that "the divine being" can and does actually act upon the human being from without—that is, "supernaturally" (see Edwards's language at Cochran, "Consent," 641). Humans are dependent upon this sort of action from God's side of the Creator/creature distinction. For the Stoics "dependent" can only mean that the life of virtue cannot be established in any other way than by living according to nature (*kata physin*). The action in this case is entirely immanent, for all development of virtue occurs within the ambit of natural human powers.

13. For example, she says, "As is the case with other parallel features between Edwards and the Stoics, Edwards's account of moral formation does not perfectly mirror that of the Stoics" (Cochran, "Consent," 642).

14. Seneca, *Epistles* 92.30.

15. Seneca, *Epistles* 95.52.

This is not, however, to say that God and world are strictly interchangeable, that Stoic grammar would allow us to use "world" each and every time we wanted to say "God." God, rather, is the more precise word for what is ultimately rational in what is—the order of the world, or the laws by which we are to live, or the reasoning faculty within the human being itself. "Creative reason," Seneca instructs Lucilius, is the first cause of all things—"in other words, it is God."[16] Human reason is "the same" as divine reason, precisely "because it is derived from divine reason."[17] Epictetus, too, teaches his students in Nicomedia that we are "intertwined with God through reason."[18] And Marcus Aurelius could not agree more: reason constitutes human divinity, he tells himself; the mind of each is "God."[19]

As such language shows, though God and world are not always exact synonyms, God is not distinct from the world but is more an eternally abiding "grain of the universe," including the rational faculty found in human beings. God, for the Stoics, is simply written into what is.[20] God is not a personal, sentient being, someone who relates to us (in any normal sense of the word "relates") or who can intervene in the world's affairs from without. Stoic "prayers" are not, contra a surface reading of their texts, addressed to someone in particular. They are rather exhortations to remember the kind of world in which the Stoics found themselves and the kind of life toward which their philosophical work is directed.

This is true even for Epictetus, whose warmly pious tone is admittedly remarkable—indeed, with the possible exception of Cleanthes's famous hymn, unparalleled in other Stoic speech. Epictetus constitutes something of a special case: when reading him one has to hold together, as Epictetus himself did, the tone or flavor of his speech with the metaphysical *dogmata* of his teaching. For Epictetus, the latter call forth the former. "Piety toward the gods," he once taught, "is chiefly having right opinions about them."[21]

Despite the incisiveness of A. A. Long's recent study, God in Epictetus is not quite a "universal mind," as if God or God's "thoughts" were distinct from the world in which his *pronoia* comes to pass.[22] Nor could Epictetus be called

16. Seneca, *Epistles* 65.12; see also, e.g., *Epistles* 90.29.

17. Seneca, *Epistles* 92.1.

18. Epictetus, *Discourses* 1.9.5.

19. Marcus Aurelius, *Meditations* 12.26.

20. If we ask, "Who, then, is the writer?" we arrive at Anselm's famous argument very quickly. But this is not a question that makes sense in Stoic cosmology.

21. Epictetus, *Manual* 31.1.

22. A. A. Long, *Epictetus: A Stoic and Socratic Guide to Life* (Oxford: Clarendon, 2001),

a panentheist, as if all things were somehow in God, because all things are not "in" some other thing called God, or even intertwined with some other thing called God—for the simple reason that there is no distinction in the *Discourses* or *Manual* that would allow God to mean "another thing." All things, so Epictetus teaches, are united as one, and a particular pattern of that one is what the word "God" means.[23] What inspires Epictetus is not his relation to a personal being but something much more like the overwhelming beauty and majesty of the world's rational order. The world is finally quite sublime, Epictetus senses, and he responds to and articulates its sublimity with the grammar of awe and thanksgiving.[24]

What, then, of the language of providence? The Stoics, after all, are well known for their affirmation of the direction of the cosmos. Marcus Aurelius, for example, repeatedly poses the Epicurean alternative as a way to remind himself of this central Stoic belief: "Remember the alternative," Marcus says to himself, "either Providence or atoms!"[25] Even the works of Fortune—the Stoics' acknowledged bane of existence—"are not divorced from Nature or from the interweaving and binding of the threads by the guiding hand of Providence. From such guidance come all things."[26] Epictetus, too, never loses confidence in the guidance of Providence, and Seneca even wrote an entire treatise on the topic (*De Providentia*). When he comes to counsel Lucilius, he says his pupil ought to recall that "the whole universe about us go[es] by turns, that whatever has been put together is broken up again, that whatever has been broken up is put together again, and that the eternal craftsmanship of God, who controls all things, is working at this task."[27]

Providence for the Stoics is not the word for the guiding hand of a

148, prefers "universal mind" as a way to describe Epictetus's God. Yet at 148 n. 5 Long articulates another reason—in addition to the one given above—why we should not speak this way: "In Stoic doctrine God is 'embodied' in pneuma, literally 'breath.'" On the same page, Long also speaks of Epictetus as a panentheist, but this, too, is problematic for the reasons given above.

23. For example, Epictetus, *Discourses* 1.14.1–10.

24. This character of the world has affected countless people down through ages and is not a kind of piety that is strange to us. Many of the Romantics had a piety of this sort, as did Pierre Hadot (see especially the conversations in P. Hadot, *The Present Alone Is Our Happiness: Conversations with Jeannie Carlier and Arnold I. Davidson*, trans. Marc Djaballah and Michael Chase [Stanford, CA: Stanford University Press, 2009]).

25. Marcus Aurelius, *Meditations* 4.3.2; 8.17; 9.28.

26. Marcus Aurelius, *Meditations* 2.3; see also 2.11.

27. Seneca, *Epistles* 71.14.

sentient God who superintendently works upon the eternal dissolution/reconstitution cycle of the cosmos from without. Providence, rather, is the Stoic word for the ordering principle inherent within. Where Christian grammar requires robust teleological affirmations to accompany its use of Providence, Stoic grammar does not. The eternal cycle—or flux, as Marcus often refers to it—is not going anywhere in particular, aims at nothing down the road, has no purpose that lies beyond itself. Or, rather, we could say that for the Stoics the cosmos is going somewhere but only in the sense of going toward the great, fiery combustion (*conflagratio/ekpyrōsis*) and then away from it, again and again in a process of eternal self-renewal through change. The repeated dispersion of reason through the cyclical process—both in terms of the overarching order of the cosmos and the human capacity for self-direction in line with this order—is what Providence is.[28] To here speak of intention—Reason intends to do this again and again—is to move toward hypostasization and to say far too much. There is no will that is able to intend. Things are just this way, so the Roman Stoics thought. To speak of the benevolence of Providence, therefore, is not to say much more than that the Stoics take such eternal reasonableness to be a good.[29] Providence, in Stoic teaching, names the recurrent reasonableness of the way things are, the fact that it will always be so, and the Stoics' evaluation of such reasonableness as good. Aligning ourselves with Providence thus means in Stoic teaching that we are to live, as they never tired of putting it, "according to nature." That is, our virtues are displayed exactly to the extent that we join the perpetual movement of our dissolution and dispersion in another arrangement.[30]

28. Chrysippus was of course known for his "determinism," but Stoic views of providence do not leave out the freedom of the human to be in accord with nature (or to refuse such accordance). See Suzanne Bobzien, "Stoic Conceptions of Freedom and Their Relation to Ethics," in *Aristotle and After*, ed. Richard Sorabji (London: Institute of Classical Studies, 1997), 71–89, as well as Bobzien, *Determinism and Freedom in Stoic Philosophy* (Oxford: Oxford University Press, 2001).

29. Cochran argues that Edwards shares with the Stoics the notion that virtue is "consent to a benevolent providence" ("Consent," 624).

30. Though I have read some of Edwards, I am no scholar of his thought. But it seems to me that this is a far cry from what he means by virtue as consent to "Being in general," or God's benevolent providence, or "love to God and joy in Christ" and so forth. If Cochran is right about Edwards himself, it makes it harder for her to be right about the Stoics or Edwards's material dependence upon them.

Stoic Insights and a Pattern of Life

Cochran speaks of the "Stoic insights" that Christians can retrieve and put to use in their own formulae.[31] Yet the Stoics themselves did not conceive of philosophy as a group of insights that were transportable from one place to another. They thought, rather, that Stoicism was a pattern of life, a style of being, or an existential trajectory. The "insights" that were Stoic were so because they corresponded to a lived intellectual structure, not an independent set of noetic truths. Moreover, the Stoic style is not most fundamentally a "receptive process" but a very active one, a way of being that both depends upon and results in discrete disciplines and exercises—physical as well as spiritual.[32] This point is not new. It was made in 1954 by Paul Rabbow in his classic book on the spiritual/intellectual disciplines antecedent to Ignatius and, more recently, by a host of writers on ancient Greco-Roman philosophy.[33] But for those who wish to use ancient philosophy for their own ends, it is nevertheless profoundly important to understand.

Ancient Stoicism was more like what we have learned to call a religion than what we now call philosophy in the modern university.[34] When we treat

31. "Christian virtue ethicists have tended to neglect the Stoics' insights" (Cochran, "Consent," 623).

32. Cochran, "Consent," 624.

33. Though the constructive side of his thought is less well known, the historical work of Pierre Hadot is now widely read. To take only a few other examples, see Ilsetraut Hadot, *Seneca und die griechisch-römische Tradition der Seelenleitung, Quellen und Studien zur Geschichte der Philosophie; Bd. 13* (Berlin: de Gruyter, 1969); Gabriele Kuen, *Die Philosophie als "dix vitae": Die Verknüpfung von Gehalt, Intention und Darstellungsweise im philosophischen Werk Senecas am Beispiel des Dialogs "De vita beata"—Einleitung, Wortkommentar und systematischer Darstellung* (Heidelberg: Winter, 1994); and John Sellars, *The Art of Living: The Stoics on the Nature and Function of Philosophy* (Burlington, VT: Ashgate, 2003). Occasionally, this focus on "living" is taken to imply that the emphasis upon "logic" had waned. For an argument against this impression and for the ongoing importance of logic in the Imperial period, see Jonathan Barnes, *Logic and the Imperial Stoa* (Leiden: Brill, 1997).

34. For a classic formulation of the modern view of philosophy, no one is perhaps clearer than Hegel. See Hegel's 1825–1826 *Lectures on the History of Philosophy*: "In what sense do we wish to treat the history of philosophy, namely, the history of free, concrete thought, or of reason? Nothing counts as reason that is not the result of thinking. *Thought that is free is thought that relates itself to itself.* So we have expressed the question as follows: In what sense do we wish to treat the history of thinking reason? What is its significance? The answer is straightforward. *The history can be expounded in no other sense than that of thought itself.* . . . In all other instances we can ask about the sense of the significance of the object. Thus in the case of art, or of language, or religion too, or other enterprises . . . we

Roman Stoicism as a repository of thinking on some topic—virtue, wisdom, divinity, and so on—we create an abstraction that severs ancient thought from its pragmatic position within distinctive options of how to live a good human life. Anthologies can tell us where to go to begin reading on particular topics, but they should not be taken to give us "Stoic thinking" on the virtues. Stoic thinking on the virtues was Stoic precisely because it was embedded within the particular style of existence called Stoicism. One cannot think both as an Aristotelian and as a Stoic vis-à-vis the virtues or passions, for example, principally because one cannot live both ways at once. What Stoicism presented in the ancient world was a choice—a distinctive set of disciplines designed to bring the Stoic, as Marcus Aurelius put it, "into another life."[35] When one becomes a Stoic, the ancients thought, then one will learn how to think Stoically—that is, to work wisely and virtuously inside the essential unity between insights and patterns of being.

The Retrieval of the Stoics

Ancient Stoic philosophy is often a port of call for ethicists of a variety of normative commitments. L. C. Becker, for example, has recently offered an "ethical naturalism" on the basis of a retrieval of the ancient Stoics.[36] And Richard Sorabji is particularly well known for his provocative work at the

ask about their sense or significance, about their value, their moral value. The significance of this sense is the essential thing; it is what is universal or substantial about such an object, and this substantial aspect of the object is the concrete thought of the object. In such cases two factors are always in play: the sense or the thought, and the presentation of expression of the phenomenon in perception. We have something outward and something inward; we have an external phenomenon, and a significance on its own account that is quite simply the thought. *But since our topic now is thought itself we do not have two factors, an inward element and an outward reality. Thought alone has significance on its own account.*" Georg Wilhelm Friedrich Hegel, *Lectures on the History of Philosophy*, ed. Robert F. Brown, trans. R. F. Brown and J. M. Stewart with the assistance of H. S. Harris (Oxford: Oxford University Press, 2009), 48; emphasis added.

35. Marcus Aurelius, *Meditations* 8.2; see also 7.2. For example, Pierre Hadot, *The Inner Citadel: The Meditations of Marcus Aurelius* (Cambridge, MA: Harvard University Press, 1998), analyzes Marcus Aurelius's *Meditations* along the lines of three core Stoic disciplines (judgment, desire, action). The *Meditations* are not, that is, just thoughts. They are thought-in-practice, thought-doing-work.

36. See Lawrence C. Becker, *A New Stoicism* (Princeton: Princeton University Press, 1999).

intersection of ancient (often Stoic) and modern philosophies of the self.[37] But as the four areas of the preceding discussion ought to make clear, Roman Stoicism presents a particularly difficult case for fruitful conversation with contemporary Christian theology/ethics. The chief reasons are three. First, Stoic philosophy hinges on an anthropological claim that Christian theology must resolutely deny—that human beings are safe and self-sufficient in their inner fortresses. Second, Christians and Stoics do not mean the same thing with the words "God" and "Providence"; indeed, the meanings are incommensurable. Such incommensurability, however, is not limited to the ways in which we abstract from life in order to think but is in fact a practically shaped difference. So, third, precisely because the difference is both so deep and so practical, one cannot live as a Stoic and as a Christian at the same time. We cannot simply extract Stoic "virtues" from Stoic lives and plop them into a Christian form of life without losing that which makes them Stoic virtues in the first place.[38] Christianity and Stoicism are in the end existentially thick choices; they are patterns of existence—ethics in the broad sense—that rule each other out.

It is true that Christians have long engaged the Stoics and learned much from them.[39] Yet the time has come for a kind of critical reflection upon the

37. See Richard Sorabji, *Emotion and Peace of Mind: From Stoic Agitation to Christian Temptation* (Oxford: Oxford University Press, 2000), and Sorabji, *Self: Ancient and Modern Insights about Individuality, Life, and Death* (Chicago: University of Chicago Press, 2006). There are some, of course, who think the Stoics unpalatable or simply unbelievable. See, for example, Bernard Williams's response to Sorabji (Williams, "Stoic Philosophy and the Emotions," in Sorabji, *Aristotle and After*, 211–13).

38. Virtues are not abstract conceptions—capable of detachment from the lives in which we see them—but are particular patterns that always occur inside of larger lived narratives. We must say "narratives" because the continuity of "selves" is itself something that is narratively shaped (Alasdair MacIntyre, *After Virtue* [Notre Dame, IN: University of Notre Dame Press, 1981], 190–209). In short, virtues receive narrative exemplification and must also, therefore, receive narrative explication.

39. For (part of) the history of the Christian encounter with Stoicism, see Marcia Colish's expansive work, *The Stoic Tradition from Antiquity to the Early Middle Ages*, 2 vols. (Leiden: Brill, 1985). For a focused treatment of the theme of this longer work, see her "Stoicism and the New Testament: An Essay in Historiography," *Aufstieg und Niedergang der römischen Welt* II.26.1 (1992): 334–79. It is of course true, as Colish argues in the 1992 article, that we can discern a wide range of ideological tendencies by reading the history of the way scholars from different fields have conceived the relation between Stoicism and Christianity. Rather than uncovering a single "historical" core of truth about Stoicism's relation to Christianity that persists from one author to another, says Colish, study of the historiographies of different scholars primarily provides an entrée into historically irresponsible ideologies—the

ethics of retrieval itself. Precisely to the degree that we cleave the ancient connection between thought and life, we, first, deny the Stoics the seriousness with which they took their philosophy, which is to say the shape of their lives as they tried to live in patterns of therapy and healing; and, second, we use them for our own constructive ends in ways that minimize the existential gravitas of their thought and obscure their claims to wisdom and truth. The Stoics believed that by living as a Stoic one discovered wisdom. Our modes of retrieval, however, run the risk of saying that we can have the Stoic wisdom without the Stoicism. There is nothing inherently wrong with a kind of Christian bricolage—using what pieces seem good to use[40]—but when it comes to the Stoics, we should admit that such a piecemeal retrieval treats the Stoics not as Stoics but as repositories of useful information. To put it very starkly, a retrieval such as Cochran's uses the Stoics as encyclopedias. The Stoics cease to be real Stoics.

This is not to say that when reading the Roman Stoics we will be unable to find areas of important agreement or that we cannot learn from them how better to reason Christianly about ethics, but it is to say that what we will learn most of all is that the Christians and the Stoics cannot both be right about how to live, and that ethics is not detachable from our form of life but flows from it. In short, what Christians will learn by a close reading of Seneca, Epictetus, and Marcus Aurelius is that we conflict. The significance for Christian ethics of a retrieval of Stoicism is thus not that we gain this or that insight into abstract general notions called "God" or "Providence," or that we see more deeply into "virtues" that somehow exist apart from their exemplifications in particular forms of human life. The significance, rather, emerges through the process of a slow and patient education in how to engage a historically deep and productive

scholar's deeper normative commitments, so Çolish thinks, that drive the use of the Stoic material and prevent sound historical (i.e., non-ideological) scholarship. Yet as almost any philosopher nowadays could point out, the desire for historiography that is non-ideological is in vain. Indeed, given that we cannot escape the way we think, it is utterly unsurprising to find history yoked to contemporary concerns. The same deconstructive procedure Colish employs on her chosen scholarly victims could be conducted on her own essay, then immediately thereafter on my reading of her reading, and again on that reading of my reading of her reading, ad infinitum. Precisely because there is no ideologically disinterested inquiry or representation of the past, the turn of this screw never ends. The best thing to do, therefore, is to acknowledge the interweaving of all historical reconstruction with deeper normative interests, declare these interests up front, and get on with the readings.

40. The most articulate argument for the moral necessity of bricolage in general remains Jeffrey Stout, *Ethics after Babel: The Languages of Morals and Their Discontents* (Boston: Beacon, 1988).

conflict of traditions. Through a dialogue with the Roman Stoics, Christians can gain deeper learning in how to talk with people whose pattern of life, were it to be true, would falsify ours (and vice versa). We can thereby come face to face with a serious alternative to Christianity.[41] That this is itself a task of great ethical weight, both in antiquity and today, requires no further elaboration. It is a task, however, that requires a great deal of further work.

41. In putting things this way, I obviously side with those who think Stoicism still works in many ways as a call to a certain kind of (or even new) existence. As a literary example, we may think of Conrad Hensley in Tom Wolfe's 1988 novel *A Man in Full.* From the real world, as it were, James B. Stockdale, *Courage under Fire: Testing Epictetus's Doctrines in a Laboratory of Human Behavior* (Stanford, CA: Hoover Institution, 1993), makes a compelling case for the contemporary vibrancy of Stoicism from his own seven-year experience in a Vietnam prison camp. The fact that we cannot reproduce all the ancient conditions that surround Stoic life is, of course, not unique to Stoicism. It is true also for Christianity, Judaism, and any other form of life from the ancient world. So, too, the fact that modern neuroscientific research (e.g., Antonio Damasio) and psychology (e.g., Timothy Wilson) render problematic Stoic notions of how judgment/assent works is not as damaging to the Stoic project as it might first appear. See the chapter "What Is Missing from the Judgmental Analysis? Brain Research and Limitations on Stoic Cognitive Therapy" in Sorabji, *Emotion and Peace of Mind*, 144–55.

God, Greek Philosophy, and the Bible

◆ A RESPONSE TO MATTHEW LEVERING

"I set the brake up by connecting rod and lever."—Yes, given the whole of the rest of the mechanism. Only in conjunction with that is it a brake-lever, and separated from its support it is not even a lever; it may be anything, or nothing.[1]

Professor Levering's recent article "God and Greek Philosophy in Contemporary Biblical Scholarship" is a wonderful example of the kind of work this journal hopes to foster and the crucial theological questions integrative conversation can raise.[2] Levering is known not only for including scripture in his constructive theological proposals but also for taking the time to read what scholars who labor daily with the Bible are saying about its texts.[3] This reading

1. Ludwig Wittgenstein, *Philosophical Investigations*, 4th ed. (Oxford: Blackwell, 2009), §6.

2. Matthew Levering, "God and Greek Philosophy in Contemporary Biblical Scholarship," *JTI* 4 (2010): 169–85.

3. Of his many excellent books, see in particular Matthew Levering, *Christ's Fulfillment of Torah and Temple: Salvation in Thomas Aquinas* (Notre Dame, IN: University of Notre Dame Press, 2002); *Scripture and Metaphysics: Aquinas and the Renewal of Trinitarian Theology* (Oxford: Blackwell, 2004); *Ezra and Nehemiah*, BTCB (Grand Rapids: Brazos, 2007); *Participatory Biblical Exegesis: A Theology of Biblical Interpretation* (Notre Dame, IN: University of Notre Dame Press, 2008); and *Biblical Natural Law: A Theocentric and Teleological Approach* (New York: Oxford University Press, 2008).

"God, Greek Philosophy, and the Bible: A Response to Matthew Levering" was originally published in *Journal of Theological Interpretation* 5 (2011): 69–80. Republished with permission of Pennsylvania State University Press: A Division of the Pennsylvania State University Libraries and Scholarly Communications; permission conveyed through Copyright Clearance Center, Inc.

habit is the work that makes intelligible the background sophistication evident throughout this most recent essay. This sort of sophistication, however, is not simply about erudition. More significantly, it also illustrates how a habit of reading widely outside our narrowly construed fields can prompt a return to a serious study of scripture in an effort to think well about some of the most basic theological questions Christians need to ask. Properly understood, Levering's essay forces us to articulate what we think about fundamental matters such as the knowledge of God, the proper disciplining of truthful theological speech, the way words mean, the unity of the intellectual and moral life, and the practice and significance of careful exegesis of scripture.

Because a main point implicit in Levering's reading of biblical scholarship is that serious constructive theology requires scriptural reasoning, his essay provides an occasion for a response that asks in what way his reasoning is itself scriptural. Levering, that is, does not simply want to endorse Richard Bauckham's arguments or caution us against overlooking the importance of Greek philosophy for understanding the theological tradition; he also wants to learn how better to think theologically by engaging the Bible and its close readers. At its heart, this is the question about the extent to which we need the Bible to reason well about God.

However, rather than examine the scriptural shape of Levering's thinking in a kind of crassly simplistic or direct way—checking his citation of 1 Timothy 1:17, say, against a careful exegesis of the Greek text—I will pursue this question via a response to his reading of my recent book, *World Upside Down: Reading Acts in the Graeco-Roman Age*.[4] The reason for this choice is not so much an attempt at clarification of my argument in *World Upside Down* as it is a judgment that Levering's discussion of this book in particular reveals the deeper assumptions that shape his thinking on the question of God and Greek philosophy throughout his essay—and, further, that these assumptions are precisely those that need scrutiny if we are to learn how to think along with scripture about this crucial question.

Levering's basic point is that Greek philosophy can on its own "independent" terms attain "true insights" into "philosophical ontology" and "God" and that the Bible and subsequent Christian tradition take these insights without fundamental change into their own constructive statements about God, supplementing them where needed with Jewish/Christian belief.[5] Levering

4. C. Kavin Rowe, *World Upside Down: Reading Acts in the Graeco-Roman Age* (Oxford: Oxford University Press, 2009).

5. Supplementation of this sort can, of course, be more or less critical, depending on the

therefore criticizes those who think that the Bible and pagan philosophical traditions were not fundamentally compatible and that the NT in particular offers a "rival narrative" to those that can be found in the wider Mediterranean world. Surely, argues Levering, the early Christians could and did make use of pagan philosophical truth on their way to expressing their views about God. Where true insights are concerned, pagan philosophy and Christian theology will not conflict, for these insights pertain, for both the Christians and the pagan philosophers, to the "Father and Maker of all the universe."

Levering's way of thinking coheres remarkably well, of course, with a division between philosophy and theology held by many prominent Catholic thinkers. Indeed, Levering's essay can be read as evidence of the way an answer to the question of scripture, God, and Greek philosophy will be determined if one already thinks within the scheme of this basic philosophy-theology division. In practice, that is, it appears as though Levering does not so much "think with" scripture about the Greek philosophical traditions as use the already-held position on the division between theology and philosophy to make sense of the complex cluster of questions surrounding the relation of the NT to the Greco-Roman world. Of course, all human inquiry employs regulative intellectual patterns (schemata) to read the past. There is nothing wrong in principle, therefore, with reading scripture explicitly with our own patterns of thought, and this for the simple reason that we can do nothing else. In fact, however, the division between philosophy and theology produces and/or reinforces several other fundamental divisions that do turn out to damage scriptural reasoning about God and pagan philosophical life. In my judgment, there are three interrelated issues that emerge out of Levering's treatment of *World Upside Down* that—when taken together—disclose the kind of divisions in Levering's thinking that prove disabling for a scripturally disciplined articulation of Christianity's relation to pagan philosophical life.[6] The three

quality or depth of the true insight or the degree to which it is intertwined with problematic ways of worship, behavior, and so forth.

6. It is important to note that Levering engages only a very small part of the argument of *World Upside Down* (principally, my reading of the Areopagus speech in Acts 17) and presents this small part as the whole. By oversimplifying one side of my argument about Acts and the Greco-Roman world, Levering obscures the dialectical relation I sought to establish and, as a consequence, presents a rather lopsided analysis of the book. The whole of chap. 3 especially does not figure in Levering's discussion, but the entirety of that chapter assumes Luke's legal learning and ability to reason within Roman law. Paying closer attention to that chapter would have helped considerably with the problem of oversimplification (I do not, for example, assume that Greek philosophy is "at war" with the Christian story). It is also necessary to say that Levering's implicit point against reading the Bible as a culturally

issues are (1) how words mean, (2) the relation between "philosophical" words and a pattern of life in ancient pagan philosophy, and (3) the importance of the "pressure" of the biblical text for a theoretical elaboration of the human knowledge of God. Clarifying the central matters involved in each of the three issues will result in a different overall picture from the one Levering paints. In the effort to see its main features, we turn now to these three issues—with the final caveat that this response to Levering is offered in the spirit of a communal *fides quaerens intellectum* and with the purpose of generating further discussion of the crucial theological points raised by his essay.

How Words Mean

The first issue is a question about how words mean—their relation to their larger semantic contexts—and therefore a question also about philosophy. Levering seems to think that words mean on their own, that when we find a phrase such as "the father and maker of all this universe is past finding out," we know that the words mean the same thing whether the phrase occurs in Plato's *Timaeus* or the Bible or Augustine or presumably—were it to turn up there—in the Upanishads or a random piece of papyrus, and so on. By contrast, I reject this view of language and instead think that words mean what they mean in relation to their larger linguistic setting.[7] The "him" of "in him we live and

pristine document—free from the "influence" of Hellenism and the like—may have had a good target in the biblical theology movement of the 1950s in the United States, or in certain moments of liberal Protestant scholarship in nineteenth-century Germany, but these targets have entirely disappeared from biblical/historical scholarship (regardless of sociocultural location or theological *Tendenz*). No significant NT scholar of the last sixty years believes that the Bible is pristine in the sense against which Levering argues. The focus on "influence" is a distraction. The question is not whether the Bible is influenced by the world in which it was born—how could it be otherwise?—but whether words as we find them in the Bible mean elsewhere what they mean in the Bible. For example, I say many times over that Luke phrases things in Acts 17 in accordance with the wisdom of the Greek poets and philosophers. The point, however, is that their wisdom is transformed hermeneutically by the location of the statements inside a Christian theological grammar.

7. As Wittgenstein once said, "A smiling mouth *smiles* only in a human face" (*Philosophical Investigations*, §583: "Ein lächelnder Mund *lächelt* nur in einem menschlichen Gesicht"). For those who wonder why we then use particular words rather than others—"Is it not because of their inherent meaning?" they ask—we can say rather simply that we tend to use words based on the history that carries them along, traditions of using them to mean certain things rather than others, and not because they inherently mean certain things irrespective of the context in which they are employed. Recognizing the importance of traditions of

move and have our being" in Acts 17:28, for example, may well be called "the Deity" or "God" in Stoic cosmology, but what the Stoics mean by God is what the Christians mean by the world/creation/nature. With allowance for nuance here and there, the Stoics are basically pantheists (*Natura* and *Deus* are fundamentally interchangeable in their philosophical/theological grammar). Were we to encounter the phrase "in him we live and move . . ." in a Stoic philosophical text, therefore, the "him" of whom the text speaks would not be the God of the Christian tradition but instead a part of creation. To refer to that part of creation as "God" would then be to make an illegitimate theological move, otherwise known in Christian theological grammar as idolatry. The "him" does not in Stoic thought mean the Christian God. It means something else.

When Levering says, therefore, that Paul's (Luke's!) statement in Acts 17:28–29 that God cannot be represented by human technical skill and imaginative power is an "insight he shares with many Greek philosophers," the basic difference in the referent of "deity/God"—for the one, the world, for the other, the God of Israel—is simply ignored. So, too, when Levering commends Bauckham's discussion of the attribute of "eternity" in Hebrews, he follows Bauckham by invoking a general category of "deity" about which both the Bible and the Hellenistic philosophers were trying to speak.[8] But there is no such category. Or, rather, the category of a general "God/god" is neither the God about whom the author of Hebrews spoke nor that of the pagan philosophers: it is an abstraction that we can conceive only because of the extraction of particular words and their subsequent reembedding in a different grammar (the academic theorizing of religion).

The point here is that just because the exact same words can be theologically true in one context and idolatrous in another, we cannot take statements such as Plato's as evidence that Greek philosophy spoke rightly about God within the structure of its own thought. We may well like the sound or flavor of the words as *we* see them—and so use them to help us say things we want to say—but to take them as expressing true theological wisdom about the triune God, we must already have read them Christianly. Of course it is true that if we insert "the father and maker of all this universe" into Christian theological discourse—voilà!—we will have an agreement between the words written by Plato and Christian teaching. But this is best explained by the

---

word use for word meaning explains, of course, how word meaning can be *both* relatively stable *and* always changing.

8. See Levering, "God and Greek Philosophy," esp. 182–84.

linguistic-and-therefore-also-and-always-philosophical point that the meaning of the words is determined by the discourse in which they are placed. Invoking the term "philosophy" or a sense of indeterminacy does not, therefore, establish a neutral ground wherein the meaning of similar words can be equated irrespective of the larger philosophical/theological grammar in which they are employed. There is no such thing as word meaning by itself. Words will have a Christian meaning only when they are read within a Christian (linguistic) framework.[9]

What all this means in relation to scripture in a wider sense seems rather obvious. We cannot simply take the words of the Bible—a sentence here, a phrase there—and line them up with similar-sounding words from other texts/thinkers to gain an equivalence of meaning, not least about an abstract category called "God/god." A procedure such as this eliminates scripture itself as the normative grammatical context in which scriptural words have their meaning. By establishing a new linguistic context for meaning—the one created by the scholarly compiler—a new meaning is fashioned, and equivalence emerges. Here, the language of invention describes the hermeneutical move far better than that of discovery. The agreement is produced in the "mind" of the scholar by virtue of the context he himself has created for the assembly of his collected phrases (e.g., ancient views on "Deity/deity").[10] In this sense, contra Levering, the "truth" of the words he cites from Romans 1, 1 Timothy, and James[11] does depend "upon their placement within the biblical narrative of the Creator God" because in fact without that placement they mean something else.

9. To relate this point to other areas in philosophical discussion, we might observe the similarity between this linguistic point and the Anscombe/MacIntyre position that an intelligible intention/action is a more fundamental concept than an intention/action per se (see G. E. M. Anscombe, *Intention* [Ithaca, NY: Cornell University Press, 1957], and Alasdair MacIntyre, *After Virtue*, 3rd ed. [Notre Dame, IN: University of Notre Dame Press, 2007]). Levering's argument enjoins us to reverse this order. But the order cannot in fact be reversed. Cf. the discussion about the per se significance/knowledge of bees and fig trees, pp. 224–26 below.

10. Cf. Jonathan Z. Smith's perceptive essay "In Comparison a Magic Dwells," which makes exactly this point in relation to so-called comparative investigations in anthropology/religious studies (in *A Magic Still Dwells: Comparative Religion in a Postmodern Age*, ed. Kimberly C. Patton and Benjamin C. Ray [Berkeley: University of California Press, 2000], 23–46).

11. Levering, "God and Greek Philosophy," 184.

Ancient Philosophy and Modern Dichotomies

The point about word meaning is also a point, however, about the embeddedness of words in life. As Nock, Hadot, Brisson, Sorabji, Kuen, and others have stressed, ancient philosophy was not an intellectual discussion in abstraction from a pattern of life; it was instead more like a thinking life. By assuming that we can extract words and phrases from philosophical texts for their "insight," Levering obscures the embodied nature of ancient philosophy and overlooks yet another (philosophical!) point about language: it was lived. To be true to ancient philosophy we can no more remove the words from the philosophical grammars of the texts in which they occur than we can extract the texts from the lives of those who sought to live by them. (To be more precise, of course, we *can* remove texts from their role in the lives of those who used them and read these texts without reference to their embeddedness in life. But when we then discover insights in them that teach us more about what we already know to be true—that is, Christian faith—we should not be confused about the location of the generative discourse of meaning.) Though there were changes in the ways the various philosophical schools were constituted, the underlying point of having a "school" or "community" remained the same: philosophy—whether Platonism, Aristotelianism, Stoicism, or something else—was training in how to live (*ars vivendi*). To turn ancient philosophy into a textual repository for Christian insights (or insights that, when discovered, agree with already-held Christian teaching) is already to have reproduced the modern dichotomy between thought and life and moved well away from what ancient philosophy actually was.

Remembering that ancient philosophy was fundamentally about a scheme of life is critical to understanding the practical shift that occurs when words from pagan philosophical traditions are inserted into a Christian grammar. I do not, for example, argue that "when incorporated into the Christian story, Greek philosophical insights are no longer *philosophical*."[12] The point, rather, is that because Greek philosophical words are words that are inextricably intertwined with a pattern of life—not simply thoughts floating around for the taking—one cannot introduce pagan philosophical words into Christian discourse without losing the practical sense or lived shape of the pagan words. The way of life that the words explicate will have been divorced from the words themselves, and the words will now be taken to speak of the shape of life called Christian. One cannot, that is, actually live the statement "in him we live and

12. Levering, "God and Greek Philosophy," 179.

move and have our being" simultaneously as both a Christian and a Stoic. Praxis, in its richest sense of the living of life, really is that deeply connected to word meaning.[13] The argument in *World Upside Down* about "incommensurability" between Christian life and Greco-Roman philosophical lives is thus as much about the fact that we cannot live more than one life as it is about the nature of independent intellectual inquiry. Even Clement of Alexandria, perhaps the most philosophically literate person in the early church, did not think he could live two lives. Much to the contrary, for Clement, the philosophical life *is* the Christian life. As Henry Chadwick once cleverly remarked, Clement "loves Plato and Homer, but he does not read them on his knees."[14] Removing words from their contexts by reading them as insights into this or that Christian truth thus runs the risk not only of fundamentally changing the meaning of the words but also of denying the people who wrote them the seriousness with which they took the shape of their lives—which is to say, in its ancient sense, the seriousness of *philosophia* itself.

The "Pressure" of Scripture

Levering presents his case as if the main difference between *World Upside Down* and his way of seeing things is a competing theory (or account) of knowledge. I would rather talk about our differences vis-à-vis the attempt to read with the grain of the biblical text. This is a crucial point because were Levering's epistemological account to allow for a better reading of scripture, I would need to rewrite my exposition of Acts. But, in my view, Levering's account does not make for a better reading of the Areopagus discourse in Acts 17. In fact, as far I can see exegetically, this passage contradicts the heart of Levering's argument about "independent insight into philosophical ontology." His argument, therefore, resists or deflects the pressure the text puts on his view. Moreover, Levering's claim fares far worse with Acts as a whole or—to take only one more example—Paul's letter to the Romans (Paul's argument in Rom. 1 makes it clear that, despite God's self-revelation in the cosmos, the Gentiles did not know him). Levering wishes I would extend the insight of

13. To put it in communal terms, one has to move from the Academy or the Lyceum or the Garden to the Ecclesia. The Ecclesia is the hermeneutical community within which the practical sense of the once-pagan words now takes Christian shape.

14. Henry Chadwick, *Early Christian Thought and the Classical Tradition* (Oxford: Oxford University Press, 1966), 37.

my "Biblical Pressure" article to philosophy;[15] I wish him to take seriously the pressure the biblical text exerts on his theory of theological knowledge.

Of course, Levering may reply that he is not so much trying to do exegesis as he is thinking about the larger speculative features of Christian knowledge. But this would be insufficient precisely because Levering is trying to think Christianly about the questions he raises, and part of doing that well is the willingness to be normed in the direction of our thought by scripture. In this case, the norming force of scripture points in two directions. On the one hand, if my reading of Acts is exegetically compelling, then Levering should be willing, at least in principle, to adjust how he thinks about these issues (however much this adjustment would run against certain streams of our inherited tradition—but see, for example, Chrysostom's homilies on Acts for a counterexample). On the other hand, if Levering is right, then his conceptual structure ought to help us to read Acts better. In short, we cannot escape exegesis: Levering owes us a better reading of Acts 17.[16] Indeed, until we receive a better reading of Acts, it will continue to look suspiciously like Levering's argument is with Luke rather than with Rowe.

Conclusion

In support of the larger argument throughout his essay, Levering cites a fascinating passage from Gregory of Nazianzus's *On God and Christ: Five Theological Orations.* Gregory, says Levering in an attempt to establish the importance of independent insight into the truth of the world, "suggests that some shared knowledge about the existence of bees is possible: 'bees devise honeycombs which hold together with hexagonal, matching cavities, made elaborately firm by a partition and by the subtlety of alternate straight lines and angles, in hives too dark for them to see the structure of the comb.'" From such observations, Levering argues, "Gregory of Nazianzus finds in the intelligent hive-

15. C. Kavin Rowe, "Biblical Pressure and Trinitarian Hermeneutics," now in part 1 of this volume. The crucial feature of "pressure" is not that we need ontological specification (as if somehow ontology names an altogether independent sphere of thought) but that our conceptual resources have to be able to receive the pressure of the text (which—of course—will include ontological specification within its ambit). Using what the world has to offer in order to receive the pressure of the biblical text is, in dogmatic terms, nothing more than the elucidation of the interconnection between creation and redemption.

16. And that, of course, is just the beginning. His reading of Acts 17 will need then to open up on the larger book of Acts, Rom. 1, and so forth.

construction by non-intelligent bees evidence that God exists and gives order to the universe." This does not, however, mean that pagans cannot see the truth of Gregory's observations about the physical nature of beehives. "Nonetheless," as Levering says, "some truth is attained that can be shared by people whose 'entire pattern of life' differs: beehives and budding leaves shape our narratives and indeed have a certain independence to which rival narratives must conform. In some sense, there is an 'independent order,' if only because beehives and budding leaves do not conform themselves to our narratives."[17]

From this use of Gregory of Nazianzus's wonder at bees and the implication that non-Christian thinkers can agree with Gregory's description of the art of hive-making, one might think that rejecting the notion that pagan philosophy speaks Christianese requires the correlative denial that the world is God's creation. Μὴ γένοιτο! Christians, I assume, should always be generous to all the world's knowledge; indeed, this is the epistemological posture required by a theology of creation. But not only is it significant that Gregory of Nazianzus is a Christian theologian—as if his view of the bees' witness to an ordering God were somehow unrelated to his willingness to read the world through Christ—it is also difficult to know what really to make of the per se truth of bees.[18] The reason is quite simple: independent order does not tell us anything independently.

Indeed, to move to Levering's next example, Jesus's fig-tree remark in Luke 21:29–30 ("Look at the fig tree . . .") is entirely unclear without the narrative theological context of the gospel in which it occurs—which is to say, once again, that the common per se truth of fig trees does not occur by itself but is subsumed within a larger (Christian) hermeneutical pattern of meaning (the saying is in fact apocalyptic). More strongly put, we do not ever know the per se truth of bees, trees, or anything else. We do not—because we cannot—think like this. The pressure the world exerts on our reading of it is always received within wider assumptions and accounts of what it is that is received. The fact that Christians can find agreement with non-Christians on a wide variety of things is hardly surprising given the fact that we inhabit the same created world (we can agree with many others on, for example, the molecular composition of water, the fact that most bees sting, that some flowers produce pungent odors, and virtually countless other matters). What would be surprising would be if we were somehow to discover this sort of agreement

17. Levering, "God and Greek Philosophy," 177–78.

18. Presumably, like all ancients, Gregory thought the queen bee was the king. In this, he was wrong with the rest. Cf. n. 19 below.

through reflection on the per se truth of the objects under our gaze.[19] But this surprise will not come. What agreement we have will always show up as agreement because of what we take the objects to be and how we read them, receive them, interpret them.

The most intellectually arresting description known to me of the importance of ordering schemata in what we could ever take the per se truth of a bee or a fig tree to be comes in the preface to Michel Foucault's *On the Order of Things.* The passage is worth citing in full.

> This book first arose out of a passage in Borges, out of the laughter that shattered, as I read the passage, all the familiar landmarks of my thought—*our* thought, the thought that bears the stamp of our age and our geography—breaking up all the ordered surfaces and all the planes with which we are accustomed to tame the wild profusion of existing things, and continuing long afterwards to disturb and threaten with collapse our age-old distinction between the Same and the Other. This passage [in Borges] quotes "a certain Chinese encyclopedia" in which it is written that "animals are divided into: (a) belonging to the Emperor, (b) embalmed, (c) tame, (d) sucking pigs, (e) sirens, (f) fabulous, (g) stray dogs, (h) included in present classification, (i) frenzied, (j) innumerable, (k) drawn with a very fine camelhair brush, (l) *et cetera*, (m) having just broken the water pitcher, (n) that from a long way off look like flies." In the wonderment of this taxonomy, the thing we apprehend in one great leap, the thing that, by means of the fable, is demonstrated as the exotic charm of another system of thought, is the limitation of our own, the stark impossibility of thinking *that.*

As Foucault goes on to explain, it is not the "fabulous" animals that are impossible to think. Rather, and this is the crucial point, "what transgresses the boundaries of all imagination, of all possible thought, is simply that alphabetical series (a, b, c, d) which links each of those categories to all the others."[20] When Levering says that "there is an 'independent order,' if only because bee-

19. Even more surprising, however, would be if we could make something specifically Christian out of our agreement about beehives. By no means must the intelligent ordering of a beehive by a nonintelligent bee point toward anything other than the strangeness/beauty/and so on of the phenomenon itself.

20. Michel Foucault, *On the Order of Things: An Archaeology of the Human Sciences* (New York: Random House, 1970), 5, xv–xvi. Significantly, in light of the preceding discussion about the meaning of words, the French title of Foucault's study is *Les Mots et les choses*—"Words and Things."

hives and budding leaves do not conform themselves to our narratives," we cannot quarrel with him if he means only that the world exists independently of our attempts to understand it. But he seems to mean considerably more than this because in the next sentence he speaks of the "speculative apprehension" of the per se truth of bees and leaves. At this point, we have to disagree. What Foucault shows here is that things even such as bees and trees do in fact conform to our narratives, at least in the very basic sense that our ordering modes of thought—the interconnections named by the letters *a, b, c, d*—will in fact determine how things will show up to us. Any time we attempt to say what the per se significance of anything whatsoever is, we will only be able to speak about this per se significance within the larger framework we use to think, analyze, order—in short, to read the world. To a startling degree, this larger framework is simply given in daily life and inherited by virtue of where we live our lives in the flow of history (cf. the importance of ordinary language in Wittgenstein, or Gadamer on the historicity of human reflection/being). The agreement we reach in "speculative apprehension," therefore, may be best explained by the fact that we share not only a common world but also a common linguistic/interpretive horizon or tradition. How much agreement would there be in the speculative apprehension of cosmological phenomena, for example, between someone who lived in the fifteenth century BC and someone who lived in the modern West today?

No Christian should deny, therefore, that there exists all kind of truth in the world—there are even parables of the kingdom!—and no Christian should deny the basic givenness of creation and the corresponding pressure this givenness puts on our accounts of its parts. But I fail to see how this amounts to saying that the NT and Plato speak the same language about the same God or that there is a space human beings can inhabit that has its own intellectual basis and allows "independent insight" into the fundamental workings of Christian grammar. Were Levering to reply that with the phrase "independent insight" he is hardly talking about a truly independent space but more about how the triune God has ordered creation, then of course we would already be inside a Christian reading of the world. Pagan philosophers would not—and, as it turned out, did not—put it like that.

It would be a dull reader indeed who could not appreciate Levering's acuity and learning. His essay "God and Greek Philosophy in Contemporary Biblical Scholarship" is in many ways a model for serious theological engagement with scripture and its attentive readers both past and present. Nevertheless, it is significantly hampered by divisions of thought that remain basic to the way he formulates the issues. As his constructive engagement with *World Upside*

Down illustrates, Levering proceeds on an intellectual basis that allows him to separate word meaning from grammatical context, philosophical thinking from living, and close biblical exegesis from a theory of theological knowledge. Of course, simply by writing an essay in which he engages the biblical material and its scholarly exposition—and in much of his other excellent work—Levering works against these separations in his own thought. Would that he give them the final boot.

Part 3

CHRISTIANITY AND THE HUMAN

Becoming Human

◆ DEIFICATION IN THE IMAGE OF JESUS CHRIST

What I will do in this brief essay is, first, name a few areas where I think Khaled Anatolios's book *Deification through the Cross* makes important contributions to our reception and understanding of Christianity—a rather large thing to say, but said this way on purpose—and, second, raise a couple of questions that might require additional or different thought than I was able to see in the book. So, to the contributions.[1]

Contributions

Of the many contributions the book makes, I will mention four. First, Anatolios chose the Byzantine liturgy as an organizing hermeneutical guide to the whole of scripture, a frame within which Holy Writ could be taken in and seen for what it's trying to say as a whole. On this side of the advent of historical criticism, whose interpretative modes have made us all aware of the vast historical and literary complexities within and across the scriptural texts, it is not always easy to say what scripture amounts to as a whole. Canonical reading that attends to the realities of history is laborious work, and even those who

1. I have retained the colloquial style of presentation from the conference.

"Becoming Human: Deification in the Image of Jesus Christ" was originally published in *International Journal of Systematic Theology* 25, no. 1 (2023): 39–46. This essay stems from a paper originally delivered to the 2021 conference held at the University of Notre Dame called "An Ecumenical Symposium on Christian Salvation," which focused on the recently published monograph of Khaled Anatolios, *Deification through the Cross: An Eastern Christian Theology of Salvation* (Grand Rapids: Eerdmans, 2020). It was then published in its present form in an issue of the *International Journal of Systematic Theology* that contained a Book Forum on Anatolios's book.

attempt it often get stuck in methodological prolegomena or in the tangles of particular textual problems. Anatolios does not avoid historical questions about scripture (e.g., he has clearly digested N. T. Wright's theory about Israel's ongoing sense of being in exile). But neither is he dominated by them. Indeed, I found Anatolios's liturgical choice hermeneutically illuminating. This might seem a surprising praise from an exegete since we are typically known to have almost allergic reactions to large-scale hermeneutical proposals for reading scripture. We tend to worry that such reading strategies flatten out the distinctive contours of the biblical witness and make texts that don't say the same thing wind up saying the same thing. But as Brevard Childs once pointed out in his magisterial work on biblical theology, it is actually "obvious that much of the most profound and critical reflection on the Bible operated with various philosophical and theological categories, often as a vehicle for the critical, descriptive task." Even "the giants of biblical study from the nineteenth and twentieth centuries (de Wette, Baur, Wellhausen, Bultmann, Käsemann, von Rad) all worked within certain dogmatic and philosophical traditions."[2] Of course, in some ways this is unsurprising. We can't not work with philosophical positions, and all assertions to the contrary are self-defeating inasmuch as they are themselves evidence of the particular philosophical position that supposes you can. The question is whether the hermeneutical lens with which you read scripture clarifies, brings things into focus, enables perception. In my view, Anatolios's liturgical reading does do these things—not perfectly but well. He avoids what Bruce McCormack calls "big idea theology"—a seizing on one point of the various systematic theological coordinates to the neglect of all others—and instead adopts a frame of reference that is generous and expansive enough to encompass much, maybe most, of the scriptural narrative.

Second, perhaps it is unnecessary to say, but a real strength of the book is its focus on sin and the way it reestablishes God as the center of the sin problem. Nearly half a century ago, Karl Menninger famously asked, "Whatever

2. Brevard Childs, *Biblical Theology of the Old and New Testaments: Theological Reflection on the Christian Bible* (Minneapolis: Fortress, 1993), 12. Cf. Gadamer's remark on the insight-producing relation of past and present, which he contrasts with what we could ever learn on the basis of the ideal of pure objectivity: "It could very well be that only insignificant things in historical scholarship permit us to approximate [the] ideal of totally extinguishing individuality, while the great productive achievements of scholarship always preserve something of the splendid magic of immediately mirroring the present in the past and the past in the present." Hans-Georg Gadamer, "The Universality of the Hermeneutical Problem," in *The Gadamer Reader: A Bouquet of Later Writings*, ed. Richard E. Palmer (Evanston, IL: Northwestern University Press, 2007), 80.

became of sin?" and noted its replacement by psychological and medical vocabularies of one sort or another (illness, disorder, etc.).[3] Anatolios's broader point about God and sin could rephrase Menninger's question as "Whatever became of God in our account of human sin?" In much contemporary discourse, Paul's "all have sinned and fallen short of the glory of God" could be said to mean something like "human beings have sinned against each other in a wide range of ways, perhaps most especially in ways that are socially and economically unjust and that therefore require repair in social and economic terms." Anatolios does not deny such realities, but he does notice that Paul's statement—as does other sin language in the NT—speaks most directly of God. By drawing on scripture's language and notable moments in the history of doctrine, Anatolios shifts the focus back to God. I take this to be a gain not only because that seems to be what Genesis 1–3 is plainly saying (and how Paul reads that section of the story) but also for the simple but incredibly important reason that horizontal sin, as it were, ceases to be sin when we lose sight of the vertical dimension of human error and evil. Without God in the picture of sin, relationships between human beings—and human beings' particular problems—can easily be reduced simply to the way things are. Certain phenomena of the world cease to show up as sin and simply show up as, well, phenomena of this or that sort among other phenomena. Or, differently put, absent a transcendent grounding, the moral/metaphysical background against which sin makes sense or shows up as sin is lost, and sin is no longer sin.

Third, Anatolios takes the existential dimension of doctrine seriously, which is to say that he knows that all Christian belief is tethered to the believers who believe it. This connection between believer and what is believed does not mean, of course, that the content of the belief is dependent for its existence or truth on our believing it—as if God's triunity did not eternally precede our knowledge of it. But it does mean that our believing certain things should make a difference in our lives—a difference, that is, to us. Whether we call this experience, as Anatolios does, or the subjective side of God's self-revelation, or the *Anknüpfungspunkt*, or something else, what Anatolios rightly emphasizes is the fact that doctrine is aimed somewhere; it has a telos, or—to say it differently—it seeks us out and wants to root itself in our lives, express itself in our affective dispositions, habits, and so forth. The truth of doctrine, rightly seen, is for us and our salvation.[4]

3. Karl Menninger, *Whatever Became of Sin?* (New York: Hawthorn, 1973).

4. See also Geoffrey Wainwright, *For Our Salvation: Two Approaches to the Work of Christ* (Grand Rapids: Eerdmans, 1997).

Finally, and briefly, Anatolios attempts to overcome doctrinal differences that have ecclesial weight, thereby—I think—hoping to overcome some of the ecclesial differences that have undesirable existential and missional weight. I do not know enough about some of the Eastern theologians and theology to know whether Anatolios is successful in their eyes, but I can say that as a Protestant reader I found myself swept up in a much larger and more hospitable theological vision than is regularly displayed in the United States. Now, my Protestantism is the sort that means I'm constantly wandering around on the shore of the Tiber and dipping my toe in, and that disposition may account for some of the welcome I sensed in Anatolios's vision. But at a more interesting level perhaps, the attempt to overcome—or at least hold in tension—what others have taken to be stark either/or alternatives suggests to me a dialectical pattern of thinking that is not altogether foreign to certain Protestant theological luminaries.[5] Anatolios does not frequently mention Karl Barth—nor is Robert Jenson in the picture—but there may be an intellective similarity in the way they do theology. Tensions are for them theologically productive places within which to think. Anatolios may or may not welcome such similarities, but I think they exist; or at least I hope so.

Questions

I turn now to two questions that I would like to pose. They are interrelated questions inasmuch as both questions emerge from the effort to think christologically about Anatolios's book. Let me first acknowledge, however, that Anatolios is unfailingly Trinitarian in the way that he thinks, and his effort to reason christologically is also abundantly clear. My questions, therefore, are not about whether he does or does not reason christologically but about the sort of christological reasoning scripture requires—and the effects of such a requirement on how we think about God, humanity, and our eschatological future.

The first question has to do with what Barth once famously called *Die Menschlichkeit Gottes*, the humanity of God, and whether the humanity of God is thought through enough for how we understand deification. I will put my point in light of three interpenetrating observations.

First, and all too briefly, reading the NT makes it plain that the image in which human beings are created is the image of Jesus Christ.[6] The *imago Dei*

5. See, e.g., Anatolios's discussion of the atonement (penal substitution, Christus Victor, etc.).

6. Jesus is the *eikōn/morphē* of God; 2 Cor. 4:4–6; Phil. 2:5–11; etc.

does not refer, that is, to some general image-bearing capacity, reality, and so forth, but to something—or, rather, someone—specific. Jesus Christ is the *eikōn* in whose image we were made. Not only as the Son of God is he the New or Second Adam, thus confirming and redoing our humanity at one and the same time; he is also the one through whom the original Adam was made and is sustained.[7] Anatolios draws on von Balthasar to elaborate our participation in the Trinity's intra-relations from the "specific location of the Son,"[8] and on Anselm to say that "human beings' likeness to God is specifically correlated to the Son's likeness to the Father,"[9] but it is unclear to me whether the Son here is too close to a cipher for an independent subject, an unknowable Logos or Person or someone who exists unhumanly, as it were, back behind the specificity given in Jesus Christ. As I understand it, there is no Son who isn't already the-human-Jesus-to-be. From eternity, God's self-determination is to be himself in time. Our humanity, our being in the image of God, is thus finally dependent on a prior humanity—namely, the humanity that is the "I am before Abraham was." For all the discussion in Christian history about what the *imago Dei* really is or in what it really consists, it seems to me that focusing

7. See especially the creation hymns in Col. 1 and 3. There is no such thing as a human being who is not in the image of Christ. In order to maintain that there was such a creature, one would have to make such terrific hash of the doctrines of the Trinity/creation/incarnation that one would unravel the basic fabric of Christian belief altogether. One cannot, for example, conceive of creation in abstraction from Christ; the NT is clear on this point, and the doctrine of the Trinity thus requires it. To think that there was such a thing as a human not made in the image of Christ would be to say that somehow God made some humans without making them as Trinity (i.e., the Godhead would be severed in the act of creation; God would somehow "go around" himself, skirting the Second Person, and "make" humans without the Son/Christ). By reading Gen. 1 in light of Christ, the NT authors committed Christians thenceforth to a christological understanding of creation and of humanity within it. Adam and the New Adam are anthropologically inseparable. There is no possibility of thinking of our image apart from Jesus; this would be an abstraction. Even sinful humans are in Christ's image. There is nothing in sin—even willful, unrepentant sin—that can erase the ontological condition of human existence as such. A human being exists as the image of Christ or it does not exist. It can rebel; it can stay in rebellion, and so forth. But it cannot overturn the fact of its existence (suicide is a refusal to live with this existence, but it does not overturn the fact that the conditions of the suicidal person's existence are the conditions of all human existence). Saying that the human could erase the ontic significance of the *imago Christi* would be to grant the human the power of the Creator himself, as if we could with our power unwrite the biblical story that says that all things were made in/through Christ.

8. Khaled Anatolios, *Deification through the Cross: An Eastern Christian Theology of Salvation* (Grand Rapids: Eerdmans, 2020), 301.

9. Anatolios, *Deification through the Cross*, 303.

on the NT concentrates our attention on a single point: we are in God's image because we are human. The incarnation ultimately shows us why we are said to be in God's image. God expresses himself, images himself, as a human because that's his likeness, or who he is. When God creates in his image, he creates humans because of Jesus. We don't show up as cats or dogs or rocks or trees. We're human because God is. Or we have our humanity because of God's. Our participation in God's life is from the location of our humanity in Jesus's humanity, not from the Son qua Son. In short, I wondered about the degree to which the hypostatic union was dissolved and the significance of the human Jesus sidelined.

Second, there is the epistemic priority of the economic Trinity and the consequence this way of knowing God has for our account of who God is as God. To put it simply, we know God's deity through his humanity, which is to say that we know the triune God from Jesus Christ and not apart from him. Any account of God's deity apart from Jesus Christ is an account of a god we do not know in Jesus Christ—that is, an abstraction. If we think through Jesus Christ toward what we want to say about who God really is, then we want to say that God's deity—God's Godness, what it is for him to be God—includes his humanity. As Barth once put it, "God requires no exclusion of humanity, no non-human humanity . . . in order to be truly God."[10] Jesus is not incidental to who God is in eternity. God really does determine himself to have human form. We know the Son becomes flesh not because we somehow know the divine person called the Son and happen then also to know that the Son takes flesh—two pieces of knowledge about God we somehow get to—but because we know Jesus and know that to say what we need to say about this flesh, we have to learn to speak of the Son of God and to speak of the Son of God's human form. These are inseparable commitments. I am not saying, of course, that the human Jesus is the Second Person of the Trinity without remainder, as it were, but I am saying that we cannot allow simple notions of linear time—the Son and then after a while comes Jesus—to override the significance of the fact that we know the Son because we know the human Jesus. There is no "time" in which God the Son was not linked to the Jesus he "later" became.[11]

10. Karl Barth, *The Humanity of God* (Louisville: Westminster John Knox, 1960), 50.

11. The most recent significant book on this entire question was published after I delivered these remarks. It is Bruce McCormack, *The Humility of the Eternal Son: Reformed Kenoticism and the Repair of Chalcedon* (Cambridge: Cambridge University Press, 2021). There is no room here to do this book justice, but I regard it as the most important current Christology biblical scholars can read other than—or alongside—Barth and Jenson. (I do not know enough yet about Bulgakov to make a judgment, but McCormack's remark about

Third, points one and two mean that when we think of deification, we should not think of a reduction of our humanity or obliteration of it but an increase, a fullness, a completion, a restoration of it. This is part of the point, I take it, of saying that the Creator/creature distinction is not one that deification overcomes. It is an eternal distinction. Jesus's human flesh and our human flesh are constitutive for what we make of our becoming like God. Our becoming like God is becoming the humanity that is God's humanity.

This takes me to my second larger question, which has to do with the contrition part of doxological contrition that continues on eschatologically.

At the end of the systematic theological portion of the book, Anatolios says, "A final question that we can deal with, even if in an equally tantalizing and incomplete fashion, is whether the dialectic of doxological contrition in some way perseveres even in the final state of humanity's deification."[12] He then turns to Irenaeus for "an authorization of an affirmative response to this question" and concludes "in company with Irenaeus" that "even in the final state of human glorification and deification, there will still be a glorified contrition in which humanity *will repent of its sins* not in sorrow and shame but only in eternal gratitude for God's salvation and in everlasting praise of the glory of his love and mercy."[13]

There is a legitimate exegetical question here—namely, whether Irenaeus says what Anatolios thinks Irenaeus means—but I want to focus on the substance of the point about eschatological contrition. I'll oversimplify it: Will we be contrite in heaven? My answer is no—or, more subjectively, I sure hope not. Or more accurately, not if contrition means what contrition means to us. Why? The simplest reason seems to be that there will be nothing for which to be contrite. There are two sides to this reason.

The first side is that we leave our suffering and our sin behind when we become fully human—that is, when we are made like Jesus Christ. Sin makes

how Bulgakov's *The Lamb of God* makes "most works in the field appear in comparison like so many casual conversations at a bus stop" is intriguing.) Among other things, McCormack's main contention that the Eternal Son is "ontologically receptive"—and all that this entails about the telos of his eternal generation, the human Jesus, and the repair of Chalcedon—merits sustained reflection, as does his argument against what he calls "substantialist ontology." David Bentley Hart criticizes an earlier version of McCormack's thinking in his *Theological Territories: A David Bentley Hart Digest* (Notre Dame, IN: University of Notre Dame Press, 2020), chap. 5. It is probably fair to say that Hart would be right about God's "decision" were McCormack to think something as crude as Hart suggests, but McCormack does not. On the questions of God's impassibility and simplicity, the debate is a live one.

12. Anatolios, *Deification through the Cross*, 382.

13. Anatolios, *Deification through the Cross*, 382–83; emphasis added.

us less human; leaving it behind makes us more so. Deification is that by which this leaving behind, this entrance into our full humanity, happens. To say that we become like God in general or even like the Son without naming Jesus is to risk losing the christological specification that funds the knowledge of deification in the first place, and it is to lose the christological specification that says exactly who it is that we become like. To say that we become fully human like Jesus is to say that we become God's image eschatologically and in a way that has left sin entirely behind. God's image is sinless and so shall we be. To think that we will be contrite in heaven but without quite being actually contrite or having something for which to be contrite strikes me as an attempt to press the interpretative scheme of doxological contrition too far forward, a kind of eschatological overreach, as it were. In systematic terms, eschatology is overridden by soteriology.

The second side is related to the crucifixion of Christ and the participation of Christians "in Christ," or, as NT scholar Michael Gorman has put it, the cruciform character of *theosis*. As Gorman shows, for St. Paul at least, our participation in Christ means our union with him takes on the character of cruciformity. We are crucified with Christ. But this ongoing, active being-conformed-to-the-Crucified-One is in the meantime, the overlap of the ages, prior to our deaths. We are not eternally co-crucified. And there is not only an eschatological reason for this but an absolutely critical christological one: Jesus is not eternally being crucified. He was crucified only once and once for all (Rom. 6:10, *ephapax*; cf. Heb. 7:27; 9:12; 10:10, *ephapax*). Were we to imagine crucifixion (or contrition, which I'm taking here as its corollary) as an eternal dialectic, we would have turned the once-for-all, historic event of the cross of Christ into a psycho-mythological symbol about our ever-present sense of the need to be forgiven—a kind of commentary on the human being's inability to defeat its feelings of shame and guilt. The symbolic cross—in this sense—would then be yet one more focal instance of a particular story we humans tell about mystery of our drama.

One might wonder here about the stigmata. It is true, of course, that Jesus retains the evidence of his crucifixion. But the stigmata, at least as they appear in the biblical text, no longer afflict him and are therefore no longer wounds; they are evidence of his once-for-all crucifixion and serve to anchor the resurrected Jesus's continuity in the earthly Jesus the disciples knew. To think that we will have our wounds from sin in ways that mean they remain wounds—that is, remain something for which we should be contrite—is once again to confuse the magnitude and uniqueness of the cross and resurrection with our eschatological healing.

In short, doxological contrition seems to me to describe Christian existence very well when we think about its texture prior to our deaths or to the restoration of all things when God will be all in all (1 Cor. 15:28). But when we turn to these final matters, *doxology* is the only word one needs.

Why should we care about this? Because it seems to me that if it is to take human sin and suffering seriously, deification must mean that such sin and suffering is repaired—fully. And since I take deification to mean that we become fully human as we are conformed to the image of God, who is Jesus Christ, as we become who we were always meant to be, we discover that our sin and suffering really is taken away; it does not persist as some shadow side of heavenly reality—where we're still repenting *sort of*, in some over-spiritualized way, with memory but without memory that has the posture that goes with the things we remember—in other words, that we're still contrite-ish for things that no longer exist.[14]

Conclusion

Looking back through my two questions for Anatolios, one can see how they both stem from trying to think through his book christologically. The attempt has been to avoid abstractions that do not name Jesus of Nazareth as constitutive of what we think about deification, to state the implications of the claim that human beings are in the image of Jesus Christ, and, finally, to draw out the importance of these matters for what happens to sin and suffering when we think about deification as becoming fully human in the way in which God himself actually is.

14. A longer discussion could also be had here about an Augustinian understanding of sin as a parasitic, negative reality, evil as *privatio boni*, which by definition could not exist in heaven—which, in turn, makes it unclear how memory could retain memories of sin.

Christianity's Surprise

◆ NEW TESTAMENT FOUNDATIONS OF THE HUMAN

"The Christian account of reality introduced into our world an understanding of the divine, the cosmic, and the human that had no exact or even proximate equivalent elsewhere and that made possible a moral vision of the human person that has haunted us ever since, century upon century." So David Bentley Hart.[1]

It is surprising that Christianity exists at all. It did not have to be. There is nothing in the evolution of humanity's self-consciousness, the history of religions, the dynamics of ancient society, or any other dimension of life that makes it *necessary.* Seen from a purely human vantage point, the world would have gone on without Christianity. After two millennia of its existence, we have largely forgotten this.

The Focus and the Procedure

Every layer of the NT testifies that Christianity's entrance into the world came as a shock. It is true that the NT texts narrate and presuppose the advent of Jesus of Nazareth in continuity with the history of God's dealings with his people from Adam through the election of Abraham to Moses and King Da-

1. David Bentley Hart, *Atheist Delusions: The Christian Revolution and Its Fashionable Enemies* (New Haven: Yale University Press, 2009), 203.

"Christianity's Surprise: New Testament Foundations of the Human" was originally published in *A Scribe Trained for the Kingdom of Heaven: Essays on Christology and Ethics in Honor of Richard B. Hays*, ed. David M. Moffit and Isaac Augustine Morales, OP (Lanham, MD: Lexington Books/Fortress Academic, 2021), 175–96. Republished with permission of Rowman & Littlefield Publishing Group, Inc.; permission conveyed through Copyright Clearance Center, Inc.

vid and beyond. The NT's citation and echoing of the OT and the language of "fulfillment," "plan," "foreknowledge," and the like require a continuity with the past to make any sense at all. This connection to the past, however, is best understood hermeneutically as a process of interpreting the continuities within an overall strategy of "reading backwards."[2] What has always been there—latently, perhaps, but really there—and is of enduring, non-substitutable significance is grasped not by tracing a simple historical line from past to present, as if the Old obviously leads straight to the New, but through the dialectical reading and rereading of Israel's history generated by the new revelation in Israel's Christ. Reading backward discloses the truths that God's work is self-consistently continuous, that history is the medium of his action, and that the Jewish people are the people whom Christians should call home. Yet it would be profoundly false to infer from such continuities that there was nothing new. There was something new. Nothing in the NT texts can hide the fact that Jesus himself was a surprise as the Messiah, that his death and resurrection were a surprise to his earliest followers, and that the Christian mission and subsequent growth was a surprise in the wider Roman world.

There are multiple features of this overarching surprise, but for this essay we shall focus on only one central aspect: the view of the human being that arrived with Christianity. With such a large topic, I obviously cannot aim for comprehensive coverage. Instead I use some thematically representative texts from the NT to sketch the foundations of the view of the human that entered the world with the advent of Jesus of Nazareth. At its heart, it is this human that over time came to be received by the church, broadcast to Roman society, and layered into culture after culture. Of necessity, we will pass over many finer exegetical details on the way to the most important judgments the texts require for their intelligibility and sense.[3] I focus here not on the constitutive parts of the human being, but rather on what the human is taken to be as it appears in the world: when one encounters the human, one encounters "this sort of thing"—this is what shows up in the world as the human in light of Christianity's arrival; the human is now this and wasn't yet. That is what I am after in this essay. I aim to mark a path of reflection on the NT that is generative for further work.

2. Richard B. Hays, *Reading Backwards: Figural Christology and the Fourfold Gospel Witness* (Waco, TX: Baylor University Press, 2014).

3. This essay is thus a representative sketch of the sorts of things that could be profitably traced in the reception history of post-NT early Christianity.

Texts

There have been many studies of NT anthropology in the modern period.[4] To my knowledge, however, my grouping of the texts is not the path typically taken. I presuppose the fruitfulness of reading canonical scripture inside the judgment that these various texts speak together. I am thus less concerned here with the historical distance and differences between, say, Romans and Revelation and more concerned with the directive judgments the texts make when considered together. In NT theological reasoning, we understand the human by understanding that to think the human is first to think Jesus, the "true human."

Jesus Is the Human

Romans 5:12–21

In what is arguably one of the strongest thoughts in Paul's thinking—at least in terms of its organizing or gravitational power relative to other thoughts—Paul sets Jesus Christ in typological relation to Adam, the first human. "Sin came into the world through one *anthrōpos* and thus death to all humans because all sinned" (v. 12).[5] Though all sinned, Adam was unique in that he was the fountainhead of the human problem and was thus "a *typos* of the one to come" (vv. 13–14). Paul then compares Adam and Jesus, the two *anthrōpoi* that reach all humans, in order to show the dramatically lopsided nature of the sin/grace and death/life relation: sin and death are defeated by the greater abundance of grace and life. "Thus, just as one man's trespass led to condemnation for all humans, so also one man's righteous act led to the acquittal of life for all humans" (v. 18).[6] At first glance, it may seem that the only comparison here is that of "headship": Adam stands at the head of a period of history, as does Jesus, only more so (into eternity). But the point of the typology actually runs

4. See, e.g., Matthias Konradt and Esther Schläpfer, eds., *Anthropologie und Ethik im Frühjudentum und im Neuen Testament: wechselseitige Wahrnehmungen: Internationales Symposium in Verbindung mit dem Project Corpus Judaeo-Hellenisticum Novi Testamenti (CJHNT), 17.-20. Mai 2012, Heidelberg*, WUNT 1/322 (Tübingen: Mohr Siebeck, 2014); Michael Laban and Outi Lehtipuu, eds., *Anthropology in the New Testament and Its Ancient Context* (Leuven: Peeters, 2010); Jason Maston and Benjamin E. Reynolds, eds., *Anthropology and New Testament Theology*, LNTS 529 (London: Bloomsbury T&T Clark, 2018).

5. Translations are my own unless otherwise noted.

6. As many scholars have noted, "the many" is a Hebraism that means "all."

much deeper. What it is to be *anthrōpos*, Paul suggests, is signified in Adam. And what it is to have the *anthrōpos* remade is signified in Jesus Christ. We all stand in Christ Jesus. The Human and the Human Remade—or, to put it only slightly differently, the damaged human made all over again into the human it was intended to be, the reestablishing of God's image in the midst of time. Human beings are thus, according to the thought of Romans 5, Adams remade and given life in Jesus Christ. To see an Adam is to see one who stands in Jesus Christ.[7]

2 Corinthians 3–4; Colossians 1:15–20; Philippians 2:5–11

In a section of 2 Corinthians, Paul explicitly states that Christ is "the image of God" (2 Cor. 4:4; cf. Col. 1:15). This could initially be surprising to a reader of Paul given his critique of idolatry in Romans 1, in which he clearly states that one form idolatrous worship takes is the fashioning of "images" of God as human beings, the confusion of creature with Creator (1:23). Paul's point in the context of 2 Corinthians, however, is not to criticize pagan worship but to argue that, by the gift and power of the Spirit, the Corinthian community of Christians is exhibiting transformation into the image of God the human being was originally intended to be. "We all, with unveiled face, beholding the glory of the Lord are being transformed into his image (εἰκόνα) from glory into glory" (3:18). In this way, the Corinthian Christians are the public letter of Christ, there for all to read.

Being transformed into the image of God is exactly being transformed into the image of Christ for the simple reason that, according to Paul, the human image of God is Jesus Christ. The anthropological possibility for Paul's way of putting it is not only Christ's resurrection but also the inseparable connection between the human in Genesis 1:26–27 and Christ: the former is (re)made in the image of the latter even as the latter is what the former truly is.[8] In Paul's way of thinking, there can be no division between the foundational Genesis *imago* text and Jesus Christ.

The well-known hymn in Colossians 1:15–20 also assumes the impossibility of reading Genesis 1:26–27 apart from Christ Jesus. Jesus Christ, says Paul, is

7. The uptake of this standing in the life of Adam is the living out of "new creation" (2 Cor. 5:17). The defeat-of-death part is, as Paul puts it in his argument about the resurrection in 1 Cor. 15, this: "For as in Adam all die, so also in Christ shall all be made alive" (v. 22).

8. So also Rom. 8:29 and Col. 3:10. On these passages, as well as Col. 1:15, see my "New Testament Iconography?," in *Picturing the New Testament: Studies in Ancient Visual Images*, ed. Annette Weissenrieder et al., WUNT 2/193 (Tübingen: Mohr Siebeck, 2005), 289–312.

"the image (εἰκών) of the invisible God, the firstborn of all creation" (1:15). Colossians does not, however, speak only of the moment of Christ's fleshly form-taking; it also presses back behind that to sing of him as God's *imago* from "before" creation. "For in him all things were created . . . all things were created through him and for him; and he is before all things" (1:16–17). The creation of the *Adam* in Genesis is thus the self-imaging of God through Christ in time, the "entire fullness" of God pleasingly dwelling in the human Jesus Christ (1:19). Because Christ is also "the firstborn from the dead," the vocation of the human image of God now encompasses reconciliation and eternal life (1:18–20).

Paul makes a substantively similar point in the so-called hymn he incorporates in his letter to the Philippians (2:5–11). "Have this mind about you," says Paul, "that was also in Christ Jesus."[9] Christ Jesus existed "in the form of God" (μορφῇ θεοῦ), emptied himself, took "the form of a slave" (μορφὴν δούλου), was born "in the likeness of human beings" (ὁμοιώματι ἀνθρώπων), and was found "as a human in the scheme of human life" (σχήματι . . . ὡς ἄνθρωπος). The collection of terms echoes Genesis 1:26–27 and connects the movement of Christ into the world with the (re)creation of Adam, the image/form of God. As with Adam, so with Christ: death was the way of the human scheme.[10] Precisely because the human Jesus was resurrected/exalted, however, the human scheme gets extended in light of its future hope. The humble and exalted Christ Jesus is the human image of God that opens the way for what *anthrōpos* comes to mean and be. Adam's history was Jesus's future even as Jesus's history became Adam's future.[11] The Philippians learn that to be human—to be Adam, in the form and likeness of God—is now to move in the pattern of Christ Jesus, for that is what the human is and has become.

In sum, when Paul thinks of the *imago Dei*, the thing that it is to be in God's image, he thinks first of Jesus Christ and then, derivatively, of the humans that were and are in that image. Paul also knows that this exact connection (that between humans and God through his imaging himself in them) brings

9. The imperative φρονεῖτε is much more here than "think" or have this "mind" in any purely noetic sense. It is more like "become the kind of person whose center of judgment-making capacity and behavior" reflects the pattern of Christ Jesus.

10. There is no substantive difference between μορφή and εἰκών; ὁμοίωμα echoes the ὁμοίωσις in the Genesis text ("likeness"). Of course, Jesus's particular "death on a cross" is a remarkable difference that should not be minimized, but at the present the point is simply that the form of execution would be a difference within the same outcome of death.

11. This is the logic of 1 Cor. 15 and much patristic reasoning: Christ becomes like our Adam so that our Adam can become like his.

the danger of travel in the other direction—namely, that they will image him as themselves (Rom. 1:23). But Paul *also* knows that in the proper order it is exactly this imaging that is the Christian gospel put to life: the human images the God who images himself in the human.

Lukan Genealogy

In contradistinction to the Gospel of Matthew, which traces Jesus's genealogy forward from Abraham through David to demonstrate Jesus's Jewish messianic credentials, the Gospel of Luke moves backward, from Jesus through David to Moses to Abraham to Adam, who was "the son of God." Luke's genealogy reaches back before the election of Israel and the division into Jew and Gentile to the original human, God's son, the one whom God made in his image. By means of this tracing, the story juxtaposes Jesus the Son of God and Adam the son of God. The point is not hard to discern: the Son of God has returned. Adam is figured in Jesus.[12]

The theological purpose of the genealogy's placement in the narrative is clear from the fact that the immediately ensuing scene is the temptation. As the son of God once moved from advent to temptation, so the Son of God once again moves from advent to temptation. As the human son of God once carried the history of the human in his act, so the human Son of God once again carries the history of the human in his act. "*If* you are the Son of God," the devil begins, echoing the question of obedience and decision that permeates the Genesis account. Jesus's subsequent victory over the devil is, according to Luke's narrative, a new creation—the human redone, its possibilities renewed, its requirements amplified, and its true identity (re)disclosed. For the Gospel of Luke, as for Paul, the *Adam*—the human—is Jesus the Lord, the Son of God. As the story moves on and even into Acts, the Lord Jesus carries forward in

12. On the way figuration works in the Gospels, see Richard B. Hays, *Echoes of Scripture in the Gospels* (Waco, TX: Baylor University Press, 2016). J. R. Daniel Kirk, *A Man Attested by God: The Human Jesus in the Synoptic Gospels* (Grand Rapids: Eerdmans, 2016), argues that the Synoptic Gospels do not have a "high" Christology but a human one. Kirk is correct that the Synoptic Gospels present Jesus as the human par excellence—the *Adam*—but wrong to set this presentation over against the features of the text that bind his identity together with God's. In its criticism, Kirk's book is only the negative of the current image in scholarship on "early high Christology"; he simply inserts a "no" where other scholars say "yes." The critical case is unsuccessful (even caricaturing). But the book's positive case helps to deepen our appreciation of Jesus's humanity. In short, reading Kirk alongside some of the studies he criticizes—rather than fully over against them—shows the range of things one needs to address to deal adequately with synoptic Christology.

his person what the human is, and thus reconfigures the understanding of humanity as that which exhibits the image of Adam-Christ.

It is a startling thought, but in significant strains of the NT's witness to the human the claim is that Jesus of Nazareth, the Christ and Lord, is what the human is. In the context of a modernity that has taught us to think of the human in terms of essences or rational capacities or desires—or many other things besides—the NT speaks a different and surprising word: to think the question of the human is to think Jesus Christ. The *imago Dei* language in Genesis 1 is taken to mean that, at bottom, the image in whose image the human is made is that of the Son of God, Jesus. How interesting, then, that we have flesh. With that thought, we turn to the other side of the question.

The Human Is the Image of Jesus

One of the most important material judgments in NT ethics is reflected in the move that extends Jesus's humanity into humanity as such. According to many important strains within the NT, to be made in the image of God, as Genesis 1 says the human is, is to be made in the image of Christ, who is the true image of God. To see the human being is to see the image of Christ. Paul's understanding of human participation "in" Christ, for example, depends on the possibility of an anthropological unity, as does Paul's "body of Christ" ecclesiology: to the extent that one encounters a Christian or the Christian church, one encounters Christ (or, quite possibly, his contradiction).[13] For Paul, baptism may be the (usual) means by which this unity is effected, but that baptism can be seen to do this at all presupposes an understanding of humanity as bearing the image into which it can be transformed and healed. In order to show this understanding more broadly, I will examine three representative texts/themes.

Matthew 25:31–46

In the last of Jesus's major teaching sections in the Gospel of Matthew, he tells several parables, concluding them—and his teaching as a whole—with

13. In modern Pauline studies since at least Albert Schweitzer's *Mysticism of the Apostle Paul*, many scholars have understood Paul's theology of "participation in Christ" to be "real" participation (i.e., not simply metaphorical or existentialist). E. P. Sanders, *Paul and Palestinian Judaism: A Comparison of Patterns of Religion* (Philadelphia: Fortress, 1977), is the most well-known advocate of this interpretation.

a whopper: the sheep and the goats. The imagery used to speak of the future judgment is intended to shock and unsettle, and the parable's point for the present is to engender action. It is straightforward and clear: care for the poor with your actions and you are a sheep; care not for the poor with your actions and you are a goat. The first way is blessing and life; the second, judgment and death. What is most striking for our purposes, however, is the anthropological claim embedded in the parable, that which gives the parable its sense and force as a command for Christian action and discipleship.

When in the parable the King says, "I was hungry and you gave me food, I was thirsty and you gave me drink, I was a stranger and you welcomed me, I was naked and you clothed me, I was sick and you visited me, I was in prison and you came to me," he begins a radical identification with the lowly. The question then comes, "But when did we see you a stranger and welcome you, or naked and clothe you? And when did we see you sick or in prison and visit you?" The King's answer is absolutely astonishing: "Truly, I say to you, as you did it to one of the least of these my brothers, you did it to me." Citizens of modern liberal democracies struggle to imagine what a true king was in all his power and splendor, but in the ancient world everyone knew that to say the king was lowly was to say water was dry, a snail was fast, an attacking lion harmless, Nero nice, Domitian docile.[14] The contradiction was blatant. The parable turns on this drastic contradiction and the picture of the human it presupposes and engenders.

The parable requires a much more specific anthropological understanding than a simple "representation"; namely, the poor, destitute, and imprisoned represent something more than their mere appearance would initially suggest. The King speaks of a closeness of kinship that means the lowly are so much the King's family that when they are encountered, the King himself is encountered. In short, they bear his image. When one encounters the lowly, therefore, one sees the image of the King, and they are to be treated as one would treat the King. The lowly, as it turns out, are nothing less than kingly. Which is to say that the lowly are the image of Jesus, who is obviously the King.[15]

Paul wrote letters and Matthew a gospel, but the substance of their judgment about the human as it appears in the world is strikingly similar: the human is the image of Jesus Christ. The human—from kings to beggars—is Christoform.

14. Two studies that help to contextualize "king" in NT times are Peter Richardson and Amy Marie Fisher, *Herod: King of the Jews and Friend of the Romans*, 2nd ed. (New York: Routledge, 2018), and David C. Braund, *Rome and the Friendly King: The Character of the Client Kingship* (1984; repr., New York: Routledge, 2014).

15. In the parable and all the way through Matthew's Gospel; in this context, see esp. 25:31–34.

Philemon and the "Body of Christ"

Paul's short letter to Philemon and the church that meets in his house is replete with details that are interesting to anyone who wonders about the early Christian view of the human. Chief among them is Paul's pastorally seasoned plea for the freedom of Philemon's slave, Onesimus. Paul does not overtly say, "Philemon, you must grant Onesimus his freedom." Instead, he makes use of the public setting in which the letter would have been read aloud to guide and pressure Philemon toward "his own" right judgment about his slave. Paul praises Onesimus, praises Philemon, assures him that he, Paul, knows that Philemon will do the right thing—all the while knowing that the people gathered in his house are listening, waiting to see what Philemon does. The Christian community is a witness to the Philemon-Onesimus relationship and, in an important sense, drawn in by Paul's letter as participants and stewards of it. Philemon's perception of Onesimus—how the complex entity that is Onesimus shows up to him—is now indelibly relational and communal. The human becomes what it is, shows up as what it has become, in the context of the community that is now its home.

The anthropological presupposition on which Paul's reasoning depends is not that of the American Declaration of Independence: that all people are created equal and have the same basic rights. Christian reasoning about the human may well eventually want to say something similar to this, but Paul himself thinks in a different register. His register is that of a family, one whose origin is their common life "in the Lord." If it is true, says Paul, that I am a brother to you and Onesimus is a brother to *me*—an apostle, one who is "bold enough to command you to do what is required" (v. 8)—how much more so is it true that Onesimus is a brother to *you*. The anthropological shift Paul calls Philemon to make is nothing short of tectonic: *he-who-was-once your-slave* is now *your-brother*. Onesimus is what Paul is, what Philemon is: the human in light of Christ. The pastoral outworking of Paul's assumptions about Onesimus's humanity is a blunt call for his full freedom: "If, therefore, you consider me your companion, receive Onesimus as you would receive me" (v. 17).[16]

16. Of course, Paul makes sure to mention that he is coming to visit later on (i.e., I'll be there to check in person that you've done what you now know you're supposed to do). On the question of slavery in early Christianity, see esp. Ilaria L. E. Ramelli, *Social Justice and the Legitimacy of Slavery: The Role of Philosophical Asceticism from Ancient Judaism to Late Antiquity* (New York: Oxford University Press, 2009).

Though obviously unique in many of its specific details, this brief letter encapsulates the practical sense and implication of Paul's much more widely developed "body of Christ" theology (see, e.g., Rom. 12; 1 Cor. 12). In Paul's way of thinking, Jesus Christ provides the unity within which the members of the church are comprehended as human beings. "For just as the body is one and has many members, and all members of the body, though many, are one body . . . for by one Spirit we were all baptized into one body—Jews or Greeks, slaves or free—and all drunk of one Spirit" (1 Cor. 12:12–13). As he puts it only a little later in relation to caring for each other: "If one member suffers, all suffer together; if one member is honored, all rejoice together" (1 Cor. 12:26). To reason about what humans are and require is to reason theologically about their identity in Christ and the ecclesial society that marks this identity in real time and space. In contrast to strong streams common to many anthropologies in modernity, for Paul there is no individual as such. The human can be powerfully thought in its individual instantiations—Onesimus—but the individual shows up as what it is in light of the body to which it belongs.[17]

Indeed, for Paul one cannot even think "cosmos" apart from the Lord Jesus Christ through whom it was created (1 Cor. 8:6; Col. 1:15–20).[18] The importance of what might be called cosmic Christology for conceiving the human being is multifaceted, but the principal point here is that precisely because the entirety of what is is related to Christ—made through him—all human beings, wherever they may be found in the widest reaches of the cosmos, are to be seen in relation to Christ. There is no corner of the world in which the human can dwell apart from Christ.

The Good Samaritan

The parable known in the Anglophone world as the Good Samaritan occurs only in Luke's Gospel and encapsulates many uniquely Lukan themes. A long-popular reading of the parable takes the summary injunction—"go and do likewise"—to apply generally in this way: go be a good person like the Samaritan (and negatively, do not be like the passersby). To be sure, the world can always

17. The contrast here with influential streams of classical liberal Protestantism is both obvious and stark. Adolf von Harnack, e.g., famously saw much of the essence of Christianity as the relationship between the individual and God ("God and the soul, the soul and its God"). See *What Is Christianity?* (Philadelphia: Fortress, 1986), 142 (cf. 11, 56, et passim).

18. See Sean McDonough, *Christ as Creator: Origins of a New Testament Doctrine* (New York: Oxford University Press, 2009).

use more such people, but the point of the parable lies elsewhere. The questions posed by the lawyer that elicit the parable and the question posed by Jesus at the end that requires the lawyer to answer his own question hold the key.

The lawyer's question, "Who is my neighbor?" is not the feeble comeback it is often taken to be. For first-century Jews, doing what the law required meant being clear about how to fulfill its commandments in practice. If the law says that one is to love one's neighbor, one needs to know who counts as "neighbor." The lawyer asks Jesus to be specific so that he knows whom to love.

As with many of his parables, Jesus constructs the scene to lead the hearer's expectations in a direction that he subsequently subverts. In this case, the parable unfolds with the expectation that the "neighbor" is the one who has been violently robbed, the priest and the Levite those who do not love their neighbor as they should, and the Samaritan the one who exemplifies the love of neighbor. While this in itself would be surprising to Jewish sensibilities, Jesus's precisely phrased question turns things in a different direction: "Which of these three seems to you to have become a neighbor to the man who fell among the bandits?" (10:36). By asking the lawyer who the victim's neighbor was, Jesus does not require the lawyer to draw the conclusion that the victim is your neighbor—that he may well already assume—but that the *Samaritan* is your neighbor.[19] This answer dismantles and rebuilds the categories the lawyer employs when thinking of the meaning of neighbor and works on the level of affect to draw the circle of neighbor as wide as it can get. By the end of the parable the lawyer now has to include the repugnant Samaritan when he gives the answer to his own question of who is my neighbor. The force of the parable, therefore, is not a simple "be good like the unlikely character the Samaritan" but "Samaritans are your neighbors. Show them mercy." This, one might say, is a parabolic rendition of Adam/Christ theology. Everyone is "neighbor."

The anthropological assumption that grounds "the Samaritan is your neighbor" teaching depends on the sense that "Samaritan" is now included within what is meant by the image of Jesus. The Samaritans, too, fit in the genealogy of the S/son of God.

Sin and the Possibility of Transformation

The NT view of the human as the *imago* is not, however, idealistic or optimistic. If Paul speaks of the human as the image of Adam/Christ, he also obviously understands the power of the Adam that we have been. The entirety of

19. NB: The lawyer cannot quite bring himself to say "Samaritan"; he says, "The *one* who showed him mercy."

the Corinthian correspondence, for example, is painful testimony to residual Adamic patterns in the life of the early Christians. If Luke believes that the terms of being human have been reset by the obedience of the Son of God in the desert, he also narrates the history of the church as one of sin and complicated struggle to become that which we have been freed to be. Every time Luke's parable of the tax collector and the Pharisee was read, the remainder of the old Adam was on display and held forth as honest commentary on the human: stand at a distance from the holy and cry out, "God be merciful to me, a sinner!" (Luke 18:9–14). Every time Jesus's words about the practice of forgiveness were read and repeated, the old Adam's indelible print was clearly seen on fellow travelers ("a brother"): "If your brother sins against you, and if he repents, forgive him. Even if he sins against you seven times a day and seven times returns to you and says, 'I repent,' you will forgive him" (Luke 17:3–4).[20] Matthew makes it even clearer: "Lord," says Peter, "how often shall I forgive my brother when he sins against me? As many as seven times?" And Jesus says to him, "I do not say to you 'as many as seven times' but as many as seventy times seven" (Matt. 18:21–22). Never is it even hinted that we are only the New Adam and cannot show the old. To the contrary, the NT speaks of the power of transformation and the practices that go with a people being transformed: we are Adam and on the way to Adam, being transformed into the new image we were always meant to be.

Paul puts the point precisely in his exhortation to the Colossians not to lie to one another. The reason is that they have "taken off the old man [ἄνθρωπος/*Adam*] with his practices and put on the new one [implied ἄνθρωπος/*Adam*], the one who is being renewed in knowledge according to the image of his creator" (3:9–10). The Corinthians, too, obviously still have a long way to go, but they have come a long way to become a living testimony to transformation into the Lord's image (2 Cor. 3:18). And the church in Rome is counseled not to exist in conformation with the old patterns ("this age") but to be "transformed by the renewal of the mind" (Rom. 12:2).[21]

If, as Charles Taylor has persuasively argued, the absence of the belief in the possibility of human transformation is one of the defining marks of our current age, then the prevailing anthropological judgment is exactly opposite

20. The "take heed to yourselves" in v. 3a of many English versions goes with vv. 1–2. "If your brother sins" begins the next teaching.

21. Again, "mind" here is not simply noetic, as the following injunctions regarding the Christina moral life make clear. To renew one's mind just is to exhibit "genuine love, to have what is evil, to hold onto what is good . . . to be aglow in the Spirit and to serve the Lord . . . to contribute to the needs of the saints and practice hospitality" (Rom. 12:9–13).

of the NT.[22] The NT knows of and endorses many immanent goods (marriage, children, friendship, etc.), but its view of the humans we show up as in the world is transformational all the way down. In order to deal with the reality of sin as the human image of God, and thus to be and become ourselves—the human as we were made and redeemed to be—we must undergo transformation into that *imago*, the image of Christ.

Death and Transformation

No NT text states, hints at, or presupposes anything contrary to the obvious deathward existence of the human. Even Jesus himself is not exempt from death. Postmoderns may be down on universals, but here is one we cannot duck. The human shows up in the world as a dying creature. In being *Adam*, as Paul puts it, "all die" (1 Cor. 15:22).

Yet precisely in its inescapable deathward trajectory the *Adam* longs for life. To be dying and to want to live—that is the contradiction in which the human exists. Strangely to us, perhaps, the NT writers do not know this because of their reflection on the human condition or the death around them so much as they know it because of the pattern of death and resurrection of Jesus's own life. They reason, that is, from the fact that his resurrection is a victory over death to the understanding of eternal life as that which he brings in the face of human death. The Last Adam and its image: "so also in Christ shall all be made alive" (1 Cor. 15:22). Or, as Paul says to the Romans about the significance of their baptism for their future, "For if we have been united with him in a death like his, we shall certainly be united with him in a resurrection like his" (Rom. 6:5). Indeed, the telos of transformation in Christian discipleship is "eternal life" (Rom. 6:22).

The inseparable connection between the Son of God, the human deathward predicament, and eternal life could hardly be stronger than it is in the Gospel of John and 1 John. The gospel author may not have known much, if anything, about Paul's construal of the "faith of Christ" and the human response of "faith in Christ," but the Fourth Evangelist nevertheless tirelessly emphasized faith/trust (πίστις) as the only proper posture toward the gift of eternal life.[23] "Lord,"

22. Charles Taylor, *A Secular Age* (Cambridge, MA: Belknap Press of Harvard University Press, 2007), 430–37 et passim.

23. See Richard B. Hays, *The Faith of Jesus Christ: The Narrative Substructure of Galatians 3:1–4:11*, 2nd ed. (Grand Rapids: Eerdmans, 2002).

Peter asks, voicing for the reader the theological point of reading the gospel at all, "to whom should we go? You have the words of eternal life" (6:68; cf. 3:15–16, 36, et passim). Likewise 1 John, where it is simply predicated of Jesus Christ that he is "eternal life" (5:20). Those who trust (πιστεύω) in him receive the "promise," which is "eternal life" (2:25; cf. 1 John 5:11 et passim).

The Pauline and Johannine literature are perhaps the most obvious examples of an emphasis on eternal life, but the entire NT pulsates with it. Matthew, Mark, Luke/Acts, Hebrews, the Catholic Epistles, and Revelation all testify to the future of the human because of and in light of Jesus's own living future. Put slightly differently, the *Adam* is a creature who hopes for life.

The NT texts claim that this hope is now actively written into the human *imago* by virtue of the Last Adam's life-creating resurrection (1 Cor 15:45, ζῳοποιοῦν). To be God's image—as Adam and Adam remade—is thus to have a future in God's own future. This is the extension of the claim for human transformation, its perfection and end: "we shall all be transformed . . . [and] when the perishable puts on the imperishable, and the mortal puts on the immortal, then what is written shall happen: Death is swallowed up in Victory" (1 Cor. 15:54). Thus is the human as it appears in the world a mysterious sign of that which lies beyond its appearance. Exactly in our deathward existence, do Christians gesture to life without end?

Manifesting the Human

One of the most critical questions that the early Christians faced was how they could keep alive the human that had been delivered to the world. If, that is, the human is inconceivable apart from its identity as the image of Christ, how can this image both be cared for and be displayed?

The NT is replete with a range of implied answers to this question, but they all presuppose the judgment that the human is best displayed in thriving Christian communities and the practices that constitute them. Indeed, to put it radically, there is no human apart from the interlocking strands of relationships, institutions, and communities that formed lived Christianity at its origins. Acts, for example, narrates the beginnings of the thriving church with at least six recurring features that are ingredient to the founding and formation of communities that steward the Christian vision of the human: the development of close-knit networks across time and space, the cultivation of public visibility, the provision for the weak and vulnerable, the navigation of conflict and disagreement, the articulation of core beliefs, and the willingness to suffer for the truth.[24] The point is not that these features—or any one of them in particular—overtly declare "this is our theological anthropology." The point is rather that, taken together, they enable Christian communities to generate, sustain, and nurture a view of the human that becomes phenomenologically relevant to the world. The anthropology is, in an important sense, a "look and see."

The Pastoral, Catholic, and Johannine Epistles all testify in different ways to the active tending of the communities that send forth what they now take themselves to be. Two brief illustrations from this body of material must suffice.

Perhaps more pointedly than any other text in the NT, the epistle of James sees the lethal threat to the Christian picture of the human posed by a division between word and practice. "Be doers of the word and not hearers only, deceiving yourselves" (1:22). The one who hears and does not do is like a man who views his face in a mirror, turns away, and forgets how he looks (1:23–24). James's point is that hypocrisy rests on a forgetfulness of our appearance, of how we really show up in the world, of what is on display for others to see. We look and see what we are, and then forget and show the world something that betrays our true image. Who we truly are as Christians, James teaches, depends on the unity of word and deed: we can show up either as hypocrites or as doers who act (1:25). The unification of life and word stewards the Christian understanding of the human not only as it exists in Christians themselves—we are to see this when we look in the mirror—but also in public. To present the Lord of glory in and with our humanity, we must do it in public.

The Johannine Epistles echo the sense that the human in Christ is something one can see and, as a correlate, something that can be concealed by a life that is contrary to it: "The one who says, 'I know him,' but disobeys his commandments is a liar, and the truth is not in him. But whoever keeps his word, in him truly love for God is perfected. . . . The one who says he abides in him ought to walk in the same way in which he walked" (1 John 2:4–6). For the Johannine community, that which was given in Jesus is to be enfleshed in the relationships that make human transformation a reality rather than simply a dream that lies just beyond an ever-receding horizon. The practice of confession, for example, tells the truth about the need for ongoing transformation

24. On these six features in particular, see my brief reflections on Acts and thriving communities: C. Kavin Rowe, "The Acts of the Apostles and Thriving Communities," *Faith & Leadership*, August 15, 2010, https://www.faithandleadership.com/series-acts-apostles-and-thriving-communities, now in *Leading Christian Communities* (Grand Rapids: Eerdmans, 2023).

from the old into the new and shepherds the community relationships of those who are living in the light away from the receding darkness. The secessionists from the Johannine community may pretend they have left sin behind, but the Johannine Christians know otherwise. Confession is intrinsic to becoming the people called from darkness into the light. "If we say, 'We have no sin,' we deceive ourselves and the truth is not in us. But if we confess our sins, he who is faithful and just will forgive our sins and cleanse us from all unrighteousness" (1 John 1:8–9). In a theological judgment that is materially similar to Paul's *imago* theology, 1 John grounds the human and its transformation in Jesus: because it is "true in him and in you," and because "the darkness is passing away and the true light already shining," the one who "hates his brother is in the darkness" while the one who "loves his brother is in the light" (2:8–10). That light and darkness are ways of displaying what the human is to be in Christ is memorably depicted by 1 John's description of what hating is. It is not simply a feeling or a mode of perception; it is a style of being, a way of life: "The one who hates walks in the darkness and does not know where he is going because the darkness has blinded his eyes" (2:11). So, too, love: "Little children, let us not love in word or speech but in deed and truth" (3:18).

In short, over the range of the NT, the requirements for keeping alive what the human being is are inseparable from the way that view is lived. The early Christian judgment here is what might be called a kind of evangelistic phenomenology: if what the Christians take the human to be can be kept alive, it will be kept alive by that which is on display in their communities; this display not only carries the view of the human, it also invites outsiders to look and see.

What Humans Are Not: God(s)

In the context of the ancient world, it was also important to say what the human is not, at least in one crucial respect: God. At a time when current and former rulers populated heaven and earth and were frequently taken as gods in one way or another, the NT writers knew that a sharp line had to be drawn between the king of the present world and God. That line was drawn principally by the practice of worship and the judgments that such practice carried with it and by which it was sustained through time. Drawing this line between God and earthly kings was all the more important because the human Jesus himself was acclaimed king and because he was worshiped.[25] Though

25. This issue lies at the heart of Christology, the early church debates about two natures,

the importance of this question can be detected in many different places in the NT, space limits us to considering only one example.

As Steven Friesen has persuasively argued, the entire book of Revelation can be read in light of the crisis produced by the Christian encounter with the Roman imperial cult and the refusal to participate in the worship of the emperor that the cult required.[26] Because of our tendency to think of politics as a discrete sphere of life, moderns find it hard to remember that such refusal was not the refusal to participate in an isolated ritual. The imperial cult was interwoven throughout the fabric of Roman culture and was inseparable from the ongoing experience of daily life in multiple dimensions of society.[27] The Christian refusal was thus a rejection of a vast web of things that made Roman culture much of what it was. It was, *in nuce*, an extreme refusal with far-reaching consequences, and it was based on a coordinated theological/anthropological judgment about the relation between God and the human. Revelation articulates this coordinated judgment throughout the book in various ways, but perhaps most explicitly with the language of worship.

On the one hand, Revelation speaks clearly of that which should never be worshiped: the beast and its image.[28] This language evokes the imperial cult, where the image of the emperor—of a variety of kinds—became the focus of sacrifice, and eventually, for Christians, the focus of the refusal to recant and to sacrifice.[29] For those who worship the emperor, apocalyptic fates await: "If anyone worships the beast and its image and receives a mark on his forehead or on his hand, he shall also drink the wine of God's wrath" (14:9–10).

On the other hand, Revelation speaks clearly of that which alone should be worshiped: God and the Lord Jesus Christ, the Lamb upon the throne.[30] In

---

and *theosis*. It must suffice here to say that Jesus is the only human who can be worshiped and that is because he is the incarnate Son, God of God, from eternity. All other humans are creatures and—whatever one's view about *theosis*—do not lose their creatureliness in time or eternity. The distinction between created and uncreated is an eternal one.

26. Steven J. Friesen, *Imperial Cults and the Apocalypse of John: Reading Revelation in the Ruins* (New York: Oxford University Press, 2001).

27. See the articles devoted to the NT and the imperial cult in the special issue of *JSNT* 27, no. 3 (2005).

28. Rev. 13:4 also names "the dragon" (Satan) who gives the beast his authority.

29. Lest we forget: all ancient religion was bound up with sacrifice/offerings (Christianity, too, through its transformation of the temple cult by relocating sacrifice in the person of Christ). The famous imperial cult scene described in Pliny the Younger's epistle to Trajan dealing with the Christians is an interpretative aid here (*Epistulae ad Trajanum* 110). On images in the Roman Empire, see Paul Zanker, *The Power of Images in the Age of Augustus* (Ann Arbor: University of Michigan Press, 1988).

30. On the christological significance of the throne language in Revelation, see Richard

counterpoint to the idolatry/apostasy described in chapter 14, Revelation 15 pictures those who did not cower before the imperial demand to sacrifice standing victoriously by a sea of glass with harps of God and singing "the song of Moses, the servant of God, and the song of the Lamb, saying, 'Great and wonderful are your deeds, O Lord God the Almighty! Just and true are your ways, O King of the ages! Who shall not fear and glorify your name, O Lord? For you alone are holy. All nations shall come and worship you, for your judgments have been manifested!'" (15:2–4). Not even an angel in all his glory and awe-inspiring presence can be worshiped, as the angelic deflections of the seer's prostration in Revelation 19:10 and 22:8–9 make crystal clear. What is to be worshiped? God alone, and his Christ, the King of kings.

The human in the book of Revelation is thus a worshiping creature through and through. Humans will, Revelation stipulates, worship other humans who wield the power to demand such worship unless they know how to resist and perhaps even die instead. The worship of God and Jesus Christ alone is the practice that correlates with this ability to know resistance and preference for death over idolatry as the way to be truly human. As with other books of the NT, Revelation's anthropology is also a public anthropology. Look and see "the endurance of the saints" (14:12; cf. 13:8–10) in the refusal to worship humans who claim God's place. "You have but little power," the church in Philadelphia hears, "and yet you have kept my word and have not denied my name" (3:8).

Revelation sustains the Christian view of the human by arguing that though humans are wondrous things, the human is not God or a god, and it should never be worshiped. To worship humans is to forget who and what they are and to turn life into death. The texts say, further, that humans are worshiping creatures, and will thus worship, but the only one to worship is God.

Concluding Reflections

Taking the sketch of this chapter as a whole makes it obvious that when it comes to the human, the NT does not say human beings are most essentially grasped as what they are by focusing on the existence of a soul or a mind or some other unique capacity that makes them stand out from their surroundings as worthy of special attention, comment, and treatment. Such understandings, or close correlates or versions thereof, had already long been on offer in the world and were there for the taking. The NT's fundamental picture of

Bauckham, *Jesus and the God of Israel: "God Crucified" and Other Studies on the New Testament's Christology of Divine Identity* (Grand Rapids: Eerdmans, 2008).

the human is much more startling and, historically considered, new. Jesus of Nazareth, the Christ and Lord, crucified and raised, is the human, the *Adam*. He is the true *imago Dei*, the exegesis of Genesis 1:26–27 with the pattern of his life. The human is what it is, *Adam*, as the image of him.

The move to name the *Adam* as the image of Christ engenders a radical figure-ground shift, a drastic rearrangement of the complex pieces of human life in which a new picture of the human emerges against the variegated and complicated background that is our embeddedness in the actual living of life. Though humans were obviously long on the earth, and though there were perhaps glimpses of this picture, the picture itself was hitherto impossible to see.[31] According to the NT, the picture of the human that came with the advent of Jesus of Nazareth was a gift, a revelation given to us from outside of what the human could make of itself.[32] In a profound mystery, the *Adam* who comes from the outside discloses what the human is by taking it up from the inside and being exactly that which we were and are to become.

The revelation of the *Adam* meant that wherever one encounters a human, one encounters the image of Jesus Christ: Adam is Adam. At its depth, this is a refusal of any separation of the worship of Jesus from how all people—of any stripe, Samaritans included—are to be envisioned: the human bears the image of Christ. Moreover, by tying the human to Jesus the crucified Lord as the very image of God, the Christians made the human—even the lowliest among them, the "crucified"—the most marvelous and glorious thing in the world. To see a human being is to see the King of the cosmos.

It is no wonder, then, that they had to take extra care to say clearly that the human is not God/god. For the early Christians, the distinction between Creator and creature was necessary to keep the human as the human, to preserve the right order in the extraordinary coordination between the living God and his living image. The human, says the NT, is made to be a worshiping creature,

31. The obvious major anticipation was of course in Jewish tradition of reflection on Gen. 1:26–27 and on Adam. On this question, see Jacob Jervell, *Imago Dei: Gen 1:26f. im Spätjudentum, in der Gnosis und in den paulinischen Briefen* (Göttingen: Vandenhoeck & Ruprecht, 1960). Ulrich W. Mauser, *Gottesbild und Menschwerdung: eine Untersuchung zur Einheit des Alten und Neuen Testaments* (Tübingen: Mohr Siebeck, 1971), argues compellingly that one can see in retrospect the anticipation of the christological *imago* through the OT's depiction of the anthropomorphism of God and theomorphism of humanity (e.g., in the prophet Hosea).

32. In one of the greatest double mysteries of being human, the human is simultaneously aware of itself as a mystery and mysteriously unable to penetrate beyond this awareness to a picture of ourselves that would dispel the mystery that we are, or the mystery that we know that we know we are a mystery and cannot get past it. We are anything but self-evident.

but precisely because the human can image God with its life, the risk exists that it would mistake itself as God. Self-worship, however, results in the obfuscation of the human, a confused, idolatrous exaltation of the image to the place of the reality, with the consequence that the human loses the ability to see itself as it truly is—*imago*.[33] No human is less than *imago* (*Christi*), but it is also equally true that no human is more: not even a Roman emperor can claim worship.

The early Christian picture of the human did not develop staying power all by itself, as if once seen it could never recede into the background of life and vanish.[34] The initial foothold and eventual permanence of the picture was directly related to the fact that for the early Christians there was no division between the idea of the human and the practices that articulated it, developed it, publicized it, and carried it around the Mediterranean. What the human was revealed to be required communal display and nurture, even as such display and nurture were themselves constitutive of the revelation and inseparable from it. In short, the human took political form.[35]

Christians have not, of course, always remembered what we believe about the human. Indeed, as we have struggled to keep this picture before us, we have often painfully exhibited the gap between the tarnish and the transformation and—as a result—hidden the picture of the true Adam, ignored it,

33. Precisely in the projection of ourselves onto the screen of eternity and the use of the word "God/god" do we disappear from ourselves. Feuerbach was right about that: all forms of projection that take the human to be God/god are but the exaltation of humanity in exactly such a way that we lose the ability to know that it is projection and confuse the projection with something real.

34. It was in competition with other pictures. In relation to the Roman world, my book *World Upside Down: Reading Acts in the Graeco-Roman Age* (Oxford: Oxford University Press, 2009) says something about competition with regular pagan daily life, and my book *One True Life: The Stoics and Early Christians as Rival Traditions* (New Haven: Yale University Press, 2016) about competition with Stoicism, but a similar case could be made with other traditions.

35. Christianity's political form was of course not only in relation to Roman government but also in relation to a range of other matters: e.g., the sick, the poor, the orphans and widows, abandoned infants, and so on. On these matters, see, inter alia, Gary Ferngren, *Medicine and Religion: A Historical Introduction* (Baltimore: Johns Hopkins University Press, 2014); Guenter B. Risse, *Mending Bodies, Saving Souls: A History of Hospitals* (New York: Oxford University Press, 1999); Rodney Stark, *The Rise of Christianity: A Sociologist Reconsiders History* (Princeton: Princeton University Press, 1996); K. C. Richardson, *Early Christian Care for the Poor: An Alternative Subsistence Strategy under Roman Imperial Rule* (Cascade, OR: Wipf & Stock, 2018); Gary A. Anderson, *Charity: The Place of the Poor in Biblical Tradition* (New Haven: Yale University Press, 2013); John T. Fitzgerald, "Orphans in Mediterranean Antiquity and Early Christianity," *Acta Theologica* 23 (2016): 29–48.

and betrayed it. Too easily, too quickly, and too often have we divided Christ from his image and seen the latter as something vastly less. But for all that, it is nevertheless this picture of the human that makes possible Christian criticism of the inhumane treatment of others, Christian and otherwise. Whenever Christians say, "This should not go on because human beings should not be treated this way, are not the sort of thing that can be thought of or used in X or Y way," they draw, wittingly or not, upon the anthropological foundations established in the NT. In the case of Christian mistreatment of others, the proper critical word is thus hypocrisy, but it is the assumption of what the human is that forms the background against which the call to repentance makes sense in the first place and against which Christian ethics takes its measure. In the case of non-Christian mistreatment, the assumption of what the human is funds the criticism and serves as an invitation to discover, to look and see, what we have become and most truly are.[36]

The human that arrived and emerged with Christianity was a presentation to the world of something it had not seen and did not anticipate. We became something we were not yet, and the human was in the world in a new way for all to see. That we have become such a thing—that it happened *at all*—was and still should be entirely surprising.

36. Even the staunchest critics of Christian misconduct often presuppose a view of the human delivered to them by the historically long and deep influence of Christianity itself.

Recovering Our Humanity

◆ INTERDISCIPLINARY INQUIRY AND THE UNITY OF LIFE

Christian thinkers should always be on the lookout for convergences between what we know to be theologically true and what the current intellectual scene has to offer. Such convergences will doubtless be ad hoc, incomplete, and temporary. But they are not for that reason any less important. Indeed, ad hoc convergences on the truth are not only occasions for rejoicing but may also allow Christians to provide a coherent grammar for what is often said only in bits and pieces and with great stuttering. In what follows I will explore one particularly significant current convergence.

Quite simply put, there is a growing awareness of something that Christians have long known from the doctrine of creation—namely, that things really are interconnected after all. All creaturely realities—which, of course, includes everything that is not God—are interrelated if for no other reason than that they are God's creation. Insofar as human creatures discover true things about the creation of which they are a part, therefore, they will continually discover the mutual embeddedness of creaturely life.

"Recovering Our Humanity: Interdisciplinary Inquiry and the Unity of Life" was originally published in *Pro Ecclesia* 24 (2015): 326–42. Copyright 2015 The Center for Catholic and Evangelical Theology. doi:10.1177/106385121502400305. This essay was originally given as a talk to the doctoral students in theology at the Divinity School, Duke University. I have mostly retained the talk's tone and relative paucity of scholarly notation. The question I was asked to address was this: What should theologians—in the broadest sense—pay attention to in the wider university as a way to think through the implications of their work? I chose to focus on one particular area that seemed to capture a broader swath of university intellectual trends rather than trying to take in a whole range of different things in all the various disciplines (from politics, from philosophy, and so on). I also chose not to focus on many other more obvious things worth examining—for example, why "working for the common good" is an insufficient way for Christians to conceive of their university committee work when other committee members are not Christians.

Interdisciplinary inquiry, to use my own university's term for the exploration of creation's interconnection, is gaining recognition as a particularly fruitful kind of thinking, a wide-ranging style more than a particular set of questions or theories that displays the necessary intertwining of our attempts to perceive a world that is necessarily interrelated. The recognition that we cannot think well about the world without a robust sense of the interconnections of created existence—it is not, of course, put this way in any official institutional language—is a (re)discovery that "tracks the truth."[1] The truth that it tracks, however, is not a minor point about this or that small connection but something rather more dramatic.

The argument of this essay is that interdisciplinary inquiry is nothing less than an effort to recover our humanity. Or, to put it more starkly, interdisciplinary inquiry is a cry for help, a manifestation of the fact that the human being is the thing that went missing in the way intellectual investigation was conducted in the modern period. Properly seen, that is, the human being itself is what is tracked through the "inter."

To see how our humanity is at stake in interdisciplinary inquiry, we will likely have to unlearn some basic habits formed over a lengthy amount of time—indeed, just the amount of time that it has taken us to move from our childhood to where we are now. The reason for this is that interdisciplinary thinking will require us to learn things that reverse a long-held and very powerful conception of intellectual growth: a pattern whereby the interconnections of life are slowly but surely pushed aside in favor of devotion to ever-increasing specialization and attempt at mastery. To think between and among the disciplines is not to put aside the goods of specialization, but neither is it to grow into them. Instead, to learn integrative or interdisciplinary thinking is to grow from an adult to a child, to relearn—even in the midst of disciplinary investigation—the unities of self and community. This is the heart of interdisciplinary knowledge. We must learn to become like children.

Becoming a Child

In a recent address to the incoming graduate students from all fields, the former dean of the Divinity School, L. Gregory Jones, spoke about cultivating the

1. The language is that of Bernard Williams, *Ethics and the Limits of Philosophy* (Cambridge, MA: Harvard University Press, 1985), though Williams himself is citing Robert Nozick.

habit of asking "big questions" as a way to pursue the interconnectedness of knowledge, or the indelibly interdisciplinary character of human inquiry. His address was aptly titled "Forming Questions." To introduce the skill of forming questions, Jones issued an imagination-capturing invitation to the new students: "I'm inviting you to discover again," he said, "the intellectual wonder of being a four-year old. . . . Remember when you asked big questions, 'How do airplanes fly? Why are there so many different kinds of animals? What makes people do such bad things?'"[2]

Jones went on to talk more about university-based integrative education and knowledge, but I lingered over the image of a child's questions. And in reflecting on these remarks I began to think about my (then) young son, whose questions on any given day ranged from "Why did God make black widows?" to "How much superglue would it take to glue our car to the ceiling?" to "Which makes a bigger splash, a can opener or cannonball?" to "Can we have a pet blue whale sometime?" to "Why is blood both runny and sticky?" to "What's prednisone?" It would never occur to my son that these questions were not related, that the typical well-educated adult would reflexively farm them out to respective "expert" or knowledgeable friends in the various fields of moral philosophy/theology, applied chemistry, marine science, medicine, pharmacology, and so forth.

At one level, of course, it did not occur to my son that his questions were not related because he had yet to develop—physiologically and thereafter by habit—the necessary cognitive skills that would allow him to focus on a particular issue to the exclusion of others: Why does it take so long for the adrenal glands to start producing cortisol after being chronically suppressed? is a question to which another question, such as, Why do smallmouth bass live in cold water rather than warm?, may be a moment of genuine distraction. That is to say, certain kinds of important matters—some of them even life-and-death matters—come to light when, and really only when, we learn how to develop finely tuned skills of focus and abstraction.

But at another level, the idea that questions can be divorced from one another does not occur to children because it does not occur to them that they are not unified persons or whole selves. Children do not know what it could mean to live "two lives" and would not understand our expressions "love life,"

2. A version of this address can be accessed here: L. Gregory Jones, "The Practice of Asking Questions," *Faith & Leadership*, August 25, 2009, https://divinityarchive.com/bitstream/handle/11258/5996/the-practice-asking-questions.pdf.

"work life," and "family life": for them there is just one life.[3] Said differently, the interrelation of their questions is just the unity of their lives: they themselves, in the unity that they are, hold their questions together.

Of course, by saying that it does not occur to children that they are unified persons or whole selves, I invoke a notion of the self that needs further explanation. In contrast to any anthropology that would hold that human beings can be divided up—either metaphysically into body and soul/mind or chronologically into different "stages" of life—I take it that the only way to speak meaningfully of the actual life of any particular human being is to speak in terms of the narrative unity of his or her life.[4] Following Alasdair MacIntyre's basic point in *After Virtue*, we can say that the life of a human being cannot be carved up into isolatable stages or moments that exist in independence from the rest of a person's existence. Such moments are but intellectual abstractions from the person who lives them in an unbroken physiological sequence. Indeed, even to make sense of something like the periods of life to which "old age" or "adolescence" attempt to point, we must employ a prior understanding (*Vorverständnis*) of a larger context in which these periods—or, more strictly, concepts—are placed and from which they derive their meaning.[5] If "adolescence" makes any sense to us, that is, it is because we have already employed a larger context that makes intelligible the sense the concept has. That larger context is the unity of a human life. It is the whole of a life in which it would make sense to speak of various periods such as childhood, young adulthood, middle age, and so on. The "self" as it will be used in this essay is therefore a word taken to point to this unity of life. It is shorthand for the same person who persists through the time it takes to live a human life.

Were we to discuss the variety of further conceptual moves that this notion of the self entails, we would move far afield from our immediate topic. There is,

3. For a portrayal of the division between work and family life, it would be hard to do better than Tolstoy's *Death of Ivan Ilych* (especially the depiction of Ivan's life for the first seventeen years of his marriage).

4. Alasdair MacIntyre, *After Virtue*, 3rd ed. (Notre Dame, IN: University of Notre Dame Press, 2007); Wilhelm Schapp, *In Geschichten Verstrickt: Zum Sein von Mensch und Ding*, 3rd ed. (Frankfurt am Main: Vittorio Klostermann, 1985). The narrative unity of life does not, of course, preclude our ability to make statements about certain characteristics of a life (he is married to so-and-so); it just means that we will not know what those statements mean without the narrative context that tells us who "he" is.

5. This is the anthropological correlate to MacIntyre's point—which he shares with G. E. M. Anscombe—that an intelligible action is a more fundamental concept than an action per se. We cannot know meaningfully what "adolescence" might ever mean without a more fundamental context of human life in which to place it.

however, one correlative concept that is necessary for our ensuing discussion: integrity. Integrity is a word that has come to mean many things, not least in current political life. Other meanings aside, for this essay integrity is used to mean the ability to live coherently—to be "the same person"—through all the various contexts of life.[6] We might call it a skill—something learned through practice—or we might call it a virtue, one which would be inseparable from other virtues, or we might call it a gift: something given to us in part by the conditions of our lives (favorable to our integrity). In truth, a life of integrity would require all of these descriptions. But for this essay integrity points to the refusal of self-division through a life of coherence.

The unity of the self and integrity—the skill needed to maintain that unity—are fundamental and indispensable presuppositions of the project of interdisciplinary inquiry; precisely to the degree that it makes sense, interdisciplinary investigation requires the unity of a human life through time—no self-integrity, no interdisciplinary inquiry. To see the significance of this fact, we begin by exploring the way role-playing threatens the unity of the self and the skill we need to maintain it.

Role-Playing and the Division of the Self

In contrast to children, for whom the unity of life is simply a lived fact, adults find the unity of human life much harder to perceive. As adults we have highly developed capacities for abstraction and, because of our larger social structures, have become accustomed to playing "roles" of various kinds: teacher, government administrator, family member, and so forth. By "role" here I do not, however, mean a job or a duty or a hobby per se: we can do all these things without actually playing a role. A role in the sense that is important for this essay holds a much deeper significance and is far more determinative for the shape of a human life. As Alasdair MacIntyre has shown, playing a role in this deeper, determinative sense involves the adoption and internalization of a highly particularized pattern of life within a "relatively autonomous sphere of activity."[7]

6. Cf. Eugene Garver, *For the Sake of Argument: Practical Reasoning, Character, and the Ethics of Belief* (Chicago: University of Chicago Press, 2004), who speaks of a thickening of reason toward integrity (esp. 30). As will become apparent from the example of the power executives given by MacIntyre, the loss of integrity is a concomitant loss in the ability to reason well.

7. Alasdair MacIntyre, "Social Structures and Their Threat to Moral Agency," in *Selected Essays*, vol. 2, *Ethics and Politics* (Cambridge: Cambridge University Press, 2006), 186–204.

With the image of a sphere, MacIntyre invokes the role-playing context, the overall framing of the form of life that is constituted and sustained through a set of rules by which we must play both to enter into and to stay in a particular role. And by describing this sphere as "relatively autonomous," MacIntyre points to the ways in which the standards of behavior, virtue, success, excellence, and so forth that obtain in any given sphere exist in relative independence from the influence and pressure of other role-playing contexts. As he puts it elsewhere, the sphere is where roles are "compartmentalized."[8] So, for example, the rules by which one knows what counts as constancy or excellence within the context of a family have no intrinsically necessary connection to or influence upon the rules for what counts as constancy or excellence within a governmental bureaucracy or medical center or small business—or even a very serious bowling league.

MacIntyre's chief example of what it means to play a role is particularly useful because it illustrates from "real life" a fundamental and rather frightening point: the danger to the coherence of the self that attends the incompatibility of the rules of role-playing contexts. When studying executives in the electric power industry in the 1970s, it became clear that "power company executives tended to a significant degree to answer what were substantially the same questions somewhat differently, depending on whether they took themselves to be responding qua power company executive or qua parent and head of household or qua concerned citizen." This was not because they seriously weighed alternative answers and simply happened to land on the answers their roles would have required. Indeed, not only their faculty of rational discrimination but even "their attitude" varied from role to role. Moreover, the power industry executives "seemed quite unaware" of these basic intellectual and behavioral variations. When playing the role of power company executive, that is, the subjects of the study thought only within the sphere of that activity and "were unable even to entertain, as a serious policy alternative, reduction in the overall levels of power consumption." But they "did not suffer from

8. Alasdair MacIntyre, "Moral Philosophy and Contemporary Social Practice: What Holds Them Apart?," in *Selected Essays*, vol. 1, *The Tasks of Philosophy* (Cambridge: Cambridge University Press, 2006), 104–22. In "Social Structures," he explains that "compartmentalization goes beyond that differentiation of roles and institutional structures that characterizes every social order and it does so by the extent to which each distinct sphere of social activity comes to have its own role structure governed by its own specific norms in relative independence of other such spheres" (197). See, too, the insightful essay of James Conant, "Philosophy and Biography," in *Wittgenstein: Biography and Philosophy*, ed. James C. Klagge (Cambridge: Cambridge University Press, 2001), 16–50.

the same inability when thinking and speaking as consumers or concerned citizens."[9] In short, the individuals disagreed not with others but with *themselves*—and this disagreement was masked by the power of the role to (mis) shape self-perception.

As MacIntyre's example shows, the rules of a role-playing context can conflict to such a degree that it is impossible to maintain integrity across all spheres at the same time (or even more than one). Thus if "in a policy meeting of the Midwestern power executives one of them had proposed attempting to bring about an overall reduction in power consumption . . . their remarks might be treated as a joke or ignored, but, if such a speaker persisted, they would find themselves deprived at least temporarily of their status in that sphere of activity, treated, that is, as a source of embarrassing background noise rather than a participant."[10] Offering only a slight twist on MacIntyre's example can help clarify the point. Though certain business cultures—the context in which the role of businessperson is played—may require the elision of the truth for the sake of the company's profit, the same cannot be said for the role of husband or wife. For the marriage to last—as indeed it must for the role of husband or wife to make sense—neither party can treat the other as the object of deceit, and lying is a practice to be eschewed. Were a married businessman to confuse the two sets of rules and forget which roles he was to play where, both spheres would be seriously destabilized and their legitimacy questioned, the one by rigorous honesty and the other by artful deceit.[11]

Or, to take a final example from one of the best books ever produced, in *Anna Karenina* Tolstoy paints Constantine Levin's friend Sviyazhsky as a perfect example of living self-contradiction: "Sviyazhsky was one of those people—always a source of astonishment to Levin—whose judgment, perfectly logical though never original, goes along one line while their lives, extremely definite and unwavering in direction, go along another, completely

9. MacIntyre, "Social Structures," 196–97.

10. MacIntyre, "Social Structures," 199.

11. Countless situations could be imagined to make the point: suppose his wife, an investigative reporter by trade, let us say, wanted to buy stock in the company and went to her husband to ask about the advisability of this. How could he answer the question: What should woman X—where X is his wife—be told about the company's profit? Such confusion, that is, would be fatal not just to one but to both roles. This example assumes as indisputable fact that some businesses operate in the way described. One could point out that telling the truth should characterize both spheres and that there would then be no conflict. But this is just the point. Developing integrity in the sense of maintaining a continuity of truth across spheres is what is under discussion.

independent of and almost always in contradiction with their judgment."[12] Sviyazhsky was liberal in his philosophy (i.e., he professes not to like government and noblemen) but serves as Marshal of the Nobility and, in his habits, behaves as the nobleman par excellence (e.g., goes abroad for fine living). To Levin, Sviyazhsky is a "living enigma," and after many attempts to find the "foundation" of his friend's views, Levin sees that it is impossible: "Levin saw that he was never going to find the connection between this man's life and his thoughts."[13]

To grasp the basic fact that the same person cannot play mutually exclusive roles is already to see that our roles are far from harmless, temporary postures designed to get us through the day. Indeed, such roles can become modes of being that actually divide the self—or, differently said, that render us more opaque to ourselves and make it more difficult or impossible to see that we are in fact the same person throughout all the different facets of life. As we move within the "relatively autonomous sphere[s] of activity" that both create and sustain our various roles, we begin to lose the sense of the unity and continuity of our lives and, therefore, the knowledge that who we are is not reducible to any role we play. And having lost our sense of our loves, we attempt to shift from the set of rules of one "sphere" to another and become—almost literally—the roles we play. But just because we cannot ourselves create harmony between incompatible sets of rules, we are mastered by the contexts in which we play. And we are thus dissolved; our integrity is shattered as we lose the ability to detect even our most basic inconsistencies.

The Scholar

As is obvious from some of the brief examples above, the roles that we play frequently correlate with the kind of knowledge or skill set or training we have. One of these roles, one that MacIntyre does not directly discuss, can be "scholar." Examining some of MacIntyre's insights, we can say that "scholar" as a role names a mode of being that results from inhabiting a way of knowing whose rules presuppose the intellectual viability of a relatively autonomous sphere of discourse. Scholars in this sense learn to play the role dictated by the rules of a particular sphere of inquiry—a "field"—and learn little else. Especially via the socialization that occurs during graduate school, but also later

12. Leo Tolstoy, *Anna Karenina*, trans. Joel Carmichael (New York: Bantam, 2006), 391.
13. Tolstoy, *Anna Karenina*, 350, 361.

through the broader critical edifice of their disciplines (peer-review journals, conference presentations, reputable publishers, etc.), scholars learn to screen out entire ways of reading the world and, instead, to move within a sphere whose habits of reasoning implicitly occlude the interconnectedness of life.

It is quite possible, for example, that we could learn the intricacies of molecular biology as a current discipline while maintaining a high degree of ignorance about the interdependence of scientific thought with larger conceptions of religious superstition, magic, and a world ordered perceptibly to immanent reason. Or we might work rigorously on the complicated physical science of atomic warfare while thinking little about physiological effects of thermal burns on children, or know quite a lot about medical trauma but nothing about the psychological damage incurred by the medicalization of life, or regularly ponder the set of challenges produced by a swell of the aged in modern Western society but entirely ignore the importance of the effects of poverty on actual life span. It is not that we would actively deny that such matters could be related; it is rather that because of our intellectual habits we do not know how to conceive their interrelation. Just because autonomous spheres of discourse implicitly claim self-sufficiency, they reject—in their mode of active reasoning—the interdependence of human inquiry. Playing the role of scholar, therefore, prohibits our ability to make the connections we would need to make were we ever to say how such seemingly independent matters as nuclear science and inner-city poverty all play a part in the overall unity of a human life.

Of course, the danger in specialization is not that of specialization itself. Seriously, who could learn everything?[14] It is rather that we learn to play the role of scholar by refusing to admit the radical permeability of our intellectual boundaries and thus—*precisely as a scholar*—assault the unity of the self with our mode of knowing. Exactly because we cannot simultaneously play the role of scholar and see the interconnections of life, that is, we learn to be incoherent. We may know a great deal about this or about that, but such knowledge comes at the price of the coherence of the self—and thus at the price of our integrity (to be "the same person" across the varying contexts of our lives).

To work, for example, in one's academic career for a materialist "Darwinian" account of human life and history while maintaining—in one's "personal life"—an active commitment to the flourishing of the "weak" (the handi-

14. See Stanley Hauerwas's commencement address to the Duke PhD graduates, "For Dappled Things," in *Sanctify Them in the Truth: Holiness Exemplified* (Nashville: Abingdon, 1998), 227–31. Hauerwas shows that one way to read specialization as a good is to see it as the deep and patient exploration of the richness of creation.

capped, children, oppressed minorities, and so on) would not be, as such a person might want to argue, a demonstration of intellectual course on the one hand and civic sensitivity on the other. It would be, instead, the concrete evidence of a fundamental division and incoherence, the attempt to play the role of scholar together with the role of loving parent, community advocate, and so on. Nor could a committed Nietzschean work as an activist for the political party of "equal opportunity" without the deepest self-deception—that is, just the kind that is built on self-division.[15] Despite whatever reasons we might offer for their differing commitments, such "role-players" would not be paragons of existential nimbleness—persons well adapted to the various and often competing demands of life—just profoundly confused. In both of these examples, the material commitments needed to follow the rules of the discourse unavoidably conflict with the commitments needed to develop and maintain care for the weak or disadvantaged. Were the two sets of commitments to come into practical conflict—the defense of the weak, say, would manifestly cripple the defender's bid for power—a choice would have to be made and one of the commitments jettisoned. The rules of both sets of commitments simply cannot be lived at one and the same time.

Yet, as these examples already hint, playing scholar is not only a fundamental threat to the self of the person who plays the role; it is also a threat to *others*. For to play scholar is at once to become intellectually ingrown and to read "the world" from within the rules that create and maintain one (falsely) isolated sphere. Our inward gaze turns outward not in a movement of self-broadening but in one of restriction and reduction. Caught in the pattern of our thinking, we shrink the world to exactly the size of our (semi)autonomous sphere. Others thus appear to us in the terms set by this shrunken world and are therefore interpreted within its normative rules.

Or, to put it more strongly—and in connection with the fashionable trend that everywhere spots "discourses of power"—we actively conform the other to the shape of the sphere in which we play our scholarly role. We thereby reduce them, render problematical to ourselves, whether willingly or not, the fullness of their self. Precisely because their self is divided by our antecedent

15. To be more precise: a committed Nietzschean could work for this political party if it served his own ends. What he would not do without profound self-deception/contradiction is to work for the party on the assumption that the normative commitments that fund the party's action were morally compelling (or true in any sort of strong sense). For a brief but very interesting exposition of Nietzsche's sense of truth/deception, see Bernard Williams, "There Are Many Kinds of Eyes," in *The Sense of the Past: Essays in the History of Philosophy* (Princeton: Princeton University Press, 2006), 325–30.

self-division, that is, we cannot see the others whole. Our fragmentary and incoherent grasp of our selves is thus reproduced in them, and they become, in a frightening instance of sophisticated projection, exactly who we take them to be. This does not mean, of course, that they are made to look like us, but rather that we construe them in the image of our intellectual boundaries: its shape, its rules, are their shape, their rules. Our divided self is their divided self. In short: the loss of our fullness is the loss of theirs.

Playing the role of scholar therefore disables us intellectually and as a precise correlate of this fact threatens human community. By inhabiting autonomous spheres of knowledge and discourse, we are literally rendered unable to make the connections on which the unity of our lives and the lives of others depend. We confuse, that is, the role of scholar with being human, on the one hand, and a human being with the role of scholar, on the other.

Hysteria, the Scholar, and Society

That the development of disciplines in the modern sense tends to reinforce rather than overcome the human tendency to divide the self and play roles is not something that has, to my knowledge, received much discussion in intellectual or university circles. This may partly be because on the face of it the idea seems rather preposterous, an entirely overblown worry due more to hysteria than to rigorous reasoning. Surely, we might say, studying complex color change in chameleons does not lead to the division of the self; focusing intensely on the surgical techniques needed to repair the retina does not predispose us to read another human being as less than a whole person; learning to decipher Egyptian hieroglyphs does not shrink the world; and so on and on virtually ad infinitum. To all such questions, there is a rather simple reply: But of course!

The point is hardly that we should stop organizing knowledge for concentrated attention. Think only of pre-anesthesia surgery! It is rather that we have forgotten what disciplines—positively conceived—are meant to be and how not to confuse disciplined attention with a whole way of knowing. At their best, that is to say, disciplines are moments of concretized or focused speculative reflection in the overall unity of a life. In this way disciplines enable us to discover the complexity of the world and can thereby enrich, almost immeasurably, our appreciation for the wonders of the world in which we live. But disciplines are not in any sense the way to read the world in toto or, worse, who or what a human being actually is.

To put the matter this way, however, is once again to risk delirium. After all, who really thinks a retina is a person? Or again, even the heartiest or most obstinate Marxists know the difference, do they not, between theoretical reflection on the economic drivers of human existence and the actual human beings who are thus driven. And yet the danger inherent in any nonintegrative thinking remains: the connections of life are occluded, and by intellectual habituation into such occlusion, we lose the ability to reflect on the significance of the radically limiting character of disciplinary thought and the fundamentally porous nature of human life.

If, for example, we inhabit a sphere of discourse whose rules bind our attention to genetics, to history, and to race, and then from this vantage point turn outward to read the world, we risk taking these fields of attention for what constitutes a human being. Precisely in our role as scholar, we risk mistaking whatever we take a person's genetics or race to be with the totality or unity of their life. The consequences of such a mistake, of course, are potentially far from simple intellectual error.

One could, for example, split the self of a Jewish person, even one who was at one point a colleague or friend in another context, and instead read him as "Jew" in a very specific sense: the kind of thing, that is, that should not be admitted into the realm of scholarly discourse par excellence—the university—but instead to be handed to the Nazis. In so doing the relational dimension of human knowledge would be destroyed—his Thou turned into an It—and the ability to see him as fellow researcher or teacher or family friend would be lost: these aspects of the overall unity of his life would simply have been elided by a habit of thinking whose intellectual structure implicitly denied the importance of the interpenetration of different facets of existence in one human life.[16]

Or, to stay with this particular context, if we played the role of medical scientist in the Germany of the 1930s and early 1940s, we could divorce scientific medical knowledge from the human being toward which it is properly aimed and, in our role as scientist, accept "Jew" to be "the-kind-of-thing-upon-which-it-is-legitimate-to-experiment." Precisely because our role-playing would prevent us from making the connections necessary to sustain a vision of human wholeness, we could screen out the humanness of those whom our colleagues in racial theory and in politics delivered to us. Both of these examples point to a further and—once again—quite alarming problem: the ability

16. Conversely, maintaining a sense of the unity of another's life or the interpenetration of different "spheres" potentially allows the other contexts—family friend, colleague, and so on—to exert positive moral pressure upon the deforming effects of self-division.

of role-players to engage in collaboration precisely in their various roles as X or Y. Of course, to say collaboration may already be to say too much, for the relation between the role-players is not one of radical interdependence—a questioning of the rules of one sphere by the recognition of different rules in the other—but is instead more like a tacit collusion: a mode of working together in which each role-player furthers the role-playing of another. If we play the role of church leader in such a way as to avoid political struggles, we collude with the politicians who play the role of the führer and his supporters. We can thus attend church on Sunday morning and the Nazi rally later in the afternoon with little to no sense of the discord, reinforcing the deadly power of the one and the political impotence of the other.

By such collusion, the playing of roles is reinforced, enhanced, and extended, thus magnifying its effects: the refusal of integrity literally takes on a life of its own as it becomes systematically embedded in a societal way of being. Regardless of the few individual exceptions, society now as a whole lacks the ability to make the connections that preserve the unity of the self and, hence, the wholeness of the other. Indeed, in its role-playing collusions, it actively reinforces division: it is a society of incoherent or divided selves.

Postmodernity and the Reach for Our Humanity

Seen in the light of the dangers inherent in role-playing, interdisciplinary reflection is nothing less than an attempt to maintain the unity of a human life—both our own and those with whom we live. Which is to say that in advanced or postmodernity we have finally begun to realize that we must recover our humanity in our thinking no less than in our living. The deep rationale or interdisciplinary reflection, therefore, is the recognition that to see whole persons we need to work in our intellectual or research habits against the division of the self while simultaneously maintaining the goods to which specialized knowledge can lead.[17]

To put it differently, at bottom interdisciplinary reflection finally makes good sense only insofar as it presupposes the unity of the self—the ability of a

17. By putting it this way, I indicate my enduring commitment to the goods achieved by specialized knowledge and simultaneously suggest that these goods come with large risks. Precisely because such goods come with large risks, interdisciplinary training is a necessary part of the overall way we think about organizing and marshaling our efforts. That is, without interdisciplinary reflection we have little to no check against the risks. With it, our risks in specialized knowledge are at least exposed for us to see and actively counterbalanced.

person to be the same person through time, one who traverses all the various contexts of life as oneself—and therefore as someone who is able to hold them together in his or her person. There is no such thing as "interdisciplinary" if there is no person that moves through time as the same self who is able to hold together various "disciplines" in an overall unity of life. Insofar as we presuppose the ability to relate different disciplines to one another, we presuppose the unity of the person through time who will do that relating. To work interdisciplinarily is thus to work for the wholeness of the self and against its division, to reach out for our full humanity in an attempt to recover and maintain it.

In just this way, interdisciplinary reflection constitutes a limit to our scholarly role-playing and works, at least implicitly, toward our overall integrity. Indeed, it is an active mode of resistance, a manner of cultivating intellectual tendencies that make it difficult to retain the notion of an autonomous sphere of discourse. Or, to state it positively, interdisciplinary reflection is a mode of intellectual repair and maintenance—a kind of training that educates us into being human precisely by making explicit the interconnection of the various moments of our lives.

Of course the emphasis on interdisciplinary work in the postmodern period is a marked difference from modern conceptions of inquiry. Modernity was the time when we believed that the world could be mastered by dividing human knowledge into disciplines. Divide and conquer, if not said outright, was nevertheless the implicit epistemological posture of modern disciplinary division. This procedure, so it was thought, would leave us with a unified world, and with a way to know it in its fullness. Each part would contribute to the whole. But disciplines did not do this. Instead they produced mind-boggling difficulty in every area of inquiry—theoretical and experimental alike—and seemed to require unending further division and subdivision (witness any major university's natural sciences faculties). Ironically, then, rather than solidifying the unity of the world and ordering our lives within it, disciplinary inquiry contributed substantially to a dramatic fracturing of knowledge and helped to make human life all the more confusing.[18] In the terms of this essay,

18. Cf. the remarks of Ernest Becker, *The Denial of Death* (New York: Simon & Schuster, 1997), 209: "The great characteristic of our time is that we know everything important about human nature that there is to know. Yet never has there been an age in which so little knowledge is securely possessed, so little a part of the common understanding. The reason is precisely the advance of specialization, the impossibility of making safe general statements, which has led to a general imbecility. What I would like to do in these few pages is to run the risk of simple-mindedness in order to make some dent in the unintended imbecility brought about by specialization and its mountain of facts."

the self was pressed ever more forcefully toward division and confusion. Modernity, in short, was the fracturing of the self and the world.[19]

Postmodernity took off from this fragmented character of self and world and proclaimed that this fragmentation was in fact the deeper logic of the way things are. We were thus free to play—play among and between disciplines, for, after all, there was no unity to which we were accountable. Or play roles: if there is no self—no final unity of our lives—we are free to move from sphere to sphere with no worries about whatever contradictions may arise. Such contradictions do not actually touch us, for there is no substantive "us" for them to touch, only role-playing moments in otherwise un-unified chronological engagements. Postmodernity is thus the celebration of the self's fragmentation, the jubilant response to the loss of our selves as the necessary correlate of the loss of the unity of the world. It might thus be thought that interdisciplinary inquiry is the hallmark of postmodern fragmentation thinking, an explicit license to play various roles in whatever way we might see fit.

But to see things this way is to misread, philologically no less than philosophically, the meaning of *inter*disciplinary inquiry. In fact, postmodernity can be the time that we realize the interconnection of our endeavors—we are all implicated in other spheres of discourse—and its irrefragable presupposition: that there is someone who is there to discover such interconnection. Discovering that the notion of an autonomous sphere of inquiry is ultimately a fiction is just the rediscovery of the self and the indispensability of human community.

In realizing the interdependence of spheres of life, that is, we simultaneously discover a sort of unity toward which we are directed. As all good doctors know, for example, to think well as a physician is not simply to analyze the disease that happens to come with a patient attached to it. It is rather to think of the patient's disease inside of a much thicker context of human life, one in which economics, family dynamics, work responsibilities, and so forth all play a part in what it means to "diagnose" and "manage" a serious illness. Only in this way will the physician's treatment of the disease display the particular texture needed to be most effective and, indeed, to earn the name "care." And, as all thoughtful patients know, to lose this larger context of life in the treatment

19. George Steiner, *Tolstoy or Dostoevsky? An Essay in the Old Criticism*, 2nd ed. (New Haven: Yale University Press, 1996), xi–xii, speaks of the "triumph of the inhuman at the heart of the century." Steiner largely has in mind the violence of the twentieth century with its two world wars, for example, but his description is exactly on target for the end of modernity's larger intellectual habits.

of their disease is, to put it brashly, to be reduced to a disease. Thus both doctor and patient are bound together in the effort to maintain the interconnections of life that emerge precisely in the context of their mutual dependence upon another for the gift and reception of healing and care. The unity toward which they are directed, that is, transcends the reach of an individual role just because it depends upon them both: gift and reception are reciprocal and mutually constitutive. This is, of course, to say considerably more than the role of physician reinforces and is reinforced by that of patient. In this case the rejection of autonomous spheres is rooted in the realization that our interdependence directs us toward our common humanity.[20]

We have also learned, to take only one more example, that the way we treat our spouses does actually have a deep connection to our public service, as countless resignations and scandals rightly attest. Despite the oft-given impression to the contrary, the general public outrage over philandering politicians is not priggery. It is instead the expression of an intuitive grasp of the only hope for a life of integrity: a refusal to accept the proposition that politicians can play by one set of rules in one sphere (honesty/trustworthiness) and another, contradictory set in a different sphere (deceit/betrayal). Here, the outraged segment of the public knows tacitly—even if the politicians do not—that such divisions in the self threaten the core of human society.[21]

To see the interconnection and interdependence of so-called autonomous spheres is to realize that the contradictions between the rules by which we play our various roles are crucially important because, in a word, they stay put. We cannot escape them by moving to another sphere, attempting to play still yet another. Precisely because the various spheres are mutually overlapping, "mixed" together, or reciprocally constitutive of one another, where we play roles we become caught in the incompatibility of their different rules of play and tear ourselves asunder by means of the contradictions we try—but necessarily fail—to live. Role-playing contradictions, that is, are part of the lives we (fail to) live.[22]

20. See Paul Ramsey, *The Patient as Person: Explorations in Medical Ethics* (New Haven: Yale University Press, 1970), and Stanley Hauerwas, *God, Medicine, and Suffering* (Grand Rapids: Eerdmans, 2000), esp. 115.

21. That we object to such behavior, however, may well be historically determined inasmuch as we inhabit a political/moral society long and deeply shaped by Christianity. The ancient Romans, to take an obvious example, did not care about philandering to the degree that modern Americans do. But it would be a mistake to think that they didn't see the unity of life, for in fact they did. They just had other kinds of objections based on other kinds of "roles" that their politicians were to play (e.g., think of Cicero or the Stoics' recurrent lauding of Cato).

22. That contradictory and failed lives are painful is obvious. We can think, for example, not only of physicians who lose sight of the human beings they treat but also of

The paradox of postmodernism, therefore, is that while it proclaims the fragmentation of reality, it literally and simultaneously invites the insight that everything is interconnected. And as it turns out, this insight is that which allows us to maintain our humanity. Of course, it is only human beings who think about these problems in the first place. Cats, for example, do not. But then, that is just the point.

Eschatological Humanity

There is one final argument against the idea that interdisciplinary inquiry works toward a recovery of our humanity. This argument can be stated bluntly: what has been presented as the inner anthropological logic of interdisciplinary inquiry is yet one more version of wishful liberal humanism, a kind of thinking that—quite in the face of all the past accumulated evidence to the contrary—stubbornly believes that the next "initiative" or "program" or "project" will at last be the one to solve our problems of division, lack of integrity, and brokenness. Interdisciplinary thinking on this view is but the name of the latest fantasy of the humanities, and its advocates no more than naive hawkers of an ultimately futile fad.

Had I a conception of the self that elided its eschatological determination, or a Pelagian anthropology, this objection would be entirely correct. Just because it ignores the fact that sin is still with us, the type of humanism that ignores the provisional, even stuttering, nature of all inquiry and ascribes a salvific importance to human efforts—in this case, habits of thought—is entirely out of keeping with real life. We will not recover our full humanity simply by thinking in interdisciplinary ways.

But any serious Christian thinker would know that even those who embody integrity will embody it imperfectly. For Christian thought, it is simply a given that interdisciplinary inquiry cannot keep us from all acts of injustice or evil and that the restoration of the fullness of our originally created selves comes only at the eschaton. Truthfulness about our ongoing failures, in fact, points directly toward the eschatological determination of the self.

Interpreting interdisciplinary inquiry as an attempt to recover our humanity is thus at its deepest level a claim that this way of thinking is a longing for the eschaton. Whether its practitioners explicitly recognize this longing or not, interdisciplinary thought grasps something of the fact that we were meant to

ministers whose double lives deeply wound the church upon their exposure—and countless other matters.

be whole selves, that our fracturing and incoherence is damaging and reproduces patterns of the fall rather than of our redemption and our final hope.

Interdisciplinary inquiry will not, of course, quicken the eschaton's arrival. But, after all, that does not change the fact that there are better and worse ways to work through life—rhythms that correspond more to our eschatological redemption and rhythms that do not. Nor does it alter the fact that within such rhythms there are habits of thought that render the unity of life more opaque and those that render it less so, those that make role-playing and self-contradiction easier and those that make it harder. If the thesis of this essay is near the mark, interdisciplinary inquiry requires habits of thought that move with the rhythms of eschatological redemption and the recovery of the human creature itself. In this way interdisciplinary thinking acknowledges the wholeness of our original creation and—with all the necessary qualifications—adumbrates its restoration.

Christianity's First Millennium

◆ REFLECTIONS ON ROBERT LOUIS WILKEN'S MAGNUM OPUS

In the second letter to his pupil Lucilius, Seneca the Younger offered some advice about reading. Read only the good books, said Seneca, and read them over and over again. Reading, he thought, was writing on the soul. Why write on your soul with anything other than the best? Lay down lines worth following, Seneca counseled, and trace them again and again and again.

There were fewer books back then than there are now, but the ranking of books is surely as old as the writing of the second book. And the task has always been hard. Even today university literature departments argue bitterly over what constitutes a good book. It would be difficult to contend that any of the learned volumes produced by academics would rank among the books worth reading repeatedly to write on our souls. But Robert Wilken's book *The First Thousand Years* is about as good as the academic sort can be.[1]

To call it learned, however, is to point only to the remarkable erudition behind every page, not to the style. The style, in fact, is anything but the typical prose of the academic. Wilken writes briskly and with a sense for what a lively tale can do. Far too often professors kill their subject matter with their lack of style. Not so Robert Wilken. And for this he deserves full praise. If Christianity is anything at all like what Christians think it is, how could a millennium's worth of its life be boring?

An engagement with a book of this kind is, almost by definition, less interesting than the story the book itself tells. Still, for the purposes of this symposium at least, there are three features of Wilken's work that invite further

1. Robert Louis Wilken, *The First Thousand Years: A Global History of Christianity* (New Haven: Yale University Press, 2012). Hereafter, page references appear in the text.

"Christianity's First Millennium: Reflections on Robert Louis Wilken's Magnum Opus" was originally published in *Nova et Vetera* 13 (2015): 1261–67. It is reproduced with permission.

comment and reflection. Of all the things that I thought about while reading the book—and this would fill many pages—these three features are those that I see as education in the more significant sense of helping to shape our perception of what Christianity was and is (and may come to be).

First, Christianity is memory. Insofar as we are able to say what the word "Christian" means, we will have to remember its past use. "The past doesn't vanish at once," says Wilken; "it dies slowly." But, "if remembered, the dead maintain their ground and live among us" (1). As general statements, such comments could sound banal, and in one sense we already do know this (or should). Yet I would wager—an educated wager, I hope, from both experience and study—that none of my colleagues at Duke or elsewhere will have gone through this book without startling new discoveries about Christian history, or, at the very least, without learning a surprising amount about people or places that have simply not been on our received intellectual maps (geographically expressed in maps 2 and 3 at the end of the book). More specifically, and perhaps most importantly in this regard, Wilken shows the truth of memory's importance in an arresting way: we Western Christians have forgotten the East. "From the perspective of the West, Christianity in the East seems part of a vanished past" (359). Wilken's point is not that we lack specialists in Syriac or the early Syrian church or St. Ephrem, nor is it the now wearisome point about Western imperialism (or imperialistic epistemology)—that it has tended to exclude non-Westerners. It is rather that the typical picture of the broad sweep of a millennium's worth of Christian history has been *fundamentally* misshapen: we Westerners, Wilken implies, do not really know the story of our own faith. Even with all the various correctives in recent years to "colonialist" histories, we have been telling ourselves—at best—only some of what Christianity has been. And we have therefore distorted our sense of what it is. Our intellectual cartography has been radically deficient, as deficient as if we were to make a map of the world and leave off Asia and India and China.

In Wilken's reading of the first half of our history, Christianity has always been a global phenomenon. We now hear much talk of the globalization of the Christian faith, its move toward the Southern Hemisphere (and its corresponding decline in the Northern), its emergence in China, and the like. While there are doubtless deep differences in both locale and substance between Christianity's original reach and its current global shape, Wilken's book would teach us that the current trends in world Christianity point toward a re-globalization rather than a first one. In other words, if Wilken is right about the shape of the first millennium of Christianity, and if the third millennium of its life is less about the North Atlantic West than elsewhere, then the time that is Western

Christianity will look dramatically less like a remarkable achievement with staying power and more like an interlude in Christianity's global development. Of course, no one knows how a thousand or more years of history from today will unfold. But the point remains that we are and have been fundamentally forgetful and that such forgetfulness imposes serious constrictions on our understanding of the Christian faith. Christianity, Wilken would forcefully remind us, was born a global faith. To conceive of "world Christianity" is not thereby to think of something northern and western with important new additions from elsewhere. It is to think, rather, of a movement beginning in an eastern part of the world and expanding from there to all corners of the earth. Conceptualizing the Christian faith in accordance with its historical shape, Wilken says, is a matter of keeping Jerusalem as the center of our interpretative map (see Warren Smith's essay in this book symposium for further reflection on Jerusalem).[2]

Second, Christianity's global history is not only a history of remarkable growth and civilization creation but also one of dramatic decline and eventual eclipse. "The extraordinary success of Christianity in the first millennium," says Wilken, "must be set alongside the dramatic rise of Islam and the decline of Christianity in historic Christian lands" (3–4). Christianity is rightly maligned for its crusades as a betrayal of the core of Christian conviction about the way God was in Christ, but what is often missed in such maligning is the fact that in a large part of its geographical reach Christianity was fading fast and becoming extinct during the latter part of the first millennium. Indeed, "in North Africa, Christianity disappeared and no indigenous Christians remain in countries such as Libya, Tunisia, and Algeria" (4).

It is a sobering fact to think of Christian history as one of decline and disappearance. We do not normally think this way in the West, but were we to write the history of Christianity in vast parts of its former habitats, we would be forced to say something like this: it was here, and then began to disappear, and then went away—no Christian children to raise, none to teach, no pastors to shepherd their flocks or bury their dead. Only the Prophet Muhammad and his One God. "Set against the success of Islam and its staying power, the career of Christianity is marked as much by decline and attrition as it is by growth and triumph" (358). Sociologically speaking, in a wide area of the world Christianity was defeated by the rise of Islam.

Anyone who pays attention to the decline of Christianity in Europe would do well to see from the growth of Islam that a decline in Christian commu-

2. J. Warren Smith, "'If I Forget You, O Jerusalem': Zion's Place in Global Christianity," *Nova et Vetera* 13, no. 4 (2015): 1269–81.

nities does not have to end in renewal; it can go all the way to extinction. We are often theologically invested in the attempt to stem decline—and for many good reasons—but Wilken's focus on the historical power of Islam reminds us that it is possible to fight a losing battle.

Christians do not, I think, have a fundamental stake in self-preservation, especially if the cost of such preservation is violence—in which case we betray our very reason for staving off diminution and extinction. We trust in the resurrection of the dead in Christ, whether God chooses to prosper our communities in the here and now or to let them die and raise us at the end. Still, a world without Christianity as a global force is a world without the truth of all things in its midst in a palpable and public sense. Such a world may come to exist, but if so, I pity those who will have to live in it. If nothing else, Wilken's description of Christianity's decline helps us to think about the importance of Christian existence simpliciter. What is it that the world owes to the existence of Christianity?[3] Such a question points further toward the importance of mission as a dynamic internal to the existence of Christianity as a form of life. Wilken repeatedly notes the missionary drive from the beginning of Christian existence. As long as there are Christians, there will be mission. Yet, as the Islamic case shows, it does not follow that as long as there is mission there will be Christians en masse. With around two billion Christians today, it is admittedly hard to conceive—I do not mean hard to believe—but it is not impossible that over time we could, once again, be a very small group.

Third, Christianity is a form of life that is inescapably structural in a very concrete sense. In an age in which many people look on structural religion with suspicion, mistrust, and disdain, it is worth remembering that without institutional patterning from beginning to end Christianity would not have been the phenomenon it has become. To put it slightly differently, if the story Wilken tells is anything like the phenomenon Christianity was, there is no such thing as Christianity in and through time without institutions that shape, hold, and carry its life. "Wherever Christianity was adopted a structure was put in place, through the person of the bishop, that provided continuity with the Christian past and spiritual unity with Christians in other parts of the world. . . . There is no evidence for enduring Christian communities without the office of the bishop" (356–57). The point Wilken makes is, of course, that of historical truth—it was this way in fact—but the lesson is of no less theological

3. For a good exploration of this question in our time, see David Bentley Hart's *Atheist Delusions: The Christian Revolution and Its Fashionable Enemies* (New Haven: Yale University Press, 2009).

importance: Christianity is a religion in which authority is indispensable. All the preaching in the world about the priesthood of all believers and, in its modern French Revolution echo, "egalitarianism" cannot rid the past of the fact that the Christian faith flourished through authoritative structure and not apart from it.

The ordered community of monastic life was no less important in the first millennium. Today, among many Western Protestants at least, it is inconceivable that human beings can go their entire lives without sex. In the older world, says Wilken, a "chaste community" was an indispensable part of the way Christianity established and maintained its existence. The monks and nuns witnessed to a new reality, to God's work on earth through the form of life that practiced the awaiting of the final consummation (not a seeking of its earthly analogues). "By the end of the third century small groups of men or women lived chaste lives in community. . . . [Later] wherever Christianity was adopted, one found monks. In some cases, in the Syriac-speaking East, in the Slavic world, and in the Latin West, monks carried the gospel to new peoples" (357).

So, too, from the first days of the earliest church, Christianity was something to be learned and therefore to be taught (Acts 2–4). Christianity was always a religion of the book, implying at the least that it needed ways to train interpreters of scripture and those who could communicate its truth to the faithful. Illiteracy was the norm in antiquity regardless of locale—though in terms of social groups it was lower among the Jews than among others—and Christians thus tried to establish educational means wherever they set up shop for any length of time. Intellectual life was always nourished, but it was not for curiosity's sake as much as it was for the working out of the logic of the faith. The Christians knew that faithful thinking was not ultimately rooted in individual intellectual talent but in the truth that had been handed on from generation to generation. Their controversies showed their willingness to innovate and learn new things, but, as Wilken illustrates, what endured were the innovations that drew most deeply from the wells of tradition. The practice of thinking thus involved remembering, and this remembering required education. One had to learn what to remember, and what was remembered had to be passed on. "Wherever there were churches," Wilken says, "Christians forged a learned tradition and handed on a cultural inheritance" (358).

In short, according to Wilken, "Christianity came into the world as an ordered community and made its way as a corporate body with institutions and offices, rituals and laws. Christianity is inescapably social. Its spread among new people had little to do with the conversion of individuals and everything to do with building a new society" (358). Wilken's denial of the importance of individual conversion is overdone—why must we always have the dichotomy between communities and the people who make them up?—but the drift of his remarks is crucially important: Christianity was and is a total way of life. It is not only a matter of the heart—but it is this!—nor is it personal preference, such as the color of ink in which you prefer to write; it is a *regula vitae*, a rule of the lives we live from the broadest social dynamics down to the thoughts we think only to ourselves. This hardly means that on Wilken's view Christianity lacked profound internal difference or avoided complicated contestation over its legitimate expressions. "The global outreach of Christianity in the early centuries is a testimony to its cultural adaptability and diversity. Christianity as practiced among the Armenians differed from the ways of the Greeks or Ethiopians. . . . The differences in language, customs, liturgical practices, architecture, and art gave birth to distinctive spiritual and cultural forms of life across the Christian world" (356). But it does mean that there was enough of a "thing" called Christianity to see where, when, and what it was. And, Wilken's book argues, the defining conditions of this thing were structural and institutional all the way down.

In conclusion, let us say it out loud: there are only a handful of people with the erudition and stylistic gracefulness to write a book like this. Many would aspire and some have tried. But Wilken has written a readably elegant book that covers a millennium of Christian history without either dumbing it down or pretending to know things he does not. And he has taught us much.

But it is just this achievement that makes one finish the book worried as much as satisfied. The worry is this: the habits of learning that Wilken's scholarship presupposes are dying off. We specialize so rabidly now that we risk losing the educational conditions that could help to produce other Wilkens. Specialization is not, of course, a problem in itself; indeed, it can be a way we come to see something of the richness of God's creation. The knowledges that specialization both requires and creates are a reflection of the unfathomable height and depth of our world. Finite creatures, after all, can see the grandeur of creation only in bits and pieces.

But it is still true that academic culture cultivates research trajectories that over time reduce our capacity for seeing the larger pictures that contain the central stuff of our history. We will doubtless see volumes upon volumes on many of the things Wilken mentions throughout his book—and rightly so. But where are the scholars who can see something of a whole, get it into a readable story that neither ignores nor fixates upon the tangles of Christianity's complex existence, and produce a book that shows us a millennium's worth of humanity's most significant form of life? Of course, in one sense it takes a whole career to get to the point where one can write this sort of book; but in another sense the habits of study and thought throughout that career are what give one the capacity for grander vision. I do not know Robert Wilken very well at all, so perhaps he would contradict my sense of how he has studied. But if so, his book would speak against him and for me. A thinking through of the necessary intellectual habits presupposed by such a book should be part of every younger scholar's reaction to it. Hopefully such thought will lead to other books of this sort in the future. For now we can read Wilken.

Bibliography

Anatolios, Khaled. *Deification through the Cross: An Eastern Christian Theology of Salvation.* Grand Rapids: Eerdmans, 2020.

Anderson, Gary A. *Charity: The Place of the Poor in Biblical Tradition.* New Haven: Yale University Press, 2013.

Anscombe, G. E. M. *Intention.* Ithaca, NY: Cornell University Press, 1957.

Augustine. *De doctrina Christiana.* In *Select Library of the Nicene and Post-Nicene Fathers of the Christian Church*, edited by Philip Schaff. 1st series. Edinburgh: T&T Clark, 1980.

Aune, David E. *Revelation 17–22.* WBC 52C. Nashville: Thomas Nelson, 1998.

Aurelius, Marcus. *Meditations.* Translated by C. R. Haines. LCL. Cambridge, MA: Harvard University Press, 1916.

Ayres, Lewis. *Nicaea and Its Legacy: An Approach to Fourth-Century Trinitarian Theology.* Oxford: Oxford University Press, 2004.

Barclay, John M. G. "Humanity under Faith." In *Beyond Bultmann: Reckoning a New Testament Theology*, edited by Bruce W. Longenecker and Mikeal C. Parsons, 79–100. Waco, TX: Baylor University Press, 2014.

———. "An Identity Received from God: The Theological Configuration of Paul's Kinship Discourse." *Early Christianity* 8 (2017): 354–72.

———. "'O Wad som Pow'r the giftie gie us, To see oursels as others see us!': Method and Purpose in Comparing the New Testament." In *The New Testament in Comparison: Validity, Method, and Purpose in Comparing Traditions*, edited by John M. G. Barclay and B. G. White, 9–22. LNTS. London: T&T Clark, 2020.

Barnes, Jonathan. *Logic and the Imperial Stoa.* Leiden: Brill, 1997.

Barr, James. *The Concept of Biblical Theology: An Old Testament Perspective.* Minneapolis: Fortress, 1999.

———. "The Literal, the Allegorical, and Modern Biblical Scholarship." *JSOT* 44 (1989): 3–17.

———. *The Semantics of Biblical Language.* Oxford: Oxford University Press, 1961.

———. "Wilhelm Vischer and Allegory." In *Understanding the Poets and Prophets:*

Essays in Honour of George Wishart Anderson*, edited by A. Graeme Auld, 38–60. Sheffield: JSOT Press, 1993.

Barth, Karl. *Church Dogmatics.* Vol. I/1, *The Doctrine of the Word of God.* 2nd ed. Edinburgh: T&T Clark, 1975.

———. *Church Dogmatics.* Vol. I/2, *The Doctrine of the Word of God.* Edinburgh: T&T Clark, 1956.

———. *Church Dogmatics.* Vol. II/2, *The Doctrine of God.* Edinburgh: T&T Clark, 1957.

———. *Church Dogmatics.* Vol. IV/4, *The Christian Life.* Edinburgh: T&T Clark, 1960.

———. *The Humanity of God.* Louisville: Westminster John Knox, 1960.

———. "Rudolf Bultmann: An Attempt to Understand Him." In *Kerygma and Myth: A Theological Debate*, edited by H.-W. Bartsch, 2:83–132. London: SPCK, 1962.

———. "Vorwort zur zweiten Auflage." In *Der Römerbrief*, vi–xviii. Zurich: Evangelischer Verlag, 1947.

———. "The Word of God and the Task of the Ministry." In *The Word of God and the Word of Man*, 183–217. New York: Harper & Row, 1957.

Bauckham, Richard. *The Climax of Prophecy: Studies on the Book of Revelation.* Edinburgh: T&T Clark, 1993.

———. *God Crucified: Monotheism and Christology in the New Testament.* Grand Rapids: Eerdmans, 1998.

———. *Jesus and the God of Israel: "God Crucified" and Other Studies on the New Testament's Christology of Divine Identity.* Grand Rapids: Eerdmans, 2008.

———. *The Theology of the Book of Revelation.* Cambridge: Cambridge University Press, 1993.

Baur, Ferdinand Christian. *Vorlesungen über neutestamentliche Theologie.* Darmstadt: Wissenschaftliche Buchgesellschaft, 1973.

Becker, Ernest. *The Denial of Death.* New York: Simon & Schuster, 1997.

Becker, Lawrence C. *A New Stoicism.* Princeton: Princeton University Press, 1999.

Behr, John. *The Formation of Christian Theology.* Vol. 1, *The Way to Nicaea.* Crestwood, NY: St. Vladimir's Seminary Press, 2001.

Berger, Klaus. *Theologiegeschichte des Urchristentums: Theologie des Neuen Testaments.* Tübingen: Francke, 1994.

Birley, Anthony. *Marcus Aurelius: A Biography.* New Haven: Yale University Press, 1987.

Blowers, Paul M. "The *Regula Fidei* and the Narrative Character of Early Christian Faith." *ProEccl* 6, no. 2 (1997): 199–228.

Blumhofer, Christopher. *The Gospel of John and the Future of Israel.* Society for

New Testament Studies Monograph Series. Cambridge: Cambridge University Press, 2019.

Bobzien, Suzanne. *Determinism and Freedom in Stoic Philosophy*. Oxford: Oxford University Press, 2001.

———. "Stoic Conceptions of Freedom and Their Relation to Ethics." In *Aristotle and After*, edited by Richard Sorabji, 71–89. London: Institute of Classical Studies, 1997.

Boyarin, Daniel. "The Gospel of the *Memra*: Jewish Binitarianism and the Prologue to John." *Harvard Theological Review* 94, no. 3 (2001): 243–84.

Braund, David C. *Rome and the Friendly King: The Character of the Client Kingship*. 1984. Reprint, New York: Routledge, 2014.

Brueggemann, Walter. "Against the Stream: Brevard Childs's Biblical Theology." *ThTo* 50 (1993): 279–84.

Bultmann, Rudolf. *The History of the Synoptic Tradition*. Translated by John Marsh. Rev. ed. Peabody, MA: Hendrickson, 1994.

———. "Is Exegesis without Presuppositions Possible?" In *Existence and Faith: Shorter Writings of Rudolf Bultmann*, 289–96. New York: Meridian, 1960.

———. *Jesus and the Word*. Translated by Louise Pettibone Smith. New York: Scribner, 1958.

———. *Theology of the New Testament*. Translated by Kendrick Grobel. 2 vols. New York: Scribner, 1951–1955; Waco, TX: Baylor University Press, 2007.

Burnett, Richard E. *Karl Barth's Theological Exegesis: The Hermeneutical Principles of the* Römerbrief *Period*. Grand Rapids: Eerdmans, 2004.

Cadbury, H. J. "The Peril of Archaizing Ourselves." *Interpretation* 3 (1949): 331–37.

Caird, George B. *New Testament Theology*. Completed and edited by L. D. Hurst. Oxford: Clarendon, 1994.

Calvin, John. *Institutes of the Christian Religion*. Edited by John T. McNeill. Translated by Ford Lewis Battles. 2 vols. Philadelphia: Westminster, 1960.

Cavanaugh, William T. *The Myth of Religious Violence*. New York: Oxford University Press, 2009.

Cavell, Stanley. "Knowing and Acknowledging." In *Must We Mean What We Say?*, 2nd ed., 220–45. Cambridge: Cambridge University Press, 2002.

Chadwick, Henry. *Early Christian Thought and the Classical Tradition*. Oxford: Oxford University Press, 1966.

Chapman, Stephen B. *The Law and the Prophets: A Study in Old Testament Canon Formation*. Forschungen zum Alten Testament 27. Tübingen: Mohr Siebeck, 2000.

———. "Reclaiming Inspiration for the Bible." In *Canon and Biblical Interpretation*, edited by Craig Bartholomew et al., 167–206. Scripture and Hermeneutics Series 7. Grand Rapids: Zondervan, 2006.

Childs, Brevard S. *Biblical Theology in Crisis*. Philadelphia: Westminster, 1970.

———. *Biblical Theology of the Old and New Testaments: Theological Reflection on the Christian Bible*. Minneapolis: Fortress, 1992.

———. "Critical Reflections on James Barr's Understanding of the Literal and Allegorical." *JSOT* 46 (1990): 3–9.

———. *Introduction to the Old Testament as Scripture*. Philadelphia: Fortress, 1979.

———. "Old Testament in Germany 1920–1940: The Search for a New Paradigm." In *Altes Testament: Forschung und Wirkung*, edited by Peter Mommer and Winfried Thiel, 233–46. Frankfurt am Main: Lang, 1994.

———. "The Sensus Literalis of Scripture: An Ancient and Modern Problem." In *Beiträge zur Alttestamentlichen Theologie*, edited by Herbert Donner et al., 80–93. Göttingen: Vandenhoeck & Ruprecht, 1977.

———. *The Struggle to Understand Isaiah as Christian Scripture*. Grand Rapids: Eerdmans, 2004.

———. "Toward Recovering Theological Exegesis." *ProEccl* 6, no. 1 (1997): 16–26.

Cochran, Elizabeth Agnew. "Bricolage and the Purity of Traditions: Engaging the Stoics for Contemporary Christian Ethics." *JRE* 40 (2012): 720–29.

———. "Consent, Conversion, and Moral Formation: Stoic Elements in Jonathan Edwards's Ethics." *JRE* 39, no. 4 (2011): 623–50.

Colish, Marcia. "Stoicism and the New Testament: An Essay in Historiography." *Aufstieg und Niedergang der römischen Welt* II.26.1 (1992): 334–79.

———. *The Stoic Tradition from Antiquity to the Early Middle Ages*. 2 vols. Leiden: Brill, 1985.

Conant, James. "Philosophy and Biography." In *Wittgenstein: Biography and Philosophy*, edited by James C. Klagge, 16–50. Cambridge: Cambridge University Press, 2001.

Cullmann, Oscar. "The Plurality of the Gospels as a Theological Problem in Antiquity." In *The Early Church: Studies in Early Christian History and Theology*. Philadelphia: Westminster, 1956.

Dahl, Nils A. "The Particularity of the Pauline Epistles as a Problem in the Ancient Church." In *Neotestamentica et Patristica: Eine Freundesgabe, Herrn Professor Dr. Oscar Cullmann, zu seinem 60. Geburtstag überreicht*, 261–71. Novum Testamentum Supplement 6. Leiden: Brill, 1962.

Daley, Brian. "Is Patristic Exegesis Still Usable?" In *The Art of Reading Scripture*, edited by Ellen F. Davis and Richard B. Hays, 66–88. Grand Rapids: Eerdmans, 2003.

Davis, Ellen F., and Richard B. Hays, eds. *The Art of Reading Scripture*. Grand Rapids: Eerdmans, 2003.

Delling, Gerhard. "*MONOS THEOS*." In *Studien zum Neuen Testament und zum hellenistischen Judentum: Gesammelte Aufsätze*, edited by Ferdinand Hahn et al., 391–400. Göttingen: Vandenhoeck & Ruprecht, 1970.

Diamond, Cora. "The Difficulty of Reality and the Difficulty of Philosophy." *Partial Answers: Journal of Literature and the History of Ideas* 1 (2003): 1–26.

Dodd, C. H. *According to the Scriptures: The Sub-structure of New Testament Theology*. London: Nisbet, 1952.

Dulles, Avery. "Response to Krister Stendahl's 'Method in the Study of Biblical Theology.'" In *The Bible and Modern Scholarship*, edited by J. Philip Hyatt, 210–16. Nashville: Abingdon, 1965.

Dunn, James D. G. *Christology in the Making: A New Testament Inquiry into the Origins of the Doctrine of the Incarnation*. 2nd ed. Grand Rapids: Eerdmans, 1996.

Ebeling, Gerhard. "The Meaning of 'Biblical Theology.'" In *Word and Faith*, translated by James W. Leitch, 79–97. Philadelphia: Fortress, 1963.

Engberg-Pedersen, Troels. "The Past Is a Foreign Country: On the Shape and Purposes of Comparison in New Testament Scholarship." In *The New Testament in Comparison: Validity, Method, and Purpose in Comparing Traditions*, edited by John M. G. Barclay and B. G. White, 41–61. LNTS. New York: Bloomsbury, 2020.

Englehardt, H. Tristan. *The Foundations of Bioethics*. 2nd ed. New York: Oxford University Press, 1996.

Epictetus. *Discourses, Books 1–2*. Translated by W. A. Oldfather. LCL. Cambridge, MA: Harvard University Press, 1925.

———. *Manual*. Translated by W. A. Oldfather. LCL. Cambridge, MA: Harvard University Press, 1925.

Epp, Eldon Jay. "Western Text." In *Anchor Bible Dictionary*, edited by David Noel Freedman, 6:909–12. New York: Doubleday, 1992.

Esler, Philip. *New Testament Theology: Communion and Community*. Minneapolis: Fortress, 2005.

Farley, Edward. *Theologia: The Fragmentation and Unity of Theological Education*. Philadelphia: Fortress, 1983.

Fee, Gordon D. "Christology and Pneumatology in Romans 8:9–11—and Elsewhere: Some Reflections on Paul as a Trinitarian." In *Jesus of Nazareth: Lord and Christ; Essays on the Historical Jesus and New Testament Christology*, edited by Joel B. Green and Max Turner, 312–31. Grand Rapids: Eerdmans, 1994.

———. *God's Empowering Presence: The Holy Spirit in the Letters of Paul*. Peabody, MA: Hendrickson, 1994.

Ferngren, Gary. *Medicine and Religion: A Historical Introduction*. Baltimore: Johns Hopkins University Press, 2014.

Fitzgerald, John, ed. *Friendship, Flattery, and Frankness of Speech: Studies in the New Testament World*. Leiden: Brill, 1996.

———, ed. *Greco-Roman Perspectives on Friendship*. Atlanta: Scholars Press, 1997.

———. "Orphans in Mediterranean Antiquity and Early Christianity." *Acta Theologica* 23 (2016): 29–48.

Fitzmyer, Joseph. "The Semitic Background of the New Testament *Kyrios*-Title." In *The Semitic Background to the New Testament*, 115–42. Grand Rapids: Eerdmans, 1997.

Fletcher-Louis, Crispin H. T. "The Worship of Divine Humanity as God's Image and the Worship of Jesus." In *The Jewish Roots of Christological Monotheism*, edited by Carey C. Newman, James R. Davila, and Gladys S. Lewis, 112–28. Supplements to the Journal for the Study of Judaism 63. Leiden: Brill, 1999.

Foucault, Michel. *On the Order of Things: An Archaeology of the Human Sciences*. New York: Random House, 1970.

Fowl, Stephen E. *Engaging Scripture: A Model for Theological Interpretation*. Malden, MA: Blackwell, 1998.

Frei, Hans W. *The Eclipse of Biblical Narrative: A Study in Eighteenth and Nineteenth Century Hermeneutics*. New Haven: Yale University Press, 1974.

———. *The Identity of Jesus Christ: The Hermeneutical Bases of Dogmatic Theology*. Philadelphia: Fortress, 1975.

Friesen, Steven J. *Imperial Cults and the Apocalypse of John: Reading Revelation in the Ruins*. New York: Oxford University Press, 2001.

Fürst, Alfons, Therese Fuhrer, Folker Siegert, and Peter Walter. *Der apokryphe Briefwechsel zwischen Seneca und Paulus—Zusammen mit dem Brief des Mordechai an Alexander und dem Brief des Annaeus Seneca über Hochmut und Götterbilder*. Sapere 11. Tübingen: Mohr Siebeck, 2006.

Gabler, J. P. *De iusto discrimine theologiae biblicae et dogmaticae regundisque recte utriusque finibus* (1787). In "J. P. Gabler and the Distinction between Biblical and Dogmatic Theology: Translation, Commentary, and Discussion of His Originality." Edited and translated by J. Sandys-Wunsch and L. Eldredge. *SJT* 33, no. 2 (1980): 133–58.

Gadamer, Hans-Georg. *Truth and Method*. 2nd ed. New York: Continuum, 1996.

———. "The Universality of the Hermeneutical Problem." In *The Gadamer Reader: A Bouquet of Later Writings*, edited by Richard E. Palmer, 77–88. Evanston, IL: Northwestern University Press, 2007.

———. "Was ist Wahrheit?" In *Kleine Schriften*, 1:47–58. Tübingen: Mohr Siebeck, 1967.

Garver, Eugene. *For the Sake of Argument: Practical Reasoning, Character, and the Ethics of Belief*. Chicago: University of Chicago Press, 2004.

Gnilka, Joachin. *Die Frühen Christen: Ursprünge und Anfang der Kirche*. HThKNT Sup 7. Freiburg: Herder, 1999.

———. *Theologie des Neuen Testaments*. HThKNT Sup 5. Freiburg: Herder, 1994.

Green, Joel B., and Max Turner, eds. *Between Two Horizons: Spanning New Testament Studies and Systematic Theology*. Grand Rapids: Eerdmans, 2000.

Greer, R. A. "The Christian Bible and Its Interpretation." In *Early Biblical Interpretation*, edited by J. Kugel and R. Greer, 107–208. Philadelphia: Westminster, 1986.

Gregg, Robert C., and Dennis E. Groh. *Early Arianism—a View of Salvation*. Philadelphia: Fortress, 1981.

Griffiths, Paul J. "On the Future of the Study of Religion in the Academy." *JAAR* 74 (2006): 66–74.

———. *Problems of Religious Diversity*. Oxford: Blackwell, 2001.

Gunton, Colin. "The God of Jesus Christ." *ThTo* 54, no. 3 (1997): 325–34.

Hadot, Ilsetraut. *Seneca und die griechisch-römische Tradition der Seelenleitung, Quellen und Studien zur Geschichte der Philosophie; Bd. 13*. Berlin: de Gruyter, 1969.

Hadot, Pierre. *The Inner Citadel: The Meditations of Marcus Aurelius*. Cambridge, MA: Harvard University Press, 1998.

———. *Philosophy as a Way of Life*. New York: Blackwell, 1995.

———. *Plotinus, or, The Simplicity of Vision*. Chicago: University of Chicago Press, 1994.

———. *The Present Alone Is Our Happiness: Conversations with Jeannie Carlier and Arnold I. Davidson*. Translated by Marc Djaballah and Michael Chase. Stanford, CA: Stanford University Press, 2009.

———. *What Is Ancient Philosophy?* Cambridge, MA: Harvard University Press, 2002.

Hahn, Ferdinand. "Exegese, Theologie und Kirche." In *Studien zum Neuen Testament. Band I. Grundsatzfragen, Jesusforschung, Evangelien*, edited by Jörg Frey and Juliane Schlegel, 17–28. WUNT 191. Tübingen: Mohr Siebeck, 2006.

———. *Theologie des Neuen Testaments*. 2nd ed. 2 vols. Tübingen: Mohr Siebeck, 2005.

Halbertal, Moshe, and Avishai Margalit. *Idolatry*. Translated by Naomi Goldblum. Cambridge, MA: Harvard University Press, 1992.

Hannah, Darrell D. *Michael and Christ: Michael Traditions and Angel Christology in Early Christianity*. WUNT 2/109. Tübingen: Mohr Siebeck, 1999.

Harink, Douglas. *Paul among the Postliberals*. Grand Rapids: Eerdmans, 2004.

Harnack, Adolf von. *Das Wesen des Christentums*. Gütersloh: Kaiser/Gütersloher Verlaghaus, 1999.

———. *What Is Christianity?* Philadelphia: Fortress, 1986.

Hart, David Bentley. *Atheist Delusions: The Christian Revolution and Its Fashionable Enemies*. New Haven: Yale University Press, 2009.

———. *Theological Territories: A David Bentley Hart Digest*. Notre Dame, IN: University of Notre Dame Press, 2020.

Hauerwas, Stanley. "Bearing Reality: A Christian Meditation." *Journal of the Society of Christian Ethics* 33 (2013): 3–20.

———. *Cross-Shattered Christ: Meditations on the Seven Last Words*. Grand Rapids: Brazos, 2004.

———. "For Dappled Things." In *Sanctify Them in the Truth: Holiness Exemplified*, 227–31. Nashville: Abingdon, 1998.

———. *God, Medicine, and Suffering*. Grand Rapids: Eerdmans, 2000.

———. *With the Grain of the Universe: The Church's Witness and Natural Theology*. Grand Rapids: Brazos, 2001.

Hays, Richard B. *Echoes of Scripture in the Gospels*. Waco, TX: Baylor University Press, 2016.

———. *Echoes of Scripture in the Letters of Paul*. New Haven: Yale University Press, 1989.

———. *The Faith of Jesus Christ: The Narrative Substructure of Galatians 3:1–4:11*. 2nd ed. Grand Rapids: Eerdmans, 2002.

———. "Humanity Prior to the Revelation of Faith." In *Beyond Bultmann: Reckoning a New Testament Theology*, edited by Bruce W. Longenecker and Mikeal C. Parsons, 61–78. Waco, TX: Baylor University Press, 2014.

———. *The Letter to the Galatians*. In *The New Interpreter's Bible*, vol. 9, edited by Leander E. Keck. Nashville: Abingdon, 2000.

———. *The Moral Vision of the New Testament: Community, Cross, New Creation; A Contemporary Introduction to New Testament Ethics*. San Francisco: HarperSanFrancisco, 1996.

———. *Reading Backwards: Figural Christology and the Fourfold Gospel Witness*. Waco, TX: Baylor University Press, 2014.

———. "Reading Scripture in Light of the Resurrection." In *The Art of Reading Scripture*, edited by Ellen F. Davis and Richard B. Hays, 216–38. Grand Rapids: Eerdmans, 2003.

———. "Reading the Bible with the Eyes of Faith: The Practice of Theological Exegesis." *JTI* 1 (2007): 5–21.

Hegel, Georg Wilhelm Friedrich. *Lectures on the History of Philosophy*. Edited by Robert F. Brown. Translated by R. F. Brown and J. M. Stewart with the assistance of H. S. Harris. Oxford: Oxford University Press, 2009.

Hester, Lee, and Jim Cheney. "Truth and Native American Epistemology." *Social Epistemology* 15 (2001): 319–34.

Hittinger, Russell. *A Critique of the New Natural Law Theory*. Notre Dame, IN: University of Notre Dame Press, 1987.

Hübner, Hans. *Biblische Theologie des Neuen Testaments*. 3 vols. Göttingen: Vandenhoeck & Ruprecht, 1990–1993.

Hurtado, Larry W. "Does Philo Help Explain Early Christianity?" In *Philo und das Neue Testament: Wechselseitige Wahrnehmungen*, edited by Roland Deines and Karl-Wilhelm Niebuhr, 73–92. WUNT 172. Tübingen: Mohr Siebeck, 2004.

———. *Lord Jesus Christ: Devotion to Jesus in Earliest Christianity*. Grand Rapids: Eerdmans, 2003.

Irenaeus of Lyons. *Against Heresies*. In *Ante-Nicene Fathers: The Writings of the Fathers Down to A.D. 325*, vol. 1, edited by A. Roberts and J. Donaldson. Edinburgh: T&T Clark, 1990.

Jeanrond, Werner. "After Hermeneutics: The Relationship between Theology and Biblical Studies." In *The Open Text*, edited by Francis Watson, 85–102. London: SCM, 1993.

Jenson, Robert W. "Scripture's Authority in the Church." In *The Art of Reading Scripture*, edited by Ellen F. Davis and Richard B. Hays, 27–37. Grand Rapids: Eerdmans, 2003.

———. *Systematic Theology*. 2 vols. New York: Oxford University Press, 1997–1999.

Jeremias, Joachim. *New Testament Theology: The Proclamation of Jesus*. New York: Charles Scribner's Sons, 1971.

Jervell, Jacob. *Imago Dei: Gen 1:26f. im Spätjudentum, in der Gnosis und in den paulinischen Briefen*. Göttingen: Vandenhoeck & Ruprecht, 1960.

Johnson, Luke Timothy. "Imagining the World That Scripture Imagines." In *The Future of Catholic Biblical Scholarship: A Constructive Conversation*, edited by Luke Timothy Johnson and William S. Kurz, 119–42. Grand Rapids: Eerdmans, 2002.

Jones, L. Gregory. "The Practice of Asking Questions." *Faith & Leadership*, August 25, 2009. https://divinityarchive.com/bitstream/handle/11258/5996/the-practice-asking-questions.pdf.

Jüngel, Eberhard. *The Doctrine of the Trinity: God's Being Is in Becoming*. Grand Rapids: Eerdmans, 1976.

Kähler, Martin. *The So-Called Historical Jesus and the Historic Biblical Christ*. Philadelphia: Fortress, 1988.

Käsemann, Ernst. "'The Righteousness of God' in Paul." In *New Testament Questions of Today*, 168–82. Philadelphia: Fortress, 1979.

Keck, Leander. "The Premodern Bible in Postmodern World." *Interpretation* 50 (1996): 130–41.

———. "Problems of a New Testament Theology." *Novum Testamentum* 7 (1964): 217–41.

Kierkegaard, Søren. *For Self-Examination, and Judge for Yourselves!* Translated by W. Lowrie. Princeton: Princeton University Press, 1944.

———. *For Self-Examination/Judge for Yourself!* Translated by Howard V. Hong and Edna H. Hong. Princeton: Princeton University Press, 1990.

———. "Was Bishop Mynster a 'Truth-Witness,' One of 'the Authentic Truth-Witnesses'—Is This the Truth?" In *"The Moment" and Late Writings*, edited by Howard V. Hong and Edna H. Hong, 3–8. Princeton: Princeton University Press, 1998.

Kirk, J. R. Daniel. *A Man Attested by God: The Human Jesus in the Synoptic Gospels*. Grand Rapids: Eerdmans, 2016.

Konradt, Matthias, and Esther Schläpfer, eds. *Anthropologie und Ethik im Frühjudentum und im Neuen Testament: wechselseitige Wahrnehmungen: Internationales Symposium in Verbindung mit dem Project Corpus Judaeo-Hellenisticum Novi Testamenti (CJHNT), 17.-20. Mai 2012, Heidelberg*. WUNT 1/322. Tübingen: Mohr Siebeck, 2014.

Konstan, David. *Friendship in the Classical World*. Cambridge: Cambridge University Press, 1997.

Kuen, Gabriele. *Die Philosophie als "dix vitae": Die Verknüpfung von Gehalt, Intention und Darstellungsweise im philosophischen Werk Senecas am Beispiel des Dialogs "De vita beata"—Einleitung, Wortkommentar und systematischer Darstellung*. Heidelberg: Winter, 1994.

Laban, Michael, and Outi Lehtipuu, eds. *Anthropology in the New Testament and Its Ancient Context*. Leuven: Peeters, 2010.

Ladd, George Eldon. *A Theology of the New Testament*. Edited by D. Hagner. Rev. ed. Grand Rapids: Eerdmans, 1993.

Levering, Matthew. *Biblical Natural Law: A Theocentric and Teleological Approach*. New York: Oxford University Press, 2008.

———. *Christ's Fulfillment of Torah and Temple: Salvation in Thomas Aquinas*. Notre Dame, IN: University of Notre Dame Press, 2002.

———. *Ezra and Nehemiah*. BTCB. Grand Rapids: Brazos, 2007.

———. "God and Greek Philosophy in Contemporary Biblical Scholarship." *JTI* 4 (2010): 169–85.

———. *Participatory Biblical Exegesis: A Theology of Biblical Interpretation*. Notre Dame, IN: University of Notre Dame Press, 2008.

———. *Scripture and Metaphysics: Aquinas and the Renewal of Trinitarian Theology*. Oxford: Blackwell, 2004.

Lindbeck, George A. *The Nature of Doctrine: Religion and Theology in a Postliberal Age*. Philadelphia: Westminster, 1984.

Linebaugh, Jonathan A. "Relational Hermeneutics and Comparison as Conversation." In *The New Testament in Comparison: Validity, Method, and Purpose in Comparing Traditions*, edited by John M. G. Barclay and B. G. White, 143–58. LNTS. London: T&T Clark, 2020.

Long, A. A. *Epictetus: A Stoic and Socratic Guide to Life*. Oxford: Clarendon, 2001.

Long, A. A., and D. N. Sedley, eds. *The Hellenistic Philosophers*. 2 vols. New York: Cambridge University Press, 1987.

Longenecker, Bruce, ed. *The Narrative Dynamics of Pauline Theology: A Critical Assessment*. Louisville: Westminster John Knox, 2002.

Longenecker, Richard N. *Galatians*. WBC 41. Dallas: Word, 1990.

Lossky, Vladimir. *The Mystical Theology of the Eastern Church*. Crestwood, NY: St. Vladimir's Seminary Press, 1976.

Luther, Martin. *Luther's Works*. 55 vols. St. Louis: Concordia, 1957–1986.

Lutz, Cora. "Musonius Rufus: 'The Roman Socrates.'" *Yale Classical Studies* 10 (1947): 3–147.

MacIntyre, Alasdair. *After Virtue*. Notre Dame, IN: University of Notre Dame Press, 1981.

———. *After Virtue*. 2nd ed. Notre Dame, IN: University of Notre Dame Press, 1984.

———. *After Virtue*. 3rd ed. Notre Dame, IN: University of Notre Dame Press, 2007.

———. "Colors, Cultures, and Practices." In *The Tasks of Philosophy*, 24–51. Vol. 1 of *Selected Essays*. Cambridge: Cambridge University Press, 2006.

———. *Edith Stein: A Philosophical Prologue, 1913–1922*. New York: Rowman & Littlefield, 2006.

———. "The Intelligibility of Action." In *Rationality, Relativism, and the Human Sciences*, edited by J. Margolis, M. Krausz, and R. M. Burian, 63–80. Dordrecht: Reidel, 1986.

———. "Moral Philosophy and Contemporary Social Practice: What Holds Them Apart?" In *The Tasks of Philosophy*, 104–22. Vol. 1 of *Selected Essays*. Cambridge: Cambridge University Press, 2006.

———. "Once More on Kierkegaard." In *Kierkegaard after MacIntyre: Essays on Freedom, Narrative, and Virtue*, edited by John J. Davenport and Anthony Rudd, 339–56. Chicago: Open Court, 2001.

———. *Selected Essays*. Vol. 1, *The Tasks of Philosophy*. Cambridge: Cambridge University Press, 2006.

———. *Selected Essays*. Vol. 2, *Ethics and Politics*. Cambridge: Cambridge University Press, 2006.

———. "Social Structures and Their Threat to Moral Agency." In *Ethics and Poli-*

tics, 186–204. Vol. 2 of *Selected Essays*. Cambridge: Cambridge University Press, 2006.

———. *Three Rival Versions of Moral Enquiry: Encyclopaedia, Genealogy, and Tradition*. Notre Dame, IN: University of Notre Dame Press, 1990.

Marshall, Bruce. "Christ and Israel: An Unsolved Problem in Catholic Theology." In *The Call of Abraham: Essays on the Election of Israel in Honor of Jon D. Levenson*, edited by Gary A. Anderson and Joel S. Kaminsky, 330–50. Notre Dame, IN: University of Notre Dame Press, 2013.

Marshall, D. G. "On Dialogue: To Its Cultural Despisers." In *Gadamer's Repercussions: Reconsidering Philosophical Hermeneutics*, edited by B. Kajewski, 123–44. Berkeley: University of California Press, 2003.

Marshall, I. Howard. *New Testament Theology: Many Witnesses, One Gospel*. Downers Grove, IL: InterVarsity Press, 2004.

Martyn, J. Louis. "De-apocalypticizing Paul: An Essay Focused on *Paul and the Stoics* by Troels Engberg-Pedersen." *JSNT* 86 (2002): 61–102.

Maston, Jason, and Benjamin E. Reynolds, eds. *Anthropology and New Testament Theology*. LNTS 529. London: Bloomsbury T&T Clark, 2018.

Matera, Frank J. "New Testament Theology: History, Method, and Identity." *Catholic Biblical Quarterly* 67 (2005): 1–21.

Mauser, Ulrich. *Gottesbild und Menschwerdung: eine Untersuchung zur Einheit des Alten und Neuen Testaments*. Tübingen: Mohr Siebeck, 1971.

———. "*Heis Theos* und *Monos Theos* in Biblischer Theologie." *Jahrbuch für Biblische Theologie* 1 (1986): 71–87.

McCormack, Bruce L. "Historical Criticism and Dogmatic Interest in Karl Barth's Theological Exegesis of the New Testament." In *Biblical Hermeneutics in Historical Perspective: Studies in Honor of Karlfried Froehlich on His Sixtieth Birthday*, edited by M. Burrows and P. Rorem, 322–38. Grand Rapids: Eerdmans, 1991.

———. *The Humility of the Eternal Son: Reformed Kenoticism and the Repair of Chalcedon*. Cambridge: Cambridge University Press, 2021.

———. "The Significance of Karl Barth's Theological Exegesis of Philippians." In *Epistle to the Philippians: 40th Anniversary Edition with Introductory Essays by Bruce L. McCormack and Francis B. Watson*, by Karl Barth, v–xxv. Louisville: Westminster John Knox, 2002.

McCutcheon, Russell T. *Critics Not Caretakers: Redescribing the Public Study of Religion*. Albany: State University of New York Press, 2001.

———. "A Default of Critical Intelligence: The Scholar of Religion as Public Intellectual." *JAAR* 65 (1997): 443–68.

McDonough, Sean M. *Christ as Creator: Origins of a New Testament Doctrine*. New York: Oxford University Press, 2009.

———. *YHWH at Patmos: Rev. 1:4 in Its Hellenistic and Early Jewish Setting*. WUNT 2/107. Tübingen: Mohr Siebeck, 1999.

Meeks, Wayne A. "Moses as God and King." In *Religions in Antiquity: Essays in Memory of Erwin Ramsdell Goodenough*, edited by Jacob Neusner, 354–71. Leiden: Brill, 1968.

———. "Why Study the New Testament?" *NTS* 51 (2005): 155–70.

Menninger, Karl. *Whatever Became of Sin?* New York: Hawthorn, 1973.

Metzger, Bruce M. *The Canon of the New Testament: Its Origin, Development, and Significance*. Oxford: Clarendon, 1997.

Meyer, Paul. "'The Father': The Presentation of God in the Fourth Gospel." In *Exploring the Gospel of John: In Honor of D. Moody Smith*, edited by R. Alan Culpepper and C. Clifton Black, 255–73. Louisville: Westminster John Knox, 1996.

Mildenberger, Friedrich. *Biblische Dogmatik: Eine Biblische Theologie in dogmatischer Perspektive*. 3 vols. Stuttgart: Kohlhammer, 1991–1993.

Minear, Paul S. "Barth's Commentary on the Romans, 1922–1972, or Karl Barth vs. the Exegetes." In *Footnotes to a Theology: The Karl Barth Colloquium of 1972*, edited by M. Rumscheidt, 8–29. Waterloo, ON: Corporation for the Publication of Academic Studies in Religion in Canada, 1974.

Mitchell, Margaret. "On Comparing, and Calling the Question." In *The New Testament in Comparison: Validity, Method, and Purpose in Comparing Traditions*, edited by John M. G. Barclay and B. G. White, 95–124. LNTS. London: T&T Clark, 2020.

Mommsen, Theodor. *A History of Rome under the Emperors*. Edited by Thomas Wiedermann. Translated by Clare Krojzl. New York: Routledge, 1996.

Morgan, Teresa. "Becoming Christian." Review of *One True Life*, by C. Kavin Rowe. *Tablet*, September 15, 2016.

Novenson, Matthew V. "Beyond Compare: or: Some Recent Strategies for Not Comparing Early Christianity with Other Things." In *The New Testament in Comparison: Validity, Method, and Purpose in Comparing Traditions*, edited by John M. G. Barclay and B. G. White, 79–94. LNTS. London: T&T Clark, 2020.

Nussbaum, Martha. "Charles Taylor: Explanation and Practical Reason." In *The Quality of Life*, edited by Martha Nussbaum and Amartya Sen, 232–41. New York: Oxford University Press, 1993.

———. *The Therapy of Desire*. Princeton: Princeton University Press, 1996.

Ollenburger, Ben C. "What Krister Stendahl 'Meant': A Normative Critique of 'Descriptive Biblical Theology.'" *HBT* 81 (1986): 61–98.

Pannenberg, Wolfhart. *Systematic Theology*. 3 vols. Grand Rapids: Eerdmans, 1991–1998.

Paul, L. A. *Transformative Experience*. New York: Oxford University Press, 2014.

Pelikan, Jaroslav. *Acts*. BTCB. Grand Rapids: Brazos, 2005.

Presbyterian Church (USA). "The Brief Statement of Faith—Presbyterian Church (USA)." In *The Constitution of the Presbyterian Church (USA) Part 1: The Book of Confessions*. Louisville: The Office of the General Assembly, 1994.

Rad, Gerhard von. *Old Testament Theology*. Vol. 1. New York: Harper & Row, 1962.

Rahner, Karl. *The Trinity*. New York: Crossroad, 1998.

Räisänen, Heikki. *Beyond New Testament Theology: A Story and a Programme*. London: SCM, 1990.

———. "A Religious Studies Alternative to New Testament Theology: Reflections on a Controversial Enterprise." In *The Bible among Scriptures and Other Essays*, 15–29. Tübingen: Mohr Siebeck, 2017.

Ramelli, Ilaria L. E. *Social Justice and the Legitimacy of Slavery: The Role of Philosophical Asceticism from Ancient Judaism to Late Antiquity*. New York: Oxford University Press, 2009.

Ramsey, Paul. *The Patient as Person: Explorations in Medical Ethics*. New Haven: Yale University Press, 1970.

Ratzinger, Joseph Cardinal. "Biblical Interpretation in Crisis: On the Question of the Foundations and Approaches of Exegesis Today." In *Biblical Interpretation in Crisis: The Ratzinger Conference on Bible and Church*, edited by Richard John Neuhaus, 1–23. Grand Rapids: Eerdmans, 1989.

Rebanks, James. *The Shepherd's Life: Modern Dispatches from an Ancient Landscape*. New York: Flatiron Books, 2015.

Reno, R. R. Introduction to *Acts*, by Jaroslav Pelikan. BTCB. Grand Rapids: Brazos, 2005.

Richardson, K. C. *Early Christian Care for the Poor: An Alternative Subsistence Strategy under Roman Imperial Rule*. Cascade, OR: Wipf & Stock, 2018.

Richardson, Peter, and Amy Marie Fisher. *Herod: King of the Jews and Friend of the Romans*. 2nd ed. New York: Routledge, 2018.

Ricoeur, Paul. *Oneself as Another*. Chicago: University of Chicago Press, 1995.

Risse, Guenter B. *Mending Bodies, Saving Souls: A History of Hospitals*. New York: Oxford University Press, 1999.

Rowe, C. Kavin. "The Acts of the Apostles and Thriving Communities." *Faith & Leadership*, August 15, 2010. https://www.faithandleadership.com/series-acts-apostles-and-thriving-communities.

———. *Early Narrative Christology: The Lord in the Gospel of Luke*. BZNW 139. Berlin: de Gruyter, 2006. Reprint, Grand Rapids: Baker Academic, 2009.

———. *Leading Christian Communities*. Grand Rapids: Eerdmans, 2023.

———. "Luke and the Trinity: An Essay in Ecclesial Biblical Theology." *SJT* 56 (2003): 1–26.

———. "New Testament Iconography?" In *Picturing the New Testament: Studies in Ancient Visual Images*, edited by Annette Weissenrieder et al., 289–312. WUNT 2/193. Tübingen: Mohr Siebeck, 2005.

———. *One True Life: The Stoics and Early Christians as Rival Traditions*. New Haven: Yale University Press, 2016.

———. "Romans 10:13: What Is the Name of the Lord?" *HBT* 22, no. 2 (2000): 135–73.

———. *World Upside Down: Reading Acts in the Graeco-Roman Age*. New York: Oxford University Press, 2009.

Sanders, E. P. *Paul and Palestinian Judaism: A Comparison of Patterns of Religion*. Philadelphia: Fortress, 1977.

Sandys-Wunsch, J., and L. Eldredge, eds. and trans. "J. P. Gabler and the Distinction between Biblical and Dogmatic Theology: Translation, Commentary, and Discussion of His Originality." *SJT* 33, no. 2 (1980): 133–58.

Saussure, Ferdinand de. *Course in General Linguistics*. New York: Philosophical Library, 1950.

Schapp, Wilhelm. *In Geschichten Verstrickt: Zum Sein von Mensch und Ding*. 3rd ed. Frankfurt am Main: Vittorio Klostermann, 1985.

Schillebeeckx, Edward. *Jesus: An Experiment in Christology*. Translated by Hubert Hoskins. New York: Seabury, 1979.

Schlatter, Adolf. "Die Theologie des Neuen Testaments und die Dogmatik." In *Das Problem der Theologie des Neuen Testaments*, edited by Georg Strecker, 155–214. Darmstadt: Wissenschaftliche Buchgesellschaft, 1975.

———. "The Theology of the New Testament and Dogmatics." In *The Nature of New Testament Theology*, edited by Robert Morgan, 117–66. Naperville, IL: Allenson, 1973.

Schleiermacher, Friedrich. *The Christian Faith*. Edinburgh: T&T Clark, 1928.

———. *Der christliche Glaube: nach den Grundsätzen der evangelischen Kirche im Zusammenhange dargestellt, Zweite Auflage*. In *Kritische Gesamtausgabe*, I. 13, 1 and I. 13, 2, edited by R. Schäfer. Berlin: de Gruyter, 2003.

Schlier, Heinrich. "The Meaning and Function of a Theology of the New Testament." In *The Relevance of the New Testament*, 1–25. New York: Herder & Herder, 1968.

Schmidt, Karl L. "Le problème du Christianisme primitive." *Revue d'histoire et de philosophie religieuses* 18 (1938): 126–73.

Schüssler Fiorenza, Elisabeth. *In Memory of Her: A Feminist Theological Reconstruction of Christian Origins*. New York: Crossroad, 1983.

Schweitzer, Albert. *The Mysticism of Paul the Apostle*. Translated by William Montgomery. New York: Macmillan, 1931.

———. *The Quest of the Historical Jesus: A Critical Study of Its Progress from Reimarus to Wrede*. Baltimore: Johns Hopkins University Press, 1998.

Schwöbel, Christoph. "The Renaissance of Trinitarian Theology: Reasons, Problems and Tasks." In *Trinitarian Theology Today*, edited by Christoph Schwöbel, 1–30. Edinburgh: T&T Clark, 1995.

Seitz, Christopher R. *Word without End: The Old Testament as Abiding Theological Witness*. Grand Rapids: Eerdmans, 1998.

Sellars, John. *The Art of Living: The Stoics on the Nature and Function of Philosophy*. Burlington, VT: Ashgate, 2003.

Seneca. *Epistles*. Translated by Richard M. Gummere. LCL. Cambridge, MA: Harvard University Press, 1917.

Smith, J. Warren. "'If I Forget You, O Jerusalem': Zion's Place in Global Christianity." *Nova et Vetera* 13, no. 4 (2015): 1269–81.

Smith, Jonathan Z. *Drudgery Divine: On the Comparison of Early Christianities and the Religions of Late Antiquity*. Chicago: University of Chicago Press, 1990.

———. "In Comparison a Magic Dwells." In *A Magic Still Dwells: Comparative Religion in a Postmodern Age*, edited by Kimberly C. Patton and Benjamin C. Ray, 23–46. Berkeley: University of California Press, 2000.

———. "What a Difference a Difference Makes." In *To See Ourselves as Others See Us: Christians, Jews, "Others" in Late Antiquity*, edited by Jacob Neusner and Ernest Frerichs, 3–48. Chico, CA: Scholars Press, 1985.

Sokolowski, Robert. *Phenomenology of the Human Person*. Cambridge: Cambridge University Press, 2008.

Sorabji, Richard. *Emotion and Peace of Mind: From Stoic Agitation to Christian Temptation*. Oxford: Oxford University Press, 2000.

———. *Self: Ancient and Modern Insights about Individuality, Life, and Death*. Chicago: University of Chicago Press, 2006.

Soulen, R. Kendall. "YHWH the Triune God." *Modern Theology* 15, no. 1 (1999): 25–54.

Stark, Rodney. *The Rise of Christianity: A Sociologist Reconsiders History*. Princeton: Princeton University Press, 1996.

Steiner, George. *Real Presences*. Chicago: University of Chicago Press, 1989.

———. *Tolstoy or Dostoevsky? An Essay in the Old Criticism*. 2nd ed. New Haven: Yale University Press, 1996.

Stendahl, Krister. "Biblical Theology, Contemporary." In *The Interpreter's Dictionary of the Bible*, edited by George A. Buttrick, 1:418–32. New York: Abingdon, 1962. Reprinted as "Biblical Theology: A Program." In *Meanings: The Bible as Document and as Guide*, by Krister Stendahl, 11–44. Philadelphia: Fortress, 1984.

Stockdale, James B. *Courage under Fire: Testing Epictetus's Doctrines in a Laboratory of Human Behavior*. Stanford, CA: Hoover Institution, 1993.

Stout, Jeffrey. *Blessed Are the Organized: Grassroots Democracy in America*. Princeton: Princeton University Press, 2010.

———. "Commitments and Traditions in the Study of Religious Ethics." *JRE* 25 (1997): 23–56.

———. *Democracy and Tradition*. Princeton: Princeton University Press, 2004.

———. *Ethics after Babel: The Languages of Morals and Their Discontents*. Boston: Beacon, 1988.

Strecker, Georg. *Theology of the New Testament*. Edited by F. W. Horn. Translated by E. Boring. Berlin: de Gruyter; Louisville: Westminster John Knox, 2000.

Stuhlmacher, Peter. *Biblical Theology of the New Testament*. Translated and edited by Daniel P. Bailey with the collaboration of Jostein Ådna. Grand Rapids: Eerdmans, 2018.

———. *Biblische Theologie des Neuen Testaments*. 2 vols. Göttingen: Vandenhoeck & Ruprecht, 1991–1999.

Taylor, Charles. "Explanation and Practical Reason." In *The Quality of Life*, edited by Martha Nussbaum and Amartya Sen, 208–31. New York: Oxford University Press, 1993.

———. *Philosophical Arguments*. Cambridge, MA: Harvard University Press, 1995.

———. *A Secular Age*. Cambridge, MA: Belknap Press of Harvard University Press, 2007.

———. *Sources of the Self: The Making of the Modern Identity*. Cambridge, MA: Harvard University Press, 1989.

———. "Understanding the Other: A Gadamerian View of Conceptual Schemes." In *Dilemmas and Connections*, 24–38. Cambridge, MA: Belknap Press of Harvard University Press, 2011.

Thielman, Frank. *Theology of the New Testament: A Canonical and Synthetic Approach*. Grand Rapids: Zondervan, 2005.

Tolstoy, Leo. *Anna Karenina*. Translated by Joel Carmichael. New York: Bantam, 2006.

Troeltsch, Ernst. "The Dogmatics of the History-of-Religions School." In *Religion and History*, edited by J. Adams and W. Bense, 87–108. Minneapolis: Fortress, 1991.

Vischer, Wilhelm. *The Witness of the Old Testament to Christ*. Vol. 1, *The Pentateuch*. London: Lutterworth, 1949.

Vouga, François. *Une théologie du Nouveau Testament*. Monde de la Bible 43. Geneva: Labor et Fides, 2001.

Wainwright, Geoffrey. *Doxology: The Praise of God in Worship, Doctrine, and Life; A Systematic Theology*. New York: Oxford University Press, 1980.

———. *For Our Salvation: Two Approaches to the Work of Christ*. Grand Rapids: Eerdmans, 1997.

———. "The Holy Spirit." In *The Cambridge Companion to Christian Doctrine*, edited by Colin Gunton, 273–96. Cambridge: Cambridge University Press, 1997.

———. "Trinity." In *Dictionary for Theological Interpretation of the Bible*, edited by Kevin J. Vanhoozer, 815–18. Grand Rapids: Baker Academic, 2005.

Watson, Francis. *Text and Truth: Redefining Biblical Theology*. Edinburgh: T&T Clark, 1997.

———. *Text, Church and World: Biblical Interpretation in Theological Perspective*. Edinburgh: T&T Clark, 1994.

Westermann, Claus. "Das Alte Testament und die Theologie." In *Theologie—was ist das?*, edited by Georg Picht and Enno Rudolph, 49–66. Stuttgart: Kreuz Verlag, 1977.

Wilckens, Ulrich. *Theologie des Neuen Testaments*. 4 vols. Neukirchener-Vluyn: Neukirchener Verlag, 2002–2005.

Wilken, Robert Louis. *The First Thousand Years: A Global History of Christianity*. New Haven: Yale University Press, 2012.

———. Foreword to *Medieval Exegesis*, by Henri de Lubac. Grand Rapids: Eerdmans, 2000.

———. "Interpreting the New Testament." *ProEccl* 14 (2005): 15–25.

———. "Not a Solitary God: The Triune God of the Bible." *ProEccl* 3 (1994): 36–55.

———. *The Spirit of Early Christian Thought: Seeking the Face of God*. New Haven: Yale University Press, 2003.

Williams, Bernard. *Ethics and the Limits of Philosophy*. Cambridge, MA: Harvard University Press, 1985.

———. "Life as Narrative." *European Journal of Philosophy* 17 (2007): 305–14.

———. Review of *Sources of the Self: The Making of the Modern Identity*, by Charles Taylor. In *Essays and Reviews, 1959–2002*, 301–10. Princeton: Princeton University Press, 2014.

———. "Stoic Philosophy and the Emotions." In *Aristotle and After*, edited by Richard Sorabji, 211–13. London: Institute of Classical Studies, 1997.

———. "There Are Many Kinds of Eyes." In *The Sense of the Past: Essays in the History of Philosophy*, 325–30. Princeton: Princeton University Press, 2006.

Williams, Rowan. *On Christian Theology*. Oxford: Blackwell, 2000.

Wittgenstein, Ludwig. *The Blue and Brown Books*. New York: Harper & Row, 1958.

———. *Culture and Value*. London: Wiley-Blackwell, 1995.

———. *Philosophical Investigations*. 4th ed. Oxford: Blackwell, 2009.

Wrede, William. "The Task and Methods of 'New Testament Theology.'" In *The Nature of New Testament Theology*, edited by Robert Morgan, 68–116. Naperville, IL: Allenson, 1973.

Wright, N. T. *Jesus and the Victory of God*. Minneapolis: Fortress, 1996.

———. *The New Testament and the People of God*. Minneapolis: Fortress, 1992.

———. *The Resurrection of the Son of God*. Minneapolis: Fortress, 2003.

Yeago, David. "The New Testament and Nicene Dogma: A Contribution to the Recovery of Theological Exegesis." *ProEccl* 3 (1994): 152–64.

Young, Frances M. "Alexandrian and Antiochene Exegesis." In *The Ancient Period*, edited by Alan J. Hauser and Duane F. Watson, 334–54. Vol. 1 of *A History of Biblical Interpretation*. Grand Rapids: Eerdmans, 2003.

———. "The God of the Greeks and the Nature of Religious Language." In *Early Christian Literature and the Classical Intellectual Tradition: In Honorem Robert M. Grant*, edited by William R. Schoedel and Robert L. Wilken, 45–74. Théologie historique 53. Paris: Éditions Beauchesne, 1979.

———. "The 'Mind' of Scripture: Theological Readings of the Bible in the Fathers." *International Journal of Systematic Theology* 7, no. 2 (2005): 126–41.

Young, Frances, and David F. Ford. *Meaning and Truth in 2 Corinthians*. Grand Rapids: Eerdmans, 1987.

Young, Stephen L. "'Let's Take the Text Seriously': The Protectionist *Doxa* of Mainstream New Testament Studies." *Method and Theory in the Study of Religion* (2019): 1–36.

Zanker, Paul. *The Power of Images in the Age of Augustus*. Ann Arbor: University of Michigan Press, 1988.

Index of Authors

Index of Subjects

Index of Scripture

Index of Other Ancient Sources